AVENGING CHILD SEX ABUSE

This book explores the subjects of child sex abuse, flaws in the justice system, cultural support for vigilantism, prison violence, and the socio-legal philosophy of punishment. Child sex abuse leaves a scar that lasts a lifetime. Can any legal punishment balance the scales of justice? Can sex offenders ever repay their debt to society, or more importantly, to the victim? For some victims of this traumatic abuse, the debt remains unpaid, and it accrues interest. Vigilantes seek to avenge child victims by hunting down sex offenders in the community. Sometimes prisoners in correctional facilities conspire with rogue correctional officers to mete out their own form of "convict justice" on people who hurt children. While their motives and methods differ, these outraged citizens seek retribution through violence because they are disgusted with a justice system they believe shows extraordinary leniency toward child sex abusers.

Whether this violence occurs in the community or in jail cells across the country, the message these vigilantes broadcast is the same: if the government won't seek retribution, they will.

The story is told through a series of case studies based on interviews with real-life vigilantes, most of whom are serving life sentences for their crimes. For the first time, vigilantes have been given a chance to tell their own stories. Patrick Drum, Steven Sandison, Joseph Druce, Jeremy Moody, Jon Watson, James Fairbanks, and others have shared their personal insights to help us get inside the vigilante mind. For some readers, these accounts will humanize people considered to be simply murderers. For others, it will demystify the popular portrayals of vigilantes in our society.

Joshua Long is an Assistant Professor of Criminology and Justice Studies at the University of Massachusetts-Lowell, where he studies prison violence and rehabilitation programs. He has extensive experience interviewing prisoners across the United States and believes that letting prisoners tell their own stories is the best way to learn about life behind the walls.

Jason Vukovich is currently incarcerated in Alaska and, for the first time, has decided to share his complete story with the public. He writes about his own journey from a survivor of child abuse to vigilante to philosopher. He understands the vigilante mindset better than anyone, and he has one message for his supporters "you are well advised to never walk my trail…"

AVENGING CHILD SEX ABUSE

Vigilante Violence in Prisons and the Community

Joshua Long and Jason Vukovich

Routledge
Taylor & Francis Group

NEW YORK AND LONDON

Designed cover image: © Getty Images

First published 2024
by Routledge
605 Third Avenue, New York, NY 10158

and by Routledge
4 Park Square, Milton Park, Abingdon, Oxon, OX14 4RN

Routledge is an imprint of the Taylor & Francis Group, an informa business

ISBN: 978-1-032-49443-2 (hbk)
ISBN: 978-1-032-49069-4 (pbk)
ISBN: 978-1-003-39384-9 (ebk)

DOI: 10.4324/9781003393849

We dedicate this book to the victims, survivors, and transcenders
of child sex abuse.

CONTENTS

ACKNOWLEDGMENTS

This book could never have been written without the support and encouragement of many people. I appreciate their time and willingness to share insights on difficult subjects. I have listed them here: J. Rueben Appleman, Shaun Attwood, James Bacigalupo, Allie Blanchard, Catharine Broad, Brad Chapman, Francis T. Cullen, Christopher Dalton, Joseph Druce, Patrick Drum, James Fairbanks, David Finkelhor, Clark Fredericks, Nate Gartrell (*The Mercury News*), Jennifer Hays-Grudo, David Hopps, Joseph Kelly, Konrad Kircher, Mike Lew, Angelina Lozano, Joshua Mills, Jeremy Moody, Amanda Morris, Matt Orchard, Lexi Pandell, Justine Payne, Jody Plauché, Paul H. Robinson, Peter Rose-Barry, Anna Salter, Steven Sandison, Adi Sideman, Rebecca Trammell, Vince Trant, Jon Watson, Alice Vachss, Gary York, Uso Ron (*30 to Life*), and Becky. I would also like to thank dozens of confidential correctional officers and prisoners I spoke to across the country for informally sharing their personal experiences with me. I also thank Ellen Boyne, Kate Taylor, and Riya Bhattacharya at Routledge for making this publication possible.

I would like to make a special acknowledgment of Alice and Andrew Vachss, two attorneys/ authors/activists who dedicated their careers to the pursuit of justice for the victims of traumatic abuse. Their work has been cited throughout this book. Consider each citation to be a footprint that proves they came before me and said it better. Their charitable work with the group Legislative Drafting Institute for Child Protection is a worthy cause (LDICP.org).

My co-author is Jason Vukovich. Jason is currently serving a 28-year sentence in the Alaska Department of Corrections. I originally wrote to Jason to ask if he had a message for my class of criminal justice students. He wrote an eloquent treatise on punishment, incarceration, public policies, and retribution. The text of this letter is preserved in the appendix. I was impressed with his analytical skills and wrote to him again to ask if he would contribute to this book. This eventually led to a unique collaboration where we mailed drafts of each chapter back and forth, revising and "conversating" our way through the writing process until our final manuscript became something new altogether. Jason understands the so-called vigilante mindset very well, and his insights provide us with the most in-depth qualitative information on the lives and motivations of vigilantes currently available, but I should note that the majority of the cases in this book refer to homicide cases and Jason has never killed anyone. He was convicted of aggravated robbery of three child sex abusers. Without Jason's help, this book would have been a poor attempt to categorize offenders with academic precision that nevertheless misses the mark. With Jason's help, this book has become something much more vivid and realistic.

None of my contributors, correspondents, or interviewees were promised payment for their assistance. They gave their information willingly. I did provide some books, postage, and funds for writing materials to some of the incarcerated men I interviewed. All of them have given permission to print their words without censorship. I offered to conceal their identities if they preferred to remain anonymous, but every one of them insisted on having their names published. That's one of the interesting things about vigilantes. They want people to know about their actions.

Readers might want to confirm the details of this book with the incarcerated men I have listed above. If so, you can find their addresses using their institutional #ID numbers listed below. Note: Mail will not be delivered if it violates prison rules or if the address is incorrect. Please check each state's department of corrections' website to confirm their current location and read all of the rules, regulations, and warnings related to prisoner mail.

Scottie D. Allen #B01314
Florida Department of Corrections

Joseph Druce #308649
Massachusetts/Arizona Department of Corrections

Patrick Drum #784289
Washington Department of Corrections

James Fairbanks #213485
Nebraska Department of Correctional Services

Jeremy L. Moody #00359801
South Carolina Department of Corrections

Steven D. Sandison #167738
Michigan Department of Corrections

Jason Vukovich #264576
Alaska Department of Corrections

Jon Henry Watson #AA4712
California Department of Corrections and Rehabilitation

Revenge first wrought me; Murder's his twin brother:
One deadly sin, then, help me cure another.
Massinger, *Duke of Milan* **II.1**

INTRODUCTION

What is an appropriate punishment for sex crimes against children? While most people would haggle over the number of years the perpetrator should spend in prison, others are quick to respond that such an awful crime is worthy of the death penalty. Since the Supreme Court ruling in *Kennedy v. Louisiana* (2008), a death sentence is no longer possible for child sex abusers convicted in the United States (unless they kill or attempt to kill their victims), so death penalty supporters are unable to legally secure their definition of "justice." On rare occasions, a person may take the law into their own hands and become a vigilante. They might physically attack or kill the suspected child abuser, an act that places the vigilante on the court docket. The law often permits a "citizen's arrest" when a member of the public detains a suspect in a crime until law enforcement officers arrive, but the law jealously guards the power of the "judge, jury, and executioner." Punishment is off limits.

The details of individual circumstances in these cases are often quite different, but we can break the situation down into phases. The first phase is the initial crime against the child (which can inspire intense feelings of disgust and hatred in the community). The second phase is the justice system response to that crime (and if it is too lenient or too harsh it might cause outrage in the community). The third phase is the vigilante's crime that is meant to secure justice they believe was not delivered by the government (with some people calling them heroes and others condemning them for violating the rule of law). The fourth phase is the justice system response to the vigilante's crime (which again can undermine faith in the government depending on if the sentence is too lenient or too harsh). While nearly everyone in society can agree that the initial crime against the child in the first phase is morally wrong, there is a departure of opinion in the subsequent phases of the vigilante justice process.

Vigilantism can occur as a response to many types of crimes, not just child sex abuse, but the cases involving "child protection extremism" are especially salient. Human beings have a natural desire to protect children from harm. Most of us experience a visceral reaction when we see a child in danger. If you cannot protect a child in the moment of danger there is a lingering desire to "make things right." This desire can manifest itself as seeking *retribution*, which is perhaps the most controversial goal of the justice system. Clearly, this is an important and thought-provoking subject for anyone who studies or is subject to the criminal justice system of the United States (1).

DOI: 10.4324/9781003393849-1

Most people intuitively understand the difference between "revenge" and "justice." Revenge seems to be highly variable depending on each individual's emotional state, and so it is often disregarded as a basis for civilized law. Justice, however, is portrayed as a noble goal that our system is designed to approach after considering the complete circumstances of each case. But the term *retribution* can easily be mistaken for either revenge or justice. Retribution is usually defined as "punishment for the sake of justice" as if hurting an offender in some proportional way will restore some cosmic balance. This is distinct from consequentialist goals of punishment (such as deterrence) because it is not concerned with having an effect beyond satisfying the desire for punishment. Retribution is a nebulous word that can be explained as common sense, or as a supernatural goal. The only way to measure its effectiveness is to ask victims if they believe a punishment was acceptable, but each person's scales are calibrated to different standards. You might argue that if a punishment makes the victim feel better it served a utilitarian purpose by increasing the perceived legitimacy of the system, but it is difficult to design public policies that can satisfy everyone's individual degree of retributive need. The debate over proper definitions will never end, but retribution is still a primary concern of lawmakers and judges.

"Eye for an Eye and Tooth for a Tooth" justice is sometimes impossible or condemnable. As Cassia Spohn has written, if a woman runs a red light and crashes her car into a man, and the man's legs are broken, should we break the woman's legs as punishment? (2). Sometimes an equal punishment is barbaric to modern sensibilities. Modern American legislation tries to determine an appropriate conversion cost in terms of monetary fines or time in prison to "pay your debt to society." We want these converted costs to be fair (meaning they should be the same for everyone convicted of the same crime), and they should be proportional to the severity of the offense. It is impossible to make everyone happy in regards to proportionality. Some people are more vengeful than others. They want two eyes for an eye, or they might even want an eye for a tooth (3).

The retributive logic of our penal system is quite clear: people who break the law should be punished in a manner that is proportional to the severity of their offense. This is referred to as the "rank order of severity" of crimes (4, 5). It is the foundation of the legal codes of every jurisdiction of the United States and informs the sentencing guidelines for judicial decision-making. That's why we expect a murderer to get a longer prison sentence than a shoplifter. Legal philosophers and critics have long argued that a retribution-based system is cruel and ineffective at achieving its goals, but their arguments have not succeeded in replacing our laws. The vigilantes I interviewed for this book reported having retribution-based definitions of "justice." They believe that some people deserve to suffer for their crimes, and they are willing to dispense this justice themselves if they think the court system is too lax. If you are strongly associated with prohibitive qualities in regards to punishment then this book will seem like a nightmarish insight into the minds of people who fundamentally disagree with your sense of justice (6). It may be uncomfortable, but I hope it is educational.

Harsh penalties are not just the currency of retribution in our legal system. They are also explained as a symbolic gesture of government concern for the public. Does the legislator, judge, or district attorney care about the public's safety? How do they express this concern? They punish an offender and make a proud speech declaring "This punishment sends a message that this crime will not be tolerated" or "This punishment demonstrates that we take these crimes seriously." When these messages are broadcast to the voting public on a daily basis it is difficult for these same people to justify a lenient sentence. *Did they decide to tolerate the crime this time? Did they decide not to take the crime seriously this time?* Members of the public might express disbelief and outrage when the logic of the legal system fails to consistently adhere to this punitive rationale. If a severe punishment is evidence that the court takes a crime seriously, why do they occasionally show mercy to people who commit the worst crimes?

What is an appropriate punishment for raping a child? It is an egregious crime that no amount of punishment can ever "repay." The victim will never be fully restored because they can never live the life they would have experienced if the abuse had never occurred. The offender can never pay "their dues in the hard coinage of punishment" (7). And yet our legal system attempts to put a number on it. They convert this horrible crime to a legislative range of penalties. Sentencing guidelines might set a minimum number of years the offender should be deprived of their liberty. They might pay a fine or be required to register as a sex offender. Sometimes they can plead guilty to a lesser offense and get probation. The government makes these deals in order to settle the bill on the victim's behalf, like a bankruptcy court might fine a debtor with pennies on the dollar. If the victim is unsatisfied with the settlement, the debt is still unresolved in their minds, and it accrues interest over time. Some of these victims seek out their abuser and try to avenge their loss through extra-legal punishments.

A retributivist philosophy of punishment is somewhat nebulous and therefore lacks the scientific precision that many academic researchers expect. Andreas von Hirsch has defended the theory of "just deserts" as a logical, proportional system of allocating *blame*. Just as the seriousness of a crime varies, so too should the justice system response (8). Punishments are calibrated according to the relative severity of the offense. If person A receives a certain punishment for a certain crime, person B should receive a greater punishment for a worse crime. Laws may be devised that offer narrow ranges of sentences that each offense is eligible for, but if two crimes with recognizably distinct degrees of seriousness are reversed in terms of punishment severity, it upsets the balance of proportionality. Retributivist goals *can* be utilitarian if they align with the public's minimal expectations. That may occur if the laws reduce fear in society or make victims feel satisfied that their suffering was respected by the system. A general satisfaction with the justice system may increase the likelihood that they will report crimes to the authorities and decrease the likelihood that they will take the law into their own hands. Paul Robinson and Michael Cahill's book *Law Without Justice* explains how unjustifiably harsh or lenient sentences lead to a crisis of legitimacy. People might disagree on the exact measure of punishment necessary for a given crime, but they tend to agree on the rank ordering of severity for different crimes. We would be outraged if someone received a harsher sentence for stealing a car than for raping a child. When the rank ordering of offenses is disturbed, people are unhappy. People may not agree on the exact terms of a punishment, but they know *injustice* when they see it. We all know child sex abuse crimes cause immense harm, and most voters expect the government to inflict a correspondingly harsh punishment. Some people try to re-balance the scales of justice by adding more punishment than the courts authorized. Vigilantes might harass, harm, or kill a sex offender in the community. Prisoners and correctional officers might conspire to torture sex offenders in prison, maximizing the pains of incarceration. These extra-legal punishments are meant to compensate for official acts of leniency.

I hope that this book contributes to these discussions by exposing the verbal justifications that vigilantes provide for their actions. Perhaps we can find a way to reduce the number of these retaliatory crimes in the future. Even if many people share the vigilante's outrage over perceived injustice, they may agree that everyone is entitled to their constitutional rights to due process, and we must ensure that trials are fair, and punishments are appropriate. However, we cannot permit extraordinary acts of leniency for serious sexual offenses when we also give harsh punishments to less egregious crimes, like drug offenses, property crimes, or even some lesser violent crimes. The mass incarceration crisis in the United States could be addressed by reducing the use of incarceration for those lesser offenses, but in the meanwhile, the "injustice gap" is the cause of much public concern. There must be a logical and agreed-upon rank ordering of severity in punishment that corresponds to the severity of the crime being punished or the public will lose faith in the justice system. Perhaps these concerned citizens will recall judges and prosecutors and replace them with demagogues who stoke public fear. It is in the justice system's interest to issue *appropriate* punishments that satisfy the public concern without surrendering to populism.

Some people think vigilantes are heroes for bravely sacrificing their liberty to secure justice for child victims. Other people (and the government itself) consider them to be dangerous villains undermining the rule of the law. My goal in writing this book is to allow these vigilantes to tell you what they think about themselves so you do not have to rely on sensational media headlines to draw your own conclusions. I think you will be surprised at what they have to say.

Men are responsible for the majority of vigilante crimes. I do mention a few women in this book who took the law into their own hands and attacked a child sex abuser with violence, but the vast majority of all cases involve men. The small number of cases involving women vigilantes makes it difficult to draw inferences. It is true that women in prison are known to ostracize and even physically attack other women who are convicted of crimes against children, but these events are too rare to be incorporated into this discussion of mostly male vigilantes (9). It is a fascinating subject, but it is one that requires a separate investigation to truly understand. Unless I note otherwise, if I refer to a "vigilante" or a "prisoner" I am referring to men, and I make no claims about how women fit into the discussion.

Most criminal justice researchers examine large numbers of cases to find patterns. They want to know what the average case is like so they can devise effective interventions. Most researchers will remind you not to focus on outliers because your inferences will be misled, but this book is different. This is a book about rare crimes and worst-case scenarios that do not fit nicely into any confidence intervals. Some of the subjects of this book experienced the most extreme forms of child sex abuse. One was kidnapped, raped, tortured, and abandoned in the streets of Detroit. Another was isolated by his stepfather, beaten, and molested for years. Unless otherwise noted, when I use the term "sex offenses" I am not referring to the standard misclassifications routinely itemized by academics in order to defuse public alarm. These are the truly serious crimes that inspire lifelong trauma, and the desire for bloody revenge.

From the victim's perspective, labeling a concern for serious sexual abuse as a "moral panic" sounds like a disregard for serious crimes that they know occur. Where in these repeated arguments against "moral panics" do the experts make an allowance for the truly atrocious crimes? They would prefer not to mention them, lest their readers panic. This leaves the victims in a precarious state. Without some commiseration or representation of their feelings, they can feel isolated. When a vigilante murders a child sex abuser and brags about it, other victims finally feel as though their suffering was acknowledged, and they call the vigilante a hero. Victims can't always skip the "Anger" phase of coping with trauma, and they might never get to the "Forgiveness" phase that counselors place so much emphasis on, unless we acknowledge the existence of outlier cases.

Most of the vigilantes I write about in this book suffered or witnessed truly horrible acts of child sexual abuse, and they believed they were let down by the criminal justice system. They were outraged by legalistic loopholes and egregiously lenient sanctions imposed on child sex abusers. They often coped with drugs, alcohol, and risky behavior in their adolescence, and started their own prolific criminal careers. This brought them to jails and prisons where the conditions of confinement were atrocious (the prison environment is another extreme factor to include our description of these outliers). Eventually, these men had enough. They decided to avenge their lost childhoods and teach the justice system a lesson by using the skills they learned on the streets and in prison. They took up the mantle of *vigilantes* and violently attacked child sex abusers. Sometimes they had a specific target in mind. Sometimes they just selected a name from an online sex offender registry. Sometimes they killed their victims in prison, thereby fulfilling their role in the "convict justice" system. However, I do not pretend that these in-depth qualitative interviews are generalizable. This is a rare type of crime, and each of these men revealed a complex personality, background, and behavioral pattern that defies any attempt to reduce them to measures of central tendency.

Are their stories reliable? I have attempted to verify each of their claims, but often they are referring to events that happened years ago, behind closed doors. I cannot corroborate everything. I have maintained a cautious skepticism of their stories, but I am left with an overall opinion that their stories are true, for them. This line of thought is familiar to qualitative researchers who try to reconstruct events from eyewitness testimony. They know that sometimes a person deliberately lies, and sometimes they have misremembered something. If I were to censor their words and try to impose my own interpretation of events in this book it would probably only serve to corrupt the narrative even more. Therefore, I have decided to present their words without interference. I have organized their materials in a format that seemed most appropriate for answering specific research questions, but I have not censored them or re-interpreted their words. When possible, I asked for clarification and allowed them to check my summaries for accuracy.

The format of this book is inspired by the "life histories" of the early American criminologists Clifford Shaw and Edwin Sutherland. Shaw published an autobiography of a young man involved in the justice system in his book *The Jack Roller* and he appended his own comments on the subject's life (10). Sutherland did much the same in his book *The Professional Thief* (11). Both books allowed the subjects to tell their entire story in their own words, without censorship. To emulate these methods, I have asked some convicted vigilantes to write their own stories, and I have added additional material from outside sources to explain the phenomenon under investigation.

I am also inspired by books that focus on a particular type of crime and draw upon multiple sources to deliver detailed explanations of the phenomenon. Ioan Grillo's books *El Narco* and *Blood Gun Money* are good examples of how to employ media reports, historical records, personal interviews, and official statistics to explain the complex world of international drug and weapons trafficking (12, 13). Likewise, I have several chapters in this book that describe media coverage of crimes against children and vigilantism. I also report conversations I have had with victims, criminal justice system professionals, and convicted offenders. These chapters are meant to explore the scope of the problem and provide examples of how society reacts to these crimes. Two other sources of inspiration are *The Black Hand* by Christopher Blatchford (with Rene Enriquez, the Mexican Mafia Carnal who contributed from his maximum-security prison cell in California) (14), and Hervey Cleckley's *The Mask of Sanity* that cataloged case studies of his psychiatric patients who exhibited psychopathic personality traits (15). Each of these books used mixed-methods approaches to describe their respective phenomena and analyze them at individual and aggregate levels.

I do not endorse vigilante violence, and this book is not intended to encourage such acts. Some people believe that sharing the words of murderers in order to analyze their crimes is a de facto endorsement of their behavior. I disagree. This book offers nuanced detailed descriptions of situations where such violence was used, and an analysis of the causes and consequences of this violence. I reject the notion that letting these men speak in their own words is an endorsement of their actions. When they published their life histories of jack-rollers and thieves, Clifford Shaw did not support jack-rolling, and Edwin Sutherland did not support professional thievery. Ioan Grillo does not endorse weapons trafficking simply because he interviews weapons traffickers, and Chris Blatchford does not endorse prison gangs because he published the life story of a Mexican Mafia Carnal. These authors published the uncensored words of their collaborators because fearless examination is the only way to find the truth.

With that said, this book does contain graphic language and disturbing content: the conniving grooming process employed by sex offenders, their sexual abuse of children, the trauma it causes, the horrors of prison life in America, the harsh language used to dehumanize the sex abusers, and the bloody revenge sought by vigilantes are among the subjects contained in this book. These are not topics of discussion for an afternoon tea party, but they are important. This book does not pull any punches and I hope you understand just because you ignore a problem doesn't make it go away.

"–Joshua Long"

References

1. Robinson, P., & Robinson, S. (2018). *Shadow vigilantes: How distrust in the justice system breeds a new kind of lawlessness.* Amherst, NY: Prometheus Books.
2. Spohn, C. C. (2002). *How do judges decide? The search for fairness and justice in punishment.* Thousand Oaks, CA: Sage Publications.
3. von Hirsch, A. (1985). *Past or future crimes: Deservedness and dangerousness in the sentencing of criminals.* New Brunswick, NJ: Rutgers University Press.
4. Tonry, M. (2012). *Retributivism has a past: Has it a future?* New York, NY: Oxford University Press.
5. Yamamota, S., & Maeder, E. M. (2019). Creating the punishment orientation questionnaire: An item response theory approach. *Personality and Social Psychology, 45*(8), 1283–1294.
6. Churchill, W. S. (1910). House of Commons Debate, 20 July, 1910. Vol. 19, CC1326–1357. https://api.parliament.uk/historic-hansard/people/mr-winston-churchill/1910
7. Robinsons, P. H., & Cahill, M. T. (2006). *Law without justice: Why criminal law doesn't give people what they deserve.* New York, NY: Oxford University Press.
8. von Hirsch, A. (2012). Punishment futures: The desert-model debate and the importance of the criminal law context. In M. Tonry (Ed.) *Retributivism has a past: Has it a future?* New York, NY: Oxford University Press, pp. 256–274.
9. Fleischer, M. S., & Krienert, J. L. (2009). *The myth of prison rape: Sexual culture in American prisons.* Lanham, MD: Rowman & Littlefield Publishers.
10. Shaw, C. (1966). *The jack-roller.* Chicago: Chicago University Press.
11. Sutherland, E. H. (1937). *The professional thief.* Chicago: Chicago University Press.
12. Grillo, I. (2011). *El narco: Inside Mexico's criminal insurgency.* New York, NY: Bloomsbury Press.
13. Grillo, I. (2021). *Blood gun money: How America arms gangs and cartels.* New York, NY: Bloomsbury Press.
14. Blatchford, C. (2008). *The black hand: The story of Rene "Boxer" Enriquez and his life in the Mexican Mafia.* New York, NY: Harper Collins.
15. Cleckley, H. M. (1941). *The mask of sanity: An attempt to reinterpret the so-called psychopathic personality.* Maryland Heights, MO: Mosby Medical Library.

1

TED GOT WHAT HE DESERVED

On October 9, 2014, Steven D. Sandison was interviewed by two detectives in a small concrete room that was painted white. He wore a dark blue uniform with orange stripes on his shoulders (unique to prisoners in the Michigan Department of Corrections). He also wore glasses and a bright orange beanie. Steven was unperturbed, relaxed, and even broke the tension with a smile or a chuckle every now and then. He serenely answered all of the detective's questions without hesitation. He was so nonchalant you might think he was making small talk while he was waiting on a dental appointment, but actually, Steven was calmly describing the murder he had committed a few hours before in his prison cell at the Saginaw Correctional Facility. Steven had strangled his cellmate, Theodore "Ted" Dyer, with the man's own shoelaces before placing his dead body back on his bunk and covering it with a blanket. Then Steven carefully packed his belongings in anticipation of being transferred, climbed into the top bunk, and went to sleep. When the body was discovered the next morning, Steven was taken to the interrogation room where he told the story of how he had murdered a "child molester" (1).

Detective: Okay, like I said, we're investigating the incident that happened last night that you were involved in. Why don't you just go ahead and tell us what happened.

Sandison: Alright. I've been locking with Ted for about two months. Never asked him what his crime was. Never really cared. We got along okay. I never had any real problems, and then, like two days ago somebody said that he was in prison for CSC so I asked him about it and he kind of never answered me. Then last night about nine o'clock at night I guess he decided to clear his conscience or something, but you know he told me what he was in prison for, that he had you know, was accused of raping an 11-year-old girl, and he got 25 to life for it, and you know I told him that's enough. I don't want to hear anymore, but he just for some reason kept talking and kept talking, and then I really don't have any patience for that kind of thing. I asked him three or four times just let it go, I don't want to hear about it. He didn't, so about eleven or twelve o'clock, somewhere around there I first, you know, punched him a couple times. Still

DOI: 10.4324/9781003393849-2

wouldn't shut up. Still kept telling me he wanted to explain that he didn't do it, that he was being set up and all this stuff. I don't know I just got mad and then hit him, and then I killed him. When I knocked, I hit him and knocked him out and then I took the shoelaces out of his shoes, tied them together, wrapped it around his neck and strangled him. Then after I was done … I mean I was aware of what I was doing. You know and then I just put him on his bed and covered him up and climbed in my bed and went to sleep.

…

Detective: Okay. So, he keeps going on about his personal business: what brought him there, what he did, like you say, he's alleging that it didn't happen and he's been framed and all of that. And I'm sure that having been in this system as long as you have you hear that all the time. You know, and to be honest I'm kind of a firm believer that if you're here and you've gone through the legal system, it's been proven beyond a reasonable doubt that the crime was committed and you're here.

Sandison: Yes. And I also know that you know getting 25 years for something like that it must have been extremely bad. Because most of the time people with CSC get really easy cases. You guys know that. There's no reason for us to talk about it. I was going to try to get moved tomorrow because I said I had heard about it, and you know, if I don't see it I don't believe it. Because everybody spreads rumors about everybody else in prison. So I confronted him about it and at first he said no. Then I left it at that. Then like I said last night, I don't know, out of the blue said he wanted to talk to me and you know told me everything. "I got 25-to-life," "11-years old" just a bunch …

Detective: Things that you just didn't want to hear.

Sandison: Yeah. And I kept asking him you know, I don't want to hear it. And it just I don't know it just seemed to irritate me more and more, even when he didn't say anything. I think him denying it is what irritated me the most.

…

Detective: Okay. So you took the shoe laces out. Um. Obviously you wrapped them around his neck. Just once?

Sandison: Wrapped them around my hands, tied the two together. There were two shoelaces together. I tied the ends together. Wrapped it around a hand put it around his neck and held it.

Detective: How long do you think you had to hold it before you were confident that he was …

Sandison: Actually, a long time.

Detective: Long time being two minutes? Five minutes?

Sandison: I don't know. But it just seemed like a long time.

Detective: Okay. I imagine that probably your time recollection would probably not be accurate because I'm sure …

Sandison: They feel like a long time.

Detective: … you know, a little little tense a little hyped, had the adrenaline going, so … you will end up you're confident that he is now deceased. You pick him up and you said you put him back in his bunk.

Sandison: Put him in the bed and faced him towards the wall so that it looked like he was sleeping.

Detective:	So he was sleeping. Covered him up.
Sandison:	Covered him up.

…

Detective:	Okay. So, you just mentioned that you made reference to that you were sorry. I mean obviously not …
Sandison:	No. Not sorry. I'm not sorry for killing him. Oh no.
Detective:	Oh okay.
Sandison:	Oh no. I was sorry that I caused them problems.
Detective:	Oh I see. Okay, alright. I'm glad to clarify that.
Sandison:	Yeah, no, I'm not sorry at all for killing him.
Detective:	Okay, it's my understanding that you are serving a life sentence right now for homicide.
Sandison:	Yeah.
Detective:	Here again, I guess, it's neither here nor there, the details of that. I guess my question is that the kind of thing that … it appears to me that what you did was because of the crime that Ted committed.
Sandison:	I do what's necessary. I do what some people won't. I mean you guys are cops. You arrest people all the time for stuff you wish you could shoot them in the face. I already know that. I'm not stupid. You know? I mean …
Detective:	I understand…
Sandison:	There's crimes that shouldn't be committed. I don't know. I just don't have any empathy for people so…
Detective:	So basically, what you did, you figure Ted got what he deserved.
Sandison:	Ted got what he deserved. I believe that with all my heart.
Detective:	Okay. And like you say you said you were sorry, and was not sorry for the act of actually killing Ted…
Sandison:	Oh no for causing the officers problems. For having you guys to come down here and go through all this bull crap over a piece of shit, so…
Detective:	I mean, Steve at this point we've put together our report. It's gonna go to the second prosecuting attorney. He will make a decision if charges will be authorized. You're here for life as it is.
Sandison:	He'll waste everybody's money and time, and make things more difficult for everybody else. Yeah, I know that.

…

Detective:	A couple of times you said that he was trying to deny his charges with you?
Sandison:	Well yeah, because he was saying well, because it got me mad you know. First off, 25-to-life. They don't give you 25-to-life. He said it was his first offense. And then I'm thinking "Dude, 25-to-life on your first offense" and then he said um, well it was just touching, and dude, 25-to-life, I'm not a fool. That's penetration. That's bad, bad penetration. Well then he said the mother set him up, and then he said… now he was just a dick man.

———————

*The full transcription of this interrogation is included in the appendix of this book.

This exchange between the detectives and Steven Sandison offers a remarkable insight into the mindset of a prison vigilante immediately after slaying a child sex abuser. His blunt honesty and rapid responses give us a clear picture of the events that occurred, his thought process, and his post hoc rationalizations. Our interpretation of this conversation may differ depending on our preconceived opinions. Some people instantly consider Steven to be a hero regardless of whether he killed Ted to secure justice or whether he was just annoyed that Ted wouldn't shut up. Others consider Steven to be a villain because there is no justification for murder (his original murder charge that put him in prison to begin with, or the killing of Ted Dyer). And still, others are indifferent to his motives or actions because both Steven and Ted were convicts and they make no distinction between their offense types.

During the interrogation Steven said that he didn't "want someone like that on the streets." Steven also shared his beliefs about sex offender recidivism. Later in his confession, he had a conversation about why killing a child sex abuser keeps society safe. He said he has seen men released from prison only to come back shortly thereafter on new charges, and sex offenders would end up hurting another child. If they are dead, they can't hurt anyone. He said "This state has nothing. They just you know, push you out, you know they don't care what happens to the people out there on the streets. They talk about it all the time, coming back in, about what they're gonna do when they get out. Not him specifically, but I hear a lot of child molesters and rapists and crazy fucks you know, always talk about what they're gonna do when they get back out." Apparently, Steven told Ted to pack his belongings so he could be transferred to another cell. Ted reportedly said it didn't matter because "he was going to be released shortly." That is the moment Steven decided to kill him. He said, "Not on my watch." Steven wanted to eliminate the possibility that Ted would be released *just in case* he was telling the truth about his early release, even though he was 67 years old and required to serve a minimum sentence of 25 years. The "crime control" motive is a common verbal justification for vigilantism.

At his trial, Steven had this to say to the court: "You know since this all happened people think I'm some kind of hero, well I'm actually not. I just did what I thought was best in the time that I was given. I don't know, I've been getting these emails saying, you know, it's not my position to judge anybody, and I want to make it quite clear that I didn't judge him. I know God is the only judge we have. I've just set the appointment up. So, I don't feel bad for what I did. You know, I feel bad for maybe the families, his family or something, but as far as remorse or something toward him, no."

This was not the last murder of a sex offender to be reported in the Saginaw Correctional Facility in Michigan. In January of 2016, a prisoner named Jason Turnbull was serving 10 to 15 years for 3rd-degree CSC (criminal sexual conduct) and multiple convictions of 4th-degree CSC (2). Just like Ted Dyer, he was strangled to death by his cellmate. There is no known connection between this case and Steven Sandison's example, but it is not impossible to imagine that a culture of vigilantism thrives in the Saginaw facility. Perhaps throughout the American prison system. Maybe in the free world too.

Steven the Hero

Steven Sandison's interrogation video was published on YouTube by the Michigan news agency MLive. The edited version of this video is 3 minutes and 38 seconds long (perfect for quick viewing by the busy public). It is the *second most popular video* uploaded by the MLive YouTube channel (only 1 million views behind a courtroom confrontation between a mother and her child's killer). The video of Steven's interrogation was uploaded on April 22, 2015. As of October 3, 2021, this video has 15,442,441 views, over 275,000 "Thumbs Up," 4,900 "Thumbs Down," and 57,074 comments. The vast majority of these comments praise Steven for his actions. A select list of public comments is listed below with the authors' names omitted. These were chosen by sorting according to "Top Comments" (most highly rated) and choosing randomly from comments on the first ten pages.

As this guy said in court: "I'm not judging, God is the ultimate judge, I've just set an appointment" What a legendary phrase.

"Then I climbed into bed and went to sleep" My favorite part.

We have an "unspoken" Social Contract with the incarcerated. "Harm those who harm children" Steven Sandison fulfilled his side of THAT contract.

Sounds like Steven has been a possible victim of past abuse, and maybe this was part of his justice he could impart on the world.

We all know the cop talking to him is sitting there thinking "I get it buddy. I get it."

Although I condemn the murder of human beings, those who touch children are not anywhere close to being people.

"I wouldn't want a guy like that back on the street." A strong man acts within that which constrains him. "Thank you sir" children & their parents worldwide.

I'd like to buy him a drink if I could.

My favorite part is when the guy goes "You guys are cops I know you arrest people you wish you could shoot in the face all the time" …and the cop chuckles. What an honest exchange

They put that guy in the same cell with this man on purpose, cmon guys…. The warden knows his inmates.

It's so sad that you even NEED to explain why you should kill a child molester…

Thank you, Steven, for your great sacrifice.

That's the most polite killer ever. In his defense he told him to shut up.

"Two wrongs don't make a right, but it sure makes things even."

One thing every prisoner have in common is the disgust and hate of child predators. Oddly wholesome.

He deserves a thank you.

I would buy a beer for this guy every single weekend for the rest of his life.

Doing the Lord's work

The most honest man is the man who has nothing to gain, and nothing to lose.

I want to give this man a trophy.

Steven made the world a little safer …

As a victim of a priest, I have to admit some satisfaction in this outcome. I know it's wrong but there it is.

GOOD JOB!I WOULD LIKE TO BUY YOU A CUP OF COFFEE AND GIVE YOU A
SMILEY FACE STICKER!

Child molesters shouldn't be in prison. They belong underground. Why should we, as citizens
pay for them to think about what they did.

In order for justice to reign, sometimes lives must be taken.

"You guys are cops, you arrest people all the time for stuff that you wish you could shoot
them in the face"... Investigator: giggles and nods rather heartwarming interaction.

Good for him!

Prison: "New rule. All child molesters get to share a cell with this guy."

I'd love to know what happened to this guy. seriously I hope it wasn't too harsh. those of us on
the outside are really tired of all the kiddy diddlers getting off with a slap on the wrist.

One person who had mixed emotions over the murder of Ted Dyer was the mother of Ted's
victim (3). The mother's name was Mary. Her daughter was 9 years old (not 11 years old as
mentioned in Steven's interrogation). Mary lived in an apartment next door to the 67-year-old
Theodore Dyer. She trusted her daughter around Ted and his girlfriend and felt they had "adopted
my kids, I guess." One day her daughter was in Ted's apartment at a later than usual hour. Something in Mary's head told her not to knock, and to just walk in. When she did, she saw Ted in his
bedroom sexually abusing her daughter. It was later revealed that this was not the first time he
had done this to the girl. Ted was sent to prison and served ten months of his 25- to 50-year sentence before Steven killed him. When Mary heard the news of Ted's death she said "I cried and I
laughed. It was a bunch of mixed emotions." She said she never wanted to see anyone die, but also
said it was a relief for her daughter "knowing that this wasn't going to happen again." Like Steven,
Mary didn't trust that Ted would serve his whole prison sentence either.

Steven has received hundreds of letters from supporters. Most of them were victims of child
abuse. They thank Steven for validating their suffering by killing a dangerous pervert. They see
bravery in Steven that they admire. These survivors of child sexual abuse did not take the law into
their own hands, but they wish that someone (maybe the government) had protected them with
the same decisiveness that Steven used to kill Ted Dyer.

One woman wrote to pour her heart out to Steven. She suffered from PTSD her entire life
and attempted to kill herself many times. She said her abuser had raped 17 girls before he was
convicted, and one of his victims committed suicide. She wrote: "I know sitting in a cell you do
not feel like a hero, but the truth is you saved a victim from pain of knowing what survival guilt
feels like. You saved another child possibly from a monster. You saved me from myself and you
gave me hope that there is still good people in the world that protect children when the justice
system fails us." The man who raped her and 17 other victims was set to be released from prison
in 2031, and she hoped that he would suffer the same fate as Ted Dyer before that date.

Researchers have proclaimed that "more incarceration is not what most victims of crime
want" (4). Although they use an either/or measure to achieve this conclusion, they are correct
that some victims want less punishment because they are forgiving people. Maybe they had social
support and therapy that helped them get to the forgiveness stage of coping with trauma. But what
about the victims who want revenge? Should the justice system consider their desires? If the judge
shows mercy to the offender, those retribution-oriented victims may feel as though their wishes
have been ignored, so they write letters to people like Steven Sandison. Their hero.

Vigilantes and victims share a common cause. They are bonded in trauma. One victim wrote this to Steven:

> Don't ever hang your head down in shame or sweat through the night over that monster. And on Judgment Day if God has something to say so will I, to Him. I'm not really sure there is a God but I do know there are angels on Earth and you are one.

You may criticize these people for encouraging a murderer, but their trauma is so severe, their suffering so profound (even decades later), that when they watch a man confess to murder on the internet they send him gifts. They pour their hearts out to him in gratitude. There is something about child sexual abuse that leaves a deep scar in someone's mind, and these victims often lose the ability to trust others. Why would they trust Steven? Because actions speak louder than words. They believe a man who kills a child sex abuser and tells the world "Ted got what he deserved" is speaking *for them* without equivocation.

Steven the Villain

In Steven's own words, he is not "an angel." He has spent most of his life incarcerated. He was sentenced to probation for simple assault at age 14, was sent to a group home for carrying a concealed weapon later that same year, was sent to jail for six months for breaking and entering at age 17, one month in jail for joyriding at age 18, and he started his prison sentences in 1981 for various car thefts and burglaries.

In 1991, he was scheduled to be released again. He had been corresponding with a woman who offered to pick him up at the prison gate. Within a few hours of meeting her Steven strangled her to death and stole her car. His official records describe this murder in the following terms:

> He has committed serious felony offenses during every previous term of parole culminating in a 1991 Murder – First Degree that involved the defendant killing a woman that had corresponded with him during his incarceration. On the day the defendant first met the woman, he strangled her to death and stole her car. For this offense, the defendant was sentenced in July 1992 to a life term without the possibility of parole.

He has said "I deserve to be in prison … I can't function in society. I already know that. I deserve to be here and I accept that." He was never a "good" citizen, but he insists he is not a "monster." His reason? "I have never harmed anyone who did not with their hand or mind hurt a child or older person." He never explained why he thought that woman deserved to die.

While most of the YouTube commentators argued that Steven was heroic for killing Ted Dyer, some of them criticized vigilante violence. It was not easy to find disapproving remarks randomly among the ~57,000 comments, but here are some that were located in the first twenty pages:

> you actually think this guy was in anyway in the right for doing this.

> Weird to see so many people praising this man. I wonder how his girlfriend's family feels about him being called a hero.

> People complementing this guy seem to be forgetting he is a murderer.

> Let me make sure that I get it right: You praise that guy for murdering a convict in a prison cell?

The guy was trying to tell him he didn't do it! Imagine if it was true…

Some people don't realize he's in a prison for a reason. He isn't a hero, just a vigilante.

This is what I don't understand about this whole moral code that criminals pretend to have. Like gimme a fucking break. This dude was in prison for murder. He's on the same level as the guy that he killed.

Thanks for uploading a clip which adds nothing to the public sphere but to expose a number of psychopaths in the comment section glad that the U.S. runs a revenge system instead of a justice system.

Some of Steven's online critics argue that there is a slippery slope. If we do not loudly condemn vigilante violence then it is just a matter of time before society collapses and the Klu Klux Klan begins a reign of terror across the country. Others were more restrained and merely noted that Steven was a dangerous person who should not be praised for killing Ted because this might inspire more prisoners to follow his example. They believe that our legal system is flawed and that anyone labeled a sex offender might be innocent. How can we justify the execution of someone who was falsely convicted? The internet is full of debates that echo these themes, but their voices are completely overwhelmed by proud statements of support for vigilante violence. Steven's supporters tend to use a trump card in these arguments. They just call their critics "pedo lovers."

Not every critic is an amateur. Philosophy professor Peter Rose-Barry weighed in on Steven Sandison's murder of Ted Dyer when the interrogation video went viral (5). He argued for a nuanced, academic analysis of the case that was certainly not considered by the average YouTube commenter. In an interview with the MLive news network, Barry said that society's misuse of the word "evil" is partly to blame for the dehumanization of child sex abusers. "One of the concerns that some people have discussing evil at all, that we need to drop the word from our vocabulary, is that calling someone evil effectively shuts down the conversation. It's a way of artificially, sometimes, refusing to talk about the situation. Once we've decided that this guy is evil, nobody is going to speak up for him… We can all probably get our head wrapped around the idea that there are some cases of justifiable homicides. Most of us can think of some circumstances where killing another human being is justified. It's much harder, maybe even impossible, to think of circumstances… where child molestation is justifiable… There might be something so remarkably heinous about that crime that's eliciting these kinds of reactions. And frankly, that's not crazy. If you make a list about the most terrible things we can do to each other is there something besides that that's going to be on the top of the list?"

Professor Rose-Barry suggests that some crimes are considered worthy of the death penalty if it is imposed by the state (because there is a better opportunity for impartiality, due process, and it is intended to communicate a message about crimes and the law). However, due to the imperfect nature of the legal system the death penalty can be challenged on procedural grounds even if it is justifiable on retributivist grounds (Rose-Barry, 2021, personal correspondence). In any event, strangling child sex abusers in a prison cell is even less justifiable than state-imposed death penalties because it is arbitrary, capricious, and not regulated. Professor Rose-Barry received some backlash for not totally endorsing Steven's homicide. He read some hate mail and online comments that were directed at himself, his wife, and his (non-existent) children, but like most outrage on the internet, the blasphemy mobs lost interest and ceased their war of words. MLive removed the comment sections from their website, perhaps due to situations like this. Clearly, the subjects of child abuse and vigilantism provoke strong emotions.

With the exception of a few unofficial "pats on the back" by correctional officers, the authorities condemned Steven's actions. Steven pled guilty to first-degree murder for killing Ted Dyer and was given a minimum sentence of life in prison. He was already serving a life sentence for murder so this punishment was merely symbolic. A more tangible punishment came from the administrators of the Michigan Department of Corrections, who certainly did not consider Steven to be a hero. Their formal process for dealing with violent misconduct is to transfer offenders to a more restrictive setting. Steven was placed in a solitary cell at the maximum-security Ionia Correctional Facility ("the armpit of the worst prison system in America" as Steven calls it). He has been in this level of confinement since 2014.

Steven has limited human contact and sparse living conditions. He is allowed to have medical care, clothing, a mirror, a sitting surface, a writing surface, a short-handled toothbrush, toilet paper, shaving gear, three meals a day from the same menu available to the general population, an opportunity to shower three times per week, a mattress, pillow, and blanket, mail privileges (although many of my letters never reach him), and he was allowed to make one 15 minute phone call every seven days. These calls cost 16 cents per minute, and Steven cannot earn money while in segregation.

Although he is 58 years old, Steven is considered to pose a "serious threat to the physical safety of staff or other prisoners" because of his actions in 2014. Unless he has a medical emergency there is no clear path for him to step down from this level of restriction to a housing unit with more privileges. Surely, in the Michigan Department of Corrections, vigilantism doesn't pay.

Steven the Artist

The stifling boredom of this seven-year-long isolation has pushed Steven to the human limit. He writes to me that he is tired of merely "existing" and that he pours himself into his writing and his art. He was afraid that if he died his drawings would be thrown in the garbage. In one letter he told me to destroy the work he sent me, but quickly followed this with another letter telling me not to destroy them because it was his sum contribution to the world.

Steven uses his time in administrative segregation to perfect his drawing skills. Although he has Parkinson's Disease and his hands tremble, he is a talented artist. In fact, he has an Associates' Degree in art. He takes inspiration from William Blake, tattoo artists, and caricaturists. He wrote to me saying: "My man is Dali. I love art that makes people wonder. I don't care if they hate it, as long as it moves something more than their eyes." He has allowed me to print some of his work in this book (Figures 1.1–1.3). One is a disturbing piece titled "Murder 101." On this poster, he has smeared ink on the paper to depict a highly accurate human skull with a bullet hole in the forehead. The poster also contains a handgun and shell casings. On it he has written the words:

NEVER KILL ANYONE YOU KNOW. NEVER HAVE A MOTIVE. NEVER FOLLOW A DISCRENIBLE PATTERN. NEVER KEEP A WEAPON AFTER USED. BEWARE OF LEAVING PHYSICAL EVIDENCE. ISOLATE YOURSELF. HAVE NO SOUL.

One of the posters Steven mailed to me depicts a child sitting on the floor hugging his knees. He is covered in dirt, scabs, and bruises. His eyes convey deep sadness and fear. He is barefoot and wearing rags. It is a self-portrait of Steven's horrendously abusive childhood.

FIGURE 1.1   "Murder 101" by Steven Sandison

FIGURE 1.2   "Murder 101" by Steven Sandison

FIGURE 1.3   "Sandison 1974" by Steven Sandison

Steven the Victim

When Steven was two years old his mother abandoned the family. Everyone blamed Steven, who was too young to understand, let alone be responsible for such a thing. His childhood was characterized by abuse and neglect. His family was all Jehovah's Witness from England, but Steven always wondered why they were so unforgiving and cruel. They never hugged him. He didn't understand when other people were affectionate with their children. He often lived in abandoned houses by himself and his older sister would bring him food. Today, none of these family members write to him in prison. He wonders if they even bother to pray for him.

Sometimes I think I came out of my mom half-grown. She left me at 2-years-old with a male adult and two other males and a female (well, a "father," two "brothers," and a "sister," all older). I never identified with any of them as family. In fact, for a long time I thought I was found in a trash can behind Farmer Jacks. That's what my sister said.

I have not talked with anyone about this a very long time. My dad said I was born without a face and that is why my mom left when I was two. Some people are born with skin covering their face [en caul birth] and that's all it was, but to others I was a devil child.

I was blamed for my mom going back to England. I asked way too many questions and didn't understand why I was treated better by people I was told to hate than by my family. And my biggest mistake was I trusted everyone. I did what I wanted and no one cared. I wish I was beat all the time. It would have been so much better than just treated like I was not even there.

In 1974, something terrible happened. Steven was 10 or 11 years old. He was wandering around the streets of Detroit by himself because his family didn't supervise him. One day, a man and a woman in an ice cream truck offered him a ride. He asked them a lot of questions, like most naïve, innocent kids do. They humored him. For the first time in his life, he was getting attention from someone. "Someone was willing to listen, but I didn't think of the cost." These adults kidnapped Steven and locked him in the basement of their house. They only took him out to rape him, to torture him, to photograph and film his sexual abuse, or give him emergency medical care to keep him alive for longer.

I should point out that I had not asked Steven to tell me about his childhood in my letters. I asked him to tell me about the incident where he killed Ted Dyer. He sent me several handwritten letters that told a profoundly sad story of the worst kinds of traumatic child abuse. I have reproduced it for you to read below:

....

"THE DARK WOODS"

By Steven Sandison

In 1974, I was off on one of my walkabouts when everything good in me died.

I was picked up by a man and woman who liked the fact I was asking so many questions. It's the same old story. Someone was willing to listen and I didn't think of the cost.

I'm sure you don't want details, but I will say, I know pain. Real pain. I was held in a coal room in the basement of a house that must have been old. The walls were huge rocks and I could see light in cracks up top of an iron door. This is where I spent a year: raped, beaten, used in every way an evil soul could think of. Other people would come and at times I was taken into other rooms, and well, I found that monsters didn't live under the bed or in the closet. The shadows were not to be feared, it was the light and the world I learned to fear. The people who I looked to for help, for love, for hope, were my monsters.

One person would see how many thumbtacks he could put in my body before I passed out. Over time, I could stand to be covered front and back. I had learned to go to the *Dark Woods*. That is what I called it. The human mind is able to do some really odd shit. I think I had got to the point where I could go someplace other than that room. I felt nothing. It was like I really was walking around in the woods at night. I would see things, smell, feel. Some of the shit I saw... never mind. I don't need you thinking bad of me.

I know a person can leave their body and go to other places. How do you think I got through all the fucked shit that monster did to me? The problem is it takes an act of such desperation, despair, or pain to open that part of your mind. The more you go the easier it gets. We want to believe that everything in life has its place – that God is the maker and would not give us gifts that could harm us, but the longer we live the more we learn. Keep them away from the Tree of Life. So why not hide answers in a place where humans will not look – pain, despair, loneliness, and hopelessness? But all the great thinkers have suffered and every great thinker tries to open the mind, with what? From time past to now we all as humans have forced some kind of suffering on others. All I know, Josh, is we don't know shit about our-self and if we just sit back and chill and listen and watch, we will learn. If you believe in something with your soul, it will happen.

When I got too sick to use, some lady would take care of me and tell me how lucky I was. She said other kids were being used and left dead in the snow all over Detroit. Shit, I truly felt *they* were the lucky ones.

The really odd part was no matter what happened or how sick I got, every day this fat fuck would read W. Blake, O. Wilde, E.A. Blair, Nietzsche... to this day these people's beliefs are burned into my soul.

Then one day, it stopped. I was still kept in the coal room, but the only time I saw anyone was when I got my bucket empty and food. I don't know how much time passed, but one day fat ass came back and he talked. I remember every word. I can still hear what he said to this day. This was not some crazy fuck who blindly went around doing this to kids. For two days he talked and I listened and I learned.

At the end he said he would and should kill me, but he said I had already let the world kill me. The illusion was gone. He read me *Paradise Lost*. Not all of it. I did read it all years later, but this fuck had the balls to look me in the eyes and tell me he was not going to kill me because anything human in me was already dead.

They washed me inside and out, put me in an ice cream truck or whatever, and dumped me in front of a strip bar.

That was my childhood.

People flipped out. Cops came and I spent four months at Herman Kiefer Hospital. It took about a year of rehab to get my body in shape and everyone wanted to know who, what, where, and even why.

Why?

I had seen, felt, and lived what man could do, so I just didn't talk. This is in fact the only time I have talked. You just got me at a time when I know my time is short. I have endured more betrayal than anyone should and if I passed it on, then more's the pity.

You know what was the worst? Not all the questions, but the look on my dad's face. Like I disappointed *him*. He, my family, never even asked me what happened. Nothing. Like it never happened and I even questioned myself. I still had one friend, Paul. His dad was a badass Vietnam vet and he knew what happened. I stayed with them for a year and listened to every word I heard. I listened and learned.

I don't trust humans. From May 1978 to 1981 I put my thumb out and never stayed anywhere more than a few days. Anyone who came on to me I ended, or tried to. I'd go state-to-state and hang out with kids and find out who was doing bad shit to them and I'd do what I could to stop them. I got away with many, and more was blamed on others. When things got hot for me I'd come back to Michigan, get into some small shit, and cool out in a youth home. My start into the system. *Alea iacta est.*

Getting into the system is like going to school. You learn from other's mistakes. And in Michigan the system is like a playland. I could get out, do my thing, and go back in. My only redeeming fact is I never harmed anyone innocent.

I'm not sure what to say about prison. When I first came in it was very bad for me. Young, White, small. I was raped one time. I laughed and talked of my past. Letting them know with each thrust that I was going to kill them, so they better kill me. Word got around and that never happened again. Everyone tried to break me from the inmates to the babysitters.

The problem is everyone has this misconception of what evil looks like. What no one seems to understand is we all have two faces. One we wear every day and the one of our true self. Two people can be together for 50 years and never see each other's true face. We do unspeakable things to each other in the name of Justice, Hate, Love, and God.

I know I sound jaded but you must understand Josh, I know nothing else. I have never felt the touch of a love we read about. Never knew anyone who I could trust, and my own knowledge of love or passion comes from a book or poem. People think I must have feelings or why do I care what happens to kids?

It's because my true face is that of a child waiting for his father or anyone to come save him. 58 years I have waited and until then I'll kill every monster that stands in my way. I guess that makes the face I show evil.

What's really so sad is the story of loss and the realization that after all we have endured in life at the end we are all truly alone. For me, be it heaven or hell, or nothing at all, I suspect that it must be better than this.

....

Steven seemed so cool and collected in his interrogation footage you would not realize what was lurking in his past. He says he lost his soul in that basement when he was 10 years old. He was a "bomb built in Hell," as Andrew Vachss might have described him. If you believe that psychopaths are made and not born, could you devise a more effective method of creating a cold-blooded, vengeful killer than through the trauma Steven experienced in that basement? Maybe the "fat fuck" who raped him and read *Paradise Lost* to him was right. He didn't have to kill Steven, because Steven was already dead inside. In hindsight, we can argue that if Steven was given support by his family or effective therapy by mental health professionals, he might have turned out differently. But observations based on hindsight can't help Steven now. He's serving a life sentence in a maximum-security prison. It is too late for him.

Steven told me that he learned to go into "the Dark Woods" in his mind when he was an abused child. If he could separate his mind from his body he could avoid feeling pain. As an adult in a maximum-security prison, he uses this skill to travel to those Dark Woods any time he wants, like flexing a muscle. He is offended that the prison psychiatrists diagnosed him with schizophrenia. He thinks this mental transportation is a hidden talent that anyone could do if they were forced to the ultimate extremity of suffering like he was. I had heard of other cases where children "dissociate" from physical reality as a way of coping with stress. Dissociative Identity Disorder is defined in the *Diagnostic and Statistical Manual of Mental Disorders* (DSM-5) as identity disruption with various symptoms precipitated by trauma and stress. Children who suffer serious abuse might develop this disorder as a mode of psychological survival. If they can "go somewhere else" in their mind they can endure torment when they are unable to escape from the source of their suffering, much like when a lab rat develops bizarre behaviors when faced with inescapable shocks (6). This sensational phenomenon is widely misunderstood, even by trained mental health professionals, but it is an established disorder supported by decades of empirical evidence. An important feature of this disorder is that it does not resolve itself over time. It persists without targeted treatment, and it can last well into adulthood (7). Steven has experienced this separation of mind and body for almost five decades. He has learned to live with it, and he uses it to help pass the time in prison.

I wanted to corroborate parts of Steven's story. He mailed a cutout from a 1974 Detroit newspaper that mentioned he was found abandoned on the streets, but I never received the letter (about half of our correspondence is damaged or lost in the Michigan DOC mail rooms). I searched online newspaper archives so I could find this article myself, but I was unable to locate it. It is possible that he was not mentioned by name because he was a child, so I searched for "missing child" or "kidnapped child" stories. I could not find his story in particular, but I found hundreds of other cases.

In the 1970s, Detroit had a series of child kidnappings, sexual assaults, and serial killings. J. Rueben Appleman catalogs these horrifying cases in his book *The Kill Jar* (also depicted in television miniseries "Children of the Snow") (8). I spoke with Appleman about Steven's case, and while he did not have any evidence that Steven was a kidnapping victim, he believes it is a plausible story. He often receives letters from people who had similar experiences during this time period in Detroit. There was an active "child pornography ring" that would lure children into video studios, abuse them, and "dispose" of the children. The survivors did not always go to the police. They were glad to be left alive.

One child named Tim was killed in 1977. He was 11 years old. His sister, Cathy Broad, has never stopped looking for his killer. She runs the website "CatherineBroad.blog" where she organizes information on child killings across Michigan and Ohio, hoping that this cold case will be solved (9). Her blog did not have any information about Steven's kidnapping, but she also agreed that his story was plausible. She receives stories from people who suffered the same fate. Maybe the "fat fuck" who read *Paradise Lost* to Steven after putting thumbtacks in his body was one of the Detroit killers. We will probably never know.

Steven sent me a copy of his presentence investigation report compiled by the DOC in preparation for his trial in 2015. It tells the basic story about Steven's record: he had five felonies, one misdemeanor, a juvenile record, and an Associate's Degree in Applied Arts earned during one of his brief periods of parole. He had a significant psychiatric and substance abuse history. He said he used drugs to cope with the trauma of his childhood experiences, and he first started using marijuana at age 12 before using alcohol and opiates at 14. This report says that Steven "reports a particularly tumultuous childhood preceding his involvement in the criminal justice system… He has no familial or social support outside of the prison system… The defendant noted that he himself had been the victim of severe sexual molestation as an adolescent and held a strong animus for anyone that would rape a child or old person." The Department of Corrections did not use this information to design a case plan to help Steven cope with his lifetime of trauma. They used it to justify sending Steven to solitary confinement in a maximum-security facility.

In a way, Steven is still a victim today. Some might say "Don't do the crime if you can't do the time" or point out that prison is "not the Holiday Inn," but it is undeniable that life in Michigan's prison system is a painful and traumatizing experience. Steven's world has shrunk to fit the size of his 8x12 prison cell in Ionia, Michigan. He has been in prison for decades. He will never leave. Most of my conversations with Steven are about this little world. In his weekly 15-minute phone call he talks to me about the noise of "shit-talkers" in the cellblock, the lethargic mailroom employees, the books that arrive in damaged condition, and about artwork. He sent me a postcard of Blake's *Job Rebuked By His Friends*, perhaps because my questions about his crimes were interpreted as rebukes. He sent me one powerful statement that should satisfy those of you who want to know his mindset:

It is easy for a man to tell the right and wrongs of war or the horror of a life spent in fear in de-spair when they have not lived it, felt it, smelled it and tasted it. How can you expect a person to understand the depth of pain felt as your very soul is ripped from your body!

The knowledge of horror is not horror.

Justice is a concept that the people in charge came up with- If a person has caused damage to the very core of what man is then there can be no other punishment than death. He con-tradicts his self by living.

Some people say to show "restraint and temperance." How could you be willing to kill to punish some other man with that in your mind?

I do not like people who try to understand something, where to live it or have it touch your soul is to know- This is why people don't understand when I talk about the Dark Woods – To tell a person my spirit leaves my body and goes to a place other than the reality we know- I'm called "Mad."

I feel it is far worse to leave a man in a cage and take away the very thing that makes us human is far, far worse than anything else! My life is spent in a 8-foot by 12-foot cell, all day, everyday. I hear nothing but yelling and shit talk – at night the despair is so thick you can feel it pushing you down like a wool blanket.

I believe everything is one thing, only, there are some questions in my life that I don't know. I've stopped asking. At the beginning I wanted to have answers for everything. And now I respect the fact that I can't have answers for everything.

Fatal Justice

Steven Sandison's case is an invaluable resource for people who want to know more about the vigilante mindset and the harsh realities of America's prison system. Watching his interrogation footage is a fantastic substitute for a Rorschach test. Rather than showing an ink blot and ask-ing someone what they see, just show them Steven's replies to the homicide investigators. If they react with confusion they are probably not the kind of person who typically supports vigilante justice. If they react with smiles, laughter, and an immediate desire to send Steven money, then they might be pro-vigilante.

Steven received hundreds of letters from "fans" after his video went viral. Most of them were women who were sexually abused as children. They thanked Steven for doing what they wish someone else would have done in their case. They poured their hearts out to a man serving a life sentence for murder, because he boldly stated that child sex abusers deserve to die. Understanding this compulsion to get revenge against child sex abusers and to issue the death penalty so they can't hurt others is a profoundly deep subject. It reaches far back into the human psyche and puts divergent worldviews on trial. Who is more moral? The person who wants to protect child sex abusers from harm, or the person who cheers when a child sex abuser dies?

We can speculate on all of this from the comfort of our homes, but the best way to understand what happens inside the mind of a vigilante is to ask them. They have a lot to say.

The Dark Side

By "A Son of Solitude"

I needed to reach the top shelf in the pantry, and I was just too damn short to do it on my own. It was past midnight on a school night. Both my parents were sleeping, and I was standing in front of the open pantry, looking at the bag of nacho cheese Doritos on the top shelf. Real Doritos! Not the store brand. My stomach was rumbling. I had already gone to bed hungry, and now, these chips were all I could think of. Stealthily, I dragged a barstool over to the pantry, cautiously climbing to the top like an acrobat, balancing, reaching, the sound of the bag loud enough to make me cringe. Food was an ally of mine. An emotional support mechanism, and while I was far too young at eight or nine years old to realize it, I used food to medicate poisonous emotions and overwhelming feelings. I was one screwed-up little fat kid, for sure. I planned to eat just a few handfuls, but as the marvelous flavor of neon cheese powder overwhelmed my taste buds, and overrode my common sense and fear, I proceeded to eat, handful after handful on the stool that night, filling my fat little belly to bursting. I had cheese powder on my hands, my face, evidence impossible to conceal, everywhere, damning me to an as yet undetermined violent repercussion of some sort. At some point, I realized I had eaten too much. I rolled the bag tight and replaced it on the shelf, then quietly made my way back to my bed. I fell asleep immediately, as the blanket covered my face.

I was awakened harshly, being jerked out of my bed by my feet. As I hit the floor I gave a yelp of shock and terror, and the evil one, my adoptive father, quickly placed his hand over my mouth, placing his face against mine, he brusquely told me to shut up. He was slapping my face, castigating me for being a pig, a fat sneak thief. It was nearly time to go to school, and as I was tearfully pulling my clothes on, he said he would have a surprise for me when I returned home. All this sneaking around in the dark and stealing was going to come to an end... today. I remember that day clearly because I had just been moved into an advanced math class. Myself and some other student had tested well enough to be placed with some older, honor students. I could not focus on anything in school that day. I made a fool of myself and the teacher who scolded me, it was as if my brain had a disconnect switch. I was too focused on the clock and what would happen when I got home to care about school.

He picked us up in the Plymouth minivan and had a grin on his face. He was a large man. Quite fat, multiple chins, and a rotund belly, red faced, glasses, hairy. He didn't say much, but he told my brother to go play outside when we got home. He took me by the hand into the attached garage. There, on the worktable, laying flat, was a freshly cut piece of wood. He picked it up and turned toward me, taking the time to display his handiwork. It was a length of framing lumber, a 2″x4″ approximately 3 feet long. He had used a jigsaw to cut a long handle into the end and had wrapped it with black electrical tape. It was obviously made to be swung with a two-handed grip. There were holes drilled all throughout the length of it, and he had written in black permanent marker "this side up" on one side, and "The Rod" on the other. The monster had spent a considerable amount of time fashioning this implement to beat me with. He was quite proud of himself and I was terrified. My legs were visibly shaking and I was just stammering, "I'm sorry, I'm sorry." He told me to pull my pants down and put my hands on the workbench. I hesitated and he roughly spun me around. The first few blows were tolerable, but then as he landed them over and over again, on the backs of my legs, they began to swell and the pain was intense. My legs spasmed, I fell down to my knees. He immediately jerked me back up and continued. After a time, I buried my face in my own arms. I leaned all the way onto the workbench. My little kid underwear now sliding down from the veracity of the beating.

It was difficult to walk for a while after that session. My brother was waiting for me outside, and for some reason, when our eyes me, I had the understanding that a small part of me died in that garage. I was learning something about killing someone one blow at a time, but I wasn't aware of the lesson. A child's psyche is much like a clear pane of glass when it is young, pristine, and undamaged. Fragile in some ways, resilient in others. Now tip that clear psyche on its side, and smash it with a rock. Watch as it shatters, each one shattering in a unique way. Some into a million small dysfunctions, others into a few identifiable shards of trauma. It is impossible to predict how a psyche has shattered or to know how cracked and fragile it has become from repeated strikes with the stone. The cracks in the child's psyche can run far and wide, and usually blossom into untold issues and damaging behaviors later in life.

I was never again successful in any math classes after that day. I soon failed out of the advanced class I had been placed in. I recall that the formulas and equations which were familiar in the past now appeared to me like unintelligible series of marks, numerical gibberish. They became unrecognizable overnight. I had always been confident with my analytical mind. Mathematics were a certain and secure territory for me. But something damaging happened to my brain, my spirit, as a result of the beatings. I also began struggling in other classes which should have been easy for me. I couldn't focus. Schoolwork just didn't place on my list of survival priorities anymore. The incident in the garage was by no means a singular occurrence. I was beaten with that 2"x4" over and over again. It became a repeated ritual, sadistic, a dark tortuous practice which permanently changed me, altered how my brain functioned. That clear, innocent psyche was shattered, time and again, and it would never be the same again. Each time he ushered me over to the dark side for an assault, a piece of me broke off and was left behind.

The scale and scope of the effects of this and other types of child abuse cannot properly be quantified. Self-image issues, credit management issues, lack of higher education, petty crimes, debt, weight issues, and so much more. At the root of all of my criminal thinking and addictions, my ongoing life failures and poor decisions was that sense of worthlessness, the hopelessness that was driven into me as a child while I was being sexually and physically assaulted. The collective nature of all of our children determines the collective future of our society. We would be most wise to recognize this and begin quickly taking concrete steps to permanently change our existing systems of justice, somehow, our children, all of them, must be given a world where they are nurtured and protected.

References

1. Steven Sandison confesses to murdering child molester in prison. (2015, April, 22). YouTube. https://www.youtube.com/watch?v=YawI85U7QtA
2. Roose-Church, L. (2016, Jan, 19). Brighton man strangled in prison. *Livingston Daily*. https://www.livingstondaily.com/story/news/crime/2016/01/19/brighton-man-strangled-prison/79014924/
3. *Mom of sex assault victim reacts to attacker's murder*. (2014, Nov. 5). Muskegon, MI: Detroit Free Press. https://www.freep.com/story/news/local/michigan/2014/11/05/child-sexual-assault-attacker-murder/18526545/
4. Alliance for Safety and Justice. (2016). *Crime survivors speak: The first-ever national survey of victim's views on safety and justice*. http://www.allianceforsafetyandjustice.org/crimesurvivorsspeak/report
5. Hoag, A. (2019, Jan. 20). Murder of child molester in prison does not serve justice, prof says. *MLive*. https://www.mlive.com/news/saginaw/2015/02/what_degree_of_crime_does_it_t.html
6. Donovan, D. M., & McIntyre, D. (1990). *Healing the hurt child: A developmental-contextual approach*. New York, NY: W.W. Norton & Company.
7. Brand, B. L., Sar, V., Stavropoulos, P., Krüger, C., Korzekwa, M., Martínez-Taboas, A., & Middleton, W. (2016). Separating fact from fiction: An empirical examination of six myths about dissociative identity disorder. *Harvard Review of Psychiatry*, *24*(4), 257–270. https://doi.org/10.1097/HRP.0000000000000100
8. Appleman, J. R. (2018). *The kill jar*. New York, NY: Gallery Books.
9. Broad, C. (2013, Jan. 31). "Why this blog? https://catherinebroad.blog/2013/01/

2

SOWING THE WIND

I spend a lot of time thinking about the crisis of child sexual abuse and the flaws in the justice system. Society is going to have to deal with these crimes and their consequences throughout the foreseeable future. Even if we eliminated the danger posed by strangers, the majority of child sex abusers live in the victim's circle of trust – their parents, stepparents, family friends, siblings, and authority figures. According to the FBI Crime Data website, in 2019, law enforcement agencies received reports that 8,567 children between the ages of 0 and 9 were raped, and another 28,433 victims between the ages of 10 and 19 were raped. According to the CDC, one out of every four girls and one out of every 13 boys in America are estimated to be the victims of sexual abuse during childhood, and this is a *low estimate* (1). A meta-analysis of studies measuring the prevalence of child sexual abuse found that 7.6% of boys and 18% of girls reported being sexually victimized as children, but that estimates were *30 times greater* in studies that used self-report measures rather than official police records ($k = 217$, $N = 9,911,745$). Sexual victimization is notoriously under-reported due to a variety of factors. Victims feel shame, they fear stigma, they fear retaliation, and sometimes they believe that the justice system will not help them.

Fortunately, there has been a decrease in the number of reported child sex abuse crimes in the United States. Using data collected for the National Child Abuse and Neglect Data System, researchers at the University of New Hampshire discovered that there was a 62% decrease in the rate of child sexual abuse crimes reported to children's services agencies between 1990 to 2018 (ending in an estimated 62,000 sexual abuse cases in 2018) (2). Getting the numbers down is great, but each case is a profound tragedy. As anyone who spends time with victims or was a victim themselves can tell you, the trauma that these children suffer is extraordinary. It does something to their relationship with the world.

Sex abuse is well known to be an adverse childhood experience that has long-lasting and devastating consequences for the victim's physical and mental health, as well as their educational, financial, and social well-being (2–8). Some of the most severe consequences are the increased risk for anxiety, feelings of anger, guilt, shame, depression, and symptoms of post-traumatic stress disorder (9–11). The effect of child sex abuse on later outcomes may be influenced by the victim's age at the time of the abuse and the length of time that passed since the abuse occurred (12–16). Some studies have found that women survivors of child sex abuse have worse mental

DOI: 10.4324/9781003393849-3

health consequences than men, but others have not found any significant differences between genders (17–22).

The research on the deleterious effects of child sex abuse can never estimate what was *lost* when a child was abused in comparison to the life they might have had if they had been protected. Most research on child sexual abuse follows a standard format: defining the terminology, estimating the prevalence, measuring the correlation of trauma symptoms with undesirable life outcomes, and then assessing the validity of the source data. This book is not meant to tread on the toes of those experts and their important work. I am merely zeroing in on the *extreme* consequences of child sexual abuse as they relate to retaliatory violence and the public's support for such violence.

Discussions about the offenders themselves often turn into a battle of definitions. For example, Frank Dicataldo's book *The Perversion of Youth* focuses on cases of harmless indiscretion and government overreach, while Anna Salter's book *Predators: Pedophiles, Rapists, and Other Sex Offenders* focuses on the most sadistic crimes. It would be better if we did not lump all cases together or use the term "sex offender" at all because there is a world of difference between public urination misdemeanors and the rape of a child. Unfortunately, the justice system fails to make these distinctions, and juvenile mistakes often result in severe penalties while horrendous crimes are not taken as seriously as they should be (Chapter 4). I will attempt to side-step this definitional problem by focusing on cases where victims suffered long-term distress from their abuse.

In this chapter, I will explore the challenges that child victims face, including their weakened ability to trust other people, the nightmarish revictimization they suffer through contact with the court system, and their increased likelihood of engaging in criminal behavior to escape from abuse or cope with their trauma- including seeking bloody revenge.

Learning Not to Trust

While researching this book, I compiled a list of hundreds of descriptors of child sex abusers that vigilantes, prisoners, and correctional officers have given me. They all describe the same person: "dirty old man," "fat slob," "sloppy," "gross," "dumpy," "Humpty Dumpty," "sleezy," "creepy," "nasty," etc. You get the idea. "You know 'em when you see 'em." One common descriptor is "White," although most people acknowledge that other races have child sex abusers as well, they believe that White offenders are more common. Some of these stereotypes can be challenged with statistics, but this is one area where even an accurate list of probabilities can be dangerous. If you think all sex offenders are creepy, old, fat, men you might end up trusting a charismatic, young, healthy person (like the karate instructor who kidnapped Jody Plauché). You might put your children in a Baptist religious school because you think Catholics are dangerous, only to discover that religious denominations are a poor predictor of child sex abuse. You might be in complete disbelief if a *woman* is accused of abusing a child. Suffice it to say, stereotypes and statistical estimates can work in the abusers' favor. If they can avoid the stereotype, they can win your trust.

For 50 years, researchers have been challenging the "myth" that child sex abusers are often strangers. Perhaps it would be better to call this "myth" a "misperception." Yes, parents should be concerned about strangers who might hurt their children, but if you think the majority of sex offenders are strangers you might be lulling yourself into a false sense of security. Most offenders are people who knew their victim before the crime. Most non-familial sex offenders don't snatch a kid and run away. They get to know them first. They are not strangers anymore after they've introduced themselves and worked their way into the child's small world of trusted friends. We call these offenders "groomers." Sometimes they gain a child's trust by giving them access to things their parents

deprive them of, such as the "Three D's": driving, drinking, and dirty pictures (23). A good example of the techniques used by "predators" can be seen in the film *Chickenhawk: Men Who Love Boys*
(1994), where director Adi Sideman followed members of the National Man Boy Love Association
(NAMBLA) and allowed them to describe their "seduction" process in their own words.

Perhaps more to the point is an interview given by a convicted "child predator" to WRTV
Indianapolis to describe how he groomed children for abuse. Jack Reynolds spent more than
12 years in prison for sexually assaulting children in the 1980s. He had a change of heart in 2017
and told the insider secrets of how he chose his targets and secured their silence (24).

Interviewer: How did you get them alone?

Reynolds: Grooming. I would check out their family situation. I would check out their clothing
to see how well they were, you know, financially. I would check out their social interaction with other kids, you know. When we were on the ballparks or on the gym
floor I would make sure which ones I wanted to molest I would give them special attention, congratulate them, talk to them when I know that I would never be allowed
to talk to anyone else, aside from everybody. I would give them the attention that an
official is not supposed to give anybody, and it made them feel like 'Wow, he's paying
me attention.' It's a direct form of grooming.

Interviewer: Were there certain characteristics that you looked for in children before molesting
them?

Reynolds: In children, yes, but more I also looked at their families. If I thought the father was
a threat I would not approach the child. If I thought that the child had friends that
he would tell I would not approach him. If I thought the child had friends that were
in the same capacity he was I would approach him for the simple fact that if I could
molest him I could lure him into believing, groom him into believing he would enjoy it, and therefore I could manipulate him into having his other friends come and
be molested by me as well.

Interviewer: So perhaps a child that doesn't really have a lot of friends, maybe not a strong family,
things like that?

Reynolds: Yes. No spiritual values. Weak in education. Needs help in many ways. Even from
split parenting. You know, has a mother who may be having problems with the family, well, here comes superhero in to help out. 'Wow, well thank you very much.'
'No problem. You ever need me to take him away for the night so you can have a
night out. No problem.' It works.

Reynolds would not have been categorized as a "stranger" for these crimes. He was a "family
friend" when he abused those children. His crimes happened inside the circle of trust. The face-
to-face grooming process has been understood for a long time, and it does correspond to Reynold's
confession. Offenders who are fixated and determined to abuse a child work to develop a reputation of trust and authority. They locate a target that is weak and vulnerable. They begin with small
favors and work up to making themselves indispensable. They test the child by sharing secrets, then
move on to brief acts of molestation. The child has been lured into the abuser's world and they are
confused. They want to get help but they are afraid. Some abusers make an explicit threat to them or
their loved ones. The victim might be afraid of being blamed for the attack or socially stigmatized.
Often the abuser will "gaslight" the victim by trying to convince them it was their fault. This psychological manipulation can wreak havoc on the child's ability to trust others, or respect themselves.

Strange as it may seem to an outsider, some victims do not want their abuser to get in trouble. The grooming process can make the innocent child feel true affection for their victimizer. Child sex abusers benefit from two key factors: silence, and confusion. They manufacture these qualities in their child victim. Silence protects the abuser from punishments and gives them a clean reputation so they can find more victims. Imagine the guilt a child would feel if their silence lead to other children being victimized.

It is true that some "regressed" child abusers are more casual in the execution of their crimes. They don't waste much time grooming. They tend to blame sexual frustration and low self-control for their actions (some even claim not to be sexually attracted to children), but the fact remains that most child sex abusers exploit one of the most innocent aspects of childhood to achieve their goals- *the child's trust*, and this has wide-ranging consequences on the child's social development.

In the increasingly online world where children make friends and socialize, it is no surprise that sex offenders use the internet to identify targets and groom victims. Child predators/solicitors use a variety of techniques to build trust with their victims, such as misrepresenting their own age or gender (25). Grooming often involves flattery and emotional manipulation (26–29). Rachel O'Connel identified five stages of online grooming that included forming friendships (discussing mutual interests), forming relationships (discussing family, friends, and school), assessing the risk of being detected (gathering information about their parent's schedules and the target's willingness to engage in sexual behavior), developing exclusive trust by manipulating guilt, and then explicitly discussing their sexual interests (30). There is evidence that online sexual predators do not follow O'Connel's stages in order. Many offenders groom more than one target at a time in multiple online forums to increase their chances of meeting a victim, and they begin asking blunt sexual questions to gauge the child's reactions and concentrate their attention on the most responsive targets (31). Researchers have examined the chat logs of child predators who were arrested in law enforcement sting operations and found that offenders often asked about the child's parents to determine if their schedules would increase their chances of detection. These included questions such as "so are you by yourself?" and "what hours do your parents work?" (32). These behaviors indicate that child predators take steps to minimize their chances of being caught. They want to quickly identify victims who are tolerant of sexual questions and are not protected by adults.

But what if the person who is supposed to *protect* the child is actually their abuser? Tragically, the child's own parents are often the ones who abuse their trust. Andrew Vachss calls this process "*growing* your own victim" rather than grooming them. If anything will destroy a child's trust in humanity more than a stranger or acquaintance taking advantage of their naivete, it must be the trampling of their social bonds by their own parents.

Andrew Vacchs was an attorney who exclusively represented children in the legal system. He described the abuse of a child by their parent as supernaturally evil. A shocking and disturbing fact that most people could not comprehend (33). He described his own introduction to the world of parental sex abuse as follows:

I always thought of myself as a pretty tough kid. I hadn't been raised in prep schools. I was so sure I knew my way around. Some of the things that shocked my colleagues were things I had known since childhood. I knew people did all sorts of ugly things to each other, for all kinds of reasons. I knew about "child molesters," those freakish men who hung around playgrounds, with a bag of candy in their pockets and evil in their hearts. But I never knew humans had sex with babies. And, on that job, I learned the truth. Not just any babies, their own babies.

Decades before the great "controversy" – was there an "epidemic" of child sexual abuse in America, or was the country on a "witch hunt," fueled by a torrent of "false allegations?" – I saw the truth for myself. Every day. Not the statistics, not the "gray areas," not the debates. An infant with a prolapsed rectum dripping with gonorrhea is not capable of "fantasizing." A twelve-year-old girl giving birth to a baby with congenital syphilis – a legacy from her father – is not "making up a story."

What stunned me was not just the hideousness of humans who grow their own victims, but the sociopathic sense of entitlement they always displayed. I still remember one of those predatory degenerates who had just been informed that his child had syphilis, and that he was the cause of the infection. Confronted with the consequences, he looked at me, and, in a voice vibrating with outrage, said, "That's my child."

It took me a while to understand what he meant. And even longer to understand that this human was not unique. He had brothers – and sisters – all over the world (34).

Psychologist Anna Salter has spent decades studying child abuse and providing therapy to parents who abuse their own children. She has published several books and academic articles on this disturbing subject but is perhaps best known for her book *Predators: Pedophiles, Rapists, and Other Sex Offenders,* and for publishing video recordings of her interviews with her clients. One interview with a serial child sex abuser who raped over 24 children (but lost count) described how he would groom children but especially how he trained his own daughter to be his personal sexual object (35).

Offender: It was power and control. I was grooming her from the age, it started about the age of one. I was the punisher. I was the one who decided the punishment over the children. I was the one who spanked the children. I was the one who punished the children. If I seen the children do anything wrong, even bickering and arguing amongst themselves I would whip them and tell them, just kids playing, I would tell myself "She's not gonna be like that. She's gonna be the perfect mate." And I told myself that. I didn't molest her then.

Interviewer: The perfect mate?

Offender: The perfect mate. I was grooming her to fit me. To fit me.

Interviewer: At what age?

Offender: I started at about a year, started grooming her, whooping her, and telling her this, to do this, not do that. Then I molested her at 18 months old. I thought to myself, I said, well, this is going to be easy. This is gonna be easy. I'm going to have my own child, my own stepdaughter, which is really not blood-related to me, and I'm telling myself these things it's not blood-related to me, when she grows up to be 14–15 years old, I will have the perfect sexual mate for sexual purposes. Anything else didn't matter. It was sex. That was it. I didn't care about, really, honestly, I didn't love the child. I wanted the child for my own purposes.

Helping a child to overcome the psychological damage inflicted on them by their caregivers is an enormous task. How do you even attempt to undo that kind of damage? Will they ever trust an authority figure again? Will they ever trust a romantic partner? Can they develop strong bonds, or will distrust always lurk in the back of their mind? Of course, each situation will be different. Some children are extraordinarily resilient. Some derive strength from wider support networks. Others might dedicate their lives to helping other victims. Therapists have referred to these transformations as "posttraumatic growth" because the abuse led to meaningful changes in the person's life course. Andrew Vachss called them "transcenders" because they went far beyond merely "surviving" their abuse.

One of the most influential experts on childhood sexual abuse is David Finkelhor of the University of New Hampshire. He has dedicated his life to studying these crimes from every angle. He has published hundreds of academic articles and research briefs to translate the scientific knowledge to actual public policies. If one person could be said to have truly made a difference in this field of research, it is him. His book *Childhood Victimization* summarized everything known about the devastating impacts of these crimes and outlined all of the areas for hope. He has written about the developmental impact of child abuse across the life course, and he argues that just as traumatic incidents can lead to harmful outcomes, trajectories can also be directed to positive outcomes. With help, victims of child abuse can overcome these memories and thrive. David Finkelhor has seen the field of victimology develop for over 50 years, and he sees major improvements across the board.

Unfortunately, the people I have encountered while working on this book did not move from "victim" to "survivor." They had few opportunities to make that transition. They can only talk about their childhoods as a series of betrayals. They trusted their fathers and suffered tremendously for doing so. Some of them trusted their own mothers with the truth, and were betrayed again. Some told a teacher or outside authority figure and were disappointed in the results. In the worst-case scenarios, they were dragged into a courtroom and bravely testified against their abusers, only to be let down one final time by the judge. Does it surprise you to learn that they were bitter? The people who write letters of support to vigilantes in prison do so because a murderer is the only person who validated their anger with actions, not promises. As Alice Vachss has written:

> There is nothing more damaging to the soul of an abused child than the belief that his or her rape is sanctioned by the adult world.

You may ask why a lack of trust is related to vigilantism. Because a victim who is unable to rely on others learns that they can only trust themselves. Those who are abused by strangers may be afraid of forming protective and comforting relationships with outsiders. Those who are abused by family members or people in their "circle of trust" may suffer worse consequences for their social development. This becomes a fundamental characteristic of the victim's maladaptive life course. Social isolation cuts these victims off from the support they need to overcome their trauma. And despite many high-sounding child protection laws passed over the past few decades, these children quickly learn not to trust the government to help them either.

The Process Is a Punishment

Konrad Kircher is an attorney who specializes in cases where he can help the victims of child sexual abuse. Konrad has argued cases before the Ohio Supreme Court, and he is currently the President-Elect of the National Crime Victim Bar Association. He has spent a considerable amount of time working with clients who suffered sexual abuse and has seen the depth of the trauma they have suffered. I spoke with Konrad about his career, and he shared an attorney's perspective on how victims interact with a flawed court system.

I asked Konrad what some of the barriers were that kept victims from making reports about their abuse. He said his own clients struggled with reporting an authority figure. "If a peer abuses a peer, you can blame the peer. If an authority figure abuses a child, they don't understand who to blame." These authority figures use their positions of power to groom the victim and isolate them. Children are still learning how the adult world works, so victims are trained to believe abuse is "normal." If the child accepts gifts they might blame themselves for putting themselves in that situation. Above all, children think "nobody is going to believe me."

Some of Konrad's clients had been abused by Catholic Church officials. In the 1970s and 1980s, religious parents would have never believed that a holy man would hurt a child. That holy reputation has been shattered in recent years, and this might give victims more hope that they will be believed, but religiosity interferes with reporting in other ways. Some Catholic victims are afraid that if they tell their parents they were abused by a priest, that the news will crush their parent's faith. They are afraid their parents will lose their most important spiritual foundation if they report a rapist to the police. That is a powerful incentive for silence. Do you want your parents to burn in Hell for eternity?

Some victims might even have an emotional bond with their abuser. This is not uncommon, especially when the groomer has deliberately fostered a meaningful relationship with the victim to initiate the abuse. This causes the victim to blame themselves. Konrad's clients have said "I kept looking internally" for the causes of abuse, "What did I do to ask for this? What did I do to provoke a holy man?"

The consequences of abuse, self-blame, and secrecy are devastating for these children: substance abuse, suicidal ideation, and shame. Konrad observes that shame is most extreme for boys who fear being called homosexual. If a teenage boy has a sexual encounter with an older adult woman they might feel it is a badge of honor, but if they were abused by a man they are afraid of being socially ostracized.

These psychological consequences are bad enough, but when they are combined with the arduous and frustrating legal process it can be too much for most victims. What if the child took a long time to decide to make a report? They might have passed the statute of limitations. Even if the criminal statutes have been extended the civil statutes usually are not. Any victim of child sexual abuse who wants to sue for damages to pay their therapy bills might discover that their time is up. In Ohio, a victim only has one year from their age of majority to file a civil lawsuit. The criminal statute for rape allows 25 years to make a report. Why would the civil statute of limitations be any different? Even in cases when the victim is an adult, they might only have 18 months from the date of the rape to file a complaint in civil court. Considering that the criminal justice system is so slow, a person who waits for the criminal court to make a decision before filing in civil court will be left without a backup plan. Oh, the rapist was given a lenient sentence and you want to sue in civil court? You should have asked for financial damages *before* the criminal charges were filed. But what if you didn't want to be accused of seeking money during the criminal trial, as the defense attorney would love to tell the jury? Then you're out of luck. Some victims have to decide between justice in the criminal court or financial compensation in the civil court. This is a Catch-22 that Konrad Kircher believes is especially insulting to the victims of child sex abuse.

Is it any wonder that most victims do not trust adults? Their abusers have ruined their ability to trust anyone again. The courts and even their own attorneys are stuck in bureaucratic loopholes that frustrate the victim to no end. So they choose not to make a report. They'd rather avoid the spotlight, the accusations, and the headache. But then they might be exposed by others. If law enforcement catches the perpetrator and uncovers a history of abuse, they might expose the child victim before they were willing to talk about it. This imposition can cause terrible distress for the victim who just wanted to be left alone.

The law is designed to let nine guilty men walk free rather than wrongfully convict anyone. Those protections are important, but victims hate to see a justice system that is designed to protect their abusers from accountability. They see how the rapist plays the system. They see how defense attorneys question the victim's credibility (asking about their recent substance abuse and sexual experiences to discredit their testimony, as if those could not be not the result of their abuser's actions). Now, because of Marcy's Law, the victim is entitled to have an attorney present. It's not just the prosecutor and the defense attorney in the room anymore, the victim has a stake in the process too.

Konrad understands the victim's desire to bury the past and move on with their lives, but he also knows that the healing process is undermined by long delays. The consequences of waiting might make it difficult to secure a criminal conviction or receive any financial compensation that can help pay for therapy, but it also leads to the accumulation of dangerous coping experiences. The failed relationships and substance abuse episodes can lead to a downward spiral. Konrad believes that the future for attorneys in this line of work is trauma-informed practice. If attorneys cannot understand how post-traumatic stress disorder impacts their clients they can never adequately represent their needs.

Konrad told me a story about one of his clients. A girl who was 8 years old and lived on a rural, isolated road. Her parents both worked, so a nice old man who lived next door offered to help get her off the bus each day. For four years he babysat this little girl in his home while the parents worked. They thanked him for helping. They couldn't believe he was so kind. Of course, he was sexually abusing the girl the entire time. This girl kept the abuse secret until she was 16 years old. She confided in a friend who convinced her to call the police. Detectives knew there would be trouble with the case because four years had passed since the last act of abuse occurred, so they asked the victim to call her abuser on the phone and trick him into confessing. They recorded the phone call. He confessed.

The old man was arrested, but before he was even charged with a crime his defense attorney worked out a nice plea deal. He would serve two years in prison for systematically and repeatedly raping a child. The girl's family was furious. They filed a civil lawsuit to help secure some level of punishment that the criminal court was unable or unwilling to impose. Plus, any money they received might help the girl pay for therapy.

Konrad took the case, but he had a problem. The girl would not talk to him. She was introverted in the extreme. She spoke in simple, short responses. He knew she would not be able to sway the jury if she couldn't tell her story.

The old man had gathered a pool of money from his family members and friends amounting to about $35,000. His attorney offered to settle the case for that amount. Konrad told the girl she could take the money and pay for therapy, college, or buy a car. It was her money, her choice. She sat up in her chair and for the first time since he met her she spoke in a clear and powerful voice: "I want to tell my story." Konrad set the trial date. She testified in front of the jury. She told her story methodically. What happened next? Then what? Then what? Then what? Konrad remembers "You could have heard a pin drop in the courtroom."

When it was over the jury awarded her $3.6 million in damages. The jury smiled and waved to her in the courtroom. She was stunned. Konrad asked her "Did you hear what the jury said?" She said she did not. "They told you it wasn't your fault," he said. She agreed. "Yes. It wasn't my fault." The court system has many, many flaws. But when it punishes a child sex abuser it can send a powerful message to the victim: it wasn't *their* fault.

Konrad had another client who was abused in a Catholic school. The Diocese of Youngstown, Ohio responded appropriately to the crime. They validated the victim's experiences and offered money in a settlement. But the victim wasn't interested in haggling for money. She wanted to stop future crimes. She wanted to make life better for children who went through the same school. She only wanted to give a talk to children in the school system every year to warn them about the dangers of sexual abuse and to encourage them to seek help. This gave her a *voice* in the same setting where the abuse occurred. When an agency changes its policies to reduce future crimes it shows that abuse can be prevented. Non-disclosure agreements just push victims back into the shadows so more crime can occur. Fortunately, many attorneys refuse to accept non-disclosure terms. Letting victims tell their stories is a form of therapy that should not be denied to them.

When the clergy sex abuse scandal was big news (2001–2002), Konrad was hired to represent a man who was a victim of child sexual abuse. The priest, Lawrence Strittmatter, had been abusing children for decades, but nobody had filed a complaint against him. His crimes were thriving in secrecy. Konrad was willing to take the case, but he warned his client that it might be publicized. Was this victim of child sexual abuse willing to have his story told across the country? The man said "It can't get worse. Do what you have to do." The story became front-page news and Konrad received calls from other victims who wanted to tell their stories too. Eventually, Konrad was representing 24 victims of Strittmatter, and another 37 victims abused by a priest named David Kelly. When one victim comes forward they can inspire so many more to come out of the shadows. The criminal justice system should do everything in its power to make sure their bravery is respected.

The severe trauma of child sexual abuse has another devastating consequence. It interferes with legal proceedings and facilitates plea bargaining. When a child victim makes a report they might be asked to testify in court. The child might be afraid to speak in front of the judge, jury, attorneys, and especially the person who abused her. She might be too scared and make for a "poor witness." This is only made worse when the defense attorney cross-examines the child and tries to make a fool of her. Perhaps calling her a liar or deliberately confusing her in front of the jury. Does it surprise you to learn that most children don't make reports and those who do don't testify in court? It would be psychologically traumatizing for them to recount the abuse in any environment, even in video-recorded testimony. Most prosecutors don't want to lose the case so they will take a plea deal. If the defendant pleads guilty to a lesser charge they can avoid a trial. The defendant gets a much shorter sentence or perhaps no incarceration at all. Child sexual abuse may be the only crime where inflicting *more severe trauma* on a *more vulnerable victim* can actually help the defendant get a *more lenient punishment*, all to avoid a public trial.

A non-profit group called Bikers Against Child Abuse (BACA, bacaworld.org) proclaims the motto "No child deserves to live in fear." The members of this organization volunteer to meet with children who are expected to testify in court to let them know that a bunch of burly biker guys have their back. They give the child a biker jacket with a BACA logo and tell them nobody is going to mess with them again. They sometimes patrol the child's neighborhood on their bikes for a period of time to remind the child (and the community) that the kid is under their protection. However, they are not a vigilante group. They work in collaboration with local and state officials to fix a gap in the legal system's response to child victims. The bikers will personally attend any trial where the child testifies in person. They fill the courtroom and sit quietly so the child does not have to feel intimidated by the presence of their abuser at the defendant's table. The existence of BACA proves that people from all walks of life care about child victims deeply.

It also demonstrates that law-abiding citizens will step up to correct flaws in the court system if the officials are unable or unwilling to do so.

After the trial is over and a rare conviction is secured, what would be considered a "fair" punishment? Of course, it would depend on the crime, the damage done, and a thousand other factors that courts may or may not address during their proceedings. It also depends on the biases of the person who is judging the sentence's "fairness." Let's be honest. We will never settle on a definition of fair punishments for every possible scenario. That is the problem with mandatory sentencing guidelines. There will be outlier cases, and there will be outrage. That outrage is the source of much vigilante violence. Every one of the vigilantes I have interviewed or that I could study in depth through official records was at least partially motivated by their belief that punishments for sex offenders are too lenient. There might not be a punishment "appropriate" enough to satisfy them, but it is the most often repeated motivation that I heard during my research.

Despite the impossibility of reforming the justice system to satisfy everyone, perhaps courts can validate a victim's experiences by passing a judgment that sends the clear message: *It's not your fault.* The abuser has repeatedly blamed the child for the abuse. The child's family members might have said the same thing. The abuser's attorney certainly pulled that trick during the trial, otherwise, they could be accused of being ineffective counsel. But worst of all, the victims *blame themselves.* When the jury sides with the victim or the judge rules that the offender is a potential danger to other children, the victim will finally recognize that the perpetrator was the problem. If the perpetrator receives a lenient sentence, it might undermine that message in the mind of the victim. Think about this from the child's point of view. *The judge let him go home. That means he can be around other kids. He's not a danger to other kids. The problem was me.*

You can dismiss their reaction as naïve, childish, or (an academic favorite) "low-information/high-salience," but to the victim, it may be a shocking scene of injustice. A fresh trauma. Imagine how that will influence the child's moral and cognitive development from that point forward. Reformers have suggested that courts engage in therapeutic jurisprudence or restorative justice initiatives to help victims and hold perpetrators accountable, but in a dichotomous system where most people get jail or go home, the message is not transmitted to the child victim appropriately. A system that justifies its own actions on retributivist grounds can undermine its own authority when it shows leniency in serious cases. If you steal a car, possess drugs, or cheat on your taxes you go to jail… so why does a child sex abuser get another chance?

Child Protection Is Crime Prevention

Researchers know that adverse childhood experiences (A.C.E.s) can lead to horrifying life outcomes. The most commonly researched ACEs are emotional abuse, physical abuse, sexual abuse, emotional and physical neglect, domestic violence, household substance abuse, mental illness in the household, parental separation or divorce, and incarceration of a household member. These ACEs are common among American youth, with two thirds of respondents regularly reporting at least one of these experiences. Often these experiences are interrelated, and they have a cumulative impact on undesirable life outcomes. Health-related risks like smoking cigarettes, alcoholism, illicit drug use, and early intercourse are commonly linked to ACEs, as well as mental health problems, criminal victimization, and criminal offending. Tragically, ACEs are also associated with a drastically shorter life expectancy of 61 years compared to the average of 79 years for adults with no history of ACEs (36). The research on ACEs cannot be fully described in this book, but

I recommend Jennifer Hays-Grudo and Amanda Morris' book *Adverse and Protective Childhood Experiences* as the most up-to-date summary of this field of knowledge (37).

These authors proposed an integrated model to help understand just how influential ACEs can be on a developing child's brain and behaviors. They call this the ICARE model (Intergenerational and Cumulative Adverse and Resilience Experiences). They map out how ACEs can lead to neurobiological adaptation to a stressful upbringing in ways that help the child survive, but impact their long-term health and development. Every conceivable aspect of brain development may be impacted by these stressors if they are not mitigated by protective childhood experiences. Hays-Grudo and Morris draw upon a mass of research to demonstrate that untreated children may experience sleep disorders, mental health problems, school failure, violence and aggression, and substance use problems as adults. The symptoms of hyper-vigilance, impulse control problems, and problems with attachment are particularly harmful to children adapting to the adult world of relationships. They begin life in turmoil, and find it quite difficult to find stable and safe environments to heal.

One consequence of ACEs is that the child might turn to crime as an escape or a solution to their abuse. To be sure, most of these crimes are status offenses; running away from home, drinking alcohol, etc. Some fall into a broad range of minor delinquent acts that are dealt with in a juvenile court, such as shoplifting, destroying property, and drug possession. Other crimes are serious and they put the child on a path to incarceration in an adult prison, as well as "life-course" persistent offending rather than the adolescence-limited offending of other children who age out of these behaviors when they form stable relationships and take on adult responsibilities (38). Is it any surprise that research studies find a strong relationship between victimization and subsequent criminal behavior? A study of 64,329 high-risk youth in Florida found increases in the likelihood of replicating criminal behavior in adolescence if the person experienced childhood physical abuse (OR = 1.55, $p < .001$), witnessing household substance abuse (OR = 1.66, $p < .001$), and especially for sexual abuse (PR = 3.58, $p < .001$) (39).

One of the most studied theories of criminal behavior is "General Strain Theory" (GST) which was first defined by Robert Agnew in 1992 (40). This theory used components of several previous competing theories to explain how some people might respond to strains in their lives with criminal coping behaviors. When people are faced with strains and stressors in their lives, they have a choice of options. They can ignore the strains, try to fix them through socially acceptable means, or they might choose criminal means to help them cope. The moderating factor in helping make that decision can be the extent to which the individual feels negative emotions like anger, frustration, depression, and hopelessness. These emotions create pressure, and the person acts. Some people are more likely to respond to strains through crime than other people. As with every criminological theory, "it depends," but strain is a part of the recipe. The more strain, the more likely a person is to reach the threshold of their resiliency.

The strains that are most likely to result in criminal coping are those that are high in magnitude and they are perceived as being unjust. A single traumatic incident of acute child abuse can be devastating. How much more devastating is chronic abuse that lasts for years? And is there anything more obviously unjust than sexually abusing a child? Even children who were subjected to years of psychological manipulation by their abusers would recognize that these crimes are *mala in se*- evil in and of itself. It inflicts life-long suffering on an innocent child for the temporary pleasure of the abuser.

Situationally speaking, a person is more likely to resort to criminal coping when the likelihood of being sanctioned for the crime is low (or if they have nothing to lose). When people believe that crime is an appropriate response, they are also at a higher likelihood of crossing that line. A good example of this is when men believe that they should defend their honor with violence in order to be considered masculine. Another situational risk is when the person *cannot* cope through non-criminal means. For example, if a child is being ruthlessly bullied in school and none of the teachers will help them, they might defend themselves with violence. I think all three of these situations work to explain why someone who is sexually abused might resort to violence against their attacker rather than call the police. The case of Sara Kruzan comes to mind.

Starting at the age of 11, Sarah Kruzan was groomed for sexual exploitation and was forced into prostitution until she was 16 years old (41). One day she planned to murder her sex trafficker. She shot him dead in a motel and fled. Although she was 16 years old, the seriousness of her crime categorized her as an adult. She was sentenced to life in prison without the possibility of parole. She served 19 years in prison before she was released. It is an understatement to say that she killed her abuser to escape "strain," but her case fits well into the GST model. She chose violence because she might not have thought she would be punished for self-defense, she might have thought her trafficker deserved to be killed, and she did not trust the police to keep her safe. This is an extreme example of general strain theory in action.

There are other components of GST that should be described. As Agnew explains, the crime itself may be a solution in and of itself. It's not always true that crime is a way to escape or distract the offender from negative emotions; criminal behavior itself can be the end goal. Agnew says "Crime may be a way for individuals to seek revenge against those who have wronged them." This helps the victim regain a sense of power. *They're in charge now.* For some people who have been truly wronged by their abuser, they are willing to pay any cost for this revenge. Those who have nothing to lose and no other path to self-respect and justice will sacrifice their freedom for vengeance. The sad thing about this is that those children who were severely abused might have lost the ability to trust others and develop meaningful relationships with them, which limits their social connections with others and increases the chances they will have "nothing to lose." The consequences of child sex abuse accrue compound interest.

Agnew understood that many crimes precipitated by strains were not malicious. They were often crimes that were committed to distract the individual from their childhood trauma. Almost every vigilante I interviewed admitted this motive for the crimes they committed. Drugs and alcohol are one way to temporarily escape from your troubles, even if they will only increase your suffering in the long run. Sometimes people committed other types of crimes like shoplifting, burglaries, and car theft because they got an adrenaline rush from these criminal distractions. Again, short-term distraction can lead to long-term suffering.

These people accumulate significant juvenile records and started racking up "criminal history" points that would be used to justify long prison sentences using state's mandatory sentencing guidelines. They became chronic, habitual, or incorrigible offenders who were not eligible for mercy in the courtroom. Their abusers, however, often had no criminal history. These troubled victims spend a considerable portion of their lives in jails and prisons. They become experts in criminology through direct experience and through conversations with other prisoners. They tell me that most of the men and women in the justice system are victims of abuse in their past. They used drugs to cope with trauma and were swept up in the War on Drugs. But they notice that they are serving longer sentences than child sex abusers (Chapter 4). They resent this unfairness and want to set things right. They can't fix the laws, but they can informally increase punishments for sex offenders to "balance the scales of justice." For them, this is a logical explanation for the violence perpetrated against sex offenders in America's jails and prisons (Chapter 7).

Girls are more likely to be sexually assaulted than boys, and yet boys are more likely to cope with strains through crimes directed toward other people (42). This is partly because men experience "moral outrage" in response to strains. Some people have argued that "men get angry and women get depressed." This is a simplistic statement but it does reflect the averages. Women are more likely to feel shame, depression, fear, and anxiety while men feel anger. These differences can be comprehensively explained with biological and cultural differences between these two genders, but such a massive topic is well beyond the scope of this book. Suffice it to say, men have the ability to convert uncomfortable emotions into anger. They may target their abusers who they believe have personally insulted them, while women are more likely to blame themselves. When this is combined with social forces absorbed from their environments, men may find it easier to fall into gender roles endorsing violence and revenge than women. Abused women may resort to drugs and self-destructive behaviors in response to childhood trauma. In a country that criminalizes most forms of drug use rather than treating it as a mental health problem, both abused men and women arrive at the same destination: prison.

It is hard to imagine that our criminal justice system will ever be reformed to such an extent that traumatized offenders will be treated with adherence to the principles of therapeutic jurisprudence. The system is a big bureaucracy. Very little time is wasted learning *why* someone began a life of crime. I asked Steven Sandison what percentage of prisoners he thinks have histories of child abuse and sexual abuse. He said "One hundred percent. All of them. We're all broken people who didn't have a chance, and the system didn't offer us a second one." The system conveys offenders into a system that is meant to punish them into unquestioning obedience. Therapy plays a minor, optional role.

The Neglected Victims

Sex offenders are masters of the "Techniques of Neutralization." These are excuses made in order to sanitize their conscience and give themselves permission to commit their crimes again in the future. These include "denying the victim" or "blaming the victim," minimizing harm, denial of responsibility, appealing to higher loyalties, and condemning their condemners. If you've watched an episode of *To Catch A Predator* you've probably seen all of these excuses in action. Therapists often target these beliefs in cognitive-behavioral therapy in order to decrease the likelihood that the offender will use them to justify future crimes. These excuses are one of the reasons why forming a therapeutic relationship with a sex offender is so difficult for therapists. It is outrageous to hear a sex abuser blame a toddler to justify their crimes.

One of the excuses is intended to draw sympathy during the punishment phase of their trials. They often claim that *they* were sexually abused as children, and their victimization is a tragic mitigating circumstance. If the court cares so much about victims, why not feel sorry for them too? This has led to a commonly believed theory sometimes called "The Bite of the Vampire" that assumes sexually abused children will grow up to sexually abuse others. The fact that most child sex abuse victims *do not* grow up to become offenders is the best argument for skepticism of these claims. Therapists might want to address this subject with sex offenders in their care, but the rest of us can add vampirism to the list of "myths" surrounding this subject.

This "Bite of the Vampire" story has another implication though. Since the vast majority of sex offenders are men, when a young boy grows up with the shame and stigma of sexual abuse, they are afraid that they will become homosexual. Elizabeth Grunfeld, Danny Willis, and Scott Easton published a study in 2017 that shared the experiences of nine therapists who specialized in treating adult survivors of childhood sexual abuse (43). They believed that the fear of being "unmanly" or secretly gay kept these men from disclosing their abuse until much later in life. It also caused some of them to feel intense hatred of homosexuals. Another problem that these adult men faced was trying to find a treatment center that would tolerate a specifically masculine response to their trauma- *aggression, and violence-* because most psychiatrists prefer forgiveness models of therapy.

The concept of forgiveness is a major barrier for male victims of child sex abuse. Andrew Vachss worked as an attorney and legal guardian for children involved in the justice system. His fictional books often had vigilante themes and condemned sex crimes against children in the strongest possible terms. Among Vachss' books are the 18-volume "Burke Series," These novels follow a cast of characters who operate on the "other side of the tracks." They are mostly career criminals who have cast aside all pretenses of mainstream happiness that "citizens" crave. Instead, they use their knowledge of the alleyways, jails, and crime dens in the city to track down "freaks" who sexually abuse children. They do not like to be called vigilantes because they prefer to be considered mercenaries. They scam, rob, and kill child sex abusers because they believe they do not deserve legal protections. They are sometimes willing to turn sex offenders over to the police if the price is right, but they are also comfortable snapping their necks or shooting them in the head. The main characters in these books consider themselves to be members of a family because they were all raised in government institutions (orphanages, juvenile jails, and prisons), but they are also "Children of the Secret." They were severely sexually abused as children. They did not believe that forgiveness was an answer. They thought anger was more therapeutic and useful. As one character said in Vachss' first published book, *Flood*: "The social workers told me it was all right to be sad, but not to be angry. It wasn't healthy" (44). In another book he wrote "People say you can't heal until you can forgive. Fucking liars. Cowards and collaborators. A beast steals your soul, you don't get it back by making peace with him. You make peace with yourself" (45). To combat the passive/pacifist view, Vachss became a champion of "righteous rage." Even though he did not endorse his fictional characters' criminal behavior, he often said that anger was an appropriate response to child sexual abuse, and that we should all be angry. Only angry people demand justice, and therapeutic platitudes about forgiveness might drive men away from treatment.

Men who have been abused might struggle with masculine identity dissonance. In other words, they feel that men are not supposed to be victims of sexual assault because it is unmasculine. They might suppress the experience or lash out at others in an attempt to reclaim their masculinity. In this sense, boys are the neglected victims of child sexual abuse as Mic Hunter argued back in 1990 (46). Since then, the clergy sex abuse scandal swept the world and revealed that these victims were not alone. Men *can* get help today, even if our treatment modalities still have a lot of room for improvement.

One thing Hunter noticed working with male clients was their struggles with anger. He felt that a desire for revenge was natural, even if it would be impossible to achieve. The damage that occurs when an adult sexually assaults a child can never be truly reciprocated because the relationship and power dynamics will never let the abuser feel how their victims felt. Hunter said that many of his clients thought that revenge fantasies were therapeutic, but others worried that they were just as "sick" "bad" or "evil" as the abuser. They were scared of what they were becoming. Hunter said he was only afraid of clients who tried to suppress their anger, not those who could express it. He asked clients to scream or break an object to finally get their anger out. He also asked them to punch a pillow, but he warned them never to imagine the pillow was their abuser, otherwise, they might feel guilty later. Consider that. A victim feels guilty for causing imaginary pain to the person who hurt them in real life. The empathy gap is striking.

The desired outcome of most treatment programs is forgiveness or acceptance. This is extremely difficult to do when men have been the victims of sexual assault. How can you forgive someone who put their own sexual pleasure above the lifelong psychological well-being of an innocent child? Mic Hunter reinterprets "forgiveness" as a chance for the victim to forgive *themselves*. To recognize that they do not need to punish themselves for what they did or didn't do when they were a child. The individual can learn to respect himself and move on with his life. Hunter advises counselors to make sure their clients understand that forgiveness does not absolve their abusers from guilt. A child rapist's behavior is never acceptable or excusable. He asks reluctant clients to envision forgiveness as relinquishing their desire for revenge, not absolving the abuser from culpability. He says some clients have dreams during the forgiveness phase of treatment that go something like this:

> … many men have dreams in which they replicate the abuse experience, except they are saved by someone or there is some other happy ending, such as the offending person accepting responsibility for his or her wrongdoing and requesting forgiveness.

Another expert who works with male sex abuse victims is Mike Lew. His book, *Victims No Longer* was published in 2004 and has been an invaluable resource for practitioners and survivors ever since (47). Some parts of Lew's book are especially relevant to the discussion of male aggression in response to abuse. He echoes the warning that men around the world are expected to play a masculine gender role. When they are sexually abused that identity is in crisis. The victim struggles with their place in the world and might even believe they are "less than human – an irreparably damaged freak." This feeling lends itself to thoughts about how the victim can reclaim their manhood and identity. Some believe they can be restored through masculine overcompensation. What is more masculine than aggression and violence? Lew identified three roles the man might try to fulfill in order to overcome their childhood trauma.

The first role is that of *perpetrator*. In the victim's mind, the world is divided up between predators and prey. If he no longer wants to be a victim he might have to be the perpetrator. The second role they may accept is to remain a *victim*. He chooses to remain powerless and allows himself to be taken advantage of. Strangely, this provides some comfort for the victim because at least they know what to expect from life. There are no false hopes when you are hopeless. The third role is to become a *protector*. Lew describes this role as follows:

> Feeling that children are in constant danger from adults, many male survivors deal with their fear of being abused by taking on the role of protector. On a very basic level they may be attempting to give others the protection they needed as children (or still want for themselves). They may see their role of protector as the only way to achieve non-abusive closeness to other people.

Lew envisions his clients as taking on a public service profession where they work with victims of crimes. This is a great use of their abilities and it provides them with meaning in their lives. Lew has worked with thousands of clients and so he understands the big picture. Unfortunately, I have a small, cherry-picked group of child abuse victims in my sample of vigilantes. I tried to fit them into one of these groups, and I find that there may be a fourth category that is more suitable. They are indeed "perpetrators" who no longer want to be victims, but they do not prey on children like their abusers did. And they see themselves as "protectors" because they avenge the wrongs done to children. An idealistic vigilante believes they can kill two birds with one stone. They become *avengers,* a hybrid of criminal perpetrator and child protector. They can demonstrate their physical superiority to the types of men who terrorized them when they were small, and they can be the hero they wished had rescued them. In these cases, vigilantism is not just self-help crime control, it is self-help therapy. It is the only way they can imagine achieving "non-abusive closeness" with other people – by defending child victims.

One therapeutic method for male victims of child abuse is to have them "confront" their abuser. This may be impossible or inadvisable, but it is one method that can be successful for certain clients. Lew warns that this confrontation must come from a position of strength and not weakness. The purpose of the confrontation has nothing to do with the abuser. It is intended to help the victim remember that what was done to them was wrong, that they never deserved to be abused, that they were not responsible for the abuse, and that people are accountable for their actions. Lew warns that rushing into a confrontation to act out a "male revenge fantasy" like Rambo or John Wayne might feel satisfying in the moment, but it will probably not work out well in the long run. Emotions like aggression and violence are responses provoked by the abuser. If the victim wants to remain in control they must confront the abuser on their own terms. I can imagine that some of the vigilantes in this book thought that bloody revenge would cure their pain, and while few of them regret their decisions, none of them said they were cured. They regret their loss of self-control- another thing taken from them by their abusers.

This book is focused on men who take the law into their own hands in order to punish child sex abusers, but occasionally a woman also becomes a vigilante. Most of these cases involve young women who kill their fathers or their sex traffickers in situations that can easily be described as "self-defense" rather than premeditated murder. In at least one case, a woman worked with her husband to kill a child sex abuser. But sometimes there are more clearly defined cases of vigilantism perpetrated by women. For example, Ellie Nesler killed the man who was accused of raping her son William back in 1993. She shot the man five times in a courtroom (48).

Some vigilante supporters believe that murdering a child sex abuser will be therapeutic for their victims. Perhaps the children can rest easy and move on with their lives knowing that true justice was served. It didn't work out so well for William Nesler. By the age of 23, he had an extensive criminal record. One day he assaulted his neighbor and went to jail. When he was released a few weeks later he immediately went back to his neighbor's house and beat him to death. William is serving a life sentence in the California prison system. He is yet another example of how abused men might lash out with violence, even if the person who hurt him was dead. If summary execution in a courtroom doesn't help these kids move on with their lives, what will?

Do Victims Want Revenge?

Philosophers, theologians, and social scientists have argued for centuries about how victims should react to the people who harmed them. Some extol the virtues of forgiveness, and others have called for retaliation. Most believed that the punishment decision should be turned over to a higher power; either Fate, God, or the government. There is a fear that revenge is not healthy for the individual and it may unravel the fabric of society if everyone takes the law into their own hands. Some critics may take into account the individual's emotional state at the moment of retaliation before deciding if it was appropriate, while others condemn even the *thought* of revenge as a sin (49). These cosmic arguments are beyond the scope of this book, but they do stand in the background of our current discussion. Punishment for wrongdoing is one of the fundamental components of humanity's civilized evolution, but if we narrow our focus, we might be able to understand why people write letters of gratitude to vigilante murderers.

Unfortunately, there is not much research evidence to help us understand victims' attitudes toward punishments for these specific crimes. Most victim satisfaction surveys focus on police and hospital interactions, and those that look at court outcomes mix all kinds of victims together, making it difficult to parse out the desires of sex abuse victims. To my knowledge, no research in the United States has asked adults about their satisfaction with the disposition of crimes perpetrated against them when they were children, and I found no surveys asking children how they felt about the process. It is possible that victimologists are overlooking an extremely important research topic. What if lenient punishments are causing psychological distress in the minds of children (e.g. self-blame, fear, or anger)? What if severe punishments are also causing harm to children (e.g. guilt or sorrow)?

Perhaps we can learn something by looking at survey results that are less specific. The Alliance for Safety and Justice conducted the "first ever" national survey of victim's opinions about punishment and rehabilitation in 2016 (50). They contacted a nationally represented sample of 3,165 individuals, of which 800 victims of a crime were chosen for an interview. This survey identified many troubling characteristics of victimization in the United States, including the disproportionate numbers of victims who are racial and ethnic minorities, and that two-thirds of victims received no help following the incident. Those who did receive help were much more likely to receive it from their friends, family, or hospitals, but only one-tenth of them received help from the court system. The two most common reasons for not reporting victimization to the authorities were the victim's belief that the police and the court system would not do anything.

Most relevant for our discussion are the victim's opinions about the criminal justice system's response to their victimization. The United States' unnecessary mass incarceration binge and its many consequences have been evident for decades. Perhaps victims are ready to call for a new approach to crime. When asked if the United States sends too many people to prison, 38% of these victims said yes, and 29% said too few were sent to prison. They also found that for every victim who "focuses on punishment" there are two victims who "focus on rehabilitation." The authors of this study conclude:

> Perhaps to the surprise of some, victims overwhelmingly prefer criminal justice approaches that prioritize rehabilitation over punishment and strongly prefer investments in crime prevention and treatment to more spending on prisons and jails. These views are not always accurately reflected in the media or in state capitols and should be considered in policy debates.

These conclusions were based on a binary question asking if people should be punished for crimes or rehabilitated. Basic survey design would suggest that this is not an appropriate way to measure the respondents' opinions accurately, and it may have been worded this way due to the authors' (correct) belief that prisons are generally not places where effective rehabilitation programming can be delivered. However, to impose this dichotomy on the respondents deliberately interferes with the purpose of the survey, which is to assess the preference of the individual, and this may include sending some people to prison and attempting to rehabilitate them. Later they found 52% of respondents believe prison increases the likelihood of committing crimes. What about the other 48% who may be unaware of the research in this field? The survey also failed to ask if prisons should be improved in terms of humane care or investing in rehabilitation programs in prison.

Another question on the survey asked if victims would prefer shorter prison sentences in order to spend more money on prevention, and 61% answered in the affirmative. If 39% disagree, then they de facto agree that prison sentences are a priority. And this does not preclude the possibility that the other 61% are swayed by double-barreled questions like preferring "prevention and rehabilitation" to long prison sentences. Giving a victim a binary choice forces them to pick a side, and many would no doubt be willing to forgo their own desire for punishment if they thought it would reduce the likelihood of more victims feeling what they felt. The vast majority preferred spending more money to invest in education, mental health resources, and treatment in the United States than to invest more money in prisons, but again this does not ask the victim if they think we have enough prisons already or if prison resources could be spent more wisely by focusing on some crimes rather than others. Other questions related to the desire for community supervision over incarceration and "options beyond prison" are imprecise and not able to capture the victim's opinions about specific responses for specific crimes. All in all, these questions are not a good assessment of the "retribution instinct" for our purposes.

There are some other methodological limitations to this national survey. It includes a pooled sample of 800 victims of crime ranging from vandalism (50%) to the murder of a family member (12%). Rape victims comprised 9% of the sample. The decision to pool these people together and report their shared views without delineation is not advisable. Victims of bicycle theft are not speaking for rape victims. Surely they would have different opinions on the appropriateness of community supervisions, treatment, and incarceration if they were asked about specific crimes rather than national priorities for all crimes. These questions are overly general, so that victims may feel that prison was an appropriate punishment in their own case, but when asked about crime in the entire country they shift their frame of reference to endorse non-incarceration solutions. Other studies have found contradictory results, as incarceration punishments are sometimes associated with increases in victim satisfaction (51). Because of these methodological limitations, I do not think we can use the Alliance for Safety study to help us make a determination on whether victims of sexual abuse desire severe punishments for their abusers. It is more of a snapshot of how victims, in general, feel about the priorities of the system, in general, when given limited choices.

It is possible to survey people to ask about their desire for revenge. A 2004 survey of adult victims in Germany asked how often they thought about "doing something" to the people who raped them, how often they fantasized about "getting back" at them, and whether they had "feelings of revenge" (52). These questions were asked in relation to the first four weeks after their abuse, and again based on their current feelings (the average length of time since their abuse was three years). This survey uses retrospective assessments of feelings, so the individual respondents may be misremembering their initial feelings after the passage of time. The responses showed that feelings of revenge were initially high for rape victims in comparison to non-sexual assault victims ($r = 0.25$, $p < .01$), but revenge feelings were not significantly different from non-sexual assault crimes when asked about their current feelings. The respondents were asked if they believed the punishment was lenient or severe, and this was compared to their desire for revenge. The study author found no significant difference in revenge feelings for people who felt that the punishment was severe, indicating that punishment is not a major factor in long-term feelings of revenge. These results do not answer our specific research questions about sexual assault victims though, because the final analysis did not examine the feelings of rape victims separately from non-sexual assault victims, and we do not have an objective measurement of what a "lenient" or "severe" punishment was in the German courts. Still, the results show that revenge may not be a panacea for crime victims, and it may have no impact on their long-term feelings of injustice.

Other studies have found considerable differences in punitive orientations of victims depending on the nationality of the survey respondents, with Mexico, Japan, Turkey, Bulgaria, and English-speaking nations preferring prison sentences for burglary crimes, while most non-English-speaking European countries preferred community service punishments (53).

Some researchers have described a rape survivor's experiences with community service providers as "the second rape" (54). Victims who are disbelieved, blamed, or ridiculed learn to distrust "the system" and stop making reports to the authorities. As the majority of rape crimes are not prosecuted or they are pled down to a lesser charge, victims sometimes report feeling that their abuse was not taken seriously enough. For example, in Chicago in 2001, researchers interviewed 102 adult women who were the victims of a sexual assault. Most (62%) were physically injured during the crime. Only 25% of these rape crimes were prosecuted. Of these, 40% did not result in a conviction, 40% did result in a conviction, and 20% included a guilty plea. In total, 70% of the cases involving White women as the victim were prosecuted even though only 37% of all victims in the sample were White women. And despite the fact that 66% of rapes involved a person the victim knew, only 20% of prosecuted rapes were committed by non-strangers. The authors of this study interpret these results as evidence that the court system in Chicago did not consistently prioritize these rape crimes as equally deserving of prosecution. It should come as no surprise then to learn that more than half of the victims (52%) believed that their contact with the justice system was hurtful. Importantly, those whose cases were not prosecuted were significantly more likely to describe the system as hurtful than those whose cases were prosecuted. Victims found greater comfort in mental health therapy, rape crisis centers, and in their religious communities than they could find in the courtroom (55).

I was unable to find peer-reviewed academic studies that measured the punitive orientations of victims of sex crimes. There is a potential for real insight into the desires of victims that do not rely on cherry-picked anecdotal accounts that fit preconceived notions about "what victims want." The best way to listen to these individuals is one at a time, in court, as they deliver a victim impact statement. Judges and juries have an opportunity to listen to the victim's words as they weigh the totality of evidence to determine what kinds of responses are most appropriate in each case (56, 57). Unfortunately, there are many things that prevent this message from being respected, not least of which are the personal biases that decide if a victim is a "Good Victim" (58). And even if children were prepared to give an impact statement under the strain of a courtroom setting, they may not be able to understand or articulate the true extent of their injury.

I conducted a preliminary survey of attitudes toward punishment, and I included some questions about victimization experiences. This survey was meant to be a feasibility study to determine if people's punishment attitudes were related to their moral foundations, so it is not ideal for answering the research questions I would like to see answered in regards to victimization and punishments. I recruited 250 respondents through Amazon Mechanical Turk (MTurk), an online marketplace for virtual tasks. I do not make any assumptions about the generalizability of this sample to the entire United States. There are clearly many flaws in using online recruitment software. Only 204 respondents completed usable surveys. Their average age was 37 (S.D. = 9.9, range = 51), 48% identified themselves as women, and 52% identified as men. The majority of respondents were White (87.3%), 6% were Asian, 3% were Black, and the remainder were Native American or any other race. None indicated having Hispanic or Latino ethnicity.

I asked each person if they had personal experience with victimization, and 47% said they had been the victim of a violent crime at some point in their lives, 41.2% said they had been the victim of a sexual assault as an adult, and 38.2% said they had been sexually victimized before they turned 18 years old. There was almost complete overlap between these categories of victimization, so that those abused as children were likely to be victims as adults. A larger percentage of men reported being the victims of violence (47–38% for women), but slightly more women reported being the victims of both types of sexual assault (a 2% difference for abuse as an adult and as a child). The full list of questions and mean scores for each group's responses are available in the Appendix of this book (Tables D1 and D2), and this survey is explained in greater detail in Chapter 5. In these questions, a "victim" is defined as someone who was sexually abused before their 18th birthday, and a "sex offender" refers to someone who victimized minors.

The results indicate that people who experienced sexual victimization before they turned 18 were somewhat more likely to endorse "tough on crime" retributivist punishments than people who were not the victims of child sex abuse. There are some notable contradictions though. For example, victims were more likely to believe that sex offenders *can* be treated, but in another question, they were more likely to strongly endorse the statement "regardless of treatment all sex offenders will eventually re-offend." Victims were less likely to agree that punishing the" wrong person" is acceptable, perhaps indicating their personal desire for retribution against the "right" individuals, whereas non-victims may not have thought clearly on that point. Overall, both groups held permissive attitudes toward punishing sex offenders, but the average level of agreement was higher for victims than non-victims. These preliminary results are interesting enough to justify further exploration of this topic with more sophisticated research methods.

The two survey items most interesting for our discussion relate to execution and violence for the sake of revenge. When asked if they agree with the statement "*sex offenders should be executed*" the mean score (on a scale of 1–5, with 5 being "strongly agree)" was 2.68 for non-victims and 3.51 for victims. When asked "*Do you think it is ever okay for a private citizen to violently harm a sex offender for revenge?*" 24% of non-victims said yes compared to 43% of victims (Figure 2.1). While I do not believe this survey is methodologically sound enough to generalize these results to all victims, it does highlight the possibility that victims may hold retributive punishment orientations under certain situations. Future researchers should ask victims about their specific case, their

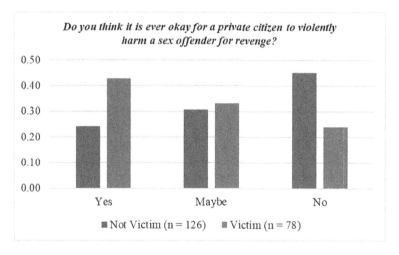

FIGURE 2.1   Responses to the question: "Do you think it is every okay for a private citizen to violently harm a sex offender for revenge?"

satisfaction with the justice system, and their support networks so we can contextualize their responses within a broader framework.

These surveys might measure someone's punishment orientations by asking victims' opinions in the broad sense of guiding policies, but they do not tell us if a victim feels better after their own abusers are punished. For that we would need to speak to victims before and after sentencing decisions are made. Even if we could detect some beneficial effects from official punishments on victim satisfaction, they may be fleeting. Other researchers have found no evidence that family members of murder victims feel closure after the perpetrator is executed by the state. Their lost family member is not returned to them after the murderer dies. In what way does the death of an offender restore the victim? (59). Perhaps the same lack of closure is evident in William Nesler's reckless behavior. He was sexually abused as a child. His mother killed his abuser. But he did not transition from victim to survivor. Maybe revenge is not a good substitute for safety, love, and professional therapy. As Andrew Vachss wrote, "You can make the perpetrator disappear from the earth, but not from the child's mind" (60).

Vengeance Is Mine

Jason Berry's book *Lead Us Not Into Temptation: Catholic Priests and the Sexual Abuse of Children* was first published in 1992 and exposed the deliberate cover-up of known felonies committed by priests for decades (61). Although the 2013 edition of this exposé included over 400 pages of detailed documentation of abuse, it only scratched the surface. *The Boston Globe*'s special investigative team known as "Spotlight" uncovered hundreds of child victims of individual priests and even more diligent efforts to obscure justice by the Archdiocese of Boston. One of the most perplexing aspects of the cover-up was not their intention to protect the church's image (which has backfired spectacularly), but that the cover-up facilitated the child abusers' efforts to find new victims. When a known and confessed child abuser was identified, they were often transferred to new parishes where they abused more children who were kept unaware of the danger posed by the offending priests.

In 2002, a man named Dontee Stokes walked into a church in Baltimore and shot Reverend Maurice Blackwell (62, 63). The bullet struck the priest's hand and side, but he survived the shooting. After he was arrested, Stokes claimed that Blackwell had molested him for a period of three years when he was an altar boy. Police records showed that Stokes had reported Blackwell's abuse back in 1993, but the investigation was dropped. The church said his allegations were not credible, but they did send Blackwell to the Institute for Living treatment center in Connecticut for three months (the same institute that treated the notorious child abuser John Geoghan in 1989, see Chapter 8) (64). Blackwell was placed on leave in 1998 after he admitted to a sexual relationship with another teenager that occurred before he was ordained.

Dontee Stokes tried to cope with the trauma of his abuse and the failure of the justice system to take his claims seriously, but he suffered from depression, dropped out of high school, and tried to kill himself. He survived this suicide attempt and tried to live a normal life, but when the Boston Globe exposé was receiving constant news coverage, he couldn't conceal his emotions anymore. He took a gun into the church and shot Blackwell. A remarkable turn of events took place during the subsequent trial. Stokes was found *not guilty* of attempted murder (he was found guilty of three charges related to using a handgun, but these charges were thrown out by the appeals court). He faced no punishment for his actions. Stokes said "This is a statement not just for me, but for every person who has been abused by anyone. This is a victory for all of them."

The prosecutor warned that this decision set a dangerous precedent and warned that vigilantes would have an "open season in Baltimore city." As he said this, his voice was drowned out by the cheers from Stokes supporters who celebrated the jury's decision (65, 66).

The tables were turned on Reverend Blackwell when *he* was charged with four counts of sexually abusing a minor. After testifying as the victim in Stoke's trial, he found himself seated at the defendant's table. Blackwell's attorneys attacked Stoke's character, said he was imagining the abuse, and told the jury Stokes was a liar (67, 68). Despite this passionate defense (or perhaps because of it), Blackwell was found guilty and faced up to 45 years in prison. Blackwell was awarded a new trial on appeal, but prosecutors dropped the case after claiming that he probably wouldn't serve any prison time even if he were re-convicted (69, 70). Blackwell was defrocked by the church and his superiors apologized to Stokes for their handling of his accusations (71). Neither Blackwell nor Stokes served prison time. This case reveals the reckless failure of both the formal and informal systems that claim to be able to determine who was a victim and who was a criminal, and it resulted in an absurd draw with no official punishments being imposed.

Expecting Justice

Supporters of vigilantes might be tempted to conclude that harsh punishments and murder will solve these problems. They believe that if the crime is avenged, then the children can grow up without fear and shame. They will be validated in their anger and the threat will be neutralized. But I do not know of any successful cases that played out this way. It didn't work for William Nesler. The trauma of child abuse cannot be ignored and it will not die with the abuser. There has been some research done to assess whether victims' desire for revenge is satiated by more severe punishments, and although the research methodology of these surveys do not fully justify broad conclusions, they do indicate that you cannot restore a victim through punishment policies alone (50, 72). I would argue that this does not give carte blanche for leniency, but it does imply that a harsher penalty may not be any more useful than one that is less severe.

Perhaps some victims cannot abide excessive mercy shown to their oppressors because of the degree of psychological suffering they endured, or because of their own indoctrination into the philosophy of retribution that our criminal justice system personifies (73). It may be difficult to convince these people that "the majority of victims" disagree, so they should abandon their deeply felt convictions. A rational criminal justice system might find a way to balance those competing interests on a case-by-case basis, but it is more likely it will overcompensate and impose extremely harsh, mandatory punishments for cases that do not require such drastic measures.

The best advice is to prevent these crimes before they occur. Prevention is like a preemptive cure. You won't have to try to undo the damage if you can prevent the damage in the first place. When that fails (and sometimes it will) we need to give effective therapy and true social support to victims of child abuse. People who were abused as children *can recover*. They can live meaningful lives and experience true happiness and loving relationships. It happens all the time. But we need to increase the number of successful cases. This means we need to expand our available resources to give individualized treatment to people with different needs. In extreme cases, we need to be proactive. We need to defuse the bomb before it explodes. The sooner we act, the better. "Taking mental health seriously" sounds like a slogan, but if we don't help these victims, we will reap the whirlwind one way or another (74).

Perhaps the best people for the job are people who suffered this type of abuse themselves. Just as a mentor in Alcoholics Anonymous can truly understand their mentee's mindset, a counselor who knows about the challenges of overcoming abuse can truly help victims. They understand exactly why a child would keep their abuse a secret. They can convince these victims that they are not alone. If we can recruit these survivors of child abuse to join the ranks of therapists, advocates, and investigators, we can help the survivor to have something meaningful to live for. All of the vigilantes I spoke to for this book had a profound lack of meaning in their lives. They had nothing to lose. Their vigilante actions were a quest for significance. Most of them tried to drown their sense of despair in drugs, alcohol, and lawlessness before they decided to go out with a bang and take some of sex offenders with them. If they had known of a better way to fight this war maybe they wouldn't be in prison today.

Sexual abuse is a serious concern for millions of children, and the public has a right to be worried. These statistics and descriptions of widespread criminal exploitation and abuse of children are staggering. We live in a dangerous world, and there is no guarantee that your family will avoid contact with the perpetrators of these crimes. When you drive through your neighborhood and see the lovingly manicured lawns, the smiling faces, and the cultivated image that your neighbors show… you would never really know what happens behind their closed doors. These crimes are not limited to any social class, racial or ethnic group, or religious affiliation. Sexual crimes against children are a scourge in our society, hidden by our own naiveté, and the victims are silenced by our cultural taboos. When child victims summon up the courage to report their abuse we need to take their claims seriously and take active steps to prevent harm, and heal the harm that has been done. Part of this response will include an appropriate legal response in regards to the perpetrator. I cannot offer specific recommendations for every possible child sex abuse crime, but I hope that court actors will consider the effects that their decisions will have on the child victim. As Charles Dickens wrote:

> In the little world in which children have their existence whosoever brings them up, there is nothing so finely perceived and so finely felt as injustice.
>
> *Great Expectations*

Silence…

By "A Son of Solitude"

It's a poisonous intimacy, this is why I stay silent. You taught me about closeness and physical contact, in the most terrible way. My mind and my body were never really my own, not even in the most precious and wonderful of times, my childhood. Do you hate your own body like I hate mine? I was never given the time or the space to love myself. As I grew, you reminded me that my life was meaningless. At any moment, my happiness or joy could be taken away.

It was a poisonous intimacy; this is what made me silent. You showed me that life was full of darkness and pain, you gave me this lesson, then reminded me as often as you chose too, that it would always be the case. Do they clench their bodies into a ball each night… the other kids? No one ever spoke of their father touching them, so I didn't know that I should speak of what you did to me. I'm still paying the price now. I should have said something, but to who?

It's the poisonous intimacy, this is what made me silent. You took away my ability to trust, piece by piece, one beating at a time, each night when you came in my room, to violate me in a sexual way. Each trauma was a brick, one to smash my consciousness, one taken away from my foundation. You left me with nothing solid to stand on. I had nothing to build a life on. Anything. Everything. It could all go away. Any time. You taught me this.

It's a poisonous sort of intimacy, this is what makes us silent. You showed me all of the reasons why my voice doesn't matter. In the beginning, I cried out in pain. You kept beating me. I fell on the floor. You kept beating me. Tears ran down my face. You kept swinging. In the end, I knew my pain, my desires, my wishes, my voice… meaningless. We were surrounded by people, your people, and they never asked. I cannot walk properly today. No one asked why. I cannot sit down today. No one asked why. I cannot run at all today… no one asked… I'll continue to be beaten… no one will ask… you know this. It emboldened you.

This poisonous intimacy, this is what made me silent. You created a world for me which was different than most everyone else's. I question every person I encounter. In my mind, I wonder, what does this coach or this teacher, or this pastor do to his children at home? At night? After school? You created a world for me that had much terror. Few joys. The joy I do have is always tempered by the knowledge that you can take it anytime you wish. This taught me that I am powerless over my own world.

It's a poisonous intimacy, and this is what causes victims of abuse to be silent. A terrible bond is formed during these moments of trauma. This bond is reinforced each time the abuser returns. You see your abuser, and your body reacts. You see your abuser, your mind reacts. You hear their voice, you react. This is evidence of that bond, that dark intimacy which is rarely spoken of. Even now, years after the man who repeatedly molested and violently assaulted me has died, I must be cautious not to invoke his spirit by guarding my mind. This is how powerful the bond is, which is formed through this sort of intimacy. I believe it is the same for all of us, survivors of this sort of trauma, we are bound to our abusers, psychologically, and perhaps there are methods and means to sever those ties, but if they exist, they have not been made known to me. So, I burned them, and I heaped any distractions I could on top of those live, electric connections, chemicals, danger, drama, anything to separate me from the past. In the end, it blossomed and bloomed, into the series of assaults on sex offenders which I am currently serving time in prison for. And so, I have no freedom. I have few joys, and it would appear as though the bond still exists.

And yet, because of that poisonous intimacy, I will no longer stay silent.

References

1. Center for Disease Control and Prevention. (2021, April, 30). Preventing child sexual abuse factsheet. https://www.cdc.gov/violenceprevention/childsexualabuse/fastfact.html
2. Donovan, D. M., & McIntyre, D. (1990). *Healing the hurt child: A developmental-contextual approach.* New York, NY: W.W. Norton & Company.
3. Finkelhor, D., Saito, K., & Jones, L. (February 2020). *Updating trends in child maltreatment, 2018.* Durham, NH: Crimes Against Children Research Center.
4. Kendall-Tackett, K. A., Williams, L. M., & Finkelhor, D. (1993). Impact of sexual abuse on children: A review and synthesis of recent empirical studies. *Psychological Bulletin, 113*(1), 164–180. https://doi.org/10.1037//0033-2909.113.1.164
5. Boden, J. M., Horwood, J. L., & Fergusson, D. M. (2007). Exposure to childhood sexual and physical abuse and subsequent educational achievement outcomes. *Child Abuse & Neglect: The International Journal, 31*(10), 1101–1114.

6. Maniglio, R. (2009). The impact of child sexual abuse on health: A systematic review of reviews. *Clinical Psychology Review, 29*(7), 647–657. https://doi.org/10.1016/j.cpr.2009.08.003

7. Young, J. C., & Widom, C. S. (2014). Long-term effects of child abuse and neglect on emotion processing in adulthood. *Child Abuse & Neglect, 38*(8), 1369–1381. http://dx.doi.org/10.1016/j.chiabu.2014.03.008

8. Salter, M. (2012). *Organised sexual abuse.* Oxfordshire, UK: Routledge.

9. Cutajar, M. C., Mullen, P. E., Ogloff, J. R. P., Thomas, S. D., Wells, D. L., & Spataro, J. (2010). Psychopathology in a large cohort of sexually abused children followed up to 43 years. *Child Abuse & Neglect, 34*(11), 813–822. https://doi.org/10.1016/j.chiabu.2010.04.004

10. Mills, R., Scott, J., Alati, R., O'Callaghan, M., Najman, J. M., & Strathearn, L. (2012; 2013). Child maltreatment and adolescent mental health problems in a large birth cohort. *Child Abuse & Neglect, 37*(5), 292–302. https://doi.org/10.1016/j.chiabu.2012.11.008

11. Nanni, V., Uher, R., & Danese, A. (2012). Childhood maltreatment predicts unfavorable course of illness and treatment outcome in depression: A meta-analysis. *The American Journal of Psychiatry, 169*(2), 141–151. https://doi.org/10.1176/appi.ajp.2011.11020335

12. Campbell, R., Dworkin, E., & Cabral, G. (2009). An ecological model of the impact of sexual assault on women's mental health. *Trauma, Violence & Abuse, 10*(3), 225–246. https://doi.org/10.1177/1524838009334456

13. Dworkin, E. R., Menon, S. V., Bystrynski, J., & Allen, N. E. (2017). Sexual assault victimization and psychopathology: A review and meta-analysis. *Clinical Psychology Review, 56*, 65–81. https://doi.org/10.1016/j.cpr.2017.06.002

14. Miller-Graff, L. E., & Howell, K. H. (2015). Posttraumatic stress symptom trajectories among children exposed to violence. *Journal of Traumatic Stress, 28*(1), 17–24. https://doi.org/10.1002/jts.21989

15. Perry, B. D. (2009). Examining child maltreatment through a neurodevelopmental lens: Clinical applications of the neurosequential model of therapeutics. *Journal of Loss and Trauma, 14*, 240–255.

16. Hambrick, E. P., Brawner, T. W., Perry, B. D., Brandt, K., Hofmeister, C., & Collins, J. O. (2019). Beyond the ACE score: Examining relationships between timing of developmental adversity, relational health, and developmental outcomes in children. *Archives of Psychiatric Nursing, 33*(3), 238–247.

17. Ashraf, F., Niazi, F., Masood, A., & Malik, S. (2019). Gender comparisons and prevalence of child abuse and post-traumatic stress disorder symptoms in adolescents. *Journal of the Pakistan Medical Association, 69*(3), 320–324.

18. Thompson, M. P., Kingree, J. B., & Desai, S. (2004). Gender differences in long-term health consequences of physical abuse of children: Data from a nationally representative survey. *American Journal of Public Health (1971), 94*(4), 599–604. https://doi.org/10.2105/AJPH.94.4.599

19. Walker, J. L., Carey, P. D., Mohr, N., Stein, D. J., & Seedat, S. (2004). Gender differences in the prevalence of childhood sexual abuse and in the development of pediatric PTSD. *Archives of Women's Mental Health, 7*(2), 111–121. https://doi.org/10.1007/s00737-003-0039-z

20. Homma, Y., Wang, N., Saewyc, E., & Kishor, R. N. N. (2012). The relationship between sexual abuse and risky sexual behavior among adolescent boys: A meta-analysis. *Journal of Adolescent Health, 51*(1), 18–24. https://doi.org/10.1016/j.jadohealth.2011.12.032

21. Chaplo, S. D., Kerig, P. K., Modrowski, C. A., & Bennett, D. C. (2017). Gender differences in the associations among sexual abuse, posttraumatic stress symptoms, and delinquent behaviors in a sample of detained adolescents. *Journal of Child & Adolescent Trauma, 10*(1), 29–39. https://doi.org/10.1007/s40653-016-0122-z

22. Dworkin, E. R., Menon, S. V., Bystrynski, J., & Allen, N. E. (2017). Sexual assault victimization and psychopathology: A review and meta-analysis. *Clinical Psychology Review, 56*, 65–81. https://doi.org/10.1016/j.cpr.2017.06.002

23. Plauché, J. (2019). *Why gary why? The jody Plauché story.* Dallas, TX: Inspired Forever Book Publishing.

24. WRTV Indianapolis. (2017, Nov. 9). Convicted child predator Jack Reynolds describes how he groomed young boys before molesting them. YouTube. https://www.youtube.com/watch?v=m7VMY8aZHVk

25. Quayle, E., Allegro, S., Hutton, L., Sheath, M., & Lööf, L. (2014). Rapid skill acquisition and online sexual grooming of children. *Computers in Human Behavior, 39*, 368–375.

26. Craven, S., Brown, S., & Gilchrist, E. (2006). Sexual grooming of children: Review of literature and theoretical considerations. *Journal of Sexual Aggression, 12*, 287–299. http://dx.doi.org/10.1080/13552600601069414

27. Katz, C. (2013). Internet-related child sexual abuse: What children tell us in their testimonies. *Children and Youth Services Review, 35*, 1536–1542. http://dx.doi.org/10.1016/j.childyouth.2013.06.006

28. Tener, D., Wolak, J., & Finkelhor, D. (2015). A typology of offenders who use online communications to commit sex crimes against minors. *Journal of Aggression, Maltreatment and Trauma, 24*(3), 319–337.

29. Wolf, M. R., & Pruitt, D. K. (2019). Grooming hurts too: The effects of types of perpetrator grooming on trauma symptoms in adult survivors of child sexual abuse. *Journal of Child Sexual Abuse, 28*(3), 345–359.

30. O'Connel, R. (2003). *A typology of cyber sexploitation and online grooming practices.* Preston, England: University of Central Lancashire. http://image.guardian.co.uk/sys-files/Society/documents/2003/07/17/Groomingreport.pdf

31. Briggs, P., Simon, W. T., & Simonsen, S. (2011). An exploratory study of internet-initiated sexual offenses and the chat room sex offender: Has the internet enabled a new typology of sex offender? *Sexual Abuse, 23*(1), 72–91. https://doi.org/10.1177/1079063210384275

32. Black, P. J., Wollis, M., Woodworth, M., & Hancock, J. T. (2015). A linguistic analysis of grooming strategies of online child sex offenders: Implications for our understanding of predatory sexual behavior in an increasingly computer-mediated world. *Child Abuse & Neglect, 44*, 140–149.

33. Grant, S. (1990, March). Suffer little children. *Time Out.* http://www.vachss.com/av_interviews/time_out.html

34. Vachss, A. (2003). Andrew vachss: Autobiographical essay. *Contemporary Authors, 214.* http://www.vachss.com/vachss/ca_2003_autobio.html

35. Salter, A. (2004). *Predators: Pedophiles, rapists, and other sex offenders.* New York, NY: Basic Books.

36. Brown, D. W., Anda, R. F., Tiemeier, H., Felitti, V. J., Edwards, V., Croft, J. B., & Giles, W. H. (2009). Adverse childhood experiences and the rist of premature mortality. *American Journal of Preventative Medicine, 37*(5), 389–396.

37. Hays-Grudo, J., & Morris, A. (2020). *Adverse and protective childhood experiences: A developmental perspective.* Washington, DC: American Psychological Association.

38. Moffit, T. (1993). Adolescence-limited and life-course-persistent antisocial behavior: A developmental taxonomy. *Psychological Review, 100*(4), 674–701.

39. Miley, L. N., Fox, B., Muniz, C. N., Perkins, R., & DeLisi, M. (2020). Does childhood victimization predict specific adolescent offending? An analysis of generality versus specificity in the victim-offender overlap. *Child Abuse & Neglect, 101*, 1–12.

40. Agnew, R. (1992). Foundation for a general strain theory of crime and delinquency. *Criminology, 30*(1), 47–88.

41. Inglis, T. (2019, June 21). Sara Kruzan, imprisoned for killer her sex trafficker, is free and fighting back. Street Roots. https://www.streetroots.org/news/2019/06/21/sara-kruzan-imprisoned-killing-her-sex-trafficker-free-and-fighting-back

42. Broidy, L., & Agnew, R. (1997). Gender and crime: A general strain theory perspective. *Journal of Research in Crime and Delinquency, 34*(3), 275–306.

43. Gruenfeld, E., Willis, D. G., & Easton, S. D. (2017). "A very steep climb": Therapists' perspectives on barriers to disclosure of child sexual abuse experiences for men. *Journal of Child Sexual Abuse, 26*(6), 731–751. https://doi.org/10.1080/10538712.2017.1332704

44. Vachss, A. (1998). *Flood.* New York, NY: Vintage Crime/Black Lizard.

45. Vachss, A. (1998). *Down in the zero.* New York, NY: Vintage Crime/Black Lizard.

46. Hunter, M. (1995). *Child survivors and perpetrators of sexual abuse: Treatment innovations.* Thousand Oaks, CA: Sage Publications, Inc.

47. Lew, M. (2004). *Victims no longer: The classic guide for men recovering from sexual child abuse.* New York, NY: Harper Perennial.

48. Associated Press. (2015, January, 14). Vigilante mom's son subject of manhunt. https://www.foxnews.com/story/vigilante-moms-son-subject-of-manhunt

49. Jonsen, A. R., & Toulmin, S. (1988). *The abuse of casuistry: A history of moral reasoning.* Berkley, CA: University of California Press.

50. Alliance for Safety and Justice. (2016). *Crime survivors speak: The first-ever national survey of victim's views on safety and justice.* http://www.allianceforsafetyandjustice.org/crimesurvivorsspeak/report
51. Laxminarayan, M., Bosmans, M., Porter, R., & Sosa, L. (2013). Victim satisfaction with criminal justice: A systematic review. *Victims & Offenders, 8*(2), 119–147.
52. Orth, U. (2004). Does perpetrator punishment satisfy victims' feelings of revenge? *Aggressive Behavior, 30,* 62–70.
53. Van Kesteren, J. (2009). Public attitudes and sentencing policies across the world. *European Journal of Criminal Policy and Research, 15,* 25–46.
54. Madigan, L., & Gamble, N. (1991). *The second rape: Society's continued betrayal of the victim.* New York: Lexington Books.
55. Campbell, R., Wasco, S. M., Ahrens, C. E., Sefl, T., & Barnes, H. E. (2001). Preventing the "second rape:" rape survivors' experiences with community service providers. *Journal of Interpersonal Violence, 16,* 123–125.
56. Davies, R., & Bartels, L. (2021). *The use of victim impact statements in sentencing for sexual offences: Stories of strength.*
57. Balfour, G., Du Mont, J., & White, D. (2018). "To this day she continues to struggle with the terror imposed upon her": Rape narratives in victim impact statements. *Women & Criminal Justice, 28*(1), 43–62.
58. Vachss, A. (2016). *Sex crimes: Then and now.* New York, NY: Pay What It Costs Publishing, LLC.
59. Christensen, T., & Eaton, J. (2014). Closure and its myths: Victims' families, the death penalty, and the closure argument. *International Review of Victimology, 20*(3), 327–343.
60. Vachss, A. (1991). *Sacrifice.* New York, NY: Vintage Crime/Black Lizard.
61. Berry, J. (2013). *Lead us not into temptation: Catholic priests and the sexual abuse of children.* New York, NY: CreateSpace Independent Publishing Platform.
62. Johnson, G. (2002, May, 15). Baltimore priest shot; alleged victim is held. *The Boston Globe.* https://archive.boston.com/globe/spotlight/abuse/stories2/051502_baltimore_shooting.htm
63. Biema, D. V. (2002, May, 19). Making a priest pay. *Time.* http://content.time.com/time/magazine/article/0,9171,238613,00.html
64. The Institute of Living. (1989). Clinical Notes: Reverend John J. Geoghan. https://www.bishop-accountability.org/docs/boston/geoghan/Geoghan_7_000339_342.pdf
65. Klein, A. (2002, Dec. 17). Stokes found not guilty. *The Baltimore Sun.* https://www.baltimoresun.com/bal-te.md.stokes17dec17-story.html
66. Willis, L. (2002, July 12). Stokes rejects plea deal. *The Baltimore Sun.* https://www.baltimoresun.com/news/bal-stokes12-story.html
67. Braun, S. (2005, Feb. 18). Ex-priest shot by former altar boy in 2002 convicted of abusing him. *Los Angeles Times.* https://www.latimes.com/archives/la-xpm-2005-feb-18-na-priest18-story.html
68. Deseret News. (2005, Feb. 18). Priest who is shot is guilty of abuse. https://www.deseret.com/2005/2/18/19877920/priest-who-was-shot-is-guilty-of-abuse
69. Chron. (2005, July, 3). No new trial for ex-priest accused of molesting boy. https://www.chron.com/news/nation-world/article/No-new-trial-for-ex-priest-accused-of-molesting-1913063.php
70. Bykowicz, J. (2005, Feb, 18). Blackwell is convicted of molesting teen Stokes. *The Baltimore Sun.* https://www.baltimoresun.com/maryland/bal-te.md.blackwell18feb18-story.html
71. Matysek, G. P. (2017, March, 23). 'Light of hope': Cardinal Keeler, basilica restorer, interfaith healer, dies at 86. *Catholic Review.* https://catholicreview.org/light-of-hope-cardinal-keeler-basilica-restorer-interfaith-leader-dies-at-86
72. Batchelor, D. (2021). Talking punishment: How victim perceptions of punishment change when they communicate with offenders. *Punishment & Society, 25*(2), 519–536.
73. Tonry, M. H., & Ohio Library and Information Network. (2011; 2012). In Tonry M. (Ed.), *Retributivism has a past: Has it a future?* New York, NY: Oxford University Press.
74. Vachss, A. (1994, August, 12). How many dead children are needed to end the rhetoric? *New York Daily News.* New York, NY.

3

THE HUNT

In his book *Sacrifice*, Andrew Vachss described how the "Children of the Secret" live hypervigilant lives, always looking for the types of people who tortured them when they were small. Now grown up, this army of abused children hear a silent whistle that brings them together in unified hatred of those who betrayed their youthful innocence. He wrote: "All things come to those who wait. Some of us wait in ambush" (1).

Ask someone you know what they think is a suitable punishment for a child sex abuser. They will probably endorse a severe punishment for these crimes. Some will say "kill them" without hesitation. Given how serious sex abuse crimes are, it is probably not surprising to learn that people become so enraged that they actually respond with violence. These incidents might happen in a moment of rage immediately after discovering the crime. It might be a father who waits with a gun in an airport to kill the man who hurt his child. A victim might seek revenge against their own abuser decades after the crime happened. Sometimes a vigilante will hunt down child abusers who never hurt them personally. For others, the vigilante act is part of a wider assault on a corrupt and failing society. Many of these crimes occur inside jails and prisons where the prisoner subculture justifies violence against "dirty" offenders by those with "clean" offenses. Sometimes an entire community will rise up as a lynch mob and collectively mete out justice that is denied to them by the court system.

Take the case of Akku Yadav who was accused of multiple murders, rapes, and armed robberies in Kasturba Nagar, India. Every time Yadav was arrested he was bailed out. In 2003 a mob of 200 women attacked Yadav, threw stones at him, threw chili powder in his face, stabbed him over 70 times, and cut off his penis. One woman who was arrested for her role in the attack said "After the murder, society's eyes opened: the police's failings came to light. That has irritated them. The police see me as a catalyst for the exposure and want to nip it in the bud. I'm not scared. I'm not ashamed. We've done a good thing for society. We will see whether society repays us" (2). The frustration these women had with the legal system caused them to take the law into their own hands. Throughout history there have been "vigilance committees," "courts of the people," lynch mobs, and lone vigilantes who have thought of themselves as morally superior to the ineffective court process (3). These groups may be lauded as heroic or vilified as the greater of two evils depending on your own personal belief systems, but you must admit, it is a fascinating subject for any psychologist, sociologist, or concerned citizen.

DOI: 10.4324/9781003393849-4

When you hear about a vigilante who kills a child sex abuser, you might remember similar news stories that have occurred during your lifetime. The prevalence of vigilante violence against child sex abusers might be overstated or understated depending on how often you read the news. Here is a sample of headlines that can easily be found on any internet search engine:

What price vengeance? A Louisiana town weighs the issue in slaying of accused kidnapper.
The Washington Post (Art Harris, March 29, 1984)

Vigilante mother cleared of murder: Child molester's killer still faces jail.
Independent (Phil Reeves, August 12, 1993)

Accused child molester impaled on a cactus.
The Arizona Republic (July 02, 2002)

Letter tells killer's reasoning for slaying 2 pedophiles.
The Seattle Times (Mike Carter, September 15, 2005).

Child molester's death ruled a homicide.
Bangor Daily News (Abigail Curtis, 2009)

The 16-year-old boy who killed his molester.
Oprah (October 18, 2010)

Convicted child molester from San Gabriel killed in prison.
The Sun (January 5, 2011)

Police: Hazelwood man attacked sex offender with hammer, claimed he was doing "God's work".
St. Louis Post-Dispatch (Valerie Schremp Hahn, 2011)

Man "grateful" for jury's acquittal in beating of South Bay priest who allegedly molested him.
CBS SF BayArea (July 5, 2012)

Supremacist gets 26 to life in killing of molester.
The Associated Press (May 4, 2013)

Husband-wife "vigilante" team killed two- planned to work way through sex offender registry "hit list".
New York Post (July 25, 2013)

Inmate confesses to killing Grand Haven child molester.
The Associated Press (February 25, 2015)

Prison inmate who killed convicted child molester gets 3rd life sentence.
The Associated Press (November 2, 2016)

Life sentence for "family vigilante" who killed his pedophile, sex abuse dad.
CBC (Kelly Bennett, November 10, 2016)

Child molester believed killed by another inmate in Lancaster prison.

Daily Breeze (September 6, 2017)

The Vigilante of Clallam County: Patrick Drum was tired of seeing sex offenders hurt children. So he decided to kill them.

The Atlantic (Lexi Pandell, December 4, 2013)

Suspects in killing thought victim was child molester.

The Spokesman-Review (Jennifer Pignolet, June 29, 2013)

Courtroom applauds as New Jersey man admits fatally stabbing Boy Scout leader he says molested him.

New York Daily News (David Boroff, June 18, 2015)

Two-time killer admits to murder of child molester in Norfolk prison.

The Patriot Ledger (September 16, 2016)

Angry parents beat convicted child molester to death, report says.

Fox4 (Clint Davis, December 10, 2016)

Vigilantes assault, rob and murder registered sex offenders.

Prison Legal News (Matthew Clarke, May 5, 2017)

Man accused of setting fire to sex offender's house in Jefferson County.

WVTM13 (August 18, 2017)

Hudson man charged with attacking sex offender with ax.

Republican Eagle (Mike Longaecker, November, 22, 2017)

Man who allegedly killed cellmate: "There's one less child molester."

CBS (February 4, 2018)

Man accused of trying to burn several sex offenders to death at Florida motel.

Tribune Media Wire (May 7, 2018)

Notorious accused child molester Clinton Don Simpson is killed in Texas prison.

New York Post (Amanda Woods, November 9, 2018)

Lake Isabella man who killed child molester will continue serving 17-year prison term, judge rules.

KGET (Jason Kotowski, July 17, 2019)

Officials investigating death of convicted child molester as a homicide at Kern Valley State Prison.

ABC News (February 3, 2020)

Ohio prisoner killed by cellmate who mistakenly thought he was a child molester.

Prison Legal News (Scott Grammar, February 4, 2020)

Inmate confesses to beating two child molesters to death in prison.

CBS News (Caitlin O'Kane, February 21, 2020)

Vigilante Justice: Maine: Stephen Marshall's true motives for murdering two men remain unknown.

Friday Night Crimes (Brianna Bennett, July 10, 2020).

Court upholds death sentence for Broward convict who murdered child molester.

South Florida Sun Sentinel (June 3, 2021)

Nebraska man gets 40–70 years in prison for killing convicted child molester.

True Crime Daily (July 19, 2021)

Richmond child molester Deandre Austin killed in prison; Cellmate held for homicide.

CBS SF (October 16, 2020)

Murder inside Marion County Jail: How an inmate was targeted and killed in 3 hours.

WTHR (August 2, 2021)

Washington dad rescues daughter from sex traffickers, kills boyfriend he believes sold her for $1,000: police.

Fox News (Pillar Arias, November 2, 2021).

Texas brothers beat stepfather to death for allegedly abusing sister – Police.

Newsweek (Gerrard Koanga, January 25, 2022)

Ex-UFC champ accused of attempted murder was targeting alleged child molester: Police.

KTVU (Lisa Fernandez, March 2, 2022)

It would be difficult to track down every case of vigilantism, but this seems like a lot of cases. Is there an epidemic of vigilante violence in America?

Richard Tewksbury conducted a survey of 121 registered sex offenders in Kentucky in 2005 (4). He found that 47% of them reported being harassed in person, and 16.2% were assaulted. Some received harassing telephone calls (28.2%) and others received harassing mail (24.8%). I do not know of any government database that measures crime with enough detail to properly estimate how often these incidents occur in a given year. Michelle Cubellis, Douglas Evans, and Adam Fera have constructed a database to track these events in the Sex Offender-Vigilante database, and they found between 1983 and 2015 there were 279 incidents listed, but these events include attacks against all types of sex of-fenders and include several types of attacks (including punching, kicking, and using a weapon) (5).

Certainly, some attacks may occur that are never linked to vigilante motives, so we will never have a precise estimate. More research and better data would help, but from what we currently know it appears that serious violent "vigilante" crimes against sex offenders are rare, with 8-9 incidents being reported by the news media each year. Of course, it is possible that the victims do not make a report, but the same limitation persists for sex crime victims as well. We can only count what is reported. I personally identified 110 cases of "serious" violence against alleged child sex abusers (see Chapter 9) where 48 attacks resulted in death, and few of them could be considered to have a "vigilante" motive. Therefore, this book is examining an *extremely rare* and special type of crime: the murder of a child sex abuser for the purposes of revenge or the public benefit. Serial killings, mass killings, and terrorist attacks are more common than vigilantes killing child sex abusers.

So why study such a rare event? When these events occur they receive a large amount of media publicity and this might lead some people to believe they are more common than the official statistics show. Perhaps they are more memorable. Can you remember the last time you heard about a drug dealer being killed? The memory is probably vague, but when you hear about a child sex abuser being killed by a vigilante you will probably remember it for a long time. There is something about vigilantism that attracts our attention, especially when the target of their wrath is someone who sexually harmed a child.

I will summarize some stories of vigilantism to demonstrate how these media headlines do not actually refer to the same type of crime at all. Each case has completely different circumstances. If you only read the headline, you will not know how distinct each situation really is. I believe these cases provide a good representation of the range of motives and circumstances surrounding the murder of child sex abusers in the community, as well as the various justice system responses that have occurred.

The Texas Father

On June 9, 2012, a Texan man saw someone kidnap his 5-year-old daughter. The alleged perpetrator, Jesus Mora Flores, carried the girl to a secluded area as she struggled to get free. The father immediately ran to her rescue. He discovered the man was sexually abusing his screaming, half-naked daughter. The father tore the man away from her and repeatedly punched Flores in the face and neck. As Flores was dying on the ground, the father called 911. He said "I need an ambulance. This guy was raping my daughter and I don't know what to do… Come on! This guy is going to die on me!" When the ambulance arrived the medical team discovered that Flores could not be saved. The police never arrested the father because the signs of sexual abuse were obvious (and later confirmed by a full investigation). In Texas "deadly force is authorized and justified to stop an aggravated sexual assault or sexual assault" (per the District Attorney overseeing the case). We do not know the father's name because he was never charged with a crime and the victim's identity was concealed by all of the media organizations who wrote about the case (6).

This event was horrifying and traumatic, but it is a clear case of when "taking the law into your own hands" is technically legal and would be considered morally justifiable to most people in our society. Sure, there might be some people somewhere in the world who lament that the offender died, but they will be hard-pressed to blame the father because he was (1) defending his daughter from a serious felonious act that was in progress, (2) he did not use a weapon or premediate his deadly assault of Flores, (3) there is some room in the law for one's emotional state during the event, and (4) he called 911 in an attempt to save the rapists' life. This is a clear case of *justifiable homicide*. It does not even qualify as "vigilantism." This Texas father killed Flores because he had to save his daughter. Nobody else could have.

The Louisiana Father

In 1984, a karate instructor in Baton Rouge, Louisiana named Jeffrey Doucet was sexually abusing a child named Jody Plauché after he had won the trust of the child's parents. Jody's father, Gary Plauché, refused to believe family members who saw Doucet inappropriately touching Jody.

Things escalated quickly when Doucet kidnapped Jody and took him to a motel in California. Doucet dyed Jody's hair a different color so he wouldn't be recognized, and he took him to Disney Land. Throughout this terrifying period, Doucet was raping Jody (7, 8).

Jody convinced Doucet to let him call his mother to tell her he was okay. The FBI traced the call and law enforcement officers raided the motel. Jody was flown home to his parents. He was examined for physical signs of abuse, and the doctors confirmed he had been raped. Jody asked his mother not to tell his father about the abuse.

When Gary Plauché learned the details, he was enraged. Gary told the news media that he felt helpless and didn't know what to do. He learned that Doucet was being flown back to Louisiana for his trial and would arrive at the Baton Rouge Metropolitan Airport on March 16, 1984. Gary went to the airport with a handgun in his boot. He was talking on a payphone when Doucet was escorted past him by several police officers. Gary knelt down to draw his weapon, turned, and shot Doucet in the head, killing him. The police tackled Gary and took his gun. One of them recognized Jody's father and yelled "Gary, why? Why, Gary?" A news crew filmed the shooting and thousands of Americans saw an enraged father killing the man who abused his son. To this day, Gary Plauché is regarded by many people as a heroic vigilante who secured a form of justice that could never have been expected from the legal system.

This case has provoked its share of controversy. Gary Plauché pled no contest to manslaughter in exchange for a seven-year suspended sentence, with five years probation and 300 hours of community service. This lenient sentence was regarded by most people as an endorsement of Gary's actions. Some people have worried that this case justified vigilantism and undermined the rule of law. It is possible that the high-profile nature of this case has inspired more vigilantes over the past 35 years to believe in the righteousness of their own behavior, but that would be difficult to prove. The former director of WBRZ news who made the decision to broadcast part of the shooting footage on television recalled how the public, who usually wrote letters to complain about violence on TV, actually demanded to see more of the footage.

> The first 24 hours we were consumed with people from around the world wanting it. And it went worldwide. It went on almost every broadcast network in the United States, and went to several around the world... at some point, we just simply said enough is enough, after the first couple of days in terms of its usage, we started trying to back up. Ironically, it's the only time in my entire career where we've gotten calls on dramatic video where people wanted to see it again, which I thought was always telling. You usually get calls complaining about, "How could you air that?".

> Because most people in this community thought this was justified it was not politically favorable to the incumbent to persecute this guy, so what we ended up getting was basically a slap on the wrist for a guy who ironically was videotaped committing a murder.

One person who believes that Doucet should have had his day in court and served a long prison sentence is the victim himself, Jody Plauché. A court system that is lenient on vigilantes would not have been lenient on a child rapist. Doucet would have suffered a fate worse than death in Louisiana's notoriously harsh prison system, and this experience would have been even worse for him, specifically, because of the nature of his crimes. Jody also believes in the rule of law and everyone's constitutional rights to due process, even though he knew very well Doucet was guilty. But Jody came to this conclusion after a lot of thought and consideration of the facts, which he has cataloged in his book *Why Gary Why?: The Jody Plauché Story*.

I had the privilege of speaking to Jody Plauché when he was a guest speaker in my graduate course on victimology at the University of Massachusetts-Lowell. His abuse was horrific and traumatizing, and this was only amplified by the media frenzy that occurred after the shooting. But Jody is the ideal example of a "survivor" of child sex abuse. As an adult, he graduated from Louisiana State University studying psychology, philosophy, and speech communications. He started working in Pennsylvania as a counselor in the Victim's Services Center where his own experiences helped him to understand the mindset of the children he worked with. He was named the Survivor/Activist of the Year by the Pennsylvania Commission on Crime and Delinquency in 2004. He even developed a great sense of humor to help other people feel comfortable talking to him without wallowing in commiseration and grief on his behalf. In 2019 he published the full account of his story in *Why Gary Why?* and speaks to people across the country to warn them of the danger of abuse so they can protect their children from harm. Jody has achieved what every victim of child sexual abuse dreams of: saving others.

The Alabama Father

Julia Maynor was eight years old when she was repeatedly sexually assaulted by her grandfather, Raymond Earl Brooks (Brooks was her mother's stepfather). When the abuse was discovered, Brooks was sentenced to prison, but he only served 27 months in the Alabama Department of Corrections. He was put on a sex offender registry but stayed close to home. Julia grew up with PTSD and struggled with relationships. Her father, Jay Maynor, watched his daughter cope with her trauma. He tried to move on with his life, be a good father, pay his taxes, and trust that the legal system did the best it could. But something was gnawing at him. For 16 years Jay brooded over the abuse his daughter suffered. He knew that Brooks was living free in society.

One day, Julia got into an argument with her father. She said something about her abuse that set him off. Jay got on his motorcycle, drove to Brooks house, and shot him twice in the head. He also shot at another man whom he suspected had abused his daughter, but did not injure him. Jay was arrested and charged with one count of murder and one count of attempted murder (9, 10).

Julia was devastated. She didn't want her father to go to prison. She was going to testify in court to explain the whole situation: her abuse, trauma, emotional outbursts, and the guilt her father suffered from for 16 years. It was a powder keg that was lit by a simple argument. Maybe her testimony would introduce mitigating circumstances to the case and her father would not get a long prison sentence.

Her father didn't want her to relive the trauma of her abuse, especially in a public trial, so in a demonstration of Southern honor, he pled guilty to spare her. She said "My father was protecting me, like a father should do. He is an amazing father – actually the best. He loves us so much." Jay was sentenced to 40 years in prison. His appeal for resentencing was denied. His family and friends have posted a petition on Change.org to encourage the governor of Alabama to commute his sentence. Julia blames herself for this crisis. "I'm going through hell," she said.

Is this a case of passion provocation or was Maynor a vigilante motivated to correct a lenient justice system response? It is easy to list this in a database as another "vigilante" attack, but when the deeply personal circumstances are explained it seems to be a case of unresolved trauma boiling over after years of simmering.

The Washington Vigilante

One might define a "true" vigilante as someone who has no personal animus toward the individual they are killing. This is up for debate, but consider how different the motives are between a man who kills their own abuser, one who kills their child's abuser, and one who kills *any* abuser.

They are not just taking the law into their own hands, they are taking the mantle of judge, jury, and executioner. They might have an emotional stake in the crime, but they are supposedly acting in lieu of government action. This is closer to the spirit of the term "vigilante" which comes from the old vigilance committees of concerned citizens who served as law enforcement in the wild west. Such is the case of Michael Anthony Mullen.

In August 2005, Michael Mullen lived in Washington state. He was 36 years old. He had a criminal history but was never convicted of a violent crime. He was outraged when he heard cases of child sexual abuse and the lenient sentences abusers received through legal loopholes and judicial indifference. He was especially disgusted with the case of Joseph Duncan, a man who kidnapped and raped children across the United States over a 27-year period. The justice system failed repeatedly in Duncan's case, releasing him for "good behavior" on many occasions until they finally convicted him of murdering five children. But it was too late for the victims he left in his wake. Mullen was baffled by the government's incompetence. He wondered why the system was so lenient toward serial rapists. He was angry, and he decided to do something about it.

Mullen logged into the online sex offender registry in Whatcom County. He searched through the names of convicted sex offenders until he found a house where three sex offenders lived together. Victor Vasquez (68) was convicted of sexually abusing children in his family over a long period of time. He served over ten years in prison for those crimes. Hank Eisses (49) was convicted of raping a 13-year-old boy in his home, and was sentenced to five and a half years in prison. They were listed as "Level III" offenders – the most likely to recidivate. A third man was also a registered sex offender, but his crimes were not as severe as the other two. Mullen paid them a visit.

When they answered the door, Mullen was wearing a blue jumpsuit and an FBI hat. He warned them that a dangerous vigilante was looking to hunt down sex offenders. He told them they were on a "hit list" and that they should be careful. Then he interviewed them about their previous sex crimes. The third man expressed remorse for his crimes, so Mullen let him leave the house. The other two men allegedly did not show remorse, and Mullen decided to kill them. He shot them dead and left the scene.

Mullen sent letters to news outlets across the state. He warned them that more sex offenders would be killed. He even explained why he let the witness live to tell the tale. "I wanted one alive to spread the message that 'we' will not tolerate 'our' children being used and abused." Despite his threatening letter, Mullen did not try to kill anyone else. He called 911 to confess the crime, then turned himself in to the police. He pled guilty to the murders and was sent to prison. His defense attorney said, "All I can say is that he is not that bad of a guy in some respects " (11–14).

Mullen was sexually abused as a child. This is a common experience among vigilantes. He said "Don't get me wrong. I am no saint. I've been haunted since childhood. I just don't want other children to grow up confused, sad, or scared. I am not proud of taking two lives. I would have gladly just given my own. But my death alone would have meant nothing. Some of these children will grow up to be drunks, addicts, thieves, or act out sexually, sometimes becoming pedophiles themselves."

Mullen was a bit of a local celebrity in prison. He was surrounded by men who were frustrated with the flawed justice system that sentenced them to long prison sentences for drug-related offenses while sex offenders came and went. One man named Patrick Drum shared Mullen's frustration and had often considered taking the law into his own hands, and he later did so (see Chapter 4).

Michael Mullen asked several other inmates to smuggle poison into the prison so Mullen could silently kill sex offenders from the inside. He wanted to use cyanide, ricin, or nicotine sulfate. There is some circumstantial evidence to suggest that Mullen took this idea from a noir fiction story written by Andrew Vachss about a prison assassin who injected candy bars with rat poison. He never carried out this plan. Perhaps he wanted to use the poison on himself. Two years after being admitted to prison, Mullen acquired a large number of pills and overdosed (incidentally, Mullen had written a suicide note and mailed it to Andrew Vachss because he was a fan of his books, and Vachss reported him to the authorities, but it was too late).

Mullen said he wanted to die so he could get to Hell before the serial rapist Joseph Duncan. He wanted to be waiting for him when he arrived.

The New Hampshire Vigilante

In 2003, in Concord, New Hampshire, a man named Lawrence Trant was looking for an apartment complex where six sex offenders lived. Then he tried to set the building on fire. He also went to an apartment building across the street from the state capitol where another registered sex offender lived. He set newspapers on fire outside his door. The fires were all extinguished, and nobody died.

Shortly after this incident, Trant saw a man walking to an Alcoholics Anonymous meeting whom he recognized from the sex offender registry. Trant chased him with an aluminum baseball bat and a knife. When he caught up with the offender he stabbed him once in the back and once in the arm.

When Trant was arrested, he did not deny his felonious conduct. He thought he was helping the police. He said "I hope I've done a service to the community. These guys are sexual terrorists. If Bin Laden moved into the house next door, wouldn't we tell people about that?" Police found a manifesto and a list of names in his house. A check mark was written next to the names of the men he tried to kill.

During his trial he told the jury "I don't want people to steal the souls of little kids... I wasn't about protecting anyone from my family. This was about protecting you!" The prosecutor said he was a danger to society, but the jury was hung. Three of the twelve jurors refused to convict him of attempted murder (although he was clearly guilty by his own acknowledgment), so he was only convicted of first-degree assault. The prosecutor was satisfied with this outcome because he knew "verdicts are based almost as much on emotion as they are on fact."

Trant was given the maximum penalty: 10–30 years in prison. He said "I think I'm a good guy. I don't think I should receive this kind of punishment. I thought people would accept it. But I was wrong." He expected that people would write him letters of support, but they didn't. He served his minimum time and was released (15–17).

When people asked Trant why he tried to kill those men he said he had been abused by a priest when he was a child, and seeing the *Boston Globe* coverage of the clergy sex abuse scandal had convinced him that nobody was protecting children. He also said the years he had spent in prison as a younger man had given him plenty of time to interact with "skinners" (child sex abusers). He hated them for stealing children's innocence and traumatizing them for life. "I'm not ashamed of it, but I'm not proud of it," Trant later said. "I did it for a reason. I'm not a monster. The monsters are the ones who victimize children."

PizzaGate

In recent years there was a massive, intricate conspiracy movement that is referred to as "PizzaGate." Users of 4chan (the online imageboard) posted a report by the FBI that linked the term "cheese pizza" with child sex exploitation because it has the same abbreviation as child pornography ("C.P."). The online sleuths began scouring the social media posts of everyone who even mentioned the word pizza on the internet and pieced together a ludicrous conspiracy about human trafficking and Satanic sacrifices. A different FBI report defined a series of symbols that criminal child abuse organizations used to advertise their businesses. One image was labeled "BLogo aka Boy Lover." It was shaped like a triangle, or maybe a piece of pizza. This same triangular shape was used as the logo for a pizzeria in Washington DC named Comet Ping Pong. The owner of this establishment was loosely connected with powerful people in Washington DC. These anonymous investigators egged each other on and cracked jokes about the whole situation, probably not expecting anyone to take action.

While most people were content to indulge in this alternate reality investigation from the comfort of their computer chairs, one person decided to visit the pizzeria with a loaded firearm to save the child victims inside. Edgar Welch, a 28-year-old man from North Carolina drove to the restaurant and told everyone to leave. Then he fired his weapon at a door, hitting a computer. He did not find any of the alleged child victims. He just found pizza ingredients. Welch peacefully surrendered to the police. He regretted his actions, apologized to the people he scared, and plead guilty to assault with a dangerous weapon and transporting a firearm over state lines. He was sentenced to four years in prison (18–20).

The PizzaGate conspiracy theory is considered to be such a danger to society that most of the original internet posts have been deleted by social media companies or they have been labeled "hoax" or "debunked" so anyone who stumbles across them will not be tempted to take the law into their own hands. At the core of this bizarre episode in 4chan history is an abiding distrust of the government. People who obsess over these conspiracies have a complete lack of faith that the government can protect children from harm. Some would find it easier to believe the entire government apparatus will facilitate child sex trafficking, torture, and murder rather than believe anonymous posts on the internet are mistaken. How did trust in the system collapse to this degree?

"Conspiracies" are not all crackpot theories invented in the fertile imaginations of paranoid or suggestible members of the public. When groups of people conspire to commit crimes against children, to avoid detection, and to mitigate their liability it can certainly be called a conspiracy, and these groups do exist. Michael Salter's book *Organized Sexual Abuse* explains how two or more adults work together to abuse children and silence them within social networks, institutions, families, and even in ritualistic fashions. Unfortunately, crying wolf over pizza parlors may give cover to the real cases where powerful organizations conspire to abuse thousands of child victims. The massive outrage over these organized forms of abuse should not be dismissed as easily as rumors about a pizza parlor.

Predator Poachers

When the government is perceived to be incapable or unwilling to get justice for children, members of the public sometimes seek their own definition of justice. Some people are merely advocates for fair sentencing. The #*MeToo* movement exposed how Hollywood and other industries fail to protect women from harassment, exploitation, and sexual abuse. The victims of Jeffrey Epstein fought non-disclosure agreements and gag orders to have their voices heard. Parents of children who were sexually abused by clergy members organized and lobbied for justice. Survivors themselves have come together to break the silence their abusers imposed on them, like S.N.A.P. (Survivors Network of those Abused by Priests). Some people create Facebook groups, run for public office, or march in protest outside government buildings. These people do not trust the system to hold the perpetrators accountable without external pressure. They are not vigilantes.

They are activists who stay within the boundaries of the law. Others might push those boundaries by taking on an unofficial law enforcement role.

The television series "To Catch a Predator" was broadcast by Dateline NBC from 2004 to 2007 and featured sting operations where men arranged to meet with underage teenagers for sexual purposes. When the men arrived at the agreed-upon location they were met by Chris Hansen and a film crew who confronted them with their sexually explicit chat logs. When the individuals fled the scene they were usually arrested by law enforcement officers and charged with crimes. The minors they were corresponding with were actually undercover volunteers who worked with the group "Perverted Justice." Altogether there were 256 suspects caught on tape attempting to meet with someone they thought was a minor, and there were at least 117 convictions in a court of law (21).

The television show was successful as far as ratings were concerned and they did secure the arrest and conviction of several men who were committing felonies, but the show was criticized as well. In some cases, the local courts refused to prosecute men caught in the operation because of questionable evidence. The case that ended the show occurred in 2006. Perverted Justice was gathering evidence against a suspect who solicited sexually explicit photopgraphs from a decoy posing as a minor. It turned out that this person was Louis Conradt Jr., an assistant district attorney in Rockwall County, Texas. The disgraced prosecutor ended his contact with the decoy and began deleting his online accounts. Law enforcement agents acquired an arrest warrant and went to Conradt's home, but he shot himself and died before he could be apprehended. *To Catch a Predator* had always been criticized for exploiting offenders to get ratings by shaming them publicly, but the deadly consequences of this case led to strong criticism from *Rolling Stone* and *Esquire*. One of Condrat's relatives sued NBC for emotional distress and she asked for $100 million in damages. She was paid an undisclosed amount. The legal liability involved in these operations contributed to the decision to cancel *To Catch a Predator*, but its legacy lived on. Amateur vigilantes began broadcasting their own sting operations on online platforms like YouTube (22).

Hundreds of "viral vigilantes" have stepped up to the plate to replace Chris Hansen with their own twist on the show. These groups will solicit child predators online by pretending to be underage. Then they invite the pedophile to meet with them in a public location. When the predator arrives the team members approach them with cameras and begin asking them questions. Sometimes the predator will run away, but the vigilantes will alert passersby that they are a pedophile. They will read the predator's own words and publicly shame them. Other times, the predators will try to argue with the strangers who are filming them saying that it was a mistake or making excuses for their behavior. Some beg not to have the video shared online because they might suffer social consequences like losing their jobs. Different vigilante groups have different methods for these operations. Some will threaten the predator that they will go to the police with the evidence unless they perform some humiliating action for the camera, like pushups, jumping jacks, eating hot sauce, or calling their mothers to confess their behaviors. These videos are wildly popular on the internet, but they operate very close to the edge of criminal behavior, especially if they are filmed in a jurisdiction where the coercive threats are considered blackmail.

Law enforcement officers, legal scholars, and many journalists condemn these groups as vigilante mobs who use harmful shaming tactics to circumvent the courts (the predator hunters agree but fail to see the problem). University of Connecticut Law School Professor Molly Land has said that the government has legitimate power because it was elected and sanctioned by the public. A journalist paraphrased her argument as "The proceedings of the judicial system are calibrated by learned people elected and appointed to the positions; they seek information and mete out sentences based on societal standards and expertise. They, as well as the legal process, can be held to account." She said "there's a reason why we have rule of law- and it's because mob justice can make mistakes." Land feared that if people were "constantly inundated" by hundreds of videos of men seeking sex with children it might distort their view of the world. Land also condemned the harm that public exposure does to men seeking sexual relationships with children. If they are exposed they can suffer "really extraordinary and significant consequences" in their lives. These critics of predator hunters have no problem criticizing the justice system's many flaws, but they believe in erring on the side of due process. Police officials reluctantly file charges when the evidence is too strong to ignore, but they do not want to congratulate the predator hunters publicly because that would be an endorsement of vigilantism. A former police chief said of the Connecticut-based predator hunter group that he was "agnostic" toward their position. He did not want to condone adult men seeking sexual relationships with children, but when balanced against the vigilantes who step into an investigative role, he could not support them. "It's a slippery slope. When we remove Constitutional protections and short-circuit the system, we lose something of living in a democracy." This unique situation has placed *grown men caught on video trying to have sex with minors* on the side of due process and the United States Constitution.

The YouTube channel "Matt Orchard- Crime and Society" has documented the questionable legality of the "Predator Poacher" movement on social media and identified several notable examples of these groups, including the "Campbell River Creep Catchers," "Dads Against Predators," "PP Toronto," "Predator Catchers Alliance," "CC Unit," and "PP Mass." The leaders of these groups tend to have the typical vigilante justifications for their sting operations that the original Perverted Justice group had on *To Catch A Predator*. They do not believe the police are able to catch all of these predators and secure appropriate punishments, so they are doing the job themselves. They think that public shaming is an effective deterrent, and at the very least it can help warn the predator's family members, employers, and friends about their secret activities. But it is also a path to online fame. The Predator Poachers and Creep Catchers are lionized by their dedicated fanbase for the public service they provide. They are considered to be heroes. Some of these groups have set up Patreon accounts or sell merchandize to fund their operations (23).

One of these viral vigilantes who stood out to me was Justin Payne, a YouTuber with over 200,000 subscribers who poses as a child on the internet in order to converse with adults who are seeking illegal sexual relationships. Justin arranges to meet with child predators and records their reactions when a tall muscular man approaches them instead of the 13-year-old they were hoping to meet. He asks them why they are willing to sexually abuse children. His methods are not as extreme or aggressive as other *TCAP*-inspired channels. He's not above using sarcasm and threats of exposure during his videos, but the predators tend to "hang themselves" with their embarrassing excuses. I spoke with Justin about his motives for making these videos and asked what advice he would give to other people who want to be vigilantes. Our conversation lasted almost two hours and we covered a wide range of topics. Nobody can say he isn't thoughtful and considerate about the implications of his channel. He offered a wealth of information on the viral vigilante phenomenon.

Justin started his YouTube channel to post funny videos and make people happy, but when trolls and haters gave him a hard time he realized he didn't care. He liked to get a reaction from confrontation. He decided to use this superpower to confront child predators. He admits that Chris Hansen's work in "To Catch A Predator" played a small role in his decision to target these offenders, but he was not obsessed with the show like many other imitators. He would enter chatrooms and use MSN Messenger to speak with strangers. The first question asked was always "asl?" (age, sex, location). He would pretend to be 13 or 14 years old. Conversations would develop from there and some predators would arrange to meet him in person. The first predator cried when he was caught and Justin described this as a surreal experience. He couldn't understand why someone would take such an obvious risk just so they could touch a child. He posted the first video on YouTube and waited for viewer comments to appear.

Most viewers were supportive of his efforts. Some people opened up to Justin about the abuse they had suffered personally and they thanked him. They believed that public exposure might lead these pedophiles to seek help or be deterred from seeking relationships with children. Some viewers were enraged that the police did not arrest the offenders immediately. The existence of amateur sting operations implies that the police can't do their job properly. Justin was also criticized for shaming people who had personal issues that drove them to such extreme behavior. Justin listened to all of these groups and tried to learn something from all of the varied responses he observed. Justin realized he had stirred up a controversy that allowed him to assess some of the deepest emotions and moral positions of a cross section of society. Justin is a curious person – a student of human behavior – and he thought this experience would help him understand human psychology and his own journey through life.

Justin hasn't been able to truly understand the most aggressive members of his audience. He doesn't know why they scream "Die, die, kill, kill" "A dead pedophile doesn't reoffend." Justin thinks of these offenders as human beings with families who will grieve even if the person did a horrible thing. "Opinions are high, common sense is low," he said. He thinks most people on the internet are like "Hungry, Hungry, Hippos" consuming media in large gulps and never being satisfied. When the entertainment value of Chris Hansen's show ended they wanted more schadenfreude and found groups online to feed them for a while. He thinks they will move on to new shows eventually. They don't really care about victims or effective methods of intervention.

He has never had a violent encounter with a predator, but he knows this is a major risk. He is putting his life on the line to do a job he thinks must be done for the greater good. He meets all of the criteria of a vigilante except he tries not to cross into any behavior that would be illegal. His advice to amateurs who want to do their own sting operations is "Don't do this at all." Not only for their own safety, but so they don't ruin the predator's lives unnecessarily.

Justin has a certain level of compassion for the men he exposes. He does not pull any punches in his criticism of their behavior, but he tries to understand their position. He believes they have a serious mental health issue that needs intervention. He hopes that his sting operations and public shaming will encourage them to get help before their behavior lands them in a prison cell. He is also considerate of their families. He would prefer not to post the videos online at all if they would only get some professional help, but few of them take up his offer. He has a code of ethics he follows to make sure he doesn't cross any moral lines when he meets with an offender. He has to have valid reasons to upload a video exposing a predator, not just looking for views. His primary reasons are to inspire some deterrence so they will seek voluntary help. If the person enters a program Justin might refrain from shaming them online (which can be criticized as blackmail). He also has a plan to go to the police any time there is a crisis, and he asks questions meant to gauge their mental health status. He doesn't want anyone to harm themselves.

Justin would be delighted if his channel ran out of material. He wishes that predators would not take his bait, but he is always disappointed to learn that there is an endless supply of adult men seeking relationships with children. He can't keep up with all of the solicitations and he knows the police can't either. "I was absolutely stunned by the number of people who were so fixated on sexual deviancy, admitting to masturbatory disorders, chronic obsessive sexual fixations who interact with me online when they read that I am 13 years old." Some of these people may not be pedo- or -hebephiles. Some are just seeking another person to interact with and they choose teenagers because they can't find anyone else. But nowadays Justin is not surprised. It is an everyday thing. He gets messages from dozens of men, phone calls, and voicemails, and offers to meet in person. He believes that most of them are delusional. They are so filled with wishful thinking that they actually believe a child would talk to them on the phone for hours and offer to meet them. They ignore all of the red flags in their phone calls and meet with him anyway. It is pathological, not rational. Justin believes this delusional mindset renders them unable to identify their own behavior problems. They think they can quit whenever they want because they don't understand their own illness. It is like a drug or alcohol addiction. One day of sobriety will not equate a lifetime of sobriety.

I asked Justin what he thinks about violent vigilantes. Those who seek to cause physical harm to child sex abusers. He said he understands their point of view. These crimes inspire strong emotions, but he cautions anyone with those impulses to follow the law. "We're not a bunch of savages killing each other. We need civilization. You can ruin your life, the offender's life, and your family's lives. It is not acceptable."

I found my conversation with Justin to be extremely insightful. It is easy enough to criticize these YouTube Predator Poacher shows, just as you can criticize any amateur group who gets attention from embarrassing others. It is reality television for people interested in crime. After speaking with Justin, I found that he had a sound rationale for his behavior and he planned his efforts. Whatever you think about the viral vigilante phenomenon, it is a form of social activism meant to draw attention to the scope of the problem and the inability of the police to handle the massive volume of these cases. Those who criticize *violent* vigilantes often recommend that they choose non-violent methods to achieve their goals. Justin's methods might not be palatable to viewers who cringe when they see people shamed and humiliated, but it is a better alternative to vigilantes who want to violently assault them. It's hard to argue with logic like that even if these activities are perilously close to criminal acts themselves.

The Nebraska Vigilante

"Hero or devil?" reads the headline from the *Omaha World-Herald* describing the case of James Fairbanks, a man who shot a sex offender seven times in May, 2020. This is a recent homicide, and it was difficult to piece together facts in the chaos of media reports, prosecutorial statements, and defense attorney pleas, but now that it is settled, James is finally ready to tell the whole story for the first time (24, 25).

James grew up in California, but he moved around a lot because his father was in the Air Force. When he was 12 years old, he walked into his house and saw a man sexually abusing a 14-year-old female family member. James didn't know what to do. The large man grabbed James and dragged him into a bedroom. He threatened to kill James, his mother, and the rape victim if anyone said anything about the crime. James was scared. He kept the secret, but he felt guilty. His relationship with the abuse victim was never the same. James was traumatized. He pushed everyone away and had angry outbursts throughout his teen years. He drank alcohol excessively throughout his youth.

James hated child abusers after that incident. He would occasionally hear a news story of a child sex abuser being killed by a vigilante, and he would smile. He thought they deserved the most severe punishments the justice system could devise, and he was outraged when he heard of lenient sentences for rapists.

As an adult with a family of his own, he was happy. His wife supported the family finan-cially while he worked third-shift jobs and took care of the children. His role as a father and husband turned him away from his reckless behaviors. He coached baseball, hosted dinner parties, and lived a happy, normal life. After 15 years of marriage, his wife left him. He was devastated and started drinking.

After the dust of the actual divorce settled and I had stopped trying to drink myself to death and sobered up I was in a bad place. I was broke... At the point when this all took place I was living with 4 other men in a house renting a room and had bought a $500.00 dollar car that was falling apart. I was spent from the divorce and feeling like I had no purpose. My youngest son and mom were still in my life but I felt like a pathetic male model for him.

James started dating a woman who had a young daughter. This family lived near a man named Mattieo Condoluci; a large, tattooed man with a handlebar mustache. When the girl needed help repairing her bicycle, Condoluci offered to help. He brushed up against the child and made her feel uncomfortable. He allegedly touched her in inappropriate places. He offered to let her come into his backyard to play on his playset. When the girl told her mother, James looked up this strange man on the internet. James discovered that Condoluci was a twice-convicted, registered sex offender. Public records described Condoluci as "a dangerous sex offender unable to control his criminal behavior."

Condoluci v. STATE

Cite as 18 Neb. App. 112

Condoluci was released on January 5, 2009, from the custody of the Nebraska Department of Correctional Services after serving his sentence for sexually assaulting a child. He was, however, immediately taken into custody by the Sarpy County sheriff and incarcerated in the Sarpy County jail, where he remained as of the time he filed the referenced appli-cation. This custody occurred because of a petition filed by the Sarpy County Attorney with the Sarpy County Mental Health Board (the Board), a copy of which Condoluci at-tached to his application. Such petition alleges that Condoluci is a dangerous sex offender. The prayer of the petition asked the chair of the Board to issue a warrant directing the sheriff to take custody of Condoluci and hold him in the Sarpy County jail pending further order of the Board.

The district court permitted Condoluci to be held in the local jail because the mental health board declared him a danger to others, but the Nebraska Appellate court reversed their deci-sion, resulting in Condoluci's release. What could James do? He wanted to protect this girl and any other children from harm. Emotionally, James was in hell. He was already thinking about suicide. He was exhausted with life. With nothing to lose, his opportunity to kill a child sex abuser seemed like a way to regain some self-respect and do what he considered to be a good deed for society.

James drove by to scope out the location and he personally observed Condoluci leering at children while he washed his car. James was worried because Condoluci was over 6ft tall, 300 lbs, and was supposedly a member of a biker gang. James knew he might lose a one-on-one fistfight, so he went home and got a rifle. James barged inside the house and confronted

Condoluci. James ordered him to go into the kitchen, but Condoluci came toward him. James fired several times, and Condoluci fell to the ground. James shot him one more time and left. Seven bullets in all.

> I felt nothing. I slept well that night and have felt nothing about him since. I believe he got what he deserved and had coming in this life. Hopefully I facilitated his reaching a new torment in his next life.
> I have no remorse for what I did. I would be lying if I said I've lost a moment of sleep caring about killing him. He was and should always be remembered as a blemish on humanity that deserved to be removed. I don't feel remorse for any of the things we did in County. Generally speaking I do believe child molesters deserve whatever punishment someone feels they want to dull out. Don't like it? Don't rape children. Seems like a pretty simple concept to me.

James was not immediately arrested. He went back to his girlfriend's house and told her what happened. She asked James not to bring her or her daughter into the courtroom, and he respected her wishes. James wrote a letter to the local media on their Facebook page. He wasn't trying to hide. He wrote:

Dear Media:

I am writing this email to let you know that I killed Matteio Condoluci Thursday May 14th around 9:45 pm… I read where he had molested (raped) two children and been convicted twice yet only served two years in prison. For RAPING CHILDREN!. One kid's mother had created a predator Facebook page about him trying to warn people about him. Her son had been assaulted by him when he was 5 and the damage he did led the poor guy to die of a drug overdose years later and his mom directly blamed that incident on him.

I've worked with kids for years who have been victimized and I couldn't in good conscience allow him to do it to anyone else while I had the means to stop him. I'm willing to turn myself in even though I'm confident I won't be caught because its my opinion that we need to fix this in our society. We cannot let this continue to happen to our children. They must be stopped. I know in this messed up judicial system that means I will face far more severe punishment for stopping him than he did for raping KIDS. But I could no longer do nothing.

James immediately received support from the community. As soon as he posted the comment on Facebook, a user replied "Thank you, whoever you are, that killed this man. Pedos deserve nothing but death." James replied, "You're welcome." The mother he cited in that Facebook post did indeed have a son who died of a drug overdose. Condoluci had raped her child back when the boy was only 5 years old. The victim was never the same after that. This mother ran a Facebook page that called attention to Condoluci's lenient sentences and other bizarre activities, such as dressing as a priest and inviting people to help him pass out food to the homeless. Condoluci was also allegedly a member of the Ku Klux Klan. This grieving mother was glad when she heard James had killed the rapist who ruined her son's life. She gathered over 13,000 signatures on a petition to have James released from prison. The court did not consider her request.

Another person who supported Fairbanks' actions was Amanda Henry the daughter of Matteio Condoluci. She had been sexually abused by her father and she was glad he was dead.

She spoke to KMTV News Now in Omaha about how she lived in fear that her father would hurt her or others.

> We might still be living, but when you molest and rape children, and your own child, you automatically took their lives. Yes, we're alive but we're not the same human beings that we should have been. I've had to live in fear for thirty-four years and it has been the worst pain that I could imagine. And so when I finally got the phone call, yes, I was relieved. I'm not at all saying I agree with murder, but when you've been violated so many times and the system has failed you so many times as it's failed me, that's the only thing you can hope for.

Amanda Henry even testified in court on *Fairbanks'* behalf during her victim impact statement. She told the courtroom:

> I was silenced until Mr. Fairbanks came along and ripped that tape from my mouth. There are so many other people that were hurt by my dad. And I don't agree with murder. But it was apparent that the justice system wasn't going to do anything to help.

It is very rare for the child of murder victim to support the killer in the courtroom.

As his next of kin, Amanda was asked to clean out Condoluci's house. She found some disturbing items inside. A little boy's khaki pants with dirt stains on the knees. Little girl's blouses. A pair of little girl's underwear. Were these pieces of clothing evidence of ongoing criminal behavior?

Condoluci's son, Joe Condoluci, completely disagreed with Amanda's version of events. He said their father was a tough disciplinarian but a generally good man who delivered groceries to food pantries. He also said the swing set in the backyard was for Condoluci's grandchildren, not for neighborhood children. He condemned Fairbanks as a delusional, cold-blooded killer. An anti-sex offender registry group called the Florida Action Committee argued that James Fairbanks should be charged with a hate crime because registered sex offenders ought to belong to a protected category.

Did Fairbanks kill a dangerous predator who was actively abusing children? We may never know, but the court certainly did not consider Fairbanks to be a hero. They took his guilty plea and sentenced him to 40–70 years in prison for murdering Condoluci (but in Nebraska most sentences are cut in half, so he is eligible for parole in 20 years). The *Omaha World-Herald* worded it rather succinctly. "James Fairbanks found out Wednesday what vigilantism costs you. Twenty to 35 years in prison, real time."

In prison, James receives letters from strangers all the time from women who were the victims of child sex abuse. Unfortunately, the Nebraska Department of Corrections has decided that these letters encourage violence and that is not rehabilitative, so two-thirds of them are confiscated. James thinks this is funny because the prison library is full of serial killer true crime novels. What a world. When a letter does pass the censors they tend to be women who hope his case will terrify their own abusers. Most of them vented their outrage at a failed justice system that permits child abuse crimes. Strangely, the mailroom does let James receive letters from apparent child sex abusers who gloat over his prison sentence. They remind him he is getting what he deserves and they hope he enjoys the crappy food. They also thank him for giving them a reason to abolish the sex offender registry he used to find Condoluci. They mock his suffering in their own gleeful embrace of retributive punishments.

James' biggest regret is being separated from his family. He knows it is difficult for them, and he hopes they understand his motives weren't selfish. A minimum of 20 years in prison is not a prize anyone wants to receive. He doesn't know if he is a hero, but he can't consider himself a devil. Not in a world where child sex abusers run rampant.

But as far as how I view myself and my case. I hurt the only people I have left in the world, my mom and my sons. I put a lot of pain on them that I likely had no right to put on them and I'm going to try and spend the rest of my life making amends best I can to them.

I hate prison and the thought of 18 more years here at least is sickening. But the realization that his victims got some relief and that he will hurt no one else does make that pain easier. It's probably more "good" than I would have otherwise done for the world.

Mistaken Identity

There are some practical dangers that must be taken into consideration for anyone who supports vigilantism or is thinking about committing a vigilante act. Remember, a true vigilante is someone who violates the law in order to secure what they define as justice. They are placing themselves in danger of being arrested and punished for their actions. They probably won't get a sympathetic prosecutor or judge to offer them a lenient plea deal. They might spend the rest of their lives in prison. For those vigilantes who are already serving life in prison, that threat loses its sting, but they still face serious consequences including reclassification to a higher security level with few privileges. Long-term administrative segregation is torturous. Most prisoners would prefer some degree of freedom to help them cope with the hardships of life in prison. It's not an easy decision to throw your life and freedom away, and perhaps that is why vigilante actions are so rare. Many people might be enraged by child sex abuser's actions, but few resort to felonious responses.

One thing a potential vigilante should keep in mind is that their actions may not be "moral" even using their own subjective criteria. Let's say a person truly believes that killing a child sex abuser is morally justified. What if their target was innocent? Sometimes our court system is just plain wrong.

Take for example the 1987 case of Frank James Harvey who was driving through Idaho with his dog (26). He picked up an adult male hitchhiker who attacked him. Harvey filed a complaint with the police. The police arrested *Harvey* because he fit the description of a rape suspect they were looking for in an unrelated case. A 6-year-old girl in the area had been kidnapped by a man who "talked funny" and had a small dog in the car. He had sexually assaulted her before dropping her off at a payphone with a dime so she could call her parents. She was sixty miles away from her home when they found her. The police didn't care that Harvey's dog was the wrong color or that the girl didn't identify Harvey in a police lineup. The police decided that she was too young to remember what color the dog was so they omitted this fact from their testimony. The prosecutor withheld the exculpatory evidence during the trial to secure a conviction. Harvey pled not guilty but was convicted and sentenced to 16 years in prison.

Because the prosecutor withheld evidence, Harvey filed an immediate appeal and the judge released him from prison after he had served four months. The investigation was reopened and a known sex offender who matched the girl's original description was put into a lineup. The girl identified him… and his dog. This man was Thomas C. Headley. He was on probation at the time, but due to the chaos of Harvey's false conviction, the jury could not reach a verdict. Headley was released and the prosecutors decided to drop the case entirely. The victim's mother said her daughter had been retraumatized by the two failed trials and she just wanted everything to be over with (27). The falsely convicted man was devastated, the guilty man was set free, and the child learned not to trust the legal system to help her. No definition of justice was achieved.

Harvey was devastated by his false conviction and the four months he spent in prison. Perhaps he was subject to some of the "convict justice" that prisoners feel is reasonable based on one's conviction status. He said "Even though I'm cleared, I don't feel like I've been cleared. A lot of people still think I am guilty. I can't get good work just because of my name alone. This all made my dad have three heart attacks, and made my parents spend their life savings." He sued the state for $50,000 in damages, but the judge refused to compensate him (28). The judge said, "That the plaintiff should be compensated in some way is obvious, but the remedy, whatever it may be, is not to be found in this court." Harvey was *guilty until proven innocent*, but even then he was still treated like he was guilty.

What happened to Thomas Headley you may ask? After being set free by the Idaho court, he went to Utah, kidnapped a 13-year-old girl, and tried to drive her into Canada. He was charged with abduction, sexual assault, two *unrelated* counts of aggravated sexual assault against another child victim, and *another unrelated* count of child rape. The prosecutor made a plea deal to drop the other charges if Headley would plead guilty to a single count of sexual abuse. He did. During sentencing, Headley's attorney pleaded with the judge that "prison will do him no good," a common phrase in courtrooms (see Chapter 4). The attorney said Headley "has come a long way in admitting the problems he's had" and said he wasn't a vicious person, that he merely *fell in love* with the child and made a bad decision. Headley was sentenced to 1–15 years in prison for this crime. He cried in the courtroom and said the prosecutors had been unfair to him.

Headley went to prison and wallowed in his own self-pity (29). He told the *Lock Up Raw* documentary film crew from MSNBC "I was charged with kidnapping somebody that was under 14. I am a man that is attracted to young women. God forbid. Ninety-nine percent of us are." He deliberately violated prison rules so he could be placed in solitary confinement where it was safe.

> There's not a safer place anywhere in the prison than where I'm at. No matter what you do, no matter how you try to approach it, you are a worthless piece of crap because you are a sex offender. You're a useless "Mo". That's all, that's the way everybody talks to you in here "Ah, you're a Mo, huh? Molester? You're one of those."
>
> But I have seen guys get stabbed. I saw a guy get a piece of a shovel handle stuck right in the side of his neck, and I seen a guy get a hammer taken to him and just get the side of his head beaten to a wreck. I've got a safety list of at least twenty names on it with people on it that's told me in no uncertain terms "You're a dead man if we ever get our hands on you."

You may be disgusted by Headley's repeated, traumatic crimes against children and his outspoken disdain for child protection laws. You might be angry that the justice system allowed him to get away with his crimes for so long. But if you think Headley deserved to have a shovel handle stuck in his neck for his crimes, then please consider that it might have been the innocent man, Frank James Harvey, who got it instead. Remember that the innocent man spent four months in prison for a crime that Headley committed. He wore the uniform that was meant for Headley. He carried the conviction charges that should have been given to Headley. He might have gotten the shovel handle in his neck too. The court system is not perfect, but it's the only "judge, jury, and executioner" we have. If I can't trust 12 "reasonable men" on a jury why should we trust one person to administer justice? Vigilantes should be concerned that official designations of guilt are fraught with error.

Mislabeling

Wrapped up into this chaos of definitions and competing interests, are misclassified child sex abusers. The justice system is full of absurd overreaches that further undermine faith in the law. Frank Dicataldo's book *The Perversion of Youth* outlines the many flaws in sex offender processing for juvenile defendants (30). He points out one case where a kid was required to register as a sex offender because he *mooned* his teacher. What would have made for a funny joke on *The Simpsons* became a lifetime sex offender label for a teenager. Should he be hunted down and shot by a wannabe vigilante? This includes the infamous Romeo and Juliet laws that convict a man of child sexual abuse on his 18th birthday for a consensual romantic relationship that was not illegal one day before his birthday. It also includes the 16-year-old who is found guilty of manufacturing child sex exploitation material *of himself* in a sext-message, or someone convicted of urinating in public. The fact that we lump "sex offenders" into the same term when their behaviors range from harmless to horrendous means we cannot even speak scientifically about the issue. Much less justify emotional outbursts against this nebulous category of people?

Common sense is sorely lacking in the bureaucratic nightmare of our legal system. A truly guilty, dangerous sex offender loves this chaos because they can hide in the crowd and pretend they are just misunderstood. It would be a shame to lump all accused people into the same category as guilty people, and similarly unjustifiable to equate all crimes as equally severe. Most of the vigilantes I have spoken to acknowledge that there are differences and they target people who have committed especially egregious crimes on very young victims.

Another problem with taking the law into your own hands is that you become an outlaw. You are not able to seek protection from danger. You're on your own. If James Fairbanks went to a sex offender's house with a gun and he'd been killed by his target, it would have been a clear case of self-defense. In a world without official law and order, Might Makes Right. Sometimes vigilantes are better off staying at home.

Fear of pain and suffering is not a problem for most of the vigilantes I identified during my research for this book. They knew what they were doing. It was a calculated "self-sacrifice." They did not expect to get the hero's welcome that Gary Plauché received in 1989. They were willing to die for their beliefs, and failing that, they were willing to lose their freedom. But to be honest, most of them had very little to live for in the first place. They wanted to secure some degree of cosmic justice and they wanted to draw attention to problems with the criminal justice system. They thought if the public knew how lenient sex offender sentences were, they could influence change. They didn't want to make a Facebook group or go door-to-door gathering petitions. They wanted to get attention through violence. But what if this attention backfired?

Some vigilantes killed people they located on sex offender registries. What if state legislatures used their attacks as proof that these registries should be abolished? We know from most research that sex offender registries are associated with increases in recidivism, not decreases, so it is possible that these warning systems will be removed in the future. Do these vigilantes think that is a good idea? Would they feel guilty if they were the reason why sex offender registries were removed? Those who support "convict justice" should also be afraid that judges will use the fear of targeted violence as an excuse to sentence sex offenders to community sanctions instead of prison. From the vigilante's perspective, that would increase sentencing disparities that justified their violence in the first place. Altogether, it is obvious that vigilante violence has some serious downsides that even a passionate supporter should take stock of.

Finally, there is the threat that vigilante violence will lead to lawlessness. This is the rationale that judges give when sentencing vigilantes to long prison sentences. They want to send a message: The government is in charge. Don't take the law into your own hands. Is this true? Will individual acts of violence lead to widespread destabilization? Will deterrence through punishment scare future vigilantes away from similar behaviors? I don't know, but it does inspire the opponents of vigilantism to rally against the supporters. These are the arguments used to justify banning free speech on social media or fundraising websites. That is why every reference to "Pizzagate" is appended with a warning that it is a fraudulent conspiracy theory.

Vigilante supporters see these bold government responses and wonder why their level of concern to protect child sex abusers is not also applied to the victims of child sex abusers. "Both sides" are bound by their preexisting beliefs, and blind to each other's point of view. When it is done correctly, a government response symbolizes the combined outrage of the community, restrained by fairness and due process. When people take the law into their own hands this outrage can be mistaken as the emotional flippancy of an individual.

Making Justice

The New Model Army song *The Hunt* described how a gang of citizens patrol the streets looking for criminals who must "pay the price" for what they've done to children. They warn the offenders that not everyone is scared of them. Vigilantes won't give them due process or follow the rules of war. There are no mitigating circumstances or lawyers to give them a second chance. The lyrics warn that citizens can wait for the justice system to solve the problem, or they can wait for a lightning bolt to strike the criminals. Both are unlikely. So, the vigilantes decided to make their own justice.

If we think of people's preferred response to child sex crimes on a scale, we can see that a vigilante response is extreme. Some people want to be activists on social media to draw awareness to lenient justice system decisions. Some want to call out perpetrators online and effectively "cancel" them through public condemnation. Some want the police to televise sting operations to shame the perpetrators. Some take that responsibility on themselves and start YouTube channels to shame alleged pedophiles. Some want to harass or threaten registered sex offenders to scare them from their neighborhoods. A few burn their houses down or physically assault them. And then, finally, at the farthest end of the spectrum, a very small number of people commit homicide. This does not imply a slippery slope exists, but it does indicate that some people feel less severe responses are not effective at achieving safety and justice for society's children.

Public support and encouragement of vigilante actions may seem strange to some people. Why would anyone support extrajudicial murder? The fact is that some people consider vigilantes to be heroes. They send them letters thanking them. They sign petitions to have them released from prison. And sometimes these citizens become "viral vigilantes" who shame and humiliate suspected sex offenders for their YouTube channels. Where is the line drawn between necessary self-defense, exploitation, and criminal vigilante crimes?

I wanted to know more about these vigilantes so I could understand them on their own terms. The minds of these vigilantes are dark and disturbing worlds plagued by trauma and abuse, but they are also marked by a profound lack of faith in the justice system. They take the law into their own hands because they do not trust "the system" to do an adequate job. They wait in ambush.

The Manor of the Devil

By "A Son of Solitude"

It saddened me deeply to see the normalcy of everyone else's lives. People in their cars, listening to music, chatting it up with each other. Folks walking through the crosswalk, a man on his bicycle, headphones on, just cruising on just another brilliant summer day. These things and many more, I could just bring into view, by craning my neck to catch a glimpse, out of the small, slivered windows of the jail transport van. I was handcuffed to the waist and shackled, jostling around in the back with the other prisoners, on our way to the courthouse for yet another hearing. Many thoughts run through your mind at a time like this. Momentary fantasies of some incredible outcome in which the judge decides to set you free. Short imaginary visions of that day, eventually, when you are able to walk out of whatever prison they put you in. Anything to detract from the weight of the years that you are expected to absorb. There is no preparation for this process, just the inevitable nature of it all. That underlying sense that it had to be like this. I really am worthless after all.

We pull into an unmarked, roll-up door around the backside of the courthouse, and after a short drive down a tight tunnel, we stop, deep in the bowels of the building. All of us, prisoners, are shackled. We are also linked together by a chain. This makes disembarking the van tricky and something of a delicate procedure. There are folks of all sorts next to me. Some sober, others not so much. Some have hygiene items and have been able to shower. Others haven't showered in days. We trundle up some short stairs, this motley chain gang of miscreants. Now on something of an industrial-sized elevator with a cage inside. We are packed into an undersized concrete cell, with a metal shiny toilet with a sink. No toilet paper is allowed. People are talking loudly, laughing, some sleeping on the floor or squeezing onto benches.

Eventually my name is called with some others, four or five at a time. They again chain us together, then we take a short walk to yet another elevator which leads us to a door into the courtroom. As the heavy wide door swings open and I am led inside. I am the so-called "Alaskan Avenger" and I am here to be sentenced for assaulting child abusers. I am hit with a wave of memories long buried in my mind. This place hasn't changed at all. It looks exactly the same as it did thirty years ago. My stomach tightened into a knot, and a rush of feelings overtook my mind. I cannot believe I am here again. I wonder if they know? Will the judge care? These beige walls, the sickening colors of the carpet, the smell of the old courthouse, it all overwhelms me and takes me right back to the first time I was here… I remember…

"We want you to be honest, but your father has already repented, and he was just being curious. He wanted to see how you and your brother were developing as men. He loves you, and only wants the best for you. He's always had your best interest in mind with everything he does. These people are outsiders. They may not even be Christians. They just want to destroy our family, and God wants our family to stay together. You need to be very careful not to say anything which could break up our family"… and the coaching and pressure went on and on…

I was still a young boy at this time, and I didn't want to talk to anyone about what my father had done to me. I was confused. I was deeply ashamed, and now my mother and this attorney they knew from our church were preparing me for my trip to the courthouse to be questioned by some strangers about the abuse taking place in our home. My brother was already gone. He had run away with his girlfriend. I was the only one called in, under an enormous amount of pressure. Of course, if I said the wrong thing, then it would be my fault that our home fell apart. Into this imposing building, down corridors and hallways, all beige, all brown, this horrible place. It just felt terrible. The air. The smell. I did not like it. The atmosphere is stifling.

They asked me a number of questions, these people. The truth of the situation being so shameful, so sickening, that I kept shaking my head no… Did I get erections? Did I ejaculate? Did he use his mouth? Did he make you touch his penis? These sorts of thing. I was already tormented in the extreme, and I didn't know how to bring these things into the light. It was too much for my little self to really comprehend. I couldn't understand what had already occurred at the hands of my adoptive father, and now, apparently, it was up to me to "save" our family. My mother had already let me know in no uncertain terms I needed to keep these outsiders out of our private family business. I am still ashamed now as I write these words. I was scared. I was too much of a coward to tell them the truth. I downplayed all that I could. I covered for this monster. I wish I would have been stronger. After hours of questioning, I was allowed to leave the room. I remember all of us lining up in the courtroom. That exact same courtroom I found myself in as an adult. The judge noted my adoptive father's associations with the church, the fact that this was his first time being accused of child abuse, and most importantly, my testimony that we really wanted him to come back home. I know now how awful it was, what happened that day. They should have known something about abused children. They should have stepped in to protect me. The judge gave him a suspended sentence. He returned home immediately. Pressuring and coercing a child to lie on behalf of his abuser is despicable at best. My own mother and her cohorts from the church doing this, seems an evil beyond comprehension.

All these thoughts passed through my mind that day. Standing in that same courtroom, listening as the judge voraciously dismantled my life, discounted my lingering PTSD as so much corollary chatter. Reminded me of how much of a wreck my life was, and then sentenced me to two and a half decades in prison for assaulting child abusers. Interesting how life can really bring us full circle. Seems a fitting ending for a kid who grew up how I did. Turns out, in the end, my adoptive father was right. I am a worthless throwaway. The State of Alaska agreed the whole way, and their commitment to protecting child abusers while not acknowledging the repercussions of that abuse, continues to this day.

I don't ever want to set foot in that courthouse ever again. Every aspect of it makes me sick. It's incredible to me that it is the place where families or citizens will end up, if seeking justice. There was no justice found in that building, nor will there every be. Not for me. It will always be the Manor of the Devil. A place of sorrow and evil. A place of lies and injustice. The motives of the government are protected there. Not the lives of the young.

In the end I grew up. I grew up on my own. Time did what none of you cared to do. It carried me away from the men who abused me. And I reached down and gathered up a handful of sand. I wanted to throw it into the eyes of everyone who had looked right through me, but the wind, it threw it right back into my face.

References

1. Vachss, A. (1991). *Sacrifice*. New York, NY: Vintage Crime/Black Lizard.
2. Prasad, R. (2005). "Arrest us all": the 200 women who killed a rapist. *The Guardian*. September 16, 2005.
3. Robinson, P., & Robinson, S. (2018). *Shadow vigilantes: How distrust in the justice system breeds a new kind of lawlessness*. Amherst, NY: Prometheus Books.
4. Tewksbury, R. (2005). Collateral consequences of sex offender registration. *Journal of Contemporary Criminal Justice, 21*(1), 67–81. https://doi.org/10.1177/1043986204271704
5. Cubellis, M. A., Evans, D. N., & Fera, A. (2018). Sex offender stigma: An exploration of vigilantism against sex offenders. *Deviant Behavior, 40*(2), 225–239.
6. Goldman, R. (2012, June 20). No charges for Texas father who beat to death daughter's molester. *ABC News*.
7. Spain, J. (1988). "Murder tonight, tape at ten." *WBRZ-TV*.
8. Plauché, J. (2019). *why gary why? The Jody Plauché story*. Inspired Forever Book Publishing. Dallas, TX.
9. Lohr, D. (2016, Nov. 28). Father who killed daughter's sexual abuser sent to prison. *Huffpost*. https://www.huffpost.com/entry/jay-maynor-alabama_n_582f4462e4b030997bbf2a1c
10. Change.Org (2018). Petition to pardon or grant clemency to the dad who killed his daughter's rapist. Change.org.https://www.change.org/p/kay-ivey-and-or-donald-trump-petition-to-pardon-or-grant-clemency-to-the-dad-that-killed-his-daughter-s-rapist?recruiter=109371870&utm_source=share_for_starters&utm_medium=copyLink
11. Blankinship, D. G. (2005, Sep. 8). Washington man admits murdering sex offenders. *The Salt Lake Tribune*. https://archive.sltrib.com/story.php?ref=/utah/ci_3010129
12. Blankinship, D. G. (2005, Sep. 6). Man held in sex offender killings, says he found victims on Web. *The Seattle Times*. https://www.seattletimes.com/seattle-news/man-held-in-sex-offender-killings-says-he-found-victims-on-web/
13. Carter, M. (2005, Sep. 15). Letter tells killer's reasoning for slaying 2 pedophiles. *The Seattle Times*. https://www.seattletimes.com/seattle-news/letter-tells-killers-reasoning-for-slaying-2-pedophiles/
14. Pandell, L. (2013, Dec. 4). The vigilante of Clallam County. *The Atlantic*. https://www.theatlantic.com/national/archive/2013/12/the-vigilante-of-clallam-county/281968/
15. Hunter, G. (2004, June 15). Ex-con "helps police" by trying to murder sex offenders. *Prison Legal News*. https://www.prisonlegalnews.org/news/2004/jun/15/ex-con-helps-police-by-trying-to-murder-sex-offenders/
16. MacQuirrie, B. (2004, Dec. 5). Man defends attacks on sex offenders. *The Boston Globe*. http://archive.boston.com/news/local/articles/2004/12/05/man_defends_attacks_on_sex_offenders?pg=full
17. Associated Press. (2006, May 21). N.H. felon 'understands' killer of sex offenders. *Sun Journal*. https://www.sunjournal.com/2006/05/21/nh-felon-understands-killer-sex-offenders/
18. F.B.I. (2007, Jan. 31). (U) Symbols and logos used by pedophiles to identify sexual preferences. *WikiLeaks*. https://wikileaks.org/wiki/FBI-pedophile-symbols.pdf
19. Eordogh, F. (2016, Dec. 7). With Pizzagate, is cybersteria the new normal? *Forbes*. https://www.forbes.com/sites/fruzsinaeordogh/2016/12/07/with-pizzagate-is-cybersteria-the-new-normal/?sh=7adbd4742b68
20. Kennedy, M. (2017, June 22). 'Pizzagate' gunman sentenced to 4 years in prison. *NPR*. https://www.npr.org/sections/thetwo-way/2017/06/22/533941689/pizzagate-gunman-sentenced-to-4-years-in-prison
21. Hansen, C. (2007). *To catch a predator: Protecting your kids from online enemies already in your home*. New York, NY: Dutton Books.
22. Lambert, B. (2019, Feb, 17). CT vigilantes who target alleged child predators draw cheers, concern. *New Haven Register*. https://www.nhregister.com/news/article/CT-vigilantes-that-target-alleged-child-predators-13623390.php
23. Orchard, M. (2021, Sep, 23). *The Predators*. YouTube. https://www.youtube.com/watch?v=ij06ti29M3s
24. Cooper, T. (2021, July, 14). 'Hero' or 'devil'? Omaha man sentenced to 40-70 years for killing sex offender. *Omaha World-Herald*. https://omaha.com/news/local/crime-and-courts/hero-or-devil-omaha-man-sentenced-to-40-70-years-for-killing-sex-offender/article_3e805a90-e4c5-11eb-a481-07ef796c4b71.html

25. Florida Action Committee. (2020, May, 20). Once fallen: The murder of Mattieo Condoluci. https://floridaactioncommittee.org/once-fallen-the-murder-of-mattieo-condoluci/

26. Deseret News. (1988, Oct. 11). Sex abuse trial to start Feb. 27. *United Press* International. https://www.deseret.com/1988/10/11/18781225/sex-abuse-trial-to-start-feb-27

27. Cousino, M. B. (2022). Frank James Harvey. *The National Registry of Exonerations Pre-1989.* https://www.law.umich.edu/special/exoneration/Pages/casedetailpre1989.aspx?caseid=387

28. Deseret News. (1991, June. 27). Montana suspect linked to '87 kidnapping. https://www.deseret.com/1991/6/27/18928100/montana-suspect-linked-to-87-kidnapping#comments

29. Hale, D. (2008) *LockUp: Raw. MSNBC.* https://www.imdb.com/title/tt1208306/fullcredits

30. Dicataldo, F. C. (2009). *The perversion of youth: Controversies in the assessment and treatment of juvenile sex offenders.* New York: New York University Press. https://doi.org/10.18574/nyu/9780814720011.001.0001

4

CONTEMPT FOR COURT

The government has a monopoly on violence. We give them this power. We turn over a portion of our liberty for the sake of safety. We want an orderly society where one group is designated as the authority over all law enforcement and punishment decisions so we do not have arbitrary and capricious acts of violence in our streets. This will prevent blood feuds between clans, and prevent terrorism from the other type of Klan. Nobody wants anarchy or a Mad Max society where might makes right. We also want a government that is restricted from taking too many of our liberties. We don't want to live under a totalitarian regime. The Constitution of the United States helps us to retain certain rights of due process in legal proceedings. Everyone should be innocent until proven guilty before a jury of our peers. All in all, the American criminal justice system promises a nice balance between liberty and safety. We are gently rocked to sleep on Lady Justice's teetering scales. Right?

You could fill several volumes the size of this book merely listing court cases where the punishment did not fit the crime. The majority of those cases in the United States would describe extremely harsh sentences, but some of them would also be egregiously lenient. Most social scientists will tell you not to cherry-pick extremes, but here is one that is too important to ignore.

In 2006, a judge in Nebraska sentenced a man to 10 years' probation for sexually assaulting a 12-year-old girl multiple times. The judge's rationale for sparing him a jail sentence was that the offender, Richard Thompson, was *too short* to endure a prison sentence. He was 5'1 and the judge feared that he would be victimized by taller prisoners. The state Attorney General appealed the judge's decision and sought a more appropriate sentence, but this was not granted. Even the American Civil Liberties Union was perplexed by the judge's decision. They had never heard of height discrimination in prison sentences before. A prison spokesman said there were many prisoners in the state who were below average height, as well as many who were physically disabled or vulnerable, but they were not spared incarceration (1).

The judge, in this case, lost her job when the public learned that the rationale for releasing the rapist would never apply to other crimes. Can you imagine a 5'1 bank robber being given probation? What if this man reoffended several times? Would his stature continue to confer immunity on him? Was this "pass" only valid once? There does not seem to be a logical reason

DOI: 10.4324/9781003393849-5

why tall people deserve prison more than shorter people, and this judge lost her career because of her decision.

These outliers might get a lot of media attention because they provoke outrage, but they are only newsworthy because they are unique. Few people deny that they exist, but when compared with the *average* sentences out of the many millions of dispositions given every year, it shouldn't be too egregious. Right?

We will never understand the vigilante mindset until we delve into these outlier cases. These are the stories that inspire the emotions that lead to violence. It is important not to wave your hand and dismiss these sensationalistic cases. Remember that most of the major tough-on-crime legislation of the late twentieth century was passed because of high-profile events. Public policy analysts can complain about the effect of the Willie Horton case on the 1988 presidential election, and they can complain about how the brutal murder of Polly Klaus by parolee Richard Allen Davis led to the infamous Three Strikes laws in California, but these complaints should serve as a warning. When the justice system fails, the people get angry. In a democracy, their anger can have broad implications beyond the individuals who sparked their fury. If you really want to prevent devastating mandatory minimum laws from being adopted the government should publicize the majority of cases that they claim to be processed correctly. Then they would have the legitimacy to argue that the government is trying its best. Unfortunately, the justice system has often shown extraordinary leniency to child sex abusers and provoked outrage from victims and concerned citizens, and in other cases, they have given life sentences to juveniles who killed their abusers (2–11).

Although these extreme examples of leniency are infrequent, they are impactful. Sometimes these cases have been cited by vigilantes who took the law into their own hands because they believed that the government had abdicated their duties to keep children safe.

The Vigilante of Clallam County

In December of 2013, Lexi Pandell published an article in *The Atlantic* called "The Vigilante of Clallam County" with the subtitle "Patrick Drum was tired of seeing sex offenders hurt children. So he decided to kill them" (12). It was accompanied by the photograph of a man being escorted by a Clallam County Sheriff's Deputy, surrounded by dozens of armed law enforcement officers with rows of patrol cars stretching into the distance. The man, Patrick Drum, is shown with his pockets turned inside out and his hands cuffed behind his back. Patrick Drum had killed two men, and he had a list of sixty more victims he would have slain if he had the chance. He was waging a war on convicted child sex abusers.

Family members of the deceased sex offenders accused Patrick of randomly choosing victims "because of the registry," but Patrick was very well acquainted with the men he killed. The first victim had a long history of criminal behavior and was a registered sex offender (he was charged with Rape 3 of a deaf and mute minor). He also pled guilty to charges of "attempted kidnapping" of a girl. In actuality, he took her to his house, held her against her will, and beat her over the head with a frying pan when she didn't obey him. He served a short jail sentence for this crime. He was also arrested for physically assaulting his 17-month-old son. He caused a spiral fracture on the child's arm, broke a rib, and broke a femur. His wife once said Gary was "misunderstood... he was just all heart." After he was ordered not to live in the same house with his abused children, he moved in with Patrick Drum. One day Patrick shot this man to death. The first of what Patrick hoped would be many killings.

The second murder victim has been described as a "man with problems" (13). He once took off all of his clothes and kidnapped two children, a 7-year-old and a 4-year-old. He carried the children to a room where he molested them. He blamed alcohol for these crimes. He was sentenced to 4 years in prison.

Patrick Drum knew the two children personally. They had been thoroughly traumatized by their victimization. Patrick wanted to avenge them, and any other children of serious sexual assault. He did not want to kill any sex offenders who were mislabeled by the justice system. He diligently searched the newspapers and sex offender registry for clear cases of predatory violence. There was no shortage of incidents. He made a list of 60 targets within driving distance of his home. Drum was only able to ambush the two men described here before being caught by a massive deployment of police, but he felt entirely justified in his actions. He left a note for the police in his car reading "It had to be done."

Pandell's article tells how the family members of the dead men grieved over their loss and feared for their lives. They claimed that they were being harassed by "Drum's followers" who spit on them and stalked them outside their homes. One victim's family member said "Tell your supporters to stop. My children and I don't deserve this... I think we've suffered enough." In court the prosecutor said that Drum's actions "diminish us all" and "there is no room for vigilantism... no one in authority will ever tolerate vigilantism." Drum interrupted "This country was founded on vigilantism." He was sentenced to life without parole. Some visitors in the courtroom called Drum a piece of shit. Others said he was going to Hell. But some thanked Drum and said, "God bless you." The divergence of opinion on his behavior hinged on public perception of the appropriateness of his actions. Why would some people condone murder? Why not trust the legal system to choose an appropriate punishment for sex offenders? Patrick Drum and his "followers" had little respect for the Washington court system. They claimed that lenient sentences for sex offenders combined with harsh penalties for comparatively minor crimes enraged them to the point of despising their government.

In September of 2021 I wrote a letter to Patrick Drum to ask him about his crimes. He said he was interested in spreading information about how citizens can legally petition the government to make legislative changes so child sex abusers would receive appropriate punishments in a court of law.

Patrick has written an essay about sentencing disparities between sex crimes and drug-related crimes. This essay is entitled "Sex, Drugs and Consequences: An Evaluation of Lenient Sex Offender Laws" and it can be found at *www.sexdrugsandconsequences.info*. The website quotes the phrase "The only thing necessary for the triumph of evil is for good men to do nothing." The article itself does not endorse or advocate for any criminal behavior to achieve justice. The author asks his readers to investigate the matter for themselves, to sign petitions, and to demand that public officials change the laws so that punishments will be administered according to the severity of the offense.

Drum's essay begins with the statement that anyone who agrees with the author's opinions should not be construed as condoning his actions. In other words, Drum is attempting to distance his strongly held beliefs about inequality in sentencing from his illegal vigilante actions so that his message can spread. He wrote to me that "the website is a more positive way of fighting what I perceive to be an injustice. It should be presented this way because I have concerns that the crime will make people not want to associate with the article/action." This essay offers us a detailed insight into the thoughts, beliefs, and attitudes of one of the most notable vigilantes of the past decade.

--- --- --- --- --- --- ---

SEX, DRUGS, AND CONSEQUENCES: AN EVALUATION OF LENIENT SEX OFFENDER LAWS

by Patrick Drum

Most citizens are too busy providing for their families and maintaining their lives to parse numerous statutes that make up the laws passed in their name. Understanding this, the intent of this article is to highlight the legislative imbalance between sentencing alternatives for drug offenders and those for sex offenders. Ideally citizens don't support their community being victimized by either category of crime, still, the imbalance between the sentence reduction and eligibility criteria is a subject worth evaluating.

The differences are found when comparing Washington State's Drug Offender Sentencing Alternative (DOSA) and the Special Sex Offender Sentencing Alternative (SSOSA). These are treatment-centric options that allow a portion of a prison sentence to be suspended and served on community custody (probation) in exchange for participating with approved treatment programs. If the offender fails to meet the terms of the sentencing alternatives, then the suspended portion of the sentence is revoked, or the offender is reclassified to serve the remaining balance of their sentence.

A person is eligible for DOSA if the conviction is not violent in nature and the violation does not involve being armed with a firearm or deadly weapon. In the case of SSOSA, a person is eligible if the conviction is not for rape in the first or second degrees. Being armed with a deadly weapon during the sex offense is not a factor of ineligibility found anywhere in the SSOSA statute. For perspective, a drug addict trying to support an addiction by pushing a store clerk out of his way when confronted for shoplifting is not eligible for DOSA. However, a pedophile who has molested a 7-year-old is eligible for SSOSA.

The inconsistencies do not stop there. A person under DOSA is sentenced to the unsuspended portion of the prison sentence of one-half the middle of their sentence range or 12 months, whichever is greater. A person granted SSOSA is sentenced to the unsuspended portion of their prison sentence of 12 months or the maximum term within the standard range, whichever is less. Said differently, the sex offender who molested the 7-year-old, which has a standard range of 129 to 171 months, cannot be sentenced to more than 12 months, so long as there are no aggravating circumstances. The drug addict who is facing a middle standard range of 6 years, 2 months for identity theft in the first degree must serve 3 years, 1 month.

The court does consider if the victim is agreeable to the sex offender treatment under SSOSA, however, the court can disregard the victim's opinion simply by writing into the court record its reasoning for doing so. Also, without access to private conversations between the prosecutor and victim, it is unclear if the victims are aware that being in agreement with the sex offender's treatment will result in the court imposing under 12 months or that there is the possibility of the sentence being served in partial confinement.

In fairness, such legislatively-permitted leniency is not limited to Washington State. In California, human trafficking of an adult (for a sex act) carries an eight-year mandatory minimum, while human trafficking of a minor carries only a five-year mandatory minimum, as displayed in People v. Richardson, 65 Cal. App. 5th 360 (2021). In Maryland, The Dupont Heir was sentenced to 0 days in prison for child molestation. We will not pivot to the reasoning behind this mindset because the link between political connections, economic status, and organized religious networks that may contribute to sex offender policies is beyond the scope of this article.

It has been my experience that the vast majority of citizens do not approve the details of these comparisons. Rather, they are typically unaware of them. Your Washington State Representative can be reached at www.leg.wa.gov. The alternative is willful blindness. Please save and share this article. When sharing the website or facts in this article on social media, please use #StopSexOffenderLeniency.

There are several important aspects of this essay that stand out as pertinent in our attempt to understand the vigilante profile. First and foremost, it is not an arrogant and violent screed justifying murder or glorifying the heroic nature of vigilantism. It is a thoughtful and concise description of perceived unfairness of the justice system that might be written by any concerned citizen. In fact, it is rather dry. You may disagree with his amateur interpretation of the law in Washington state, but you must agree that his manner of expressing his beliefs is rational and professional, and stands in stark contrast to his courtroom proclamations on the virtues of vigilantism.

This essay begins by noting that most people in society do not understand the imbalance in court sentencing when comparing drug-related offenses and those given to sex offenders. This is a common theme among prisoners I have spoken to. They do not understand how a sex offender can receive relatively lenient sentences while drug offenders (even juveniles) receive seemingly harsh and devastating punishments. Countless books and essays have been written on the devastating consequences of the War on Drugs, class warfare, racial discrimination in sentencing, and America's imprisonment binge during the "get tough" movement of the 1970s to 1990s. I believe that Drum's essay would fit in nicely among them and nobody would notice that it was written by a convicted murderer.

Drum's essay describes several sentencing options available to judges in Washington state, and explains how the law might work in hypothetical cases where a child sex abuser receives a less severe sentence than someone convicted of identity theft. He also describes how sex offender treatment programs might exacerbate this sentencing gap, because there are so many people who need drug treatment that there is no realistic way to divert them all from jail. In a letter to me, he added a description of the human trafficking laws in California where "human trafficking an adult (for a sex act) carries and eight-year mandatory minimum, while human trafficking of a minor carries only a five-year mandatory minimum, as displayed in *People v. Richardson, 65 Cal. App. 5th 360 (2021)*."

Drum makes a special mention of "The Dupont Heir." This case is famous among vigilantes and those who despair over lenient sex offender laws, so it is important that this entire case be explained here.

Filthy Rich

The DuPont family (also spelled du Pont) is a wealthy American family with roots in French nobility (14). They became extraordinarily wealthy in the nineteenth century in the gunpowder industry, chemical manufacturing, and later in the automotive industry. The family was most well-known for philanthropy and for building libraries, museums, and large, beautiful estates. In 2016, the family had an estimated net worth of $14.3 billion dollars (15). In recent years, the family has been embarrassed by high-profile scandals including a bizarre murder committed by Jon Eluthere DuPont in 1996. But the criminal case most Americans are familiar with involves Robert Richards, one of the many heirs of the family fortune.

Robert Richards was born in 1966 and lived in Delaware most of his life. He did not enter the public spotlight very often, and he seemed to be living the quiet life of a trust-fund millionaire. As an adult, Richards was a large man; 6'4 and over 300 lbs. with blonde/red curly hair and a swollen face. He was divorced in 2014 by his wife, Tracy Richards, who sued him for monetary damages related to a crime he had to plead guilty to in 2009. The crime was extremely serious. Shockingly serious. He had pled guilty to raping his 3-year-old daughter many times. He told the judge "I feel horrible. There's no excuse for what I've done to her." This multi-millionaire pled guilty to raping a toddler. How did the media fail to report this news? If his ex-wife had not sued him in 2014 we might never have known about this case at all. The DuPonts are a powerful family, especially in Delaware (16).

Judge Jan Jurden presided over Richards' case. She considered the possibility that he might not have a good time in prison. In fact, she said that Richards "would not fare well" in prison at all because he was a gentle person. She decided to be merciful to this man who admitted to raping a toddler. She said "I have concerns about this, because arguably, you should be [in jail] for what you did… but I think you have significant treatment needs that have to be addressed, and you have very strong family support. So unlike many unfortunate people who come before me, you are lucky in that regard, and I hope you appreciate that." She decided to give Richards' *no jail time*, 8 years of probation, and a fine of $4,395.

Richards did attend a local treatment program for sex offenders, but he wasn't doing well. He confided in his counselor that he might have raped his son too. This was reported to his probation officer, but he was never charged with this crime. He completed his probation in 2017, having never attended the treatment center he agreed to enter as part of the terms of his probation.

The "DuPont Heir" rape case was one of those rare events that brought the left- and right-wings of the American population together in unified and unidirectional outrage. Liberals were infuriated that rich "one percenters" could buy their way to freedom while poor people, mostly minorities, are routinely given harsh prison sentences in the incarceration capital of the world, and struggle to survive in atrocious living conditions in our nation's penitentiaries. Conservatives didn't care so much about that. They were disgusted at yet another example of the lenient criminal justice system allowing another sex offender to escape punishment.

One person who agreed with the judge's decision was the Delaware Attorney General Beau Biden (son of Joseph Biden, the 46th President of the United States). Biden wrote an op-ed in the *News Journal* to address the concerns of the outraged mobs. He said the decision to offer the sweetest of sweetheart deals had nothing at all to do with money and nothing to do with the judge's own statements (that Richards was too gentle for prison or that his family would support him). Biden said it was simply a matter of lack of evidence. He was afraid that the case would be lost in trial because the child victim was so young her testimony would not be strong enough evidence to secure a conviction. He made a deal with the devil, as so many prosecutors do, and accepted a guilty plea in exchange for the most lenient punishment that an admitted child rapist could ever receive. He argued that if Richards was on probation he could receive mandatory treatment and maybe that would prevent future crimes. It was a practical, utilitarian decision that the emotional American public wouldn't understand, so they should trust the government to sort these matters out on their behalf.

This excuse might be reasonable to those who spend a lot of time in America's bureaucratic courtrooms, but it sounded like a cop-out to most of the people who followed the case. Does anyone fare well in prison? What about the tens of millions of people who have been processed through jails and prisons since the passage of the Violent Crime Control and Law Enforcement Act of 1994 (often called the 1994 Crime Bill) that expanded death penalty eligibility, eliminated college education grants for prisoners, increased federal penalties for sex crimes, established sex offender registries that set the groundwork for Megan's Law and the Adam Walsh Child Protection and Safety Act, provided funding for truth-in-sentencing and mandatory minimum incarceration sentences, and included three-strikes provisions to give life sentences to repeat offenders? There was no pity for the offenders targeted by this bill, the majority of whom were young, impoverished, men from minority groups (17). Is sensitivity to the prison environment now to be considered an exclusionary factor in sentencing decisions? We are supposed to be a nation of laws, not men. Why do some men get special consideration before the law? Incidentally, it was Beau Biden's father who wrote that tough-on-crime bill.

Patrick Drum knows that it takes more than a prosecutor's recommendation to secure a lenient plea deal. Patrick wrote to me the following: "In exchange for a guilty plea the prosecutor agrees to *recommend* to the judge a specific term. In no state is the judge bound by that recommendation (it is required that the judge inform the defendant of this before the plea even being legally acceptable). If I have a standard range of 5–10 years, enter a plea where the prosecutor agrees to recommend 5 years, the court can absolutely sentence me to 10 years despite the recommendation… I do not know the plea terms nor the standard range of the Dupont case, but once Richards plead guilty the judge could have given him more than zero days (no ifs, ands, or buts)… Beau Biden's op-ed is absolutely a manipulation of the public's ignorance of the plea agreement process."

Perhaps the Dupont Heir is merely another case of "affluenza," where the filthy rich can afford the best lawyers while the common criminals get a public defender who encourages them to plead guilty for his/her convenience. Maybe this is not a reflection of a criminal justice system that is lenient toward sex offenders. It is just an example of how money gives an unfair advantage in the legal process. The rich get richer, and the poor get prison, as they say. But regardless of whether the judge abdicated her duties or the district attorney was a hypocrite, this case is now cataloged in the collective memory of American citizens as another example of government incompetence. It may not have been the straw that broke the camel's back and caused Patrick Drum to begin his war on sex offenders in Washington state, but it was certainly one of the straws in the bale and contributed to his deep sense of injustice. It's hard to tell a man that he has to serve years in prison for drug charges when a millionaire can rape a toddler and get probation. So, Drum killed two sex offenders and had a list of 60 others with plans to kill more. Call it a collateral consequence of extraordinary leniency.

Testing Drum's Hypothesis

There are certainly many real-life cases of egregious court decisions that could fill endless volumes merely listing the names of the defendants, but this would be cherry-picking. Yes, high-profile cases of leniency toward sex offenders inspire strong emotions and stay in our memories, but I could also find numerous cases where sex offenders were overcharged and given 100-year sentences for crimes that other sex offenders received relatively short sentences for. Do sex offenders serve shorter sentences than drug offenders? Sometimes they do. We can all think of cases where a sex offender received probation instead of incarceration. Therefore, anyone who went to jail for a drug offense has served more time than they have. There is considerable sentencing overlap for all offense types. It depends on which cases you are contrasting.

I wanted to test Drum's Hypothesis using official sentencing data. I found that most federal reports were vague in their methods and categorization of offenses, so I decided to compute the averages and graph the distributions myself. I gained access to official sentencing records contained in the National Corrections Reporting Program, 2000–2019 database, which contains sentencing information on over 13 million cases. Every state, territory, and federal court was required to send records of their correctional population to the Bureau of Justice Statistics. Six states failed to respond (Alaska, Arkansas, Connecticut, Idaho, Vermont, and Virginia), but this is a good representation of sentencing patterns in the other 44 states and the federal courts. This does not contain cases where probation was the only sentence, but it does include cases with suspended sentences (equaling zero days incarceration). The data is not perfect because there are some typos, missing fields, and incompatibilities across jurisdictions, but the large sample size helps to reduce the effects of random errors in the data. Ultimately, this may be the largest and most detailed dataset to allow for the calculation of prison sentences in the United States, and it is used by the BJS in their annual reports on average sentence lengths.

BJS identified the three most serious offense categories for each case, with multiple counts for each conviction. The total sentence length for all offenses can be calculated manually, but the BJS also separates the sentence length attributed to the first primary conviction offense for the majority of all cases. For example, an individual convicted of rape (primary offense #1), a weapons charge (offense #2), and perjury (offense #3) might receive a 15-year prison sentence, but the rape conviction is the most serious, so the proportion of the sentence attributed to that crime is listed apart from the total (for example, 10 years). Using these separate variables it might be possible to parse through the legal fog and determine the average sentence length for a single count of the primary offense, therefore isolating the "going rate" for a sex offense penalty.

My intention was to compare various sex offenses to drug-related crimes because this perceived inequity is the source of much outrage in society. I used the Bureau of Justice Statistics categories for labeling a sex offense as either rape, aggravated sexual assault, statutory rape, or lewd sexual acts with a child. Drug offenses were separated by the type of substance listed in the primary offense charge (heroin, cocaine/crack, marijuana, or "other") as well as the type of crime (trafficking or possessing). The mean sentence for one count of each type of offense is described in Table 4.1. This does not include people sentenced to probation, only those sent to a correctional institution (Note: I excluded women from these analyses and focused primarily on men because the overwhelming involvement of men in sex crimes might skew the comparisons).

From this analysis we can see that the mean sentence for a person convicted of one count of rape is 10.93 years in prison, which is a longer sentence than any of the non-sex offense crimes we examined here. Using this metric, there is a basic respect for the rank order of severity for most offenses. However, these mean values are heavily skewed. As with measurements of household income, a better measure of central tendency for skewed data is the median. We see here that one count of lewd sexual acts with a child has a median sentence of 5 years' incarceration, which is equivalent to the median sentence for someone convicted of possessing heroin. This 4-year sentence is one year less than someone faces for a single count of trafficking "other" types of drugs like ecstasy or LSD. The rank order of severity in punishment is upset when comparing the median sentences of these crimes (Table 4.1).

Simple statistics like a median or a mean is not sufficient for testing Drum's Hypothesis. We can see there is some support for his assertions, but you could also choose to interpret these

TABLE 4.1 Average sentence for one count of primary conviction offense (men only)

	n	*Minimum*	*Maximum*★	*Median*	*Mean*	*SD*
Sex offenses						
Rape	186,967	0	39.2	8.00	10.93	9.83
Aggravated sexual assault of a child	152,169	0	39.2	5.00	7.47	7.93
Statutory rape	36,698	0	39.2	9.00	10.34	7.59
Lewd sexual acts with a child	158,674	0	39.2	5.00	6.84	6.83
Drug offenses						
Trafficking other drug	126,563	0	39.2	5.00	6.73	6.15
Trafficking cocaine/crack	173,848	0	39.2	4.50	6.55	6.14
Trafficking heroin	15,896	0	39.2	4.00	5.52	5.31
Trafficking marijuana	145,361	0	39.2	2.00	2.20	1.31
Possessing other drug	158,295	0	39.2	2.00	2.96	3.03
Possessing heroin	6,904	0	39.2	4.00	4.83	5.24
Possessing cocaine/crack	71,842	0	39.2	2.83	4.60	5.82
Possessing marijuana	48,764	0	39.2	2.00	3.00	3.84

★Sentences longer than 39.2 years are considered "Life" and are therefore capped at 39.2 to match the US Sentencing Commission's definition of a Life sentence and to restrict outlier influence on the mean. BJS reports often cap Life sentences at 100 years, but this results in unrealistic means

statistics differently. Perhaps you noticed that the standard deviations are quite large for most crimes. Or maybe you noticed that some people serve *zero* days in prison for crimes as serious as rape, while other people are receiving life sentences for crimes as petty as possessing marijuana. Perhaps these outliers are extremely rare occurrences. To know for sure, it might be useful to create a visual display that shows the distribution of these sentences (Note: the units of measurement are maximum sentences rounded up to the nearest whole number, so any sentence between one day and one year is listed as "one year," and zero refers to people who were given a suspended sentence) (Figures 4.1–4.5).

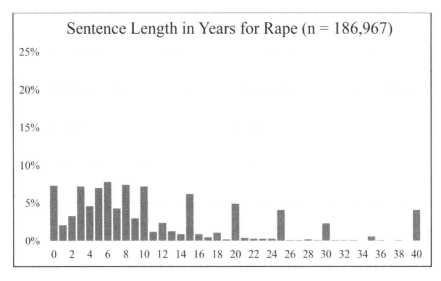

FIGURE 4.1 NCRP 2000–2019: Sentence length in years for rape

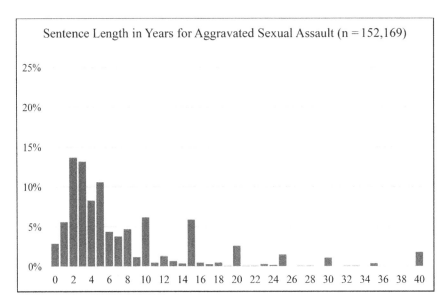

FIGURE 4.2 NCRP 2000–2019: Sentence length in years for aggravated sexual assault

As you can see, there are some long sentences given for each crime, including life sentences, but a large proportion of sex offense cases result in sentences of less than 5 years. I created a side-by-side comparison of all drug cases (combined) compared to sentences for lewd sexual acts with a child. Although a larger proportion of drug offenders receive a sentence of 0–5 years in prison, there is considerable overlap even in those sentences. This supports the anecdotal assertions made by prisoners across the United States. When they claim to share a prison cell with a sex offender who is serving less time than they are for drug offenses, they might very well be telling the

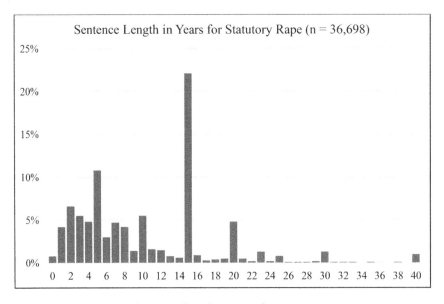

FIGURE 4.3 NCRP 2000–2019: Sentence length in years for statutory rape

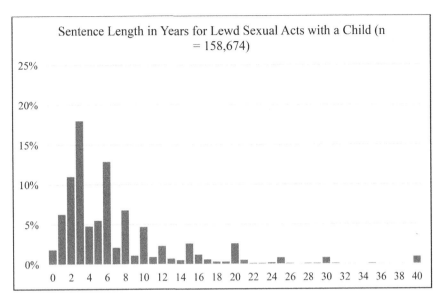

FIGURE 4.4 NCRP 2000–2019: Sentence length in years for lewd sexual acts with a child

truth. These are not isolated cases. Informing these prisoners "Yes… but the *average* sentence is longer" is unlikely to defuse their outrage. The mean sentence for lewd sexual acts with a child (6.74 years) is a hypothetical number that less than 1% of these offenders receive, and only 30% receive a longer sentence. Small comfort to the 18% of drug offenders who receive a longer sentence than the "average" child sex abuser.

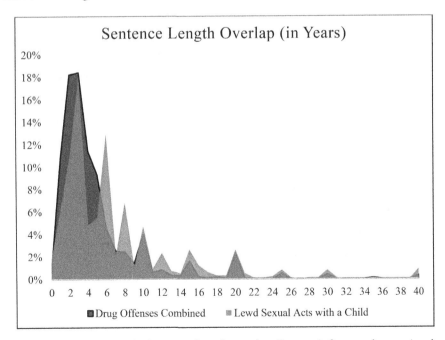

FIGURE 4.5 NCRP 2000–2019: Sentence length overlap (in years) for people convicted of drug offenses and lewd sexual acts with a child

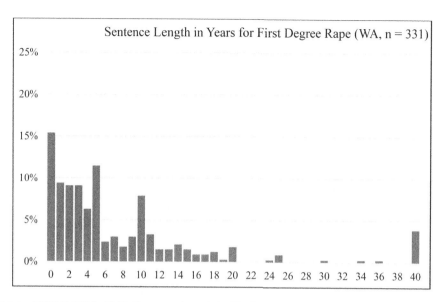

FIGURE 4.6 NCRP 2000–2019: Sentence length in Washington state for first-degree rape

I was also interested in measuring differences in sentence length across jurisdictions. Some states issued longer sentences for sex offenses than others. As a demonstration of these differences, I ranked states according to their average sentences for one count of lewd sexual acts with a child. Some states were omitted because they did not report to BJS or their legal codes did not meet the criteria for inclusion in this offense category. Georgia, South Dakota, and Arizona had the longest mean and median sentences for this crime (more than 10 years), while Colorado, North Carolina, and Nevada had the shortest mean and median sentences (Table 4.2).

How should you interpret these findings? Cautiously. Any "average" is fraught with errors. We do not want one-size-fits-all sentences for any crime. Individual case circumstances, data limitations, and legal definitions make it difficult to condemn or endorse current sentencing practices. However, I think you can use this information to answer some general questions.

Imagine you are a legislator. You need to decide if our sentencing guidelines should change. Look at these numbers, and ask yourself the following:

1 Is the rank order of severity appropriate for each crime?
2 Is the average sentence for sex crimes appropriate for the "average" sex crime?
3 Are the minimum and maximum sentences for each crime logical, or should they be adjusted?
4 What mitigating or aggravating circumstances *ought* to be considered to permit fluctuations across these sentencing ranges?
5 When is an "outlier" sentence justified?

Patrick Drum killed two sex offenders because he was particularly outraged by his perception that penalties were too lenient in his home state of Washington. I decided to take a close look at the Revised Code of Washington to make sure that the BJS categories for each crime type were not mixing cases together that are better studied apart. I decided to disaggregate these offenses and replicate my tables for each Washington state offense category. This has many advantages that are overlooked in the previous models, not least of which is the fact that rape, rape of a child, and

TABLE 4.2 Average sentence for one count of lewd sexual acts with a child (men only)

	n	Minimum	Maximum*	Median	Mean	SD
State						
Georgia	18,802	0	39.2	12.00	14.02	9.38
South Dakota	422	0	39.2	12.00	14.18	9.19
Arizona	4,972	0	39.2	10.00	11.25	5.15
Mississippi	311	0	39.2	7.00	8.08	5.44
Louisiana	801	0	39.2	6.00	9.80	10.03
South Carolina	5,134	0	39.2	6.00	7.64	6.77
Missouri	3,113	0	38	6.00	6.56	3.84
Tennessee	403	0	21	6.00	5.69	3.16
New Mexico	143	0	23	5.46	6.75	5.17
West Virginia	844	0	35	5.00	9.91	7.68
Rhode Island	886	0	39.2	5.00	7.43	7.48
New York	1,963	0	25	5.00	7.38	5.64
Oklahoma	3,608	0	39.2	5.00	7.28	7.14
Wisconsin	1,920	0	39.2	5.00	6.57	5.54
Iowa	558	0	25	5.00	6.00	3.86
Wyoming	239	0	25	5.00	5.53	3.24
Florida	11,763	0	39.2	5.00	6.82	6.39
Indiana	14,680	0	39.2	4.92	8.67	9.75
Alabama	211	0	39.2	4.00	7.36	7.88
California	62,368	0	39.2	4.00	5.22	3.94
Michigan	364	0	20	4.00	5.39	3.73
Illinois	1,237	0	39.2	4.00	5.15	4.88
New Jersey	952	0	25	4.00	4.61	3.30
Kansas	2,518	0	39.2	3.33	4.47	4.21
Texas	1,992	0	39.2	3.00	4.01	4.29
Kentucky	1,377	0	39.2	3.00	3.98	3.80
Massachusetts	541	0	35	3.00	3.96	3.92
Washington	6,569	0	39.2	3.00	3.65	3.07
Minnesota	723	1	39.2	3.00	3.86	3.48
Hawaii	302	0	39.2	2.42	3.59	4.21
Oregon	289	0	30	2.33	3.54	4.50
Pennsylvania	786	0	36.25	2.00	3.52	4.43
Colorado	1,018	0	39.2	1.67	3.36	4.83
North Carolina	8,849	0	39.2	1.67	2.01	1.89
Nevada	730	0	20.67	0.00	1.73	4.35

child molestation charges can be studied as first-, second-, and third-degree felonies. This still does not solve the problem of plea-bargaining interfering with the final conviction charges, but it is more refined than a national summary. These figures do not represent all of the sex abuse cases in Washington state. Only those reported to the BJS (Table 4.3; Figures 4.6–4.16).

In glancing through these charts and figures you can find some trends that support Patrick Drum's claims. Notice that more than half of all "third-degree rape of a child" convictions result in a 0–2-year prison sentence, exactly as Drum predicted in his *Sex, Drugs, and Consequences* essay because this sentence is eligible for a legislator-approved sentencing adjustment. It may come as a surprise that first-degree rape charges are most likely to result in a sentence of zero years in prison, with more than 15% of people convicted of this crime avoiding incarceration entirely. One really

TABLE 4.3 Washington Average sentence for one count of primary conviction offense (men only)

	n	Minimum	Maximum*	Median	Mean	SD
Sex offenses						
First-degree rape	331	0	39.20	4.25	7.00	8.84
Second-degree rape	392	0	27.50	5.00	5.32	4.54
Third-degree rape	426	0	39.20	2.54	3.78	5.38
First-degree rape of a child	1,415	0	30.00	5.56	6.01	4.77
Second-degree rape of a child	762	0	20.83	4.83	4.79	3.54
Third-degree rape of a child	1,046	0	20.83	1.67	2.67	2.46
First-degree molestation	1,690	0	28.33	3.67	4.09	3.51
Second-degree molestation	951	0	26.50	1.67	3.16	3.37
Third-degree molestation	297	0	23.33	1.67	2.71	2.81
Indecent liberties	577	0	39.20	2.00	3.82	4.08
Drug offenses						
Manufacturing drugs	749	0	20.00	3.00	4.26	3.68
Prohibited drug – A	32,207	0	39.20	1.83	2.83	2.94

strange observation from looking at these distributions is the similarity across offense types. What is the purpose of dividing crimes into first, second, and third-degree rape, or first-, second-, and third-degree rape of child, when the sentences allocated for each charge are remarkably similar to those given for "indecent liberties" and "molestation" crimes?

Do sex offenders serve shorter sentences than drug offenders? Sometimes they do. As you can see in the final graph, some drug offenders are sentenced to 10 years, 20 years, or in two cases, Life. Few people sentenced to prison for drugs get a suspended sentence. Only 116 out of 32,207 cases were given this reprieve, but suspended sentences were common for sex offenders. I also found that sex offenders served less time than their official sentence, perhaps due to "good time" or the sentencing adjustment laws mentioned by Drum in his essay. A first-degree rapist served 23% less

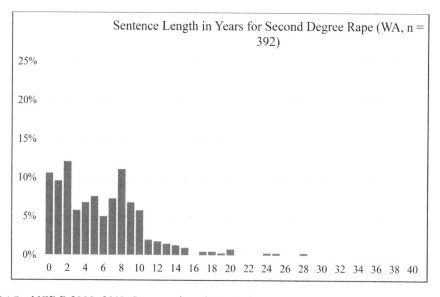

FIGURE 4.7 NCRP 2000–2019: Sentence length in Washington state for second-degree rape

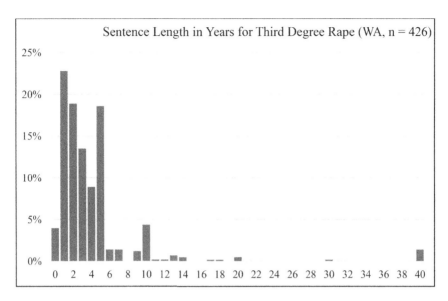

FIGURE 4.8   NCRP 2000–2019: Sentence length in Washington state for third-degree rape

time than their mandatory release date, while other types of sex offenses saw 20–55% reductions in their sentences depending on the crime, degree, and number of charges. However, contrary to Drum's hypothesis, drug offenders also saw an average reduction of 47% off their mandatory sentence, indicating that there isn't much truth-in-sentencing in Washington for any of these crimes.

A man serving 5 years for selling cocaine is shocked to learn he is sharing a prison cell with a child sex abuser serving the same time or less. They believe there should be *no overlap at all,* but the overlap is not the only consideration. Vigilante supporters want extremely long sentences for sex offenders that would not be possible under current sentencing laws. And, of course, vigilantes

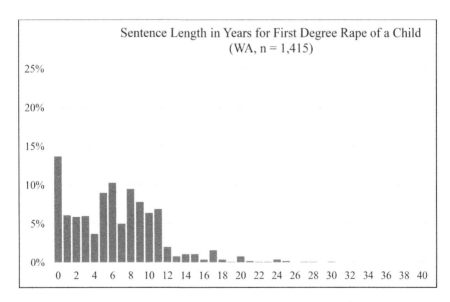

FIGURE 4.9   NCRP 2000–2019: Sentence length in Washington state for first-degree rape of a child

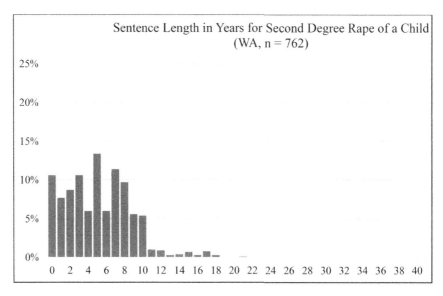

FIGURE 4.10 NCRP 2000–2019: Sentence length in Washington state for second-degree rape of a child

often prefer the death penalty to any length of incarceration. I think most people would be reasonable if you presented the facts of a specific case to them and explained practical constraints in legal terms, but the idea that anyone who rapes a child receives *zero* days in prison inspires the same outrage that others feel when they hear about a case where a life sentence was given for a petty crime. People who are trained to think of punishments in terms of relative severity want justice to be proportional, and sex offenders are expected to receive uniquely harsh penalties in comparison to lesser crimes. Justice system reformers who want to shift the discussion away from punishment entirely have their work cut out for them.

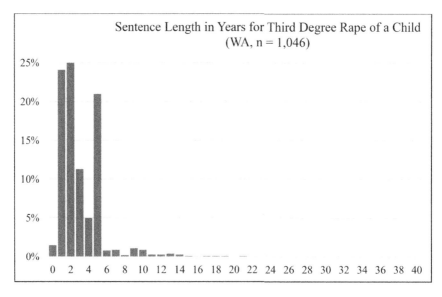

FIGURE 4.11 NCRP 2000–2019: Sentence length in Washington state for third-degree rape of a child

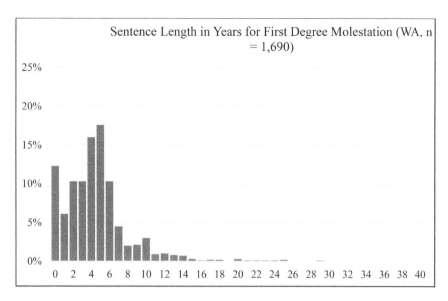

FIGURE 4.12 NCRP 2000–2019: Sentence length in Washington state for first-degree molestation

Black-Robed Collaborators

Many people share their opinions on how the justice system *ought to* work, but the ultimate decision is made by a select few. In one of his fiction stories, Andrew Vachss referred to lenient judges as "black-robed collaborators" because they define child sex abuse as a symptom of a curable disorder (18). This framing justifies treatment, compassion, and probation… anything except jailing them. Certainly, Andrew Vachss was venting his own frustrations with the system through his fictional character's opinions, but he was speaking for a large portion of the American public

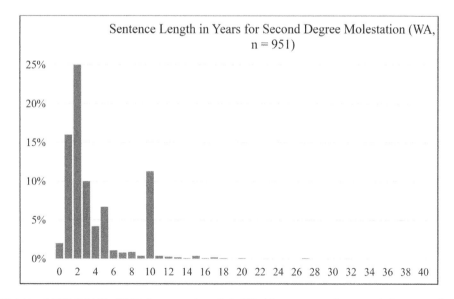

FIGURE 4.13 NCRP 2000–2019: Sentence length in Washington state for second-degree molestation

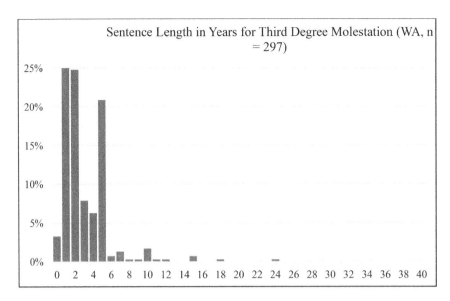

FIGURE 4.14 NCRP 2000–2019: Sentence length in Washington state for third-degree molestation

who think a few months in a compassionate treatment center is too lenient for a crime that causes so much pain. Academics can dismiss them as "low information, high salience" or the "panicky public," but these opinions are commonly held, and they hold sway in elections, so practical reformers ought to consider the genesis of these beliefs (19, 20).

Judges have been entrusted with broad decision-making powers. Judicial decisions have been evaluated to determine what case characteristics are associated with disparate outcomes. This is one area where social scientists have excelled in bold investigations of powerful people. It might be one of the most important contributions of academics to improving the criminal justice

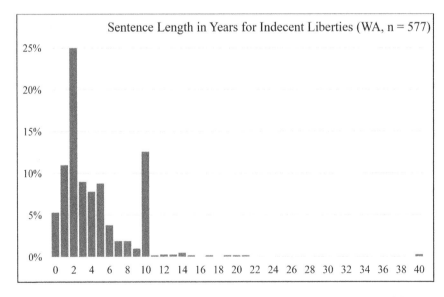

FIGURE 4.15 NCRP 2000–2019: Sentence length in Washington state for indecent liberties crimes

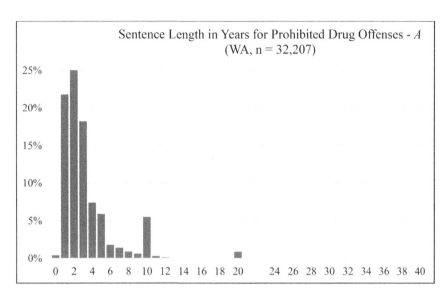

FIGURE 4.16   NCRP 2000–2019: Sentence length in Washington state for prohibited drug offenses

system. By analyzing and evaluating judicial decision-making they have been able to identify just how often decision-makers deviate from the letter of the law to give harsher or more lenient punishments to certain defendants. Mountains of research have compared sentencing outcomes for rich vs. poor, Black vs. White, women vs. men, adults vs. children, and then explored the interaction of age, race, and sex. Massive datasets help us to assess millions of court outcomes with rigorous statistical techniques to control for the effects of confounding variables in cases, as well as the "extra-legal" factors that hint of judicial bias.

Courtroom actors (such as the judge and prosecutor) decide whether to detain a defendant or release them before their trial, whether to press charges or not, which charges to press, whether to reduce charges or accept a plea bargain, sentencing decisions, and whether jail, prison, or community supervision are appropriate. Judges may not have enough information to make a fully rational decision, and they may not be able to fully process the information they do have. Focal concerns perspective (FCP) identifies potential "cognitive filters" or "perceptual shorthand" that might help explain how judges use their discretion in different cases. These concerns are typically listed as blameworthiness of the defendant, concerns for the protection of the community, and the practical limitations of making particular decisions. When crimes are less severe the courts have more discretion. When officials use this discretion, they may be relying on extralegal factors to help make a choice. While the system is designed to allow flexibility in decision-making to accommodate the unique circumstances of each case, it is possible that biases and prejudice of the official can lead to disparate treatment of defendants. The amount of disparity can differ widely between different groups of people, different jurisdictions, across the various decision points, and even within a single courtroom.

If a child sex abuser is found guilty, the judge might consider many factors that have nothing to do with their crime before deciding how to punish them. They might ask if the person is entirely blameworthy, or whether the victim shared some blame (which is why defense attorneys ask those accusatory questions of child victims to besmirch their character). As Alice Vachss explained in her book *Sex Crimes: Then and Now,* one of the most offensive subjective judgments is whether the victim is a "Good Victim" in the eyes of the court. *What was the victim wearing? How long did they take to make a report? Did they cry enough during their testimony? Did they cry too much? What race are they?* These questions have nothing at all to do with the fact that they were sexually abused, but they are questions that can change a jury's collective mind on whether or not the victim was "really" a victim (21).

The judge might also ask if the offender is really a danger to the community. If the individual has no criminal history they might appear to be a low-risk person. For example, the notorious Catholic priest John Geoghan was convicted of a single incident of touching a child's buttocks, but investigators knew of nearly 150 additional victims in his past who suffered more severe abuse. None of the other cases resulted in criminal charges. He was transferred from parish to parish by the Church and was not reported to the police. When he was finally convicted of a single offense his defense attorney used his clean record as a reason why he didn't deserve to go to prison. After all, he was an elderly priest who was involved in the community for his entire life. He would be at a low risk to re-offend. The judge disagreed and sentenced him to 8 years in prison (Chapter 8). So a person with no criminal record can be given a harsh sentence, and other judges may show leniency to a "pillar of the community" who was found guilty of many crimes.

Every criminologist knows that the greatest predictor of future behavior is past behavior. That's why every recidivism risk assessment tool includes a measure of one's prior criminal history. Sentencing guidelines are designed to set mandatory minimums and maximum sentences for each crime, but they also include sentencing enhancements if the defendant has prior offenses. Essentially, the defendant is being given an extra punishment because of their past crimes, even if they already "paid their debt to society," which violates a sense of fairness in receiving "just deserts." An argument against habitual offender provisions is that they sweep up people with a history of persistent problems. Those with unresolved drug addiction and mental health issues might rack up a large number of "prior criminal history points" and be sent to prison where their criminogenic needs cannot be properly addressed. As I mentioned in the chapter on trauma, many of the people with these persistent problems were survivors of child sex abuse, which contributes to their distrust of a system that punishes victims and shows leniency to their abusers.

"Practical constraints" refer to the consequences of making one decision over another. This may be described in terms of organizational costs to the justice system (e.g., their reputation in the community), costs in terms of resources (e.g., available jail or prison space), and costs to the offender themselves (e.g., will the punishment disrupt their ties to their children, will they personally be able to "do the time," or will it increase their chances of recidivism?). This is the point at which judges show their punishment orientations. Do they want to send a message to other sex offenders that they will not tolerate a certain crime? Or do they worry that the offender might be too short (or too rich) to endure a prison sentence? (22, 23).

Organizational concerns also include the maintenance of workgroup relationships among courtroom actors. Judges want to maintain a flow of cases and often work with the various agencies and interested parties to ensure that this flow is stable (23–26). An additional consideration that judges might take into account is the impact that their sentencing decisions have on local and state resources, including crowding in jails and prison facilities (27). In 1984, Peterson and Hagan proposed the idea that some judges might become more lenient toward drug dealers when state prisons are populated over capacity, because they did not want to contribute further to the overcrowding problem (28). This echoed a belief proposed by James Q. Wilson in 1977 when he noted that some prison facilities were in such bad condition due to overcrowding that "many judges in good conscience" chose not to sentence offenders to incarceration (29). Perhaps judges show leniency to child sex abusers because they believe the prison authorities cannot protect them from "convict justice" that is dished out when prisoners target sex offenders for violence.

That may be a far-sighted motivation for keeping child sex abusers safe in prison; it may increase the likelihood that they are sent to prison in the first place.

In 2012, Jeffery Ulmer reviewed the literature in sentencing research and identified new and necessary approaches for advancing our understanding of this topic (30). In this article, he defined "localization and social context" as a balance between the goals of the organization and the "realization and implementation" of those goals in the local jurisdiction. He pointed out how jurisdictions (even within states) vary widely in their sentencing practices, and how this might be a matter of responding to pressures unique to the local environment. The commonly recognized roles of offense severity/type, criminal history, guilty plea, gender, race, and ethnicity are all subject to interaction effects due to local courtroom factors. "In sum, substantial evidence exists that what kind of sentence one gets, and the factors that predict why one gets it, in significant part depends on where one is sentenced" (p.14). Among these county-level factors are the available resources, including county jail space (31, 32). When the jails are full, courts might sentence someone to probation or state prisons merely because of lack of resources to accommodate them locally. A reciprocal effect can be seen in a study by D'Alessio and Stolzenberg, where judges were more likely to depart from guidelines to increase the likelihood of local jail sentences when state prisons were overcrowded so that local resources would be used instead (33). This further emphasizes the link between local jail and state prison populations.

Focal concerns theories work both ways. Beliefs in blameworthiness, dangerousness, and practical constraints can also be used to amplify sex offender punishments in relation to other offenders. Perhaps the most rigorous evaluation of sex offender sentencing was conducted by Joshua Cochran, Elisa Toman, Ryan Shields, and Daniel Mears in 2020 (34). These authors examined felony sentencing data for over 1.8 million defendants in Florida who were processed between 1995 and 2011. They found evidence that showed every crime type saw an increase in the probability of receiving a prison sentence over this time period, but the increase was steepest for sex offenders. They also found that the predicted sentence length in months for sex offenses was greatest for sex offenders at all time periods, and it also increased well beyond the other types of crime they studied (violent, property, drug, and "other" offenses), whose sentence lengths all remained relatively flat over this same time period. They used a sophisticated matching model to compare similar sex offense defendants to one another in different sentencing years (to reduce the effects of individual case characteristics on outcomes). They found that a sex offender sentenced in 1995 had a 41.3% chance of being sentenced to prison and on average they were sentenced to 8.25 years in prison. In 2011, a similarly situated sex offender would have an 80.9% chance of going to prison, and they would serve 9.75 years in prison. The authors of this study believe that this increase in sex offender punishments was caused by increasing societal concern for sex crimes (especially child sexual victimization) and highly publicized cases of especially heinous offenses. This attention put pressure on legislatures and judges to give the people what they wanted: more punishment. Pro-punishment activists should be glad to see these changes. They appear to be achieving their goals of having a criminal justice system that focuses on sex offenders, even if it isn't enough to satisfy the revenge impulse of vigilantes.

Deal with the Devil

Plea bargaining is the real confounder in this research. Even if you found that a sex offender received a harsh sentence for their crimes it might not actually reflect the total number of crimes the court knew about. Imagine that a defendant has ten charges and one of them is rape.

The prosecutor offers a deal. "Plead guilty to rape and we'll drop the other nine charges." The defense counteroffers to plead guilty to the nine charges plus a misdemeanor sexual assault so the defendant doesn't have "rape" on their criminal record. The deal is made, but the judge doesn't like the deal. He gives the defendant the maximum punishment for all of the guilty charges because he is really trying to punish the rape charge. On paper, it would look like this man was given a harsh sentence for misdemeanor sexual assault. You can't look at the original charges as a better indicator because the prosecutor might hack this process by deliberately *overcharging* the defendant in anticipation of pleading them down. A good example of this is when a prosecutor charges someone for a hundred child sex exploitation material crimes, one for each image on their computer. Then they plead guilty to one charge and the other ninety-nine are dropped. Very few research studies have the level of detail necessary to conduct a rigorous statistical analysis to identify what punishment was given for which crimes.

Plea bargains interfere with categorization. If a man goes to prison for child sex abuse it is assumed that he committed far worse crimes in addition to those listed on his paperwork, but he got a plea deal to hide most of the other offenses. It is also assumed that they had committed many more crimes that were never reported in the first place. "Where there's smoke, there's fire" is the underlying justification for "smashing child molesters" in prison. The abundance of plea bargains has undermined faith in conviction offenses. This might be thought of as a collateral consequence. If a person is convicted of a sex offense and it was one of those marginal Romeo and Juliet cases where the offender had turned 18 and was *technically* breaking the law when he was not the day before his birthday, the other prisoners would just assume this person was far worse than their conviction offense showed. "One charge? How many were pled down or dropped?" This individual would be treated the same as someone who committed many serious crimes against children, just because the conviction charges are so often considered to be bureaucratic lies.

Alice Vachss (former sex crimes prosecutor in Queens, NY) has described how the plea bargaining process so often resembles haggling in a fish market. In her book *Sex Crimes: Then and Now,* she relates how a "going rate" is really determined.

> There are even some unspoken rules for what a case is "worth." The numbers vary among jurisdictions, but the considerations – the degrees of proof, the likelihood of conviction, the sentences judges tend to impose after the trial – rarely vary. It's the way social prejudices are incorporated into the entire system, not just the trial cases.
>
> Plea negotiations are what they're called: bargaining. It's very easy to lose sight of the case itself, to lose sight of anything other than bargaining. When that happens, both sides get the best bargain they can, but they often forget about justice and dignity.

Carissa Byrne Hessick's book *Punishment Without Trial* explains the crises that excessive plea bargaining has created in America's courts. While most of her book focuses on times when people under duress pled guilty to crimes they didn't commit, she does catalog the problems of lenient plea deals for sex offenses (35).

When Hessick was researching her subject she received a large envelope containing a number of troubling cases where serious sex offenses were reduced to less serious crimes. She learned that out of hundreds of cases, only 60 resulted in a jail sentence longer than one year, and 250 resulted in no jail sentence at all. Often prosecutors would deal openly with the defense team in court and admit that they were going to argue for a tough penalty so they could impress their constituents, even though they knew the deal would result in lenient punishments. This disingenuous, scripted posturing was all for show. Of course, the victims would not know that these shenanigans took place until after the court was adjourned.

Ohio Supreme Court Justice Michael Donnelly had personally investigated cases where this unethical behavior occurred. He was appalled that some serious sexual abuse crimes were covered up, so repeat offenders appeared to be non-recidivists in terms of sex crimes. He was also worried about the effect these deals had on victims. A victim knew *for certain* that they were sexually assaulted and it wasn't their own fault, but the court would reduce the charges to a low-level non-sexual assault charge. These types of charges were usually reserved for bar fights where the victim provoked the attack, but when they were applied to sexual assault crimes they implied that the victim had provoked their own sexual assault. One of these cases reduced from rape to assault involved a woman who was sleeping when a man broke into her home and sexually assaulted her. The judge, prosecutor, defense, and defendant arranged to blame the victim for this crime in order to hurry the case along. The court was deliberately blaming the victim in order to shield the sex abuser from harsh penalties.

Unethical plea deals hurt the court's reputation if they are used to railroad innocent people into taking guilt for crimes they didn't commit, and if they are used to hide the true nature of a violent sex crime. Unfortunately, our courts are overwhelmed with cases and it is unlikely that we will ever have enough resources to curtail our use of plea bargains. The Supreme Court has ruled that "creative" plea bargaining is acceptable, even if it results in final convictions that had nothing to do with the initial charges (*Padilla v. Kentucky,* 2010). We have been drawn so far away from the jury trial guarantees of the US Constitution that it would be laughable to suggest that we restrain plea bargaining in our courts. We are dependent on conveyor-belt justice. In the conclusion to her book, Hessick writes:

> Convictions no longer tell us what a defendant actually did; they simply represent the end of a negotiation between lawyers. A defendant who pleads guilty to a low-level assault in Ohio may have committed that assault, he may have committed a rape, or he may be innocent of any crime. We do not know, and widespread acceptance of plea bargaining seems to tell us that we should not care.

Sometimes a plea bargain might have a more utilitarian purpose than simply clearing the judge's docket. Law enforcement agencies might need the defendant to cooperate with them in order to catch more offenders. A horrifying case occurred in Australia where Matthew Graham was arrested for facilitating the sexual abuse, humiliation, torture, and murder of children. He paid men to create snuff videos and he hosted them on the Dark Web. He was the "CEO" of a criminal empire called the "Hurt2theCore" child sex exploitation material network. Graham might have been charged with any number of felonies for his role in hosting this customizable, streaming, pay-per-view torture porn. He was facing a lifetime of imprisonment for his crimes. But the taskforce that arrested him needed his help. He had the password to a vast online empire of brutal child sex exploitation. If he would cooperate, they could arrest dozens of other suspects and rescue their child victims. They made a deal with Graham that if he gave them access to his computer, he could plead guilty and serve his prison sentence in Australia instead of being sent to the United States where he wouldn't be treated as nicely. Graham agreed, supplied his password, and pled guilty to 13 charges. He was given 15 years in prison (36). The information taken from Graham's computer helped Taskforce Argos in their undercover sting operation inside the hurtcore forums that eventually resulted in the rescue of 85 child victims (37).

Graham's crimes against children were egregious. A 15-year prison sentence cannot satisfy the victims' or the public's desire for retribution for the manufacture of infant murder porn. Even far-left prison abolitionists would have a hard time with that case. The fact remains that this plea deal resulted in the rescue of 85 child victims, the broader network of child abusers was unraveled, and the nefarious Hurt2theCore empire was shut down. Should those 85 children have been left in the hands of their abusers just to satisfy vengeance against Graham? Plea bargains in these cases might be a deal with the devil, but the total costs and benefits must be weighed. Deals like these can also sow the seeds of distrust in these online communities and encourage more offenders to betray their coconspirators. After all, if the CEO of Hurt2theCore will give his password to the police, can they trust anyone on the Dark Web? Is there loyalty among anonymous, online, child sex abusers? This is obviously an extreme example, but it is one reason why even law enforcement officers might prefer to have plea bargains on the table.

Plea bargain reform poses many problems. If legislatures crank up the mandatory minimums or restrict prosecutor's bargaining power, they might create unintended consequences that interfere with the justice process. Defendants facing extremely long sentences will demand a trial. That will slow the system down and impose more trauma on the victims. Testifying in court under cross-examination might scare victims away. Defendants will also be less likely to assist law enforcement in breaking up human trafficking and online pornography networks. While the excuses made by prosecutors might seem dismissive or aloof, there is an argument to be made that flexibility is necessary. Otherwise, more child sex abusers will walk free. A short sentence, mandatory treatment, and community supervision might be the best they can do. Unfortunately, egregious lapses of common sense will always remind the public that the plea-bargaining process is flawed. Every rational decision will be overshadowed by cases like the Dupont Heir fiasco which stained the reputation of the entire system.

Plea bargains will be a persistent source of confusion in the court system for a long time. I do not think we can disentangle these bargaining shenanigans from the final sentencing outcome with enough certainty to truly measure differences in sex offender sentencing trends. It probably doesn't matter very much for most vigilantes. Many of them would not care if sex offender punishments were tripled or quadrupled. They want blood.

Nothing Less than Death

I think there is a hidden debate hidden under the surface of all of these arguments for and against vigilantism. It may have special significance in the United States, as it is one of few Western industrialized nations that still permits the death penalty. Americans have strong opinions about the death penalty that must shape the foundations of their beliefs on this issue. Someone who believes that government-imposed execution is justifiable may not support vigilantism, but every person who supports lethal vigilantism surely believes that death is an acceptable punishment. On the other side of this issue, people who oppose formal death sentences will never support vigilante murders (unless they are extreme libertarians who want true self-governance-wild west style).

I spoke with a philosopher about this issue. Peter Rose-Barry, the man who shared his expertise during the media frenzy surrounding Steven Sandison's murder of Ted Dyer (Chapter 1). In his initial conversation with the media, he said that it would be impossible to imagine any scenario where sexually abusing a child is morally justifiable, but he said there are arguments to be made that the death penalty serves a positive social purpose. Philosophers love to play devil's advocate if it causes people to think. I reached out to Professor Rose-Barry to see if he could help me understand the death penalty angle on this story.

Rose-Barry said there are obvious reasons why we want the state to handle executions. It is the most severe penalty we can impose. A formal procedure gives due process to the suspect. They are entitled to present evidence, confront witnesses, be represented by an attorney, and have the privilege of a jury trial. This is all meant to reduce the likelihood that an innocent person is convicted or an underserving case is given the ultimate penalty. The process is flawed, but it is certainly better than summary execution by a vigilante. Another reason why the state should have a monopoly on lethal punishment is that there are "expressive or communicative functions that state-sponsored executions might serve." Here Rose-Barry implies that the state can serve as a moral authority. Their imposition of the death penalty bears some degree of legitimacy. They speak on behalf of society. A lone vigilante speaks for themselves. They are rogue citizens sneering at the social order.

At the end of the day, these arguments in support of the death penalty hinge on the value of *retribution*. To give someone what they deserve for heinous crimes. Even if you agree with that goal and believe that death is appropriate, you would have a long way to go to prove that the state could possibly achieve a reliable degree of impartiality and rightful conviction to justify capital punishment. The system is simply too flawed to justify permanent retribution. Keep in mind, this position does not rule out capital punishment completely, it just argues that the state cannot meet the threshold of legitimacy needed to entrust them with this power. This is a "contingent proceduralist kind of abolition." Rose-Barry doesn't rule out the possibility that capital punishment for a limited class of child sex abusers might be morally justified. After all, the death penalty is already proscribed for a certain class of murderers. Taken altogether, he thinks the death penalty is an issue that extends well beyond the simplistic moral arguments commonly debated and it extends into complex legal opinions. But in no way do these arguments support vigilante violence. If we can't trust the government to kill our citizens, why should we trust an angry man who strangles people with prison-issued shoelaces?

It is extremely unlikely that the United States will ever permit the death penalty to be used as punishment for child sex abusers. In the past, there were many crimes that were eligible for a swift execution, but today the death penalty is limited to a small number of "capital" cases that meet certain criteria. In 2008, the Supreme Court ruled in *Kennedy v. Louisiana* that sex offenders do not qualify for the ultimate punishment unless the offender killed the victim or intended to kill the victim (38). Patrick Kennedy's sex crimes were the catalyst of this decision. He was found guilty of raping his 8-year-old stepdaughter. Under Louisiana law, he was eligible for the death penalty, and the jury sentenced him to this punishment. It was appealed by the defendant, and the Supreme Court ruled in a 5-4 decision to bar the death penalty for the crime of child rape. Justice Anthony Kennedy (no relation to the defendant) delivered the opinion of the Court. While he recognized the extreme severity of the rape crime (that resulted in the separation of the child's cervix from the back of her vagina), he agreed with the arguments made by the defense.

Below I have listed summaries of each argument presented by the Court in support of the Patrick Kennedy's appeal:

- The death penalty may be cruel and unusual punishment depending on the evolving standards of decency in society.
- The death penalty "risks its own sudden descent into brutality" if it seeks retribution without decency and restraint.

- Only a "narrow category of the most serious crimes" with extreme culpability are deserving of capital punishment.
- Juveniles and cognitively impaired defendants are not eligible for the death penalty because they have diminished responsibility for their crime, therefore restrictions on death penalty decisions have precedent.
- The death penalty should only be used when the crime resulted in a death of a victim otherwise it is disproportionate.
- The Court had previously ruled that the death penalty was unconstitutional when the crime was the rape of an adult woman.
- Executions for child rape were rare (the most recent execution occurred in 1964, which was 44 years before the Court ruling in *Kennedy v. Louisiana*).
- After the Supreme Court temporarily invalidated the death penalty for rape in *Furman v. Georgia, 1974*, only six states reinstated this penalty for rape, and all of these statutes were struck down in later rulings.
- Louisiana reinstated the death penalty for rape in 1995 if the victim was under the age of 13. Five other states enacted the death penalty for child rape, but they did not have strict liability as Louisiana did, or they required other aggravating circumstances.
- The remaining 44 states and the federal government did not permit the death penalty for the rape of a child. Although 31 of these jurisdictions permit the death penalty for other crimes, they do not permit it for the rape of a child.
- Rape is a serious crime with serious consequences, but it does not compare with murder because it does not result in the loss of a human life.
- The Court's decision to bar capital punishment for an adult raping an adult did not establish that it was guaranteed in the case of an adult raping a child.
- While other states had proposed laws that imposed the death penalty for crimes of child rape, most of them failed to be passed by the state legislatures. Therefore, no there was no evidence that the "consistency of the direction of change" would lead to a greater consensus among states on this issue.
- Although some states permitted the death penalty for child rape, no individuals had been executed for these crimes since 1964, implying that it was unusual and not supported by a national consensus.
- Louisiana itself only had two people on death row for a nonhomicide offense (Patrick Kennedy and Richard Davis), implying that it was an unusual punishment even within Louisiana's own jurisdiction.
- For the victim of rape, "life may not be nearly so happy as it was" but it "is not beyond repair" even for child victims who are expected to have permanent psychological, emotional, and physical impacts.
- The Court should be hesitant to extend the death penalty to crimes where the victim did not die because they were obliged to show restraint when interpreting the Eighth Amendment's prohibitions of cruel and unusual punishment.
- The death penalty is unique in its severity and irrevocability, and it must be limited to a narrow category of crimes that are an "affront to humanity" where the only adequate response is death. While rape is "morally reprehensible" it cannot be compared to murder in terms of "severity and irrevocability."
- Crimes against the State (such as treason, espionage, terrorism, and drug kingpin activity) may still be eligible for the death penalty even if they do not result in death. The Court's logic is only concerned with crimes against individuals in this case.

- If every child rapist were executed it would expand the use of the death penalty to a significant number of people, and these executions would violate our "evolving standards of decency and the necessity to constrain the use of the death penalty."
- In many cases, rape crimes will "overwhelm a decent person's judgment" and lead to arbitrary applications of the death penalty.
- Juries may not be able to understand the role of aggravating factors in a rape case as they would "common-sense core of meaning" factors in a murder case.
- Evidence cannot convincingly demonstrate that the death penalty deters crimes, including rape.
- Retribution is not justified because the death penalty is too harsh for nonhomicide crimes.
- The death penalty may not balance the wrong done to the victim.
- Child victims suffer trauma in testifying in lengthy death penalty trials.
- Child victims are not mature enough to make the moral decision on whether they should assist the state in seeking the death penalty.
- Child victims may have unreliable testimony because they are highly susceptible to suggestive questioning techniques.
- The rape of a child victim usually involves only the child and the alleged perpetrator, meaning the facts of the case are subject to fabrication, exaggeration, or both.
- Children may be less likely to report their victimization if the perpetrator faces the death penalty.
- Rational offenders might kill their victim to eliminate a witness in a capital crime, but might be more likely to let the child live if they only face life in prison as a maximum penalty (the Court recognized that the offender might also be expected to be deterred from offending in the first place, but argued that the uncertainty of this point makes it difficult to use deterrence as a justification for the death penalty).
- While each of these justifications might not be enough to render the death penalty unconstitutional, taken in sum, the Court found that they were convincing enough to bar the death penalty for the rape of a child.

"Based both on consensus and our own independent judgment, our holding is that a death sentence for one who raped but did not kill a child, and who did not intend to assist another in killing the child, is unconstitutional under the Eighth and Fourteenth Amendments."

I suppose that it is possible that *Kennedy v. Louisiana* could be overturned someday if the "evolving standards of decency" in our society shift far enough to compel a new assessment, but this is very unlikely. As the Court Opinion stated, they tend to resist any expansion of interpretations of cruel and unusual punishment. They also tend to stand with the doctrine of *stare decisis* – the precedent set by prior rulings. For now, the death penalty is off the table.

I have presented this extensive list here because it is extremely important for explaining the logic of the highest court in the land. I assume that some of my readers picked up this book because they support vigilante violence against child sex abusers. You've been thinking deeply about the various issues I've brought up throughout this book. Here you have the itemized list of reasons why *your government* excludes the possibility of killing the people you think deserve to die. You can use this list to think about your own moral priorities, then go and read the full *Kennedy v. Louisiana* decision. Read the case law cited by the Court opinion. Read the dissent proposed by Justice Alito (which may help you understand how even the people who support the death penalty for sex offenders do so for different reasons than you). Be an informed citizen who investigates these issues honestly and does not use instinctive judgments to decide what is right or wrong. It is easy for people to read a news headline and share their opinion. It is not so easy to take the time to carefully map out your rationale and weigh opposing arguments. After you have concluded your deliberations on the subject of lethal punishment you should ask if you trust *random citizens* to decide who lives or dies.

The Ultimate in Vanity

In 2008, the billionaire Jeffrey Epstein was given a "sweetheart" deal in exchange for his guilty plea to charges of procuring a child for prostitution and for soliciting a prostitute. These crimes represented only a fraction of the charges he could have faced for abusing 36 girls and young women on his private island (called the Pedophile Island by locals who saw him bring young girls into his residence). Despite the severity of these crimes, Epstein was given a "sweetheart deal" where he was allowed to serve only 13 months in a minimum-security correctional facility and was permitted to leave prison most days to work in his impossibly lucrative stock trading business.

The US Attorney who approved of this remarkable plea deal was Alexander Acosta, who claimed that he was told to "leave it alone" because Epstein "belonged to intelligence." This trusted government official was later appointed to be the United States Secretary of Labor before resigning when his role in the plea deal was scrutinized. One disturbing aspect of this case was the non-prosecution agreement that granted immunity to several co-conspirators and any "potential co-conspirators" that might be identified. This clause was rife with potential for conspiracy theorists because Epstein was well known for schmoozing with incredibly rich and powerful people (Prince Andrew, Bill Clinton, Donald Trump, Leslie Wexner, Jean-Luc Brunel, Bill Gates, and Leon Black to name just a few). How many of them were listed as "potential co-conspirators" in his crimes? Why were they given blanket protection from prosecution in Epstein's plea deal before they were ever charged with a crime? Why were the public, and even the victims, banned from knowing their role in Epstein's crimes? Was there a conspiracy involving rich and powerful people? (39).

I don't think we should underestimate the influence of the Jeffrey Epstein case in shaping the public's attitudes about the government's ability to keep them safe from sex offenders. If Epstein's criminal case were written as a book it would never be published for fear that the plot was too ridiculous. A billionaire on an island who gets away with child sex trafficking on a massive scale? His close affiliation with presidents and royalty? Government corruption and intelligence agencies? All it needed was a murder mystery to be truly outside the realm of possibility, and this was soon furnished.

Epstein was arrested again on sex trafficking charges in 2019 and was held at the Metropolitan Correctional Center in New York City awaiting his trial. He was placed on suicide watch and had another prisoner assigned to help counsel him against ending his own life. Correctional officers were required to look into his cell every 30 minutes, but they did not follow their protocol on the night of August 9, 2019. The next morning Epstein was found dead in his cell. The official cause of death was listed as suicide by hanging, but many people in the public believe he was killed in order to protect his powerful co-conspirators from being exposed in a trial. The phrase "Epstein Didn't Kill Himself" spread across the United States, and each time it was shared, posted, or sprayed onto an overpass it was a symbol of American distrust of the government. Epstein was the one child sex abuser that the public *didn't* want to die.

After his death, the conspiracy of government involvement in child sexual exploitation was amplified to a new level. At best, the federal government is perceived to be incompetent in securing justice for children who are sexually victimized. At worst, they are perceived to be complicit in this abuse. This is not a good look. No wonder large numbers of American citizens do not trust the government to secure justice in cases that do not receive the degree of media attention that Epstein's case generated. Every convicted offender who receives more than one year in prison will compare their sentence to the crimes of Jeffrey Epstein and wonder how the American "justice" system can be so unbalanced. *Your son got 5 years for stealing a car, but Epstein got 1 year for raping kids? What's wrong with this country?* This feeds the popular belief that the public cannot trust courts to achieve justice.

In 2021, a Gallup poll found very little support for the justice system in the United States (40). Only 11% of Black, 17% of White, and 35% of Hispanic adults had a great deal or quite a lot of confidence in the justice system. In contrast, 61% of Black, 41% of White, and 30% of Hispanic adults had very little or *no* confidence in the justice system. Only 36% of all US adults had a great deal or quite a lot of confidence in the Supreme Court. Despite the massive social upheaval caused by police officers' deadly use of force in 2020, 51% of US adults still had confidence in policing. The institution with the lowest amount of confidence was Congress, with a dismal 12% showing support for them. Things look bleak, but these trends are nothing new. Confidence in these institutions has been low for almost three decades. The only major shift has been in a gap between Black and White adults in regards to certain institutions.

The Justice System Perceptions Study conducted by the American Bar Association found that 74% of respondents in the US population strongly agreed or agreed with the statement "The courts let too many criminals go free on technicalities" (41). Lawyers get a large proportion of the blame in this case, and not just the defense attorneys, but the prosecutors as well.

Alice Vachss was the Chief of the Special Victims Bureau of the Queens District Attorney's Office in New York. She tried over 100 felony cases. She developed a reputation for being too tough on sex offenders. One judge said she "drank blood for breakfast." She denies this characterization. She was resolute on behalf of the brave victims who came forward to get justice. If she cut a plea deal behind their backs, it would be a betrayal. However, her unwavering approach earned her some enemies among the good old boys in the DA office. They wanted to close cases quickly, even if it meant offering lenient plea deals to serial rapists. Vachss considered some of these court actors to be so unscrupulous in their efforts to help rapists that they should be called collaborators in future sex crimes (42).

My first lesson about sex-crimes prosecution was that perpetrators were not the only enemy. There is a large, more or less hidden population of what I later came to call collaborators within the criminal justice system. Whether it comes from a police officer or a defense attorney, a judge or a court clerk or a prosecutor; there seems to be a residuum of empathy for rapists that crosses all gender, class, and professional barriers. It gets expressed in different ways, from victim-bashing to jokes in poor taste, and too often it results in giving the rapist a break.

The public often thinks of "the system" as a monolithic entity, rather than different states, counties, courtrooms, and individuals acting separately. An egregious case of leniency in Delaware might inspire a man in Washington to kill sex offenders. It is easy for "the system" to lose respect. Legitimacy in the system is important because a government "by the People and for the People" requires public trust for it to function properly. Most studies on public perceptions of institutional legitimacy hinge on excessive punishments for racial minorities in the War on Drugs. These studies find extensive support for the idea that equality under the law is a prime motivator in the public's lack of confidence. However, there is another side to legitimacy that is more germane to the subject of vigilantism. If the people think the government cannot secure a fair punishment, they might take the law into their own hands. Vigilantism is "self-help crime control" (43).

When Trust Fails

Vigilantism has a long and interesting history that is beyond the scope of this book, but there are a few incidents that should be mentioned. In 1866, Thomas Dimsdale published *The Vigilantes of Montana* which explained what life is like when the government did not have a reliable justice system. Murder, theft, chaos, and terrorism ruled the state. Violent men openly bragged about their crimes with impunity, daring anyone to challenge them. When the law-abiding people could no longer tolerate this situation, they banded together and swore to fight for mutual protection. They shot and hanged as many outlaws as they could, but all the while they petitioned the government to replace them with sworn law enforcement officers as soon as possible. Dismdale was a mild-mannered academic, but he was converted to the vigilante way of thinking (44).

> The question of the propriety of establishing a Vigilance Committee depends upon the answers which ought to be given to the following queries: Is it lawful for citizens to slay robbers or murderers when they catch them; or ought they to wait for policemen, where there are none, or put them in penitentiaries not yet erected?
>
> Gladly, indeed, we feel sure, would the Vigilantes cease from their labor, and joyfully would they hail the advent of power, civil or military, to take their place; but till this is furnished by Government, society must be preserved from demoralization and anarchy; murder, arson, and robbery must be prevented or punished, and road agents must die. Justice, and protection from wrong to person or property, are the birthright of every American citizen, and these must be furnished in the best and most effectual manner that circumstances render possible. Furnished, however, they must be by constitutional law, undoubtedly, wherever practical and efficient provision can be made for its enforcement. But where justice is powerless as well as blind, the strong arm of the mountaineer must wield his sword; for "self-preservation is the first law of nature."

Perhaps the most famous case of vigilantism in modern times was that of Bernard Goetz, the "Subway Vigilante." Like many New Yorkers in the 1980's he was fed up with the crime infesting the city. He illegally carried a gun on the subway. When he was accosted by four men he shot them, paralyzing one of them. His case was a tabloid sensation with people taking sides and debating if he was a hero or a villain. The Washington Post said, "When people feel they are not adequately protected, the force of the argument that they should not take their defense into their own hands diminishes" (45). Ultimately, the jury convicted Goetz only of weapons charges and he spent eight months in jail. Other people were frustrated with the city too, but they chose less violent methods of improving the situation. The Guardian Angels became a kind of vigilance committee. They would help citizens in distress and call the police, but they did not carry guns.

The "wild west" mentality that many vigilantes and supporters endorse is not so different from the logic used by citizens in Philadelphia in the crime wave of the early 1990s. Elijah Anderson's book *The Code of the Street* shows just how far citizens are willing to go in order to protect themselves when they have a "profound lack of faith" in the system. Young men carried guns and often killed people who merely looked at them the wrong way. They were killed because the streets were so dangerous that failure to respond with violence to any sign of disrespect would stigmatize them as weak. Easy prey. This led to an escalating war of deterrence, until the hospitals were full of gunshot victims on a nightly basis. Once again, there were those "decent" people who didn't resort to violence. Some of them marched *en masse* to crack houses where drug dealers plied their trades. Herman Wrice led the group "Manuta Against Drugs" in brave demonstrations against these drug dealers to run them out of town. All of this was done because of a lack of faith in the government's ability to handle the crisis. When the people can't trust the system, they might take action.

I believe the same lack of faith in the system influences the level of support given to vigilantes in America. Some people truly do not believe that the system that protected Jeffrey Epstein from an appropriate punishment for child sex trafficking can be expected to care about justice for other sexually abused and exploited children. Most of them have probably never looked up the statistics on average sentences. The complexity of calculating a true average is confusing and only serves to create a fog of ambiguity. *How long does a child molester really serve? Why isn't the answer easy? It should be crystal clear!* As you can see from this chapter, it is difficult to give a simple average. Too many factors shape that decision, there are too many limits to the data, and too many backroom deals to truly answer this question honestly. I have done the best I can to give you an honest answer, but I don't think it will satisfy vigilantes and their supporters. They have lost faith in the system, utterly (46).

Outlier Influence

It is impossible to define "leniency" to everyone's satisfaction, but I tracked down some concerned citizens who advocate for tougher sentencing laws in order to see how they define leniency. Christopher Dalton is a special education teacher in California who is appalled by injustices in the court system. He has a Twitter account (@DaltonReport) where he compiles news reports of egregiously lenient sentences for child sex abuse, human trafficking, and child sex exploitation material crimes. He thinks the justice system is entirely too lenient on sex offenders and he catalogs every case he can find.

As a Christian, Christopher Dalton feels it is his duty to warn people about dangers to their children and the moral degradation of our society. As of February 3, 2022 he has archived 417 cases of "pedophiles given leniency," 87 cases of police and fire officials charged with child sex abuse crimes, 151 cases of "pedophile educators" charged with child sex abuse crimes, and 565 "illegal alien pedophiles" arrested. He only started tracking these cases in January 2019, but he has already accumulated a long list of "lenient" cases across the country. Of course, his definitions of "leniency" might differ from others, but I was intrigued by his passionate stance. He does not endorse vigilante violence, but he is not surprised that some people are so outraged they choose that path. As a Christian, he would much prefer to influence change through non-violent means.

I wrote to him and asked for his opinion on some of these debates. He replied "As for inspiring change, I think it may be too late. The best we can do is inform people that pedophiles are real. It's a topic that is very uncomfortable for most people… academia and the MSM (mainstream media) have chosen the side that it is okay to be a pedophile as long as you don't act on it." He believes there is no political movement to increase the severity of punishments. "I think it's too late because politically the right and left both support criminal justice system reform. Even Trump and his daughter went all in."

I used his Twitter thread of "pedophiles given leniency" to construct a spreadsheet of different case characteristics. These cases are naturally cherry-picked, but it demonstrates the types of cases that show up in the news and are spread by concerned citizens like Christopher Dalton. This is how perceptions of sentencing are spread in the age of social media.

Christopher posts these stories along with the judge's contact information. He hopes that if enough pressure is put on these judges, they will alter their behavior. He is a grassroots activist in that sense. Most of his posts describe cases where a suspect is arrested and released on low bond amounts, but many involve final sentencing decisions after plea deals had been established. I was curious about the news reports that are leading to popular dissatisfaction with the legal system, so I systematically reviewed each of his cherry-picked cases and compiled a database. I did not include pre-trial decisions or child sex exploitation material cases in this analysis. This is because pretrial decisions are often based on the availability of local supervision resources, and child sex exploitation material cases may involve over-charging to facilitate plea deals. I am looking at final dispositions of completed or attempted contact offenses among this list.

I found 155 cases in Christopher Dalton's list that met my inclusion criteria (Figure 4.17). Only 17 of these were women, and most of these women were teachers who had illegal sexual encounters with their students. When the victim's ages were reported, they were all between the ages of 14 and 16. Slightly over half of these women received community supervision sentences instead of incarceration sentences. Those who were incarcerated were sentenced to an average of 11 months in jail. The remaining 138 convicted sex offenders were men. Their conviction offenses included soliciting sex from a minor (13.7%), sex trafficking crimes (0.7%), sexual assault/child molestation (41.0%), rape (using the UCR definition of any sexual penetration without lawful consent, 43.5%), and attempted rape (1.4%). When the age of the victim was reported the average was 12.5 years old. Ages ranged from a 1-year-old victim to 17-year-old victims. These men were most often sentenced to community control sanctions, such as probation or house arrest (49%). Some were sentenced to treatment only 2.9%). Those who given incarceration sanctions were sentenced to an average of 7 months in jail. Incarceration sentences ranged from a single day in one case to 15 years in another case. The 15-year sentence was considered to be lenient by Christopher Dalton because the individual had filmed himself raping his 1-year-old baby and

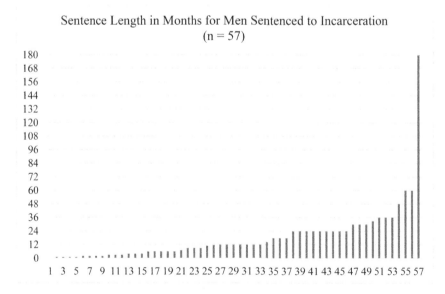

FIGURE 4.17   Sentence length in months for men sentences to incarceration in Christopher Dalton's list of "lenient cases"

uploading the video to the internet. Christopher asked why this man was not getting a life sentence for this atrocious crime. I have graphed these jail sentences below. This list of lenient cases included the crime of rape, of which only 35% resulted in a jail or prison sentence. Some of these rape sentences were as low as one month.

I read each of the news articles that Christopher Dalton posted in detail. Most of these stories told "both sides" of the issue. They presented the prosecutor's outrage at lenient sentences and the defense attorney's plea for even more leniency. Even though I acknowledge the fog of war that occurs whenever a complicated court case is summarized by the media, I found it difficult to understand the rationale behind some of these sentencing decisions. Even if the evidence was weak and a plea deal was necessary to secure a conviction, the downward departures can defy all logic.

Consider the case of 19-year-old Eli Binnion, who forced a 14-year-old girl onto a bed and raped her. She told her parents and the police what happened. Binnion was convicted of rape and sentenced to 180 days in jail followed by probation. This six-month sentence was outrageous to the victim and her family (47). Her father said:

> What is the judge telling our children when we try to teach our children to go to the police?… Let the police handle everything. Let the law do it. That's what their job is, and then this happens. You get a slap on the wrist. No victim is gonna want to come forward and go through all of the struggles and all of the ordeal that they have to go through, just for the person to get out and walk free… Be careful what judges you elect.

Binnion went to jail where he broke another prisoner's jaw, and he was given a 3-year sentence for that assault. He received a six-times greater punishment for a fight in jail than he received for raping a child. The victim's father said, "I promised my daughter justice, and obviously I was wrong because the court system is not gonna give it to her."

Another case of extraordinary leniency took place in Utah. A 22-year-old man pled guilty to raping a 12-year-old girl in an attempt to get her pregnant. He was caught in the act and left a series of text messages stating his intentions, so his guilty plea was not necessary for a conviction. The judge, Richard Mrazik, sentenced the guilty man to 20 days in jail, to be served on 10 consecutive weekends. He said "The crime is very serious. The effects of the crime are very, very serious, but I cannot consider those facts as aggravating factors." He believed that 10 weekends in jail would send a signal to the community that "the criminal justice system takes it very seriously." The prosecutor condemned this sentence as disturbing and dangerous, and she was right. The man who was given this reprieve was re-arrested within a year, this time for attempting to have a sexual relationship with a 16-year-old. A former prosecutor in the county offered his thoughts on the case. He said "Judges are good people, they certainly do their best, but they're not perfect and they can't do everything right the first time, every time… Do we fill up the prisons with all sex offenders? And leave everybody else out? Sex offense is a terrible crime, but it's not the only terrible crime that's out there." By this logic, sex offenders are set free in order to make room for non-sex offenders in prison (48, 49).

These outlier stories are not the products of a moral panic or conspiratorial imaginations. These lenient court decisions do occur in real life, and people are watching. Cherry-picked? Yes. Nonexistent? No. Maybe the Epstein and DuPont sweetheart deals are not unique. Concerned citizens are compiling a list of grievances against "the system" and they are not swayed by arguments that the system punishes sex offenders too harshly. They have long lists of cases that defy those claims. Conservative media outlets like the Daily Mail have been drawing attention to thousands of cases where people convicted for sex offenses in California serve less than one year (50). As long as stories like this happen, they will spread across the internet and contribute to the public's growing dissatisfaction with the legal system, and it might sway elections.

If you are quick to dismiss Christopher Dalton as a religious, right-wing extremist indulging in a moral panic, you should know that he is certainly not alone in his quest to understand why judges show leniency for sex crimes. Lili Loofbourow is a journalist who writes for Slate magazine. She published an insightful article called *Why Society Goes Easy on Rapists* in the wake of the Brock Turner controversy (51). She also lists cases where judicial decisions defy common sense and hint at a conspiracy of patriarchal racism and classism. She wrote:

> The result is a criminal justice system that shows an unexamined bias toward accused sexual predators—particularly those from the dominant race and class—by protecting them in advance from punishments that (in practice) very rarely materialize. And this is a hypercorrection that occurs again and again even though false claims remain statistically minuscule, and even though less than 1% of rapes result in a conviction.

Racial discrimination is a common topic when people argue about lenient sentences (I often see people comment "I wonder what his sentence would have been if the rapist was Black"). Is this an issue that liberals and conservatives can agree on? Should judges be removed from the bench if they show excessive leniency to sex offenders for extra-legal reasons? Well, don't be too hasty. There are some people who believe that punishing judges for lenient decisions will contribute to the "culture of mass incarceration" that has resulted in America's position as the number one incarcerator on planet earth. They label people who demand harsh penalties for rape as "carceral feminists" who engage in their own moral panic against sex abusers (52).

A notable example of justice system reform can be found in John Pfaff's book *Locked In: True Causes of Mass Incarceration* (20). Pfaff is a professor of law at Fordham University, and his book argues that America must reduce our level of incarceration. Pfaff's plan for violent offenders is to "rethink" how we treat them, which he explains is to "think about how to punish less" (p. 185). He writes that if we want to "scale back on incarceration, we need to start cutting back on locking people up for violent crimes." He says real reform cannot happen if we only release people "who don't scare us." He identifies several "low-level violent crimes" that he thinks can be targeted for non-custodial legal responses. These include kidnapping, statutory rape, sex abuse, lewd sexual acts with a child, forced sodomy, simple assault, aggravated assault of a police officer, blackmail/extortion, hit and run with injury, child abuse, and "other" violent crimes. He calls these "low-level" violent crimes "low-hanging fruit" that can be targeted for legislative reforms. "Given that these non-index crimes are often less severe than index offenses, they may provide more possibilities for diversion and sentence cutting" (p. 200).

Pfaff acknowledges that this will be difficult because 60% of those non-index violent crimes are sex offenses, and he laments that "current attitudes" toward sex offenders "boil down to unrelenting harshness, even in this time of reform." He fails to offer any ideas on what an appropriate punishment for kidnapping, lewd sexual acts with a child, and forced sodomy *should* be, but he does say that true reform starts with reframing how we "talk" about violent offenders. A change in language may set in motion a cultural and attitudinal change in America that will help the public think of these people as human beings and not dangerous criminals.

Although he optimistically presents this argument several times in his work, Pfaff doesn't actually think that changing words will shape the public's attitudes. He writes in his conclusion that a campaign designed to educate the public to think correctly on these issues would be "the worst sort of useless idealism." He has no faith in the public or his ability to persuade them. "Direct education will likely fail- that's the whole problem with a low-information, high-salience electorate: that it doesn't really pay attention to non-salient outcomes" (p. 232). In Pfaff's mind, the problem with the justice system in a democracy is ignorant and emotional voters. So he wants to cut the public out of the conversation entirely. He wants to "shield those in charge of the criminal justice system from a low-information, high-salience electorate" by appointing judges and prosecutors instead of electing them. That way if an offender is given a lenient sentence and commits a heinous act of violence in the community, the people will not be able to remove the judges or prosecutors from office. The reformers will be saved and they can continue to engage in their experiments in leniency. I suppose the admission here is that these polices will not be popular, so the solution is to restrict democratic interference and force the public to tolerate their dissatisfaction with the new justice system.

Pfaff asserts that America's courtrooms treat sex crimes with "unrelenting harshness." He does not offer a suggestion for an appropriate punishment. According to the National Crime Victimization Survey in 2019, there were an estimated 459,310 rape crimes perpetrated against victims who were older than 12 years of age (53). According to the FBI Uniform Crime Report in 2019, there were 66,363 rape incidents reported to law enforcement agencies, and arrests were made in 20,501 of these cases (54). Using BJS prison sentencing data, we can see that 22,583 individuals were sent to prison for rape in 2019 (55). So less than 5% of the rapes that were reported in the NCVS resulted in a state prison sentence, and only 1/3rd of those reported to the police resulted in a state prison sentence. Considering that the NCVS does not include victims younger than 12, we are only incarcerating a very small number of people who commit rape crimes in the United States. With the median time served in state prisons 4.2 years for rape, how can we possibly consider this to be an example of "unrelenting harshness" against sex crimes? (56). Many people would consider this to be outrageous leniency. Unless reformers like Pfaff are willing to assert what an appropriate legal response for rape should be, we cannot assess whether we are over- or under-punishing anyone according to their subjective standard. The "injustice gap" between lenient punishments for sex crimes compared to less serious offenses might explain the public's frustration with court decisions, but it is unlikely modifications to current sentencing practices will fully satisfy everyone (57, 58). The country is not just comprised of citizens who want tougher punishments. There are a large number of concerned citizens who believe our current punishments are too harsh. They are working to release sex offenders from prison and to reform the laws to reduce stigmatization. There is a major tug-of-war going on. We can never make both sides happy. Maybe we don't need to rewrite the laws, we just need to handle egregious cases better. We could address the uncertainty of punishment in these cases so people know what to expect. Does anyone disagree with that recommendation? Can anyone advocate for *greater* uncertainty in court practices?

It might also be useful to alter the perception of unfairness by toning down the use of incarceration for less serious crimes, so that sex offender sentences achieve the severity ranking they deserve, if not the exact sentence people desire. A 2016 report by James Austin, Lauren-Brooke Eisen, and their colleagues argued for rational and fair sentencing that did not eliminate incarceration entirely, but used it sparingly for truly dangerous offenders (59). The only time incarceration should be used is when the crime was serious, harmed a victim substantially, was committed with intent, and the offender posed a continuing threat. They estimate that 576,000 people (39% of the prison population) are incarcerated without a public safety justification. Around 364,000 prisoners (25% of the population) would benefit much more from treatment and community supervision, as an incarceration sentence will probably increase their chances of committing future crimes. Of these,

66,0000 prisoners were incarcerated only for possessing drugs. The majority of all prisoners (79%) suffer from mental illness or substance use disorders that can be treated with humane care outside of a prison and potentially resolve their risk for criminal behavior better than a prison sentence ever could. The authors recommend taking important steps to reduce the use of prison sentences for these people, but they *did not include sex crimes* in their recommendations. They suggest that serious crimes (e.g. robbery, murder, aggravated assault, and manslaughter) ought to be eligible for prison sentences, and they add to this list rape, lewd acts with a child, "serious" statutory rape (but not "other" statutory rape). If their recommendations were adopted nation-wide, the injustice gap between drug and sex crimes would be addressed, and the source of much hatred of "the system" might be abated. This reform agenda is ambitious, but not impossible, and it acknowledges that sex crimes are among those in the highest rank ordering of severity. Child sex abuse must always be considered a justice system priority. Again, to quote Andrew Vachss, "Humanity's worst crime exists in no statute book: What could the lawmakers call the theft of childhood?" (60).

It is important not to become fixated on drug and sex crime comparisons. We should look at common crimes and see how the justice system responds. Consider the recent case of Kenyon Menifeld in Michigan (61). Menifeld was a basketball coach and he didn't like the referee's decision during the game. Menifeld punched the referee and caused injuries that required hospitalization. Menifeld asked the judge for leniency because he was enrolled in an anger management program and he already served 15 months in jail waiting on the hearing. The judge sentenced him to 6 years in prison. Is 6 years in prison appropriate for punching someone, but sex offenders can be given passes? Judges are straying from the rank ordering of severity that society expects to see, and their credibility is at stake. By recalibrating the scales of punishments, we might be able to reduce perceived injustices even if we don't increase sex offender punishments at all. If the people can't get a perfectly satisfactory punishment for everyone, maybe they will settle for *relative fairness*.

Provoking Justice

Some people might question the term "vigilante" when it is applied to some of the cases I have described in this book. Prisoner-on-prisoner violence can occur for a variety of reasons that have nothing to do with avenging sex crimes. Those who seek personal revenge against their abusers might not share the true vigilante motive of inspiring societal change. But Patrick Drum is a true vigilante. He took the law into his own hands and killed two men so he could draw attention to lenient sentencing. The distinction between "revenge" and "justice" are clearly demarcated in his mind. Revenge is an impulsive desire. Justice is a goal.

I spoke with Lexi Pandell, the freelance journalist who wrote the article "The Vigilante of Clallam County" (12). She told me about how she was looking for a story to investigate for her graduate school thesis. She heard about Patrick's case and wrote a letter to him. When his trial was over he responded to Pandell and shared his entire life story. They talked on the phone. She even went to Clallam County and saw the home where one of the victims was murdered (the bullet holes were visible in the walls). She drove around the county with police, and even traveled with a convicted sex offender who was filming a documentary about sex offender stigmatization. She immersed herself completely in the story and wrote what I consider to be the best journalistic depiction of a complicated vigilante case I have read in all my research.

Pandell understood why Patrick felt as strongly as he did. The abuse he suffered as a child and the chaotic, nightmarish world that child sex abuse victims endure inspire strong emotions in any caring person. She does not endorse violence, but she understands Patrick's position. Deep down inside, he wanted to be a protector. That is a noble quality, but it was twisted into felonious conduct. Pandell's main takeaway was that Patrick was a lonely man. Completely isolated even when he was living freely in the community. His childhood experiences had separated him from humanity to a certain degree. When I told her he had been spending long periods of time in administrative segregation in prison she felt sorry for him. Pandell's father was a defense attorney. She knew how horrible and traumatic our prison system can be. This lonely man was cut off from the world physically and emotionally, yet again.

After he killed his first target, Patrick Drum left a note beside his bullet-ridden body. It told a story about the protective virtues of scorpions:

When I was younger I was at a pet shop. I saw these three scorpions in an aquarium. One was a pregnant female and two were males. As I approached, the female tucked into a protective ball. The two males got in front of her in full battle ready posture; tails up, claws out and open. Being young and curious I played a game and used my hands to circle the aquarium in different directions. Each male picked a hand and moved with it, never leaving her side and staying between the hand and her. This spirit always impressed me.

Patrick signed this note with his real name, along with a candy-coated dead scorpion. He knew he would not escape "justice." It was a calculated decision to mark the scene of his crime with bold accountability. He told Lexi Pandell that he believed his experiences gave him firsthand empathy for the issue, "but my actions were not about me… They were about my community. I suffered many failures and my overall view of things was one of hopelessness. I took that hopelessness and in turn threw myself away to a purpose. I gave myself to something bigger than myself."

No Easy Way Out

By "A Son of Solitude"

And yet… I can never forget. These memories which haunt me, continue on, even as I move on through stages of life which should be reserved for peaceful reflection and simple joys. In the evenings when I prepare myself for sleep, I must lay only on my left side, facing the wall. This is the position I developed as a child to reduce the access to my genitals, knowing my adoptive father would be coming, every night, off of this late evening shift. Under the guise of "prayer" he would silently molest my brother and I. The sexual aspect of the abuse was something new he developed as his complete control over us grew. We had already suffered years of being beaten with boards, sticks, belts, and any other implement that was at hand. Should a boy's first orgasm, the first time he ejaculates, be at the hands of his stepfather? Certainly not. What sort of curse does this place on a child who simply wants to be loved? My brother and I learned very well, early on, that the world was a place of contradiction and confusion. Raised in a household wrapped in the poisonous foil of religiosity. This deviant behavior, and all of the ramifications of its impact, the reverberations, still being felt today, had a dark, protected place to manifest. Even when their church community became aware of his deviancy, they rallied around him, covered his behavior, I specifically recall being hauled in before the church tribunal, being instructed to "forgive" him, for he had repented. I recall the day I was driven to tell my mother about the molestation, as she was already eminently aware of the beatings. They had gone on for years… She didn't believe me. My brother was mad as hell. She forced all of us to sit on barstools in the kitchen and made me present my accusations to my stepdad's face. I was terrified and he gave me a look that notified me that I would pay for this later, which I did.

I couldn't sleep last night until I rolled up on my left side. I pull my knees up slightly and I still wake up for even the slightest sound. I'm still on guard, on point. My stepfather is now dead. In a twist of fate, sometime after I was arrested for assaulting pedophiles, I received the first communication I had from my mother in many, many years. A letter stating that he was dead, and that he had left a note for me, did I want it? I never wrote her back, this woman who stayed with him to the exclusion of her own children's safety and sanity, all the way up until his death. She has never apologized or explained why she stood by his side, this abusive molester, all those years. Now reaching out to see if I'd like to hear something he had to choke forth out of his bitter mouth- no thank you. I only wish I was there to watch his body expire. To see his last breath. I would've loved to see him die. That was the only thing he could have ever given to me, which would have mattered, him leaving this earth, and yet, I still cannot sleep well at night. This man cursed me, sentenced me to sorrow and suffering. Driven by his own twisted sense of entitlement and power, flush with a deviant viral load, some sickness originating in darkness. I hope he suffered and was scared while dying, he deserved so much worse…

The memories and pain were given purpose through service for others. I began to track down pedophiles and assault them. I am not a violent man by nature. It took some doing on my part to conjure the energy required to face these men. But I found the well, the long-buried reserve in this place of pain, built and filled to the brim and overflowing from my own years of traumatic abuse. The religiosity of my youth carried over into my adult life. I was driven and guided by spirits, an intuition that was uncanny that led me to many places which were impossible in their timing and need. I found myself knocking on the front door of a house, at the exact moment when an uncle and his two young nieces were nearly blackout drunk, both the girls, 10- or 11-years-old, already in their underwear. When he swung the door open, I could see them giggling and laughing on the bed behind him, the smell of alcohol and cigarettes thick in the air. Every location I visited, I went "face-up" no mask, no gun. I wanted them to see my face. I wasn't hiding from anyone. I simply grabbed him by the collar and yanked him up out of his own home. I instructed the girls to lock the door and call their mom. I dragged him stumbling, behind me, down the stairs and out into a darkened park nearby. I sat him down on a bench, and with my gloved hand, I proceeded to open-hand slap him, back and forth, back and forth. "Have you sobered up yet, you piece of shit?" It took some time, and his face was beet red, small amount of blood running from his nose, but he was sober now. As I took my time slapping him vigorously, I was lecturing him about abusing kids and how I would not tolerate that behavior here, in Alaska, in my state. He was sobbing and crying now, trying to be repentant. Initially, it disgusted me because I know exactly how these deviants operate. They are highly manipulative and can rarely ever be trusted. Deceit and deception being the cornerstone of their disease. And yet, as he cried and sobbed, he began to describe to me the depth of his brokenness. He said that for as long as he could remember he was sexually attracted to kids. After so many years he said he now hated his aspect of himself. He had no control over his impulses, and after being released to a housing center his room had a window that overlooked the daycare facility right across the street. He said most days he would not allow himself to leave his room, he would just masturbate inside while watching the youngsters play in the playground. He asked me to just kill him, he didn't want to live with his "burden" any longer. He began begging me just to end this whole thing for him. He kept pushing me, pushing me… pushing me…

I changed the lightbulb in my lamp today. The whitish-purplish light of the old bulb reminded me constantly of the light from the little aquarium my brother and I kept a few fish in as kids. This spectrum of light constantly presented an outline of the shadow of my stepfather, as he would enter our room, night after night, to "pray" and satisfy his own diseased lust. The glow of that bulb made me feel nauseated and I couldn't even eat properly with its pall case over my cell. It's a little better now. I've constructed a lamp box, with file folders, and have taped it to the wall. Kinda looks like old-timey candlelight. I feel better. My brother and I couldn't look at each other the same.

My brother and I couldn't look at each other the same. We had always been close with him tormenting me as older brothers will, but with the introduction of the sexual abuse, even our naturally close bond was compromised. We spoke of nothing. Did he do to my brother the same things he did to me? Was I supposed to fight? Wasn't our life centered around the church and a god? Weren't their rules about this? There was no one to ask, and psychologically, we were being banished to separate island, miles apart, no way to escape, no easy way out.

I heard him enter our bedroom. I clenched my knees together and rolled over on my left side. It sickens me to remember, wishing that my brother would go first this time. What a poisonous memory to carry. I'm a good person. I wouldn't wish what happened to us on anyone. He roughly reached his hand under my blanket, jerking my underwear down. I could feel him grabbing, grabbing, trying to get his adult-sized hand around my child-sized penis. Breathing his hot, dank breath in my face, muttering some prayers, or strikingly excited words, while moving his hand up and down on my penis. I am sick to my stomach now as I was sickened then. It's as if no time has passed. I held my eyes clenched shut, and wished to be anywhere in that room, with that monster. My young body responded to stimulation exactly how it should. This response would confuse and torture me for years later in life. This was a curse, and it took away whatever my life could have been, should have been, before I even had a chance.

So, I tracked down pedophiles and registered sex offenders. I knocked on doors and slapped the shit out of grown men just like my stepfather. Would you like to tell me all of the reasons why my actions are inappropriate? Would you like to attempt to convince me that I, of all people, am acting out of line, to take up this cause, and act on behalf of others? Please do, I'm listening…

Actually, I stopped listening some time ago, listening to haughty words from power-damaged people. I've tuned out the entire world, and I only give a quarter to that which moves me. I am a simple man, and I am still healing myself. These wounds run deep. Some will simply stop bleeding. Others will never get well. So again, I ask you, why are my actions inappropriate? I didn't want to let my younger self down. I had to be there. No one did it for me, but I promise you, I was privileged, gifted with the opportunity to be there for others… worth it. After all, there is no easy way out, and I'm not scared anymore, for I am a Son of Solitude.

References

1. Inskeep, S. (2006, June 1). Too short for jail. *NPR Morning Edition*. https://www.npr.org/templates/story/story.php?storyId=5443969
2. *Tampa Bay Times*. (1991, July 20). Fixing the glitch in the rape law. https://www.tampabay.com/archive/1991/07/20/fixing-the-glitch-in-the-rape-law/
3. Higgins, L. (2014, Feb. 13). Child molester says victim to blame for injuries. *The Journal News*. https://www.usatoday.com/story/news/2014/02/13/child-molester-blames-victim-for-injuries/5471353/
4. Fantz, A. (2016, June 7). Outrage over 6-month sentence for Brock Turner in Stanford rape case. *CNN*. https://www.cnn.com/2016/06/06/us/sexual-assault-brock-turner-stanford/index.html
5. Lagoe, A. J. (2017, Feb. 2). KARE 11 investigates: Minnesota's secret sex offenders. *KARE 11*. https://www.kare11.com/article/news/investigations/kare-11-investigates-minnesotas-secret-sex-offenders/89-396022916
6. Puente, K. (2017, Feb. 1). Orange County judge sentence for sex assault of 3-year-old too lenient, appeals court says. *The Orange County Register*. https://www.ocregister.com/2017/02/01/orange-county-judges-sentence-for-sex-assault-of-3-year-old-too-lenient-appeals-court-says/
7. Associated Press. (2006, May 26). Attorney general to appeal child sex abuse sentence. *ChinaDaily*. https://web.archive.org/web/20071209032249/http://www.chinadaily.com.cn/world/2006-05/26/content_601294.htm
8. True Crime Daily. (2017, Dec. 13). Mark Berrios reveals details in Olen Lee Hepler murder from behind bars. https://truecrimedaily.com/2017/12/13/mark-berrios-reveals-details-in-olen-lee-hepler-murder-from-behind-bars/
9. Jenae, J. (2017, July 10). Jax man receives new sentence for killing accused pedophile. *First Coast News*. https://www.firstcoastnews.com/article/news/jax-man-receives-new-sentence-for-killing-accused-pedophile/77-455074689
10. Inglis, T. (2019, June 21). Sara Kruzan, imprisoned for killing her sex trafficker, is free and fighting back. *Street Roots*. https://www.streetroots.org/news/2019/06/21/sara-kruzan-imprisoned-killing-her-sex-trafficker-free-and-fighting-back
11. Martyna, B. (2013, April 2). Deal reached in Sara Kruzan's case. *National Center for Youth Law*. https://youthlaw.org/publication/deal-reached-in-sara-kruzans-case/
12. Pandell, L. (2013, Dec. 4). The vigilante of Clallam County. *The Atlantic*. https://www.theatlantic.com/national/archive/2013/12/the-vigilante-of-clallam-county/281968/
13. VigilanteJustice.Net. http://www.vigilantejustice.net/patrick-drum-sex-offender-vigilante-washington-state/
14. Dutton, W. S. (1942). *Du pont, one hundred and forty years*. New York, NY: Charles Scribner's Sons.
15. Forbes. (2020, Dec. 16). America's richest families (2020): Du Pont family. https://www.forbes.com/profile/du-pont/?sh=42fa0448253b
16. Cam, D. (2019). How a Du Pont heir avoided jail time for a heinous crime. *Forbes Dark Capital*. https://www.forbes.com/sites/denizcam/2019/06/14/how-a-du-pont-heir-avoided-jail-time-for-a-heinous-crime/?sh=5275cd7829db
17. Alexander, M. (2012). *The new jim crow: Mass incarceration in the age of colorblindness*. Revised edition. New York, NY: New Press. Chicago.
18. Vachss, A. (2001). *Dead and gone*. New York, NY: Vintage Crime/Black Lizard.
19. Leon, C. S. (2012). *Sex fiends, perverts, and pedophiles: Understanding sex crime policy in America*. New York, NY: New York University Press.
20. Pfaff, J. (2017). *Locked in: The true causes of mass incarceration*. New York, NY: New York Basic Books.
21. Vachss, A. (2016). *Sex crimes: Then and now*. New York, NY: Pay What It Costs Publishing, LLC.
22. Loeks, M. (2008, Nov. 4). Vote to oust judge impacts legal community. https://starherald.com/news/local/vote-to-oust-judge-impacts-legal-community/article_daced775-600e-5284-a258-d77435e58330.html
23. Dixon, J. (1995). The organizational context of criminal sentencing. *American Journal of Sociology*, *100*(5), 1157–1198.

24. Flemming, R. B., Nardulli, P. F., & Eisenstein, J. (1992). *The craft of justice: Politics and work in criminal court communities.* Philadelphia: University of Pennsylvania Press.
25. Ulmer, J. T. (1995). The organization and consequences of social pasts in criminal courts. *Sociological Quarterly, 36*(3), 587–605.
26. Ulmer, J. T., & Kramer, J. H. (1996). Court communities under sentencing guidelines: Dilemmas of formal rationality and sentencing disparity. *Criminology, 34*(3), 383–408.
27. Steffensmeier, D., Ulmer, J., & Kramer, J. (1998). The interaction of race, gender, and age in criminal sentencing: The punishment cost of being young, black, and male. *Criminology, 36*(4), 763–798.
28. Peterson, R. D., & Hagan, J. (1984). Changing conceptions of race: Toward and account of anomalous findings of sentencing research. *American Sociological Review, 49*(1), 56–70.
29. Wilson, J. Q. (1977). The political feasibility of punishment. In J. B. Cederblom and W. L. Blizek, (eds.), *Justice and punishment.* Ballinger Publishing Co., Cambridge, MA.
30. Ulmer, J. T. (2012). Recent developments and new directions in sentencing research. *Justice Quarterly, 29*, 1–40.
31. Ulmer, J. T., & Johnson, B. (2004). Sentencing in context: A multilevel analysis. *Criminology, 42*(1), 137–178.
32. Johnson, B. D. (2006). The multilevel context of criminal sentencing: Integrating judge and county level influences. *Criminology, 44*, 259–98.
33. D'Alessio, S. J., & Stolzenberg, L. (1997). The effect of available capacity on jail incarceration: An empirical test of Parkinson's law. *Journal of Criminal Justice, 25*(4), 279–288.
34. Cochran, J. C., Toman, E. L., Shields, R. T., & Mears, D. P. (2021). A uniquely punitive turn? Sex offenders and the persistence of punitive sanctioning. *Journal of Research in Crime and Delinquency, 58*(1), 74–118. https://doi.org/10.1177/0022427820941172.
35. Hessick, C. B. (2021). *Punishment without trial: Why plea bargaining is a bad deal.* New York, NY: Harry N. Abrams.
36. Johnston, C. (2016, May 14). Lux captured: The simple error that brought down the world's worst hurtcore paedophile. *The Sydney Morning Herald.* https://www.smh.com.au/national/lux-captured-the-simple-error-that-brought-down-the-worlds-worst-hurtcore-paedophile-20160513-goum54.html
37. Safi, M. (2016, July, 12). *The takeover: How police ended up running a paedophile site. The Guardian.* https://www.theguardian.com/society/2016/jul/13/shining-a-light-on-the-dark-web-how-the-police-ended-up-running-a-paedophile-site
38. *Kennedy v. Louisiana, 554 U.S. 407 (2008).*
39. Sommerlad, J. (2021, Dec. 30). What was Jeffrey Epstein's 'Lolita Express'? *Independent.* https://www.independent.co.uk/news/world/americas/crime/lolita-express-jeffrey-epstein-b1966996.html
40. Jones, J. M. (2021, July 14). In U.S., Black confidence in police recovers from 2020 low. *Gallup.* https://news.gallup.com/poll/352304/black-confidence-police-recovers-2020-low.aspx
41. Stein, R. (2007). Causes of popular dissatisfaction with the administration of justice in the twenty-first century. *Hamilton Law Review, 30, 499.*
42. Vachss, A. (2016). *Sex crimes: Then and now.* New York, NY: Pay What It Costs Publishing, LLC.
43. Black, D. (1983). Crime as social control. *American Sociological Review, 48*(1), 34–45. https://doi.org/10.2307/2095143
44. Dimsdale, T. J. (1866|2003). *The vigilantes of Montana.* Guileford, CT: Morris Book Publishing, LLC.
45. *The Washington Post.* (1984, Dec. 28) On New York's subway.
46. Makubetse, S., & Louw, A. (2011). *Violent justice: Vigilantism and the State's response.* Pretoria: Institute for Security Studies.
47. Hecker, I. (2021, June 9). Father calls out judge for giving daughter's rapist a light sentence. *Fox 11.* https://www.foxla.com/news/father-calls-out-judge-for-giving-daughters-rapist-a-light-sentence.amp?taid=60c434cda6698a0001b87c52&utm_campaign=trueanthem&utm_medium=trueanthem&utm_source=twitter&__twitter_impression=true
48. Cramer, A. (2021, June 17). Summit County attorney decries 'leniency' in sentence for child sex abuser. *Park Record.* https://www.parkrecord.com/news/summit-county/summit-county-attorney-decries-leniency-in-sentence-for-child-sex-abuser/

49. McGurk, N. (2022, May 20). Convicted rapist re-offends less than 1 year after sentencing, police say. *ABC4 Utah.* https://www.abc4.com/news/local-news/convicted-rapist-re-offends-less-than-1-year-after-sentencing-police-say/amp/

50. Boswell, J. (2022, Nov. 28). 'It's frightening for society.' Thousands of convicted pedophiles in California are being released from prison in less than a year for horrific acts, including rape, sodomy and sexual abuse of kids under 14, DailyMail.com investigation reveals. *Daily Mail.* https://www.dailymail.co.uk/news/article-11453859/Thousands-convicted-pedophiles-California-getting-year-prison-time.html

51. Loofbourow, L. (2019, May 30). Why society goes easy on rapists. *Slate.* https://slate.com/news-and-politics/2019/05/sexual-assault-rape-sympathy-no-prison.html

52. Phillips, N. D., & Chagnon, N. (2020). "Six months is a joke": Carceral feminism and Penal populism in the wake of the Stanford sexual assault case. *Feminist Criminology, 15*(1), 47–69.

53. U.S. Department of Justice, Bureau of Justice Statistics. (2020). *Criminal victimization, 2019.* Table 1.

54. Federal Bureau of Investigation (2019). *Crime data explorer* Washington, D.C. https://cde.ucr.cjis.gov/LATEST/webapp/#/pages/explorer/crime/crime-trend

55. U.S. Department of Justice, Bureau of Justice Statistics. (2021). *National Corrections Reporting Program, 1991–2019.* Washington, D.C.

56. U.S. Department of Justice, Bureau of Justice Statistics. (2016). *Time served in state prison, 2016.* Table 1.

57. Sekhonyane, M., & Louw, A. (2011). *Violent justice: Vigilantism and the State's response.* Pretoria: Institute for Security Studies.

58. Exline, J. J., Worthington, E. L., Hill, P., & McCullough., M. E. (2003). Forgiveness and justice: A research agenda for social and personality psychology. *Personality and Social Psychology Review, 7*(4), 337–348.

59. Austin, D., Eisen, L.-B., Cullen, J., & Frank, J. (2016). *How many americans are unnecessarily incarcerated?* New York, NY: Brennan Center for Justice, Twenty Years.

60. Vachss, A. (2016). *Another chance to get it right.* Milwaukie, OR: Dark Horse Books.

61. Reagle, M. (2022, Jan. 12). Michigan man who punched local referee sentenced to six years in prison. *WPSD Local 6.*

5
MORAL MURDER

In the previous chapter, I addressed the belief that punishment for sex crimes is too lenient. I showed that "lenient" is a subjective term, and our best estimates are corrupted by the multitude of factors that influence a judge's decisions. Ultimately, I concluded that even if punishments were more severe, they would not reach the threshold that satisfies most vigilantes: the desire to inflict the death penalty on child sex abusers.

This leaves us with an interesting question. Are vigilantes committing their crimes for the sake of justice? Perhaps they are merely displacing their personal frustrations on sex offenders or they want their crimes to imbue them with some degree of heroism among their supporters. Anything is possible, but my assessment of the men I interviewed for this book is that they genuinely believe that killing sex offenders is a *moral* action. They do not believe that shooting, stabbing, strangling, or bludgeoning a child sex abuser is immoral. They know it is a crime, but they were willing to sacrifice their freedom to do something they thought was morally necessary. Some of them couldn't sleep at night with the guilt they felt because they hadn't *yet* killed a child sex abuser. They are not alone in this belief. They often have thousands of supporters who praise them as heroes who did a good deed for society. How can murder be considered morally justified?

This is a deep subject that has been carefully considered in *Shadow Vigilantes* written by Paul and Sarah Robinson. This book explores the subject of vigilantism as a form of self-help crime control spurred by a lack of faith in the system (1, 2). These authors explain in detail each of the elements that contribute to various vigilante acts. They itemized the factors that help determine whether or not a vigilante crime was illegal, and yet still "moral." I have used these factors to help assess two completely different cases of vigilante violence, and I have shared the list with other vigilantes who have helped me to unpack each rule one at a time. I believe this is the first time that the Robinsons' rules have actually been presented to real-life vigilantes in order to hear their thoughts on this characterization of their behaviors.

Ten Rules for Vigilantes

Paul Robinson and Sarah Robinson identified several high-profile and influential cases of absurd government incompetence and describe how private citizens took the law into their own hands

DOI: 10.4324/9781003393849-6

to finish the job that the police and courts were unable to achieve. The authors do not deny that some vigilante justice is socially acceptable even if it is illegal, but they identify "ten rules" that vigilantes must follow in order to potentially be considered "moral vigilantes." These rules are listed here with the permission of the authors:

1 **Don't act unless there is a serious failure of justice.**

 Any vigilante action will be disruptive. It cannot justify itself unless it produces more benefits than the disruption itself costs.

2 **Don't cause more harm than is necessary and just, and avoid injury to innocent bystanders.**

 Part of doing justice means recognizing that society has an interest in minimalizing damage to all, even unlawful aggressors.

3 **Don't act unless there is no lawful way to solve the problem.**

 The law often allows citizens to use force in defense of unlawful aggression against themselves, others, or property. Individuals should stay strictly within the requirements of this legally authorized force if that response will provide the needed protection against lawlessness.

4 **Don't act alone.**

 The vigilante is one who acts for the community, not himself; vengeance is not vigilance. If a person's conduct is to reflect community views, that fact must be demonstrated by having the vigilante action be group action.

5 **Before acting, be sure of the facts, and take full account of all relevant mitigations and excuses.**

 Prospective vigilantes must understand that they are in a credibility contest with the official criminal justice system. To win the battle for hearts and minds, the vigilantes must actually do justice better than the system is doing it, not worse. Doing justice requires taking account of the mitigating or excusing factors in a case, not just the aggravating factors.

6 **Show restraint and temperance, not arrogance or vindictiveness.**

 The goal is to be responsible, even if the government is not. A vigilante is not the wrath of God, but just a means of shaming the government into doing what it ought to do: namely, take justice seriously. Vigilantes should not just adhere to the moral vigilante rules, but make it clear that they are adhering.

7 **Warn the government that it is in breach of its social contract with its citizens, and give it an opportunity to fix the problem, unless it is clear that such a warning would be useless.**

 Ideally, this means laying out the specifics of the system's failures of justice, as well as giving the authorities the time and opportunity to make things right. It is always preferable to have the official criminal justice system do justice, no matter how well respected a vigilance community may be.

8 **Publicly report afterward what you have done and why.**

Failure to publicly take responsibility for your vigilante actions simply adds to the problem of perceived lawlessness. The community cannot judge the justness and reasonableness of a vigilance committee's actions unless it is given the details of what has been done and why.

9 **Respect the full society's norms of what is condemnable conduct.**

Do not act in pursuit of justice for an offense unless it is clear that the larger society sees the offender's conduct as truly condemnable. Taking action based upon a peculiar view of the world lacks the basis for moral vigilante action.

10 **If it becomes clear that the problem cannot be fixed through vigilante action, then withdraw from further action.**

If it becomes clear that the criminal justice system literally cannot be changed no matter how dramatic and thoughtful the vigilante action, then further action toward that goal cannot achieve its purpose. Vigilante action must be a temporary and transitional state that moves the system to fix itself, not a permanent substitute for official conduct.

As a law professor at Penn Law, Robinson's ten rules serve as a guideline for how juries might weigh the appropriateness of a vigilante's behavior under certain situations. I should remind any readers who have found their own limitations to Paul and Sarah Robinson's rules that their list was designed to encapsulate *all* forms of vigilantism, not just targeting child sex abusers. When rule five says "take into account all mitigating factors and excuses" the authors clearly did not mean to imply that child sex abusers could have an excuse. This language might only apply to other less serious crimes.

Let us examine two cases of vigilante justice against child sex abusers to demonstrate how one might be considered "morally justified" according to these rules, while the other is clearly immoral using the same criteria. Although both are still illegal, the court might have considered these issues when choosing an appropriate punishment for the vigilante. Prosecutors, judges, and juries might be more likely to consider mitigating circumstances in a case when the vigilante acted with moral intentions.

Clark Fredericks' Search for Meaning

The first example is the homicide committed by Clark Fredericks in New Jersey in 2012 (3). Clark was a happy and outgoing child who was involved in sports and the Boy Scouts. His Boy Scout leader was Dennis Pegg, whose full-time job was a lieutenant in the county sheriff's department. Pegg became a close family friend and would take Clark on special trips (4). The grooming process moved from keeping secrets to sharing alcohol, to touching, and finally to rape that was so horrific it caused him to question the existence of God. During one violent rape incident, Clark was crying in pain and Pegg's dog was barking in confusion. Pegg forced Clark to watch as he beat the dog to death in front of the terrified child, sending the message that Clark would suffer the same fate if he talked.

At age 12, Clark changed. He kept the secret, but it was festering inside him. He lost interest in sports and school and started using drugs. One day a rumor spread that Dennis Pegg was sexually assaulting detainees in the county jail. Clark's father asked him if Pegg had ever been inappropriate with him. Clark said no. A lie he regretted. He had every symptom of PTSD but drowned them in alcohol. As an adult he became a gambling addict and accumulated insurmountable debts.

One day in 2011, Clark saw Pegg enter a deli with a small boy. The child was calling Pegg by a nickname; the same nickname that Clark had been forced to call Pegg when he was the child's age. Clark ran out of the deli, quit his job, and fell into a deep depression. On television, he saw news coverage of Jerry Sandusky and his lawyers preparing for their legal defense on 52 charges of child molestation. Clark had a feeling that justice would not be served in that case, and in his own case Pegg would never be appropriately punished because the statute of limitations had expired. Clark drank an excessive amount of alcohol, snorted cocaine, and went to Pegg's house with a knife. A supportive friend drove him there and watched what happened next (5, 6).

Clark saw his abuser sitting in a chair watching TV. Clark burst inside and brutally stabbed Pegg to death, leaving a trail of blood all across the living room. He went home and got blackout drunk. When he woke up, his house was surrounded by police. He went outside and hoped they would shoot him on the spot, but they took him into custody. He was charged with murder. In court he said: (7)

> For all those years after Dennis Pegg raped me he was still untouchable because of who he was and what he represented. He was a respected law enforcement officer. He was an expert with guns. He was a Boy Scout leader. No one would ever believe my word over his. In November of 2011 Jerry Sandusky from Penn State was arrested. This also caused me to flash back to my abuse at the hands of Dennis Pegg … my reaction to seeing Sandusky get out of that car with his lawyer was that Dennis Pegg would never be held accountable ….
>
> I started stabbing Dennis. I said over and over to him "How does it feel raping little kids now?" I also repaid … repeated "It's not so fun raping little kids now is it?" At the end I slit his throat.

The courtroom applauded after hearing this testimony. The prosecutor and the judge believed that Clark had several mitigating circumstances relating to his childhood abuse, and that his PTSD and substance use were evidence that he should not be convicted of murder. Instead, he was able to plead guilty to passion/provocation manslaughter and served four and a half years in prison. The Sussex County Assistant Prosecutor Gregory Mueller said "We feel it is a fair and appropriate result given all the circumstances."

Clark used his time in prison to read widely. He discovered Viktor Frankl's *Man's Search for Meaning* and found a quote that changed his perspective: "When we are no longer able to change a situation, we are challenged to change ourselves." Clark decided to do something important with his life. He served his four and a half years without incident and then became an advocate for legal reform. The previous statute of limitations in New Jersey said that children who were victims of sexual abuse had to make a report before they turned 20 years old in order for charges to be pressed, but the average age for people to talk about their abuse was ages 48–52. Clearly the law created a safe haven for child rapists in New Jersey. They knew if they could keep a traumatized child silent until they were past the reporting age they could get away with their crimes. Clark had a mission in life: fix the loophole.

He started writing and speaking. He traveled to schools and universities. He even spoke at the local jail he had been held in after his crime. Eventually he went to the state legislature. A man who was "eating prison food surrounded by insane inmates" was eating with state senators. His message was powerful and the people were ready for a change. A bill was passed to give victims of child sex abuse until the age of 55 to come forward with their allegations. Clark – the vigilante – became a force for change. Now other people in his "hopeless" position can seek legal solutions to their injustice.

In considering this case we can apply Paul and Sarah Robinson's ten rules of moral vigilantism. The first is, "don't act unless there is a serious failure of justice." In Clark's case he never came forward to report Pegg's crimes, so the justice system didn't have a chance to fail him. However, the expectation that a child abuse victim will make a report before age 20 is completely out of touch with the complexity of PTSD and the fear and shame that victims experience. The statute of limitations made it impossible for Pegg to be held accountable, and by the time Clark was ready to get help, it was too late.

The second rule is "don't cause more harm than is necessary and just, and avoid injury to innocent bystanders." Was a brutal death by stabbing more harm than was necessary? The court did punish Clark with prison time so they clearly understood that murder is not the *least severe* action Clark could have taken, but they also took into account his drug and alcohol use prior to the crime as well as the passion/provocation circumstances that weakened his ability to choose a lesser form of justice. Clark's rage was directed only toward Pegg. No innocent bystanders were harmed. This is another rule where Clark's case is somewhat morally justified.

The third rule is "don't act unless there is no lawful way to solve the problem." As mentioned previously, Clark believed there was no way that he could have achieved justice because of the statute of limitations and the lack of physical evidence in the intervening decades since his assault occurred. He knew it happened and he knew it would be impossible to get justice through the legal system as it existed in 2012.

The fourth rule is "Don't act alone." Vigilantism is meant to help the community, not merely get revenge. If other people support the vigilante then there is some level of consensus. This makes the act less secretive and personal. On the night of the murder Clark was accompanied by a friend. Clark told his secret to this friend shortly before the murder. His friend was supportive and was willing to help Clark get justice. Together they conceived the murder and went to Pegg's home. Technically this meets the Robinsons' criteria for moral vigilantism because the friend was an outsider who did not have a personal grudge against Pegg. He was an external observer who supported Clark's decision. Mob justice is usually an undesirable element of vigilante justice, but this rule appears to be met in Clark's case.

The fifth rule is "Before acting, be sure of the facts, and take full account of all relevant mitigations and excuses." The Robinsons' did not create this list of rules with child sex abuse in mind specifically, so this may seem out of place here. Clark would have personally known that Pegg was guilty, even if outsiders didn't, and there are not any convincing mitigating circumstances or excuses that an adult could have to justify raping a child, so this rule is also not a problem for Clark, but it may be for outsiders who appraise the morality of his behavior.

The sixth rule is "Show restraint and temperance, not arrogance or vindictiveness." Brutally stabbing a man to death, cutting his throat, and repeating "how does it feel raping little kids now?" are not signs of restraint and temperance, but again, the inebriating substances and passion/provocation excuses somewhat mitigate the application of this rule. One clear piece of evidence, in this case, is the lack of arrogance or vindictiveness. Clark was clearly in emotional distress after the murder and choked back tears throughout his court proceedings. He did not consider himself a hero or even encourage other people to follow in his footsteps. He gives speeches encouraging people *not* to take the law into their own hands. The evidence here is mixed, but on the surface, it is possible that Clark showed as much restraint as he was able to. He did not glorify his actions.

The seventh rule is "warn the government that it is in breach of its social contract with its citizens, and give it an opportunity to fix the problem, unless it is clear that such a warning would be useless." This is good advice. If the police could have arrested Pegg and charged him with a crime, then Clark should never have taken the law into his own hands. If the system has failed to appropriately respond to a crime, then citizens in a democracy can remind them of their failure and seek redress through non-violent means. In Clark's case, the statute of limitations made it impossible to fix his immediate sense of injustice. The likelihood of making sweeping legislative changes must have seemed remote if not impossible. This does not *justify* his violent actions, but in the mind of a prosecutor, judge, or jury member it may be considered a mark in his favor. This might not apply to other types of crimes where you could "blame the victim" for not making a report sooner (e.g., if your car is stolen ten years ago), but given the traumatic nature of child sex abuse crimes some blame can be attributed to the misguided statute of limitations rules in New Jersey at the time.

The eighth rule is "publicly report afterward what you have done and why." Clark did not have an opportunity to report his crimes because he went home and passed out from alcohol consumption before the police arrived. He also did not immediately confess to the police because it is always good advice to consult an attorney. However, he did make a complete confession down to the description of how he sharpened his hunting knife before he left, clearly indicating premeditation and potentially hurting his own case for the passion/provocation charge.

The ninth rule is "respect the full society's norms of what is condemnable conduct." This rule is meant to apply in cases where the crime being avenged is actually immoral. Clearly, raping a child is seen as immoral by all but a few individuals in our society, so Clark was justified in thinking that Pegg was in the wrong.

The tenth rule is "if it becomes clear that the problem cannot be fixed through vigilante action, then withdraw from further action." This is the one rule that Clark would have a difficult time convincing his case to reasonable and rational people. Murderous revenge is a solution to this single case of injustice only insofar as it incapacitated Dennis Pegg from harming others ever again, and it satisfied some community-level need for retribution. It did not solve the problem of irrational statute of limitation laws. That problem was fixed through the democratic process. There was a unanimous vote by the New Jersey legislature to revise the laws and permit the justice system to prosecute child abusers. Murder was the catalyst for this reform by bringing attention to the problem, but murder cannot fix the problem.

If Clark had gone to trial rather than pleading guilty he might have faced a jury of twelve random citizens. They would have compared his story to the crime scene photos. They would have seen the smears of blood across the floor and the mangled body of Dennis Pegg. Maybe they would have considered some of the ten rules listed above to help them decide if this "vigilante" was morally justified in his behavior. They might not have a checklist with clear definitions, but intuitively they would have wondered how they would have acted in the same position. Perhaps they would have come to the same conclusion as the prosecutor in this case. Justice is not served by giving Clark life in prison, but neither is it served by letting him off scot-free. Is four and a half years a suitable punishment for a semi-moral vigilante? If you are struggling to fit this case into a typical murder conviction category, you understand now how difficult it is to apply rules to complex real-life situations. Clark's passion-provocation homicide was considered close enough to "moral" behavior that the prosecutor gave him a lenient deal.

The Habitual Line-Stepper

Let's contrast Clark Frederick's case to that of Jeremy Moody. Jeremy was the son of a preacher, but he spent most of his life as an atheist. He finished high school in a small town and graduated from a private religious college. He claims that he was never abused as a child.

Jeremy got involved in the Skinhead movement through music. He was friends with the members of famous bands and was invited to write songs for *Definite Hate*'s "Welcome to the South" album. He attended hate-rock and Rock Against Communism festivals. He always considered himself to be a true believer in the Skinhead cause, and he was dismissive of "peckerwoods" and drug abusers in the movement. He despised the wolves in sheep's clothing, like August Kreis, who professed to be moral leaders of the White race, while they were sexually abusing White children (a "child molesting piece of shit" according to Jeremy). He always thought that the White race needed to clean their own house before they could fight against outside forces.

The first thing you notice about Jeremy is the tattoo across his neck reading "SKINHEAD." He has nothing to hide. He is proud of his White-supremacist beliefs. He has written two books about his view of the world (8, 9). One is titled *Yesterday, Today, and Forever* and it catalogs his views on the skinhead movement, racial differences, Jewish power and influence around the world, the 9/11 terrorist attacks, homosexuality, and communism. He is an extremist in every sense of the term. He also wrote a special sub-chapter on the appropriate punishment for child sex abusers that is reproduced here with the permission of the author:

CHILD ABUSER (I SEEK YOUR DEATH)

by Jeremy Moody

> Child abuse casts a shadow the length of a lifetime.
> *Herbert Ward*

I know that this topic does not flow with the overall theme of this book, but it's a topic that I'm passionate about just the same. Child abuse and molestation takes place every day, inside unsuspecting homes, from the most unsuspecting families. It's one of the most appalling offenses that can ever be done to a child .... In most cases when a person is arrested for child abuse, he or she will serve two to three months in a penitentiary. The sentence is taken into consideration by the defendants past run-ins with the law, or felonies, or on parole. But in most cases, the individual will spend a month or two, get out on good behavior, and that is that.

The people at www.childmolestationvictims.com report that, *roughly 33% of girls and 14% of boys are molested before the age of 18, according to the U.S. Justice Department. Nearly two-third of all sexual assaults reported involved minors and roughly one-third involved children under the age of 12. In most cases, however, child molestation goes unreported. Estimates are that only 35% of sexual abuse is reported. Kids can be frightened or embarrassed and many times do not say anything.* If a person is convicted of child molestation, it's a bit different than child abusers. Conviction of child molestation carries a slightly higher penalty, but not by much. Again, the sentences vary depending on the persons rap sheet, whether he or she is a felon, out on parole, probation, etc. The average stay in prison for them is one to three years. If the convict is a 'model convict' which most child molesters generally are (because they take out their physical and sexual frustrations on children and not adults), they will serve 60%–80% of their time. That means, a three-year conviction will turn into about 18 months, and the convict will have to put their photo on a silly website and register as Sex Offenders.

Child abuse or neglect, when a person gets charged for this heinous crime, he or she will usually serve no more than 20 months in prison, along with their mug shot, placed on a website. That may sound like a lot to most people, but it's easy to change an appearance or to use an alias. These people are chameleons to begin with, they are your neighbors, your relatives, your friends, they are everywhere, and they blend in with any environment. These disgusting people almost always have a history of abuse in their families. Psychologists have reported that nine out of ten child abusers and molesters were abused or neglected when they were children. To me it sounds like liberal doctors are looking for a cheap excuse or explanation. Once society finds these perverts guilty of abuse or molestation, they put them in prison, where most prisons make them undergo classes and psychological examinations to try their very best to rehabilitate the convicts. It's possible to rehabilitate a drunk, drug addict or thief. It is not possible to rehabilitate a child molester. If a man has a strong sexual attraction to redheads with green eyes, no amount of counseling will stop his attraction. Pedophiles are sexually attracted to children, that is their sexual preference, whether they admit it or not. Their sexual attraction will always be there, nothing can erase it from their mind, their first sexual attack on a child will always be in their minds, and that memory will always serve as a fantasy. In prison, they will continue to fantasize about this disgusting, unforgivable, heinous crime, and will learn how to be sleeker the next time they do it.

How do we rehabilitate a sex offender? They cannot be fixed, what they can do, is convince the Psychologists that they are "fixed" and they are safe to be released into society. The only cure for child abusers and molesters is to have every member of their immediate family killed. These nefarious crimes and people should not be allowed to procreate. By destroying their immediate family member, you purify the bloodline. This is the only way to ensure that they (the pervert or family) cannot ever hurt a child again. Liberals will think that these statements are immature and that I must be empty-headed. How many people consider the children that were abused or molested? What about the mental destruction that this child has to live with for the rest of their lives? How these children will find it difficult to ever trust another person. How these children may possibly never be able to have children of their own, because they were raped so severe, that it damaged them permanently? I don't think my suggestion is immature, I think it's the only answer, and if you don't agree, then you too should be destroyed.

This manifesto is quite clear in its justification for murder. In some ways it is not much different from the commonly held beliefs of a large portion of American society, and his references to lenient sentences echo those made by Patrick Drum in the previous chapter. But the final paragraph is where Jeremy Moody departs from all of the other vigilantes I have interviewed. He takes a strong *eugenicist* stance against crime because he believes that pedophilia is incurable and heritable. He wants to kill child sex abusers who have identified themselves through their criminal actions, and he wants to eradicate their bloodline by killing their relatives.

Who will wage this war on pedophiles? Jeremy says: "Anyone that is willing to shed their blood or risk their lives for something far greater than they are, makes them definitively a *hero*." Strong words. But anyone can be a tough guy on paper. The internet is full of keyboard warriors who write about all the things they *would* do in a certain situation, but how many actually do it? Jeremy wanted to make sure nobody could call him a keyboard warrior.

Jeremy and his wife Christine Moody looked up the names of child sex abusers on a sex offender registry in South Carolina. They found a suitable target: Charles Parker, a two-time offender who lived in a convenient location (remote from neighbors, but near a highway). The next Sunday, after church, Jeremy and Christine went to the man's engine repair shop and pretended that their car needed service. Parker's wife, Gretchen, opened the door. Jeremy didn't plan for anyone else to be home, but he was not going to abort his mission. He pointed a gun at Parker and his wife. Parker said he didn't have any money, and Jeremy said "I am not here for your money. I'm here to kill you because you're a child molester." He shot Parker in the stomach and watched him collapse on the sofa. Then he turned his gun on Gretchen and shot her above her collarbone.

At this point, Jeremy helped Christine cut Gretchen's throat with a knife. Jeremy coldly describes this gruesome action with the following words "I was surprised by how easy the blade pierced her skin. I pressed with all my strength & bodyweight until I felt resistance. What I felt was her spine." Gretchen died. Jeremy has no remorse for this "innocent bystander" because he considered her to be guilty by association with Charles Parker.

Jeremy believes he was too hasty during this homicide. He didn't expect Parker to have a wife at home, and he didn't know that a security camera recorded solid proof of his crime. Jeremy and Christine were both quickly arrested and given life sentences.

Jeremy has recounted all of these events in his second book *The Jewish Scourge: Answers for the American People,* a racist polemic he wrote in prison and published on Lulu.com, a private publishing company (the title reflects his belief that Jews have "subverted" American society and they are the ones allowing sex offenders to escape punishment). His account of the crime differs somewhat from the news reports and court testimony that is published online, but they are not entirely incompatible (most reports claim that his wife Christine was enthusiastic in stabbing Gretchen to death without Jeremy's help, but Jeremy says she just got in the way and he killed Gretchen himself). Jeremy concluded this book with the following observations:

As a result of my heroism, I was sentenced to serve three consecutive life sentences plus 65 additional years for two counts of kidnapping & a violation of probation & using a weapon during the altercation & commission of a violent crime. It's unfortunate that I lost my family & friends. I have no regrets. If the government cared more about children, then I wouldn't have had to do it.

Imagine a government that did not tolerate rape, sexual or physical abuse against anyone; man or child. If a sexual abuser is found, then we destroy him & purge his bloodline.

Sexual attraction to children is no different than how a healthy man might be attracted to blonds with large bosoms. There's no medicine or counseling that could erase those attractions.

Therefore, if a man is sexually attracted to children, then you can't run the risk of castration; instead, you have to destroy him completely. I personally would like to see the offenders' immediate family also liquidated; the mother, father, brothers, & sisters. Purify the bloodline. I think pedophilia is a genetic disorder; why take unnecessary risks? Kill them all.

Liberals have convinced mainstream society that these people can be cured. Society believes that with counseling, medicine, Electrical Shock Therapy (E.S.T.), & whatever other hippie bullshit might exist, they could be healed. We need a revolution. We need strong white men & women that are unafraid. We need people that are willing to make selfless sacrifices for the greater good.

We can only survive as a race & nation through gritty, rugged ruthlessness. A revolution is what we need. Who will be the spark to ignite it?

Rapists & pedophiles are the scum of all society, but they are not the threat to our American values. I contend that there has never been a more sinister, vile, & corrupt people than the Jews.

For now, I will leave it up to the reader to assess how Jeremy Moody's White-supremacist beliefs have influenced his views on vigilantism against child sex abusers, but we will return to this subject in Chapter Nine when we discuss ideologies and cultural factors. Even though he accuses a worldwide Jewish conspiracy for most of the problems in the world, he did not choose to physically attack any Jewish groups or racial minorities. He chose to wage his ideological war against a child sex abuser and his wife, who were both White. The purpose of sharing Jeremy's words at this point in the book is to assess whether his motives and behaviors meet Paul and Sarah Robinson's criteria for "moral vigilantism" as we did with the case of Clark Fredericks.

Jeremy killed a child sex abuser, but he has virtually nothing in common with Clark Fredericks. For one thing, Jeremy was never abused as a child (contrary to media reports and his defense attorney's pleas for leniency). The man Jeremy killed was a stranger he found on the South Carolina sex offender registry. Also, Clark was drunk when he killed his abuser, and Jeremy was sober and of sound mind when he killed Parker. Another difference between Clark and Jeremy is that Jeremy has no remorse for his actions. Jeremy's only regret is that he didn't kill *more* pedophiles before the police arrested him. He considers his actions as a public service and his punishment as a heroic self-sacrifice. His motives were different from Clark Fredericks in almost every way, and this highlights the problem of lumping all "vigilantes" into the same category. Seeking personal revenge and seeking a bloody revolution are not comparable motives.

In applying Paul and Sarah Robinson's ten rules of moral vigilantism we can systematically assess the situation piece-by-piece. The first rule is, "don't act unless there is a serious failure of justice." In Jeremy's mind the entire sentencing scheme of the US justice system is flawed and he wanted to impose the death penalty against a child rapist, but also against his wife who never abused a child. He defines this as a serious failure of justice, but it does not meet the spirit of the rule as portrayed by Paul and Sarah Robinson. Another problem is that Charles Parker *had* been punished by the justice system and he was abiding by the rules of his community supervision. He was registered as a sex offender and was living at the address he reported to the government. The "serious failure of justice" is one that Jeremy Moody interprets differently than the vast majority of people in society. Therefore this rule is violated.

The second rule is "don't cause more harm than is necessary and just, and avoid injury to innocent bystanders." Jeremy's decision to surprise and kill Charles Parker was already an excessive degree of harm that was meant to punish a man who had already been sanctioned by the criminal justice system and was not actively engaged in any criminal behavior. After his arrest, Jeremy spoke with some of Charles Parker's victims who said he was still actively abusing children, but this is hearsay and Jeremy did not have this information at the time of his crime. Jeremy would disagree with what is "necessary and just," but this rule is clearly violated in the murder of Parker's wife who meets every definition of an innocent bystander. Jeremy also learned that

Gretchen had been convicted of child abuse crimes in the past, so he believes she also got what she deserved, but he didn't know anything about her at the time of the crime. He merely assumed she was worthy of death because of her association with Parker.

The third rule is "don't act unless there is no lawful way to solve the problem." Jeremy could have done almost anything else to demonstrate his dissatisfaction with the justice system without resorting to homicide. In retrospect, he acknowledges that he could have boycotted Parker's business or warned his neighbors, but he did not think that would solve the problem as effectively as a bullet. He has explained how he searched for sex offenders in his community and looked at the locations of their homes on Google Maps. He did this to find those in secluded areas with nearby access to a highway. He did not target Parker for any personal reasons or any specific belief that his case was especially problematic when compared to the list of all sex offenders, or that this case needed rectifying due to a specific problem with the legal proceedings. Jeremy has described how the decision to act was somewhat spontaneous. He and his wife were talking about "murdering someone together" and that "baby-rapists" were "good candidates." There is no indication that he even considered any lawful ways to solve the problem before deciding to kill. He would disdain those milquetoast "solutions."

The fourth rule is "Don't act alone." Jeremy was assisted in these murders by his wife, so we can say that he technically meets the criteria for this rule, but her involvement does not necessarily increase the degree of morality involved because she was a full partner in the scheme and did not act as a check or balance to his actions. This rule is difficult to assess in any case.

The fifth rule is "Before acting, be sure of the facts, and take full account of all relevant mitigations and excuses." There is no evidence that Jeremy considered any mitigating circumstances for Charles Parker's crimes and he would have probably laughed if you made such a suggestion. He did not consider that Parker's previous punishments or compliance with the sex offender registry (the "silly website") were signs that Parker was not an egregious case of injustice requiring desperate action. He also did not care about Gretchen Parker because she was considered guilty by association in his mind. Therefore, Jeremy could never have met the criteria for this rule of moral vigilantism.

The sixth rule is "Show restraint and temperance, not arrogance or vindictiveness." Not only did Jeremy show no restraint during his crimes but he also flaunted his vindictiveness ever since. His book glorifies his own actions as heroic and morally superior to all other responses. After being sentenced to life in prison his wife Christine Moody said to news reporters "Killing that pedophile was the best day of my life" and Jeremy said, given the chance, he'd kill more. You might even say that the most sensational aspect of their case is their complete, unwavering belief in the righteousness of their actions. However, according to Paul and Sarah Robinson, this violates one of the ten rules of moral vigilantism because it implies that the action was not a last resort to secure immediate justice, but rather a sign that the vigilantes were reveling in the action itself for its own sake. I have had many discussions with Jeremy while writing this book, and I am most confused by this aspect of his case. I bluntly asked him if this crime was an attempt to change the world or to be seen as a hero, and he denied that selfish motive. He said he wanted to take advantage of the spotlight after his arrest to draw attention to the case. He would have been more than happy to avoid detection and continue killing child sex abusers from the shadows. For him, this crime was a syllogistic necessity. "*If* I truly believe child molesters deserve to die *then* I must kill them, otherwise I am a hypocrite." It was adherence to his principles. The gloating was not planned.

The seventh rule is "warn the government that it is in breach of its social contract with its citizens, and give it an opportunity to fix the problem, unless it is clear that such a warning would be useless." Jeremy Moody did not attempt to fix the situation through any legal means or warn anyone about his actions. His first book was published before the murder, so he did give some fair warning, but he must have known it was unlikely that his book would result in any systematic legal reform even if it were read by any government officials. He probably assumed that warning the government would be useless, so in his mind, he did meet the criteria for this rule.

The eighth rule is "publicly report afterward what you have done and why." Jeremy did not report his crime because he intended on killing several other people on the sex offender registry. He did not have a chance to make a public report until after the legal proceedings were concluded and he explained the rationale for his actions.

The ninth rule is "respect the full society's norms of what is condemnable conduct." Jeremy's manifestos on race, racism, politics, and history are all outside the boundaries of what most people in our society consider to be "pro-social." His books have been described in the news media as "racist screeds" and hate speech. His SKINHEAD neck tattoo has been described as a clear warning sign that his entire worldview is anathema to a twenty-first century, racially diverse, and safe society. His views on killing child sex abusers have some support among people who are frustrated with the justice system, but how many of them would have supported killing Gretchen Parker simply because she was married to a sex offender? It is safe to say (and he might agree) that he has *no respect at all* for the full society's norms. He wants to replace those norms with his own beliefs.

The tenth rule is "if it becomes clear that the problem cannot be fixed through vigilante action, then withdraw from further action." This one is debatable because Jeremy did believe that his actions could spur a longer war on sex offenders that would eventually result in a more perfect society and a fair justice system. However, this is another rule for moral vigilantism that most people would decide Jeremy violated, and he would disagree because of his particular worldview. If the vigilante act is meant to be ongoing rather than a temporary nudge for the official justice system to correct its policies, then it is considered immoral.

I asked Jeremy what he thought the best definition of a vigilante was. He said "A vigilante is someone who is hyper-sensitive to moral injustices." From his point of view, the crime of child sexual abuse is so immoral that any crime committed against the perpetrator is justified. He has an override switch for his morality. He is "hyper-sensitive" to moral injustices. He believes that the average "20 months" in prison for sex crimes is egregious, so he decided to fix the government's mistake by issuing the death penalty.

In summation, Jeremy Moody's actions in killing Charles and Gretchen Parker can only unambiguously meet one of the ten rules for moral vigilantism (not acting alone), and even this one fails to address the true spirit of that rule because the second-party is supposed to be a check on the vigilante's personal biases, not a full co-conspirator. We do not even need to compare his case to that of Clark Fredericks in any more detail because they are obviously different scenarios even if they both resulted in homicide (and I am sure Clark Fredericks would be insulted to have his case of passion/provocation compared to Jeremy Moody's ideologically driven actions). But that is the difficulty of lumping all acts of vigilantism together: they might all be illegal, but the court processes them differently based on their consideration of hundreds of variables and unique case characteristics that are ignored in media headlines. Jeremy's case is considered immoral by almost every measurable standard, and this is reflected in the court's decision to give him three life sentences plus 65 years for his crimes. We will discuss Jeremy's ideology and its overlap with vigilante themes later in this book, but for now, we can bookmark his case as an extreme example notable for its planning, boldness, and lack of remorse. It is a case that would challenge even the most hard-core vigilante supporters to question their beliefs.

Expert Appraisal

I asked Patrick Drum what he thought of Paul and Sarah Robinson's ten rules of moral vigilantism. He had some interesting insights. As a man who planned his own assaults on sex offender registrants, he would rank closer to Jeremy Moody's style of vigilantism than Clark Fredericks personal revenge crime, but his social and political beliefs differ from Jeremy Moody substantially. Patrick believes that six of the ten rules were important for assessing vigilante actions (rules 1, 2, 5, 6, 8, and 9), but he believed that the Robinsons failed to understand the true scope of the issues on the other elements of vigilantism. For example, rule number three says that a vigilante should not act if there is any *legal* way to respond to the abuser's crimes. Patrick said that is a fundamental reason why vigilantism occurs. There *is* a legal response, but the courts choose not to enforce the laws. "There was a lawful way to punish 'The DuPont Heir', there was a lawful way to hold accountable the police officers that violently beat Rodney King on camera, there was a lawful way to penalize the captain of the Exxon Valdez which had alcohol on his breath when he caused a major oil spill. A lawful means to solve the problem and it actually being used are two separate issues."

Patrick disagreed with rule number four (don't act alone). While the sentiment is acceptable in rule number nine (to adhere to society's norms of acceptable conduct), in a practical sense, having co-conspirators is not wise. Patrick suggested the book *Snitch Culture* by Jim Redden that explores how Americans are encouraged and incentivized to report all acts of disobedience so they can be rewarded (10). A vigilante who acts with a partner is doomed to betrayal, perhaps before they can even commit their first crime. Patrick sees that as a wasted opportunity. A wise vigilante acts alone, or they might not be able to act at all.

Patrick does not entirely trust a consensus either. The Robinson's rules were derived from the full history of vigilantism in America, going back to the original Vigilance Committees of the wild west. Patrick warns that "in the same way there is wisdom in the crowd, there is ignorance in the crowd. It is a (faction of a) group that thinks it is righteous to burn the building of small business owners when they are angry at the justice system; that thinks it is in support of White supremacy to cite facts on the number of unarmed White people that are also killed by police every year. On the other side of that subject, it was groups of good Christians that would lynch innocent Black people because it was agreed it was best for the community. It was a neighborhood conscience group of men who shot a Black man (Arbery) for simply jogging down the street. A group is not necessarily an effective check and balance system."

For rule number seven (warn the government of its breach of the social contract), Patrick says this is unrealistic. When Washington state has a backlog of cases and hasn't even analyzed the DNA from rape kits, they clearly do not prioritize sex offenders in their justice system. Warning them that they should take their job more seriously is a waste of effort. They simply don't care enough to hold rapists accountable, even when the proof is right there in the evidence room. "The government is not entitled to any notice of negligence here, it is obvious," Patrick writes.

Patrick agrees that vigilantes should take responsibility for their actions, and that they should be wary of a slippery slope. He does not believe mob justice is good for society. He just wants the justice system to do its job so the people don't have to. He does not want to comprise the rule of law entirely, he only wanted to provoke the government into responsible action. "There is a dangerous grey area between a vigilante action for the betterment of society and a terrorist action on behalf of what a person/group views as best for society. This is admittedly a slippery slope." I believe this particular insight is useful in identifying Patrick as a "true vigilante" in contrast to many other cases explored in this book that involved circumstantial actions, volatile emotions, and short-term planning. Patrick saw his behavior as a single step toward the goal of a permanent, *governmental* solution.

His criticism of rule number ten is further evidence of his long-term planning and motivations. He does not believe that "withdrawing from further action" when long-term change is impossible is good advice. He knows that vigilantism won't change anything directly (it might even result in major setbacks if sex offender registries were abolished or the government doubles down on their leniency toward sex offenders), but he believes that a vigilante crime can draw attention. People will notice the problem, argue about it, and some people will use legal, democratic methods to make long-term changes. Patrick might be interested to learn about how Clark Fredericks' brutal murder of Dennis Pegg drew attention to the need for a legislative extension of the statute of limitations for reporting child sex abuse crimes in New Jersey. In a purely practical sense (not necessarily a moral sense), Patrick might be right about this one.

I believe that Paul and Sarah Robinson's criteria for measuring moral vigilantism gives us a well-planned system for assessing important case characteristics. It certainly helps us separate the chaff from the wheat when parsing out motives and subsequent actions. However, deciding whether something is "moral" or not is always going to come down to a value judgment. Some readers might be asking how *any* murder can be considered moral by any standard. Despite these concerns, the ten rules for moral vigilantism might help us to understand how prosecutors frame their decisions and how juries might process each case differently. These rules disaggregate the case characteristics that are subconsciously processed when we make our gut-instinct determinations in such matters, and they help us think systematically about these issues.

Diverging Opinions

Some readers may be asking why this book on vigilantes and child sex abusers is even necessary. Aren't the answers obvious to everyone? Some of you are shaking your head in dismay that vigilantes would *ever* take the law into their own hands. All lives are precious and should be protected. After all, two wrongs don't make a right, and violence is never the answer. Vigilantism is always immoral and if it is permitted it will lead to a resurgence of lynch mobs and mass executions. We stand upon a precipice, and should we even consider the vigilante point of view we will go down a dark path toward anarchy and hatred. If this paragraph describes your thoughts, then you might be surprised to learn that other people disagree with you on such a deeply felt issue.

Another group of people are also asking why this book needs to be written, but for different reasons. How could our society stoop to such a level of moral degradation that we even have to justify killing a "pedo" in the first place? Death is merciful compared to the poetic tortures they would inflict if they had the opportunity. They believe vigilantes are heroes who performed "community service." The message should be clear. Touching a child in a sexual manner is unjustifiable, and if it is permitted then disgusting pedophiles will kidnap and rape *your* children next. If the government won't secure justice, the people will!

There are still others (the silent centrists) who think that child sexual abuse is always wrong *and* that vigilante violence is always wrong. They condemn both and have reasons for doing so, but they don't speak up very often.

This deep well of disagreement is an interesting dilemma. What seems obvious to you would be the subject of great divisiveness and hatred if you shared your beliefs outside of your trusted social circle. Anyone who shows the slightest hesitation or lack of enthusiasm in voicing their support of these moral perspectives would be considered a suspicious person at best, and an evil supporter of unjustifiable crimes at worst. Why do these differences exist in our society? What effects do these differences have on our justice system in a democracy that is so susceptible to public opinion? Can people be persuaded to change their minds?

Jonathan Haidt is a social psychologist and author of several books on moral psychology, politics, and happiness. His book *The Righteous Mind: Why Good People are Divided by Politics and Religion* describes the possible origins of human morality and its impact on group polarization (11). This book and his conceptualization of moral "taste buds" may be useful in understanding why people have strong divergent opinions on how child sex abusers should be treated and whether vigilantes are heroes or villains.

Haidt proposes a model containing five primary moral values. People differ in terms of how they prioritize these values when deciding whether a scenario is moral or immoral. You may think that everyone shares a core moral value system and they can simply learn to change their opinions with enough information or pressure. You will be disappointed. All of your books and lectures will fail to have their intended moralizing effect, because, Haidt says, our intuitions are like an elephant and you are simply a rider. Sometimes the elephant goes in a direction you don't want it to travel in. People have a gut reaction to their situations and they search for arguments and evidence that help them convince others they are right. They don't find evidence first and change their feelings accordingly. People aren't that rational. I have listed and described the five original moral values below.

1 *Care/Harm* – Most humans have an innate sense of caring and an appreciation for harm that others endure. If you rank very highly on sensitivity to caring and nurturing situations (such as seeing children happy and safe) and you react very strongly to situations where others are threatened with harm (such as seeing a baby seal attacked by a hunter) you have an abundance of empathy.
2 *Fairness/Cheating* – When human beings cooperate in a system or a group you expect that everyone should have a fair chance to succeed. If you saw someone had an unfair advantage or they cheated in order to have more success than others you would be upset. The more strongly you feel about this part of the human experience the more you care about equity and equality.
3 *Loyalty/Betrayal* – Human beings often form groups that stand in opposition to other groups. If you feel strongly that people should be loyal to their own group and not easily betray them, then you would have a foundation of loyalty that influences your moral outlook.
4 *Authority/Subversion* – Some people value leadership and hierarchy in their social groups more than others. They want to support obedience, respect, and submission to authority within the group, and they do not approve of disobedience, disrespect, or rebellion.
5 *Sanctity/Degradation* – Some people feel profound levels of disgust when they perceive that a situation violates a principle of sanctity, even if the violation does not actually harm anyone. Those who react most strongly to degrading situations may be experiencing an intense visceral disgust reaction.

The differences between liberals and conservatives are important. Haidt and his colleagues have conducted research on how people react to questions that push the boundaries of each moral value. He found that conservatives who are high on sanctity/degradation values are truly disgusted by the idea of someone having sex with a dead, frozen chicken carcass. Liberals, however, hesitate to condemn this behavior until they learn more about the situation to ensure that no chicken was harmed in the process, reflecting their somewhat greater emphasis on the care/harm value. In fact, Haidt and his colleagues have found that liberals have a narrow but strong sense of morality that is derived from the care/harm and fairness/cheating values. They care about loyalty, authority, and sanctity to a certain extent, but they feel so strongly about those two priority values that they have a hard time understanding conservative points of view. They are often under the impression that conservatives are evil and selfish because they don't care about empathy or equality *at all*. This is not true though.

Conservatives have a broad base for their moral values. They rank nearly as high as liberals on measures of care/harm and fairness/cheating, but they care more about loyalty/betrayal, authority/subversion, and especially on measures of sanctity/degradation. Conservatives may have a trump card. An override switch that changes the influence of the other values. That is *disgust*. If someone behaves in a way that violates the conservatives' sense of purity they would despise that person. Liberals tend not to understand the conservative overreaction to sanctity/degradation. Liberals are usually neophiles – open to new experiences. They will try more strange foods and sexual experiments than conservatives because they do not fear new things (neophobia) like conservatives. This openness to experience expands the type of people and behaviors that a liberal will feel empathy for, but the boundaries of sanctity/degradation can override a conservative's ability to empathize with people they consider "disgusting."

Based on these findings in the science of moral foundations, I wonder how these factors influence people's attitudes toward crime and punishment. Conservatives might have compassion for a criminal offender who met certain criteria, but they're not going to go out of their way to worry about the offender's feelings or emotions. They may be less empathetic than liberals in that regard. If a criminal offender commits a *disgusting* crime, then conservatives should lose their desire to empathize with them. They may not be able to understand how anyone ever could empathize with a child sex abuser. To my knowledge, no one has asked people to explain how they feel about child sexual abuse crimes after assessing their moral foundations, but it seems likely to me that people who are high on sanctity/degradation will be more likely to endorse severe punishments for the offender than people who rank low on measures of disgust.

Liberals may share this disgust to a certain extent, but based on Haidt's work it is possible that they will be more considerate of the harm done to the perpetrator by excessive punishments. In other words, they have enough compassion to go around. They feel sorry for the victim *and* the perpetrator, while conservative disgust leads to extreme emotions and the true vigilante spirit.

When a conservative opposes vigilantism it tends to be because of their opposition to "criminals" in general or undermining the rule of law (loyalty and authority values), but for liberals, there is something missing. Their compassion is selective. They empathize with a child sex abuser but cut off sympathy to the vigilante who lashes out at child sex abusers. I think this is due to the fairness/cheating value that emphasizes equality. They already distrust a judge and jury of twelve people to rule over someone's fate. Perhaps they see a vigilante as a "judge, jury, and executioner" rolled into one. They don't hate the vigilante, they hate fascism, and they equate vigilantism with yet another right-wing conspiracy to hurt others and impose moral values. Cases like Jeremy Moody (with SKINHEAD tattooed on his neck) serve to reinforce this belief.

A Preliminary Examination of Moral Foundations and Punitive Orientations

Susan Yamamoto and Evelyn Maeder designed a punishment orientation questionnaire that classifies people into groups depending on if they are permissive or prohibitive of punishments, and if they believe punishments should be utilitarian (have some effect on future behavior) or merely retributive (that punishments balance justice in and of themselves without an effect on others be-havior) (12). They ask people the degree to which they agree with statements like, "punishment is necessary because it restores the balance of justice" or "it is more important to keep innocents free from punishment than to ensure all guilty people are punished." Respondents are classified into one of four groups; 1) those who are permissive of utilitarian punishments, 2) permissive of re-tributive punishments, 3) prohibitive of utilitarian punishments, and 4) prohibitive of retributive punishments. Additionally, Dorota Wnuk, Jason Chapman, and Elizabeth Jeglic have designed a survey measuring people's attitudes toward sex offender treatment that can help us understand what policies are specifically endorsed for these types of crimes (13).

I have attempted to measure the relationship between moral foundations and punishment orientations using an online survey. I recruited respondents through Amazon Mechanical Turk (MTurk), an online marketplace for virtual tasks. I do not make any claims about the generalizability of this sample to the entire United States. There are clearly many flaws in using online recruitment software, but this is only meant to be a feasibility test for similar research in the future.

I received complete responses from 250 people, but some of the data was unusable. Two people were excluded because they did not appear to be answering the questions properly (they typed their location when asked their age). Another 44 (18%) were removed because they were "caught" by a question meant to determine if they were paying attention to their responses. After these cases were removed, none of the others showed any suspicious patterns that indicated improper answering methods. A total of 204 people were retained in the final analyses. Their average age was 37 (S.D. = 9.9, range = 51), 48% identified themselves as women, and 52% identified as men. The majority of respondents were White (87.3%), 6% were Asian, 3% were Black, and the remainder were Native American or any other race. None indicated having Hispanic or Latino ethnicity. The biggest disparity between this MTurk sample and a nationally representative sam-ple is that 88.7% of respondents had a college degree (Associates' or higher). Using a dichotomous measure, 69.6% of the sample were conservatives and 30.4% were liberals.

As Haidt predicted, self-described liberals scored higher on moral foundations measuring harm and fairness, and conservatives scored higher on measures of in-group loyalty, authority, and purity. The average scores on moral foundations for each group are displayed below. To answer the first research question ("Are conservatives more likely to be permissive retributivists than liberals?") I also graphed their mean scores on the punishment orientation questionnaire criteria. I found that conservatives did indeed have a greater mean score than liberals on the permissive utilitarian subscale of questions, and this was also evident in the permissive utilitar-ian scale. Liberals were slightly more likely to answer strong support for prohibitive retribution policies, but not more likely to answer strong support for prohibitive utilitarian policies. This implies that liberals and conservatives have some qualms about unrestricted punishments of offenders, but conservatives would be more likely to permit punishments for either retributive or utilitarian reasons.

Next, I wanted to see how liberals and conservatives compared specific questions relating to punishment. I chose questions that were most relevant to the topic of this book, but the full list of questions are available in the Appendix (Figures 5.1–5.4; Table D2).

We can see from these results that conservatives are, as predicted, more likely to endorse harsh punishments for sex offenders. They are also more likely to endorse retributive justifications for their beliefs, as can be seen in their agreement with the statement "it is more important to punish a guilty person because he deserves it than it is to punish him to benefit society." The greatest

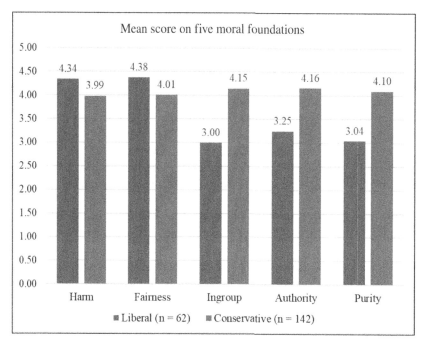

FIGURE 5.1   Mean score on five moral foundations

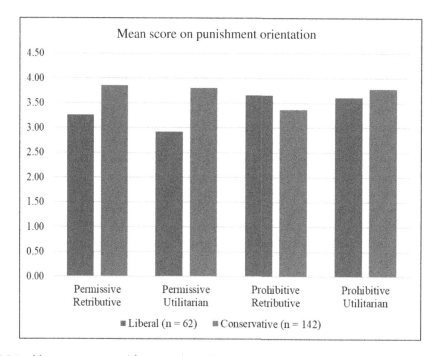

FIGURE 5.2   Mean score on punishment orientation

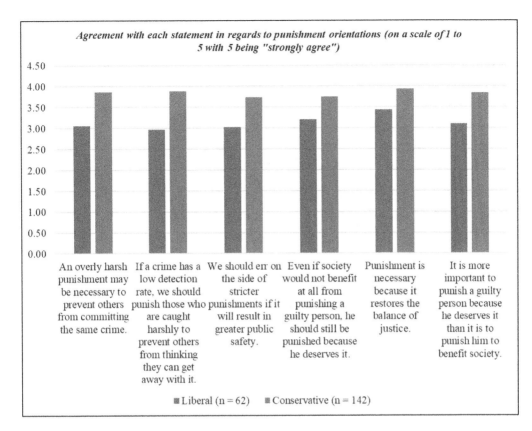

FIGURE 5.3   Agreement with each statement in regard to punishment orientations

substantive differences between liberals and conservatives are in regard to execution. Not all conservatives endorse the death penalty, but then again, not all liberals opposed the death penalty. The average scores show that conservatives are more likely to endorse the execution and life imprisonment of sex offenders than liberals.

I asked an additional question about the individual's opinion on vigilante violence. I asked, "Do you think it is *ever* okay for a private citizen to violently harm a sex offender for revenge?" This is deliberately vague. I did not have the resources to ask my survey respondents to read detailed vignettes, so I wanted to gauge their willingness to even *consider* the possibility that vengeful violence is acceptable. The differences between liberals and conservatives were stark, but not absolute: 43% of conservatives and 24% of liberals said "yes," 33% of conservatives and 31% of liberals said "maybe," and 24% of conservatives and 45% of liberals said "no." When graphed, it is almost a mirror image reversed on the degree of support for revenge.

Although this survey is far from perfect, it supports two important hypotheses: 1) conservatives are more likely to endorse extra-judicial violence for punishment's sake than liberals, and 2) even some liberals are open to the idea that violent harm is acceptable for revenge's sake. I think this is an interesting subject for future researchers to explore, but for now we can try to understand how conservatives and liberals talk about vigilante violence within their peer groups.

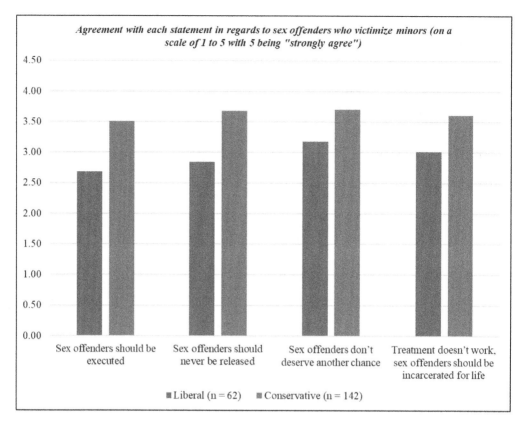

FIGURE 5.4 Agreement with each statement in regards to sex offenders who victimize minors

Conservative Morals

If Jonathan Haidt is correct, these moral values are buried deep within each individual and they contribute largely to our inability to understand or commiserate with divergent opinions. We react with hostility when anyone contradicts us because we are bound by our moral foundations, and we are blind to the priorities of other people. Haidt wrote, "Can partisans even *understand* the story told by the other side?" Haidt suggests that conservatives would find it easier to empathize with the moral perspective of liberals than vice versa because even though conservatives rank lower on moral values of care and fairness, they still hold those values very high in their broad scope of morality. Liberals, however, tend to assume the worst of conservatives. They fail to understand the conservative obsession with sanctity and degradation, and they assume that all conservatives are evil and selfish. Those assumptions go a long way toward keeping these groups from being able to persuade each other. Calling someone names is unlikely to change their opinions, but name-calling does help signal in-group virtues to your own side.

As Haidt has written, "human nature is not just intrinsically moral, it's also intrinsically moralistic, critical, and judgmental .... Morality blinds and binds. The true believers produce pious fantasies that don't match reality, and at some point, somebody comes along to knock the idol off its pedestal." This makes it extremely difficult to change someone else's mind. In a democracy we all try to get along and make laws that work to keep us safe. How can we convince people to

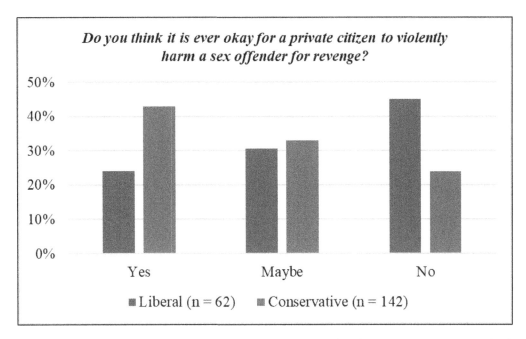

FIGURE 5.5 Answers to the question: Do you think it is ever okay for a private citizen to violently harm a sex offender for revenge?

stop being irrational and make better decisions? Haidt suggests that empathy is the key. When you get to know someone beyond a news headline or their political affiliation you might be able to think of them as a human being instead of a heuristic straw man your emotions have constructed. "Empathy is an antidote to righteousness, although it's very difficult to empathize across a moral divide" wrote Haidt.

Generally speaking, a person who endorses a conservative position may be more likely to endorse extreme punishments for child sex abusers. Just as "conservative" is nearly synonymous with "tough on crime" rhetoric, it would certainly be the case that conservatives want to increase punishments for crimes that inspire extreme levels of disgust. This may be tempered by the individual's libertarian beliefs, but even in that case, a libertarian conservative might be more likely to endorse vigilante violence against these offenders because they would not trust the government to do the job. Conservatives' high sensitivity to "disgust" on the purity/degradation moral foundation might increase the likelihood that they will endorse extreme punishments for sex offenders. Dale Spencer, a law professor at Carleton University in Canada, has argued that sex offenders are cast out of society, literally and figuratively, in order to restore the social order's "sacred" values. When sex offenders are identified on public registries it gives an "informal license to vigilantes to expel sex offenders physically from communities" (14). There is something to the idea that vigilante supporters are "right-wing" because they tend to hold extreme conservative beliefs, such as preferring smaller government but desiring a more punitive justice system. The sample of vigilantes I interviewed for this book is not generalizable to all vigilantes, but it is worth noting that most of them consider themselves to be conservative and at least two of them are members of far right-wing extremist groups. They all use the term "disgusting" to refer to the child sex abusers they attacked.

Disgust is an interesting phenomenon in moral/emotional psychology. Disgust is an autonomic evolutionary response that keeps contaminants from compromising an organism's health. This explains our natural disgust at the sight of maggots, rotting meat, and the stench of decomposing bodies. It can also apply to sexual desires. Zoophilia, necrophilia, and pedophilia are *disgusting* to people who cannot imagine being sexually aroused by animals, dead bodies, or children. As psychologist Reid Meloy has said in regard to terrorists who dehumanize their enemies, you are not *angry* at a cockroach when you step on it (15). You feel a different emotion. Disgust is a preservation instinct. You kill to be rid of the feeling of disgust. This is incidentally a survival fitness benefit to society. Killing bugs and rats keeps humans safe. That is why terrorists (and vigilantes) have a clean conscience after they kill their victims. They consider them to be less than human, and unworthy of pity.

The notes I took while interviewing the men who murdered child sex abusers include universal feelings of disgust for pedophiles. One murderer, Joseph Druce, drew a picture of a cockroach being killed by a flyswatter and labeled the dead bug as a "pedo." Scottie Allen (on death row in Florida, Chapter Seven) said:

To me, they're like cockroaches. Killing that pedophile was like stepping on a cockroach. I felt no satisfaction or discomfort. It was like killing a disgusting cockroach. Not sorry you had to do it, but sorry it existed in the first place.

Scholars have noted that anger, by itself, is not associated with acts of targeted violence. If you are angry you might write a strongly worded letter to your congressional representative. The moral/emotional sequence that passes from anger, to contempt, to *disgust* is a distal factor associated with lone actor terrorism. David Matsumoto has argued that the ANCODI (anger, contempt, and disgust) sequence is vital to understanding how violent people are able to dehumanize their enemies to the point that killing them *en masse* is morally acceptable (16). However, disgust may be an atavistic evolutionary trait in the sense that we may be disgusted with other humans and it leads us to violent acts contrary to the functioning of a civilization based on the rule of law. Dehumanization of another person allows us to sanitize our conscience and think of them as a bacilli. Child sex abusers disgust many people in our society. Stomping them, like Joseph Druce stomped on the chest of John Geoghan in his Massachusetts prison cell (Chapter Eight), is perhaps an extermination instinct uninhibited by empathy for another human being.

There has been some research on punitive attitudes and measures of disgust for sex offenders. Stevenson, Malik, Totton, and Reeves surveyed college students to assess their levels on the Disgust Sensitivity Scale, and then asked their opinion about a juvenile sex offender vignette (17). The results were not completely straightforward, but there was evidence that students who are more sensitive to disgust were more likely to support juvenile sex offender registration, and they were more likely to label the offender as a "superpredator." The authors suggest that the emotion of disgust may be triggering psychological distancing, dehumanization, and fear. Perhaps that is why other research finds that many people don't care about research evidence that demonstrates the ineffectiveness of sex offender registries (18). Emotion trumps evidence. Other researchers have found that when people are surveyed on their judgments of moral concern for humans and animals, the group they care about the *least* are child molesters, who come in dead last below terrorists, murderers, flies, wasps, ants, and worms (19).

If you see a news report about vigilante killing a child sex abuser and you have strong feelings about the case, you might want to know if other people agree with you. If you scroll down to the comment section you will probably see a colorful debate between "Nazis," "Communists," and "Pedos" that violates every one of the terms of service agreements required by the website. Usually, the news sites will close the comment section on stories that become too hostile, and the combatants take their aggression to other venues. The invention of the internet and the proliferation of social media have created an opportunity for like-minded people to congregate together and cheer each other on. Some might call this an "echo chamber" or even "radicalization," but to the group members, this is fellowship. They compete to create edgy memes that trivialize or demonize their opponents, while portraying themselves as rational and heroic. These memes can be humorous, disturbing, or both.

Pro-vigilante memes are not just created and shared by young people. I found an image of a woodchipper captioned "Pedophile Treatment Center" on Facebook. This particular meme is important because it gets at a one of the core beliefs of vigilantes and their supporters: that pedophilic child sex abusers cannot be cured, and they cannot be rehabilitated. Death is the only solution, and a gory, painful death is preferable. "Chippie the Woodchipper" has become a symbol of vigilante support online. It is common enough on social media that people will post images of a woodchipper that does not have an explanatory caption, but the image still receives hundreds of "Likes" from people in-the-know. Flippant endorsements of murder are common on the internet, but this particular image was found on a closed Facebook group for correctional officers and prison employees. At the time I downloaded this image, it had 158 "Likes" from members of the group and dozens of comments encouraging such crime control methods, including "Is the loader job bid by seniority?" and "Feet first in slow gear" and "damn Skippy!!!" The fact that it is posted by correctional officers on a Facebook page may be a cause for concern among people who believe that sex offenders should be treated with humanity and dignity by government employees. Laughing at the thought of grinding their bodies into pulp inside a woodchipper may be unprofessional.

You may not have noticed these memes before if you are isolated in parts of the internet that reinforce your own attitudes, values, and beliefs. That's how the algorithms and self-selection work. If you could step outside your normal online environment and into someone else's you might see entirely different cognitive landscapes that would help you get inside the mind of a vigilante. The use of humor in these memes might seem strange to people who condemn all forms of violence, and it may even be distasteful to most victims of child sexual abuse who do not want any part of this debate to be entertaining, but to the Meme Warriors who make and share these images, it is way to signal their own brand of virtue. If you can joke about killing a pedophile then you must *really* hate pedophiles. It goes beyond an expression of fear, disgust, or hatred. Laughing at murder is the ultimate expression of vigilante support.

It is obvious that there is a culture of pro-vigilante sentiment in America today. It might be a sub-group of people with unique characteristics (e.g., high on measures of "disgust" toward sex crimes, or conservative political beliefs). People do not often reach across the political/moral divide to learn from their opponents. They stay in their echo chambers and reinforce their previously existing beliefs.

Liberal Morals

Liberals have a more defensive position in this debate. They tend to have different priorities. They have been working diligently to reduce the size and influence of our criminal justice system for a long time while defending themselves against accusations that they care more about criminals than victims (20). This is frustrating to many liberal activists because they certainly *do* care about victims and often dedicate their lives to helping them. They just happen to have enough empathy to also feel sorry for the offender in many cases. Some of them would prefer to have *less punishment* for sex offenders, even those who abuse children. They do so because they believe that punishment is ineffective at reducing future crimes (utilitarianism), and that prison living conditions are cruel (compassion). If Haidt's Moral Foundations Theory holds true, liberals would be expected to be less likely to endorse a policy because they are disgusted with offenders. They would frame their condemnation in terms of harm and fairness. If a child were clearly harmed by a sexual assault it would certainly offend liberal sensibilities, but this leaves room for mercy in cases where the level of direct harm is ambiguous (such as in "hands off" child exploitation crimes). Liberals might also be more likely to condemn sex abuse crimes if the situation involved inequalities in relationships (such as men hurting women, or wealthy and powerful people escaping punishment). Liberals who have strong feelings about child sex abusers might agree with Andrew Vachss that child abuse is the "ultimate fascism" where people with power abuse the most vulnerable people in our society. In other words, liberals might care more about the inequality of power dynamics than the disgusting nature of the crime (21).

> The ultimate fascism is child abuse. Its victims are Prisoners of War without a Geneva Convention to protect them, hostages to terrorism … And that truth compels another: Righteous war against oppressors of humanity is the highest calling of our species.

There is an interesting phenomenon occurring behind the scenes in liberal debates about the criminal justice system. Among left-wing groups there are two competing interests: the feminists who protest lenient punishments given to male sex offenders, and the prison reformers who want to abolish or seriously reduce our use of prisons. The battle here is between the *#MeToo movement* who applauded the incarceration of Harvey Weinstein and Bill Cosby, and the *#AbolishPrisons* movement who lament the incarceration of any human being. So-called "Carceral Feminists" have been accused of being "penal populists" for wanting to punish rapists like Brock Turner who was given six months in jail for raping an intoxicated woman (22). The condemned feminists countered with the accusation that some idealistic liberals actually bolster a "rape culture" in our society because they want to eliminate punishments for sexual assault crimes. This debate is unlikely to be resolved anytime soon, but the final outcome is not necessary to draw the inference that both groups would oppose vigilantism. Liberal support for *the death penalty* is near zero in this debate, and they would balk at the suggestion that vigilante violence is justifiable against sex offenders. They are only arguing over the appropriateness of a jail sentence.

Christine McDermott and Monica Miller have researched the phenomenon of vigilante support. In 2016, they published an article describing how moral disengagement, the need for cognition, faith in intuition, and legal authoritarianism influence university student's opinions about vigilantism. Their definition of vigilantism included violence against non-sex offending targets, but it does support the idea that people who differ on deeply felt moral issues can differ in their levels of support for violence. They found that vigilante supporters had lower levels of "need for cognition" than people who opposed vigilantism. That is, they did not "enjoy thinking and processing information at a deep level." Those who had more trust in their intuitions and could disengage themselves morally from the wrongness of violence tended to support vigilantes than people who thought about the issues deeply. Perhaps these deep thinkers argued with themselves about due process, social concerns, and definitional issues (23).

While they did not measure the liberal versus conservative beliefs of the survey respondents, they did measure levels of legal authoritarianism. People with high levels of support for obedience to legal authorities were *more likely* to support vigilantism. Why would people who submit to the law endorse vigilante lawbreakers? Perhaps because they envision vigilantes as helping to achieve justice. If the vigilante went too far this authoritarianism might undermine support for vigilantes. If we compare this relationship to Jonathan Haidt's moral foundations we can see that one major point of disagreement between liberals and conservatives is the tendency for conservatives to support authorities. This counter-intuitive relationship between the support for criminal behavior and support for legal authorities indicates that liberals and conservatives have fundamentally different understandings of what a vigilante is, and how they relate to the legal system.

Then there is the liberal fear of stigmas. Michel Foucault has been a darling of liberal academics for decades. Hardly any book about the criminal justice system can be published without lengthy citations from his work, especially *Discipline and Punish* which traces the evolution of the methods and purposes of punishment in Western nations (24). Foucault believed that a primary purpose of punishment is to create a class of "others" who can serve as a reference point for "normal" people to rally against. For Foucault, punishment "compares, differentiates, hierarchizes, homogenizes, excludes. In short, it normalizes." When one group of people (such as pedophiles or child sex abusers) are labeled and punished, everyone else in society can feel a sense of community due to their shared distinctness from the "others." This violates the liberal moral foundation of equality and fairness because it puts one group of people ("criminals") below everyone else. Chrysanthi Leon describes this mode of "subject creation" by claiming that "punishment's real intent is not to discipline the offender, but to dramatize the violated norm …. Punishment maintains social solidarity by dramatizing the superiority of 'us' over 'them'" (25). According to Leon, modern sex offender registration laws like Megan's Law are "drawing social boundaries in which the subjects of offender, victim, authority figure, and moral community are regenerated." She argues that the tendency for society to rally against enemies is pernicious. A slippery slope. Alexandra Stupple has argued that the use of "disgust" language in legislative practices may dehumanize sex offenders and give permission for lawmakers to be excessively punitive (26).

This is a possible explanation for why liberal reformers are so dedicated to changing the labels used to describe sex offenders. They prefer "person-centered language" that separates the individual from their behavior. They have many reasons for making this argument and some of them appear to be quite logical (e.g., it helps in therapy if the person can separate themselves from their behavior), but the fixation to change names and scold people throughout society who use outdated terms seems petty to conservatives. Remember, conservatives are disgusted by these offenders. They often want to *kill them*. Calling them "a person convicted of a sexual offense" rather than a "sex offender" makes conservatives believe that you are trying to downplay the crime or euphemize their behavior. They believe it is just a matter of time before liberals decriminalize sex with children. The slippery slope again. This is another reason why vigilantes might fall on the conservative side of this particular issue. They think they are saving society from utter ruin. They want to "otherize" child sex abusers, they want to punish them severely, and they condemn the governmental system that allows them to run free.

Liberals may have another reason for being anti-vigilante. As flawed as the justice system is, they believe it is the only method of ensuring that individual rights are being protected. They do not want people taking the law into their own hands and killing sex offenders whenever they please. They cannot ensure that the victims of vigilantism were actually guilty or that their crimes deserved such an extreme punishment (especially because liberals tend to stringently oppose the death penalty even for truly horrendous crimes). When conservatives hear the word "vigilante" they probably think of some hero in the Wild West dishing out gunslinger justice on a bad guy. When liberals hear the same word, they probably think about the Ku Klux Klan: law-lessness, terrorism, and oppression (27). Liberals probably do not support the government because of their dedication to authority. They just prioritize fairness, and they think fairness is more likely to occur in a bureaucracy than in the fevered imaginations of vigilantes.

Moral Justice

In 1906, the jurist Roscoe Pound lectured on the causes of popular dissatisfaction with the justice system. He said:

> Justice, which is the end of law, is the ideal compromise between the activities of all in a crowded world. The law seeks to harmonize these activities and to adjust the relations of every man with his fellows so as to accord with the moral sense of the community. When the community is at one in its ideas of justice, this is possible. When the community is divided and diversified, and groups and classes and interests, understanding each other none too well, have conflicting ideas of justice, the task is extremely difficult. It is impossible that legal and ethical ideas should be in entire accord in such a society.

It seems as though we will have to agree to disagree on these issues. Juries can make determinations on a case-by-case basis and society can hope that extreme decisions will be rare. The psychological elements of one's moral outlook on life are difficult to change. Some people support the murder of child sex abusers wholeheartedly, while others decry the loss of any human life. Edgy vigilante supporters might interject that pedophiles aren't human. You see we are at another impasse. Morals are in the eye of the beholder. A determination of the morality of any murder depends on the circumstances of the case *and* the pre-existing belief structures of the observers (28).

Pure vigilantes would not sacrifice their lives and freedom to fight a war against sex offenders unless they were truly "hyper-sensitive" as Jeremy Moody said. In their minds, they are as moral as the citizens marching on crack houses in Mantua, Philadelphia, to fight drug dealers or the Guardian Angels who patrolled the subways in New York to fight the muggers. They did what they had to do. They couldn't live with themselves if they had refrained.

No list of moral qualities intended to justify murder will satisfy everyone. People are divided on many issues of politics, religion, morals, and basic standards of human decency. The world is full of people who speculate, bravely, on what they *would* do in a certain situation. Perhaps they would bravely sacrifice their own freedom to punish a child abuser … or maybe they'd scurry away and not get involved at all. Some people might declare they would *never* take the law into their own hands because they are morally superior to the emotional fools described in this book, but unless they have been put in that position themselves, they will never know for sure. Few people will be put to the test. Most people will post memes and tweets that signal their self-proclaimed moral superiority to like-minded allies on the internet.

This debate over the morality of punishment also occurs when discussing non-homicidal punishments for sex offenders. Conservatives have a reputation for being tough on all crimes and recklessly increasing the size of America's prison population, creating a crisis that certainly contributed to the "injustice gap" described in Chapter Four. Liberals have "good intentions" (as defined by their moral outlook) to save people from the degradations of punitive populism, but many of the far-left activists in this debate overlook the pragmatic issues that interfere with their utopian dreams. Joan Petersilia and Francis T. Cullen (two premier experts on the dangers of over-incarceration) wrote in the *Stanford Journal of Criminal Law and Policy*, that reformers should be liberal, but not stupid (29). That means they should combine their progressive sensibilities with pragmatism if they actually want to achieve their goals of reducing our prison population. They argue that liberals can broaden public support for their policies by including the majority of all voters who support alternatives to incarceration. That means they must communicate the research evidence that those alternatives are more effective than incapacitation.

A caveat in those suggestions is the special disdain that the majority of voters have for sex offenders. Pragmatic reform efforts are focused on non-violent, non-sex offenders because there are enough people caught up in the system who meet that criteria who can be diverted. Liberals who demand an all-or-nothing reform agenda that includes overwhelming compassion for sex offenders may isolate large numbers of people who "just don't give a #%&!" about sex offenders (18, 30, 31). I would suggest that dismissing these voters' concerns as a "moral panic" is unlikely to persuade them. Activists might want to rebrand their message if they want to communicate effectively with this population. Getting past the barrier of "disgust" may be especially important, but moralistic argumentation may not be the best method. Expressions of outrage over the moral disgust of your opponents can easily backfire (17, 26, 32, 33). I will further discuss the stigmatization and dehumanization of sex offenders in Chapter Nine when I discuss the criminology of vigilantism.

I think further investigation into the moral foundations, political affiliations, and punitive orientations of voters would be immensely valuable in helping us understand how our society is divided on these issues. Vigilante violence is a small, extreme example of how people may fall on one side or the other. Is it possible that the majority of voters actually share some common morality that would help us agree on safe and effective policies for sex offenders? While this chapter does not present any answers to these questions, I hope it has offered some possible roadmaps to investigation.

I suggest that moral psychologists replicate those famous "trolly dilemma" studies that they subject their undergraduate students to. Instead of asking if they would choose to "push a fat man" off a bridge to his death in order to save five others from an oncoming trolly, they should inform their students that the fat man is a child molester. Their answer may no longer be predicated on saving five people at all.

Cup of Clay

By "A Son of Solitude"

Anasilan brother … Anasilan … that moment after the wind stops moving, this should never fill you with dread, for silence is wisdom.

… and wisdom is a splendored and vicious Goddess, to entreat and encounter her, we must prepare ourselves….

… the vessel must be still … it must be….

… silent….

… and now, she is near … have you learned to recognize her shadow when it is cast upon you?

Every mountain stands in silence, many having absorbed the blood and bones and detritus of the many cities of bedlam. The seeker knows he must climb the mountain to reach the heights of wisdom. This must be done in silence.

The oldest tree in the forest has stood for seven thousand years or more. Having watched civilizations rise and fall, now tired, but in complete silence, its meditation has caused its roots to run deep beneath the surface, spreading wide, in directions you have not conceived of, this was achieved through silence.

The greatest bodies of water, ancient beyond comprehension, give life, first, through silence. They must be still, unmoved, from this position, creation is breathed into existence. The depths of the ocean itself, are completely silent, wrapping each form and organism with the placid and comforting embrace of a wisdom that has always been, so powerful, it can suffocate.

The Stone People, the Enyans, these are the oldest race on this planet, this is what the elders have taught us. These stones, formed of death, then life, chaos and order, destruction and creation, these Enyans, the Stone People, surround us, in silence. They can only be coaxed to speak through heat and water, and even then, only if approached and respected in a humility born of silence. Place your open palm on a stone, its stillness and silence should speak to your soul.

To the Sun we owe our life, this atmosphere and all thing which thrive within it are moved and given opportunity through the silent blessing of the sun's bounty. This light. The greatest of many, has given us all things, in complete silence. Have you ever heard the sound of a sunrise? The sound of the sun's warmth on your body? No one has, for she only stands in her full glory, in silence, this is wisdom.

Wisdom is a Goddess, and all of her acolytes are silent. Consider the stewards of Wisdom-fear, pain, joy, love, hunger, thirst, desire, longing and so many more, these only exist in silence. This is their shared lineage, a common attribute which has been venerated for centuries by the masters. The cup of clay must remain silent, must be still, for by doing so he or she becomes the proper recipient of a much water and light and darkness and hunger, then is completely sated and satiated and runs over with the mighty forces which have been seen. The force and the energy fills it to the top, then bursts over and blows away all that surrounds it ... this clay cup ... and then ... Anasilan ... that stillness ... it comes again brother ... after the raging of the winds ... this existence ... Anasilan ... this is where we find her, in her stunning beauty, Wisdom, she is no comfort to you if you have not encountered each one of her acolytes, and accepted each for its own nature. When pain first came to me, I recoiled, but then, I embraced her, and in silence, she has taught me many things. Fear, when it first came to me, I hid my face, but then, in time, I embraced her and in silence, I became strong. Solitude and loneliness, when they chased me and captured my heart, I struggled and fought, but when I relented, in silence, I gained everything. Sorrow and hunger, terrible and persistent in their glorious horror, they perused me. I hid and begged them to leave me, and then, I gave myself over to them, and in silence, we communed. They showed me wisdom. I became whatever it is I am, only in their company, gaining their respect, silently.

I am a mountain, and I have absorbed the blood and bones and detritus of the cities of bedlam ... I remain unmoved, in silence. I am a tree, and I have stood for seven thousand years or more. I have seen civilizations rise and fall. I am tired ... but, deep beneath the layers, my roots running deeper than you can imagine, listen to my silence, for even surrounded by a million other trees, I am alone. I am an ocean, and within my body, there is life, and horror, and glory, and the ability for all things to thrive, or to suffocate. I am ancient, and I will continue to be here after many things pass away. I remain, in silence. I am a sun. Can you feel my warmth on your face? Does the faithfulness of my light bring you comfort and peace? I will only come to you, in silence ....

And now I am only a clay cup, a vessel, now worn and cracked, now broken and shattered, now just so many pieces, now a handful of dust ... scattered ....

Silence is wisdom, solitude is power.

Anasilan brother

References

1. Robinson, P., & Robinson, S. (2018). *Shadow vigilantes: How distrust in the justice system breeds a new kind of lawlessness*. Amherst, NY: Prometheus books.
2. Robinsons, P. H., & Cahill, M. T. (2006). *Law without justice: Why criminal law doesn't give people what they deserve*. New York, NY: Oxford University Press.
3. Flammia, D. (2019, Oct. 3). He killed the man he says raped him – These are the lessons he learned. *New Jersey 101.5*. https://nj1015.com/he-killed-the-man-he-says-raped-him-these-are-the-lessons-he-learned/
4. Fredericks, C. (2019). 'I didn't care whether I lived or died.': Male sexual abuse survivor who retaliated against abuser advocates for child abuse laws, 'Break the silence.' *Love what matters*. https://www.lovewhatmatters.com/clark-fredericks-sexual-abuse-survivor-murder-motivational-speaker/
5. CBS New York. (2015, June 17). *N.J. man admits to stabbing boy scout leader he says molested him as boy*. https://newyork.cbslocal.com/2015/06/17/sussex-county-murder-molestation/
6. Associated Press. (2015, Dec. 11). Killer influenced by Sandusky trial gets 5 years. *The Daily Item*. https://www.dailyitem.com/news/killer-influenced-by-sandusky-trial-gets-5-years/article_6d89d0ee-a00d-11e5-8117-2b160b73ddd7.html
7. CBS New York. (2015, June 18). Clark Fredericks statement on slaying of alleged molester. YouTube. https://www.youtube.com/watch?v=8ghgSBH7cQM
8. Moody, J. (2012). *Yesterday, today, and forever*. Self-published.
9. Moody, J. (2020). *The Jewish scourge*. Self-published.
10. Redden, J. (2000). *Snitch culture: How citizens are turned into the eyes and ears of the state*. Port Townsend, WA: Feral House.
11. Haidt, J. (2012). *The righteous mind: Why good people are divided by politics and religion*. New York, NY: Pantheon Books.
12. Yamamota, S., & Maeder, E. M. (2019). Creating the punishment orientation questionnaire: An item response theory approach. *Personality and Social Psychology, 45*(8), 1283–1294.
13. Wnuk, D., Chapman, J. E., & Jeglic, E. L. (2006). Development and refinement of a measure of attitudes toward sex offender treatment. *Journal of Offender Rehabilitation, 43*(3), 35–47.
14. Spencer, D. (2009). Sex offender as homo sacer. *Punishment & Society, 11*(2), 219–240. https://doi.org/10.1177/1462474508101493
15. Meloy, R. (2022). T.R.A.P.-18 training seminar. *Mental Health Systems: Global Institute of Forensic Research*. https://drreidmeloy.com/training/
16. Matsumoto, D., Hwang, H. C., & Frank, M. G. (2017), Emotion and aggressive intergroup cognitions: The ANCODI hypothesis. *Aggressive Behavior, 43*, 93–107. https://doi.org/10.1002/ab.21666
17. Stevenson, M. C., Malik, S. E., Totton, R. R., & Reeves, R. D. (2015). Disgust sensitivity predicts punitive treatment of juvenile sex offenders: The role of empathy, dehumanization, and fear: Disgust sensitivity and attitudes toward sex offenders. *Analyses of Social Issues and Public Policy, 15*(1), 177–197.
18. Socia, K. M., Rydberg, J., & Dum, C. P. (2021). Punitive attitudes toward individuals convicted of sex offenses: A vignette study. *Justice Quarterly, 38*(6), 1262–1289.

19. Jaeger, B., & Wilks, M. (2022). A variance component analysis of the moral circle. Working paper. https://psyarxiv.com/46kws/

20. Cullen, F. T., & Jonson, C. L. (2016). *Correctional theory: Context and consequences. Second* Edition. Thousand Oaks, CA: Sage Publishing.

21. Vachss, A. (1996). The ultimate fascism. *The Zero.* http://www.vachss.com/av_dispatches/disp_9600_a.html

22. Phillips, N. D., & Chagnon, N. (2020). "Six months is a joke": Carceral feminism and Penal populism in the wake of the Stanford sexual assault case. *Feminist Criminology,* 15(1), 47–69. https://doi.org/10.1177/1557085118789782

23. McDermott, C. M., & Miller, M. K. (2016). Individual differences impact support for vigilante justice. *Journal of Aggression, Conflict, and Peace Research,* 8(3), 186–196.

24. Foucault, M. (1977). *Discipline & punish.* New York, NY: Pantheon Books.

25. Leon, C. S. (2012). *Sex fiends, perverts, and pedophiles: Understanding sex crime policy in America.* New York, NY: New York University Press.

26. Stupple, A. (2014). Disgust, dehumanization, and the courts' response to sex offender legislation. *The Guild Practitioner,* 71(3), 130.

27. Brown, R. M. (1977). *Strain of violence: Historical studies of American violence and vigilantism.* New York, NY: University Press.

28. Jonsen, A. R., & Toulmin, S. (1988). *The abuse of casuistry: A history of moral reasoning.* Berkley, CA: University of California Press.

29. Petersilia, J., & Cullen, F. T. (2014). Liberal but not stupid: Meeting the promise of downsizing prisons. *Stanford Journal of Criminal Law and Policy,* 2(1), 1–43.

30. Rydberg, J., Dum, C. P., & Socia, K. (2018). Nobody gives a #%&!: A factorial survey examining the effect of criminological evidence on opposition to sex offender residence restrictions. *Journal of Experimental Criminology,* 14(4), 541–550.

31. Sparks, B. (2021). Attitudes toward the punishment of juvenile and adult sexual offenders in Canada: The roles of sentencing goals and criminal justice motivations. *Journal of Child Sexual Abuse,* 30(2), 125–145.

32. Lynch, M. (2002). Pedophiles and cyber-predators as contaminating forces: The language of disgust, pollution, and boundary invasions in federal debates on sex offender legislation. *Law & Social Inquiry,* 27(3), 529–557.

33. Clark, J. A., & Fessler, D. P. S. P. M. T. (2014). The role of disgust in norms, and of norms in disgust research: Why liberals shouldn't be morally disgusted by moral disgust. *Topoi,* 34(2), 483–498.

6

CHARLES BRONSON BAD

Johnny Cash wasn't a career criminal. He had some run-ins with the law over drugs and spent a few weeks in jail. But he did have a strong affinity for prisoners. He identified with them. He said they were victims of the times. He wrote a song about Folsom prison sung from the convicts' point of view. He secured his place in music history (and the history of prisons) when he performed this song inside Folsom prison in 1956 in front of a crowd of cheering prisoners who were desperate for validation. Later, in 1958, he outdid himself by singing a new song called "San Quentin" inside that prison. With this song he challenged the staff, warden, and the entire system of penology by asking what good San Quentin did for society? Did anyone think the prisoners who lived in that facility would be better when they were released to the community? Or would their souls be warped? One California prisoner who admired Cash was Merle Haggard, a short-time prisoner who went on to become a legendary musician himself. He said that Johnny Cash "was there because he loved us. When he walked away, everyone in that place had become a Johnny Cash fan."

If you've heard the live recordings of these albums you know that the prisoners were an enthusiastic audience, but if you've seen the camera footage of this event in San Quentin you can also watch interviews with some of the prisoners and correctional officers. They didn't talk about music or their plans for the future. They all talked about survival. One prisoner said that a man was killed right outside his cell. The victim was hit over the head with a 2×4 and was carried away before he even noticed. "Most of the people here are paranoidic (sic)" said a prisoner. "In other words, they're all afraid something is going to happen to them in one sense or another... The first week I was here there were something like three or four killings." Some described race wars and unexpected violence. Prisoners walking from the dining hall might find themselves in the middle of a riot. Another prisoner said that he could remember a time when seeing someone stabbed would bother him, but he was getting to a point where it didn't even concern him. The overarching concern for these prisoners was survival. One correctional officer said:

> When an inmate comes in, many of them that comes in, I think are afraid. This causes them to do one of two things. They either have to join a clique of some kind, some kind of gang to survive, they have to pay protection to survive or they have to do many things even to the point of being homosexuals to survive. Many of them has to pay protection to survive, and I

DOI: 10.4324/9781003393849-7

feel that this type of thing characterizes a lot of inmates. I think practically every inmate in the whole institution has his own way of survival. This causes him to not be able to act himself. I've seen cases where inmates wrap their arms in toilet paper to make them look big and muscled up. I've seen them do many things to do this. They will give staff a bad time in order to show some other group of inmates that I am on your side or I'm a big tough guy and so forth. This is a means of survival.

California is one of the largest and most documented prison systems in the world. It gets a lot of attention. We probably know more about prison experiences in California than any other state due to the endless flow of citizens in and out of their facilities who tell us stories, public records from constant lawsuits, minute-by-minute news reports, documentary films, and the proximity of Hollywood movie productions. The concept of a "prison" that most Americans are familiar with are California-style prisons, and yet we are still confused. There is almost too much information to process, and the contradictory accounts create more confusion. Misunderstandings abound.

Most people would think that liberal California has a lenient criminal justice system, but researchers and activists know it is a brutal place that is responsible for nearly 25% of all homicides in state prisons (1, 2). California is the cradle of the deadliest prison gangs that have spread across the country from their point of origin (e.g., Mexican Mafia, Nuestra Familia, Black Guerilla Family, Aryan Brotherhood, Nazi Lowriders). California is the breeding ground for security threat groups that plague all of the other prison systems in the United States. If deterrence was an effective method of crime control, the fear of being stabbed in prison would make California the safest place in the country. But within the chaos of the California prison system there are some acts of violence that stand out as especially newsworthy. Not the riots, collective violence, gang wars, or sexual assaults. That's old news. To be famous in California's gladiator pits these days, you have to do something really special... maybe that's why people want to know more about the man who killed two pedophiles who were watching PBS Kids on television. Now *that's* a story.

In 2009, another musician entered the California Department of Rehabilitation and Corrections. He wasn't a visitor like Johnny Cash or a short-timer like Merle Haggard. His name was Jon Henry Watson. He had been the singer in a punk rock band and had a tattoo of a 1950s style microphone on his neck. He was a convicted murderer serving a 50-year prison sentence. Watson was certifiably dangerous. Literally, he had a piece of paper from a prison psychologist saying that he was too dangerous to be housed with other prisoners, and yet the staff put him in an open dorm. He told them he was going to "kill a child molester" if he was not transferred. The staff ignored him. Then one day, a known child sex trafficker was watching PBS Kids on the television, leering at the child actors. A prisoner asked if anyone was going to put a stop to this perversion. Nobody moved. Watson said "I got this," grabbed a walking cane, and beat the man to death on the spot. He walked down the corridor to report his crime to the authorities, and along the way, he saw another known child sex trafficker. "In for a penny, in for a pound," Watson said, and he beat this man to death too. Two murders in one day. A rare occurrence, even in a prison system as plagued with violence as California's.

The Reckless Ones

Jon Henry Watson was raised in a military/law enforcement family where he learned good old-fashioned American patriotism, a hard work ethic, and respect for the law. His Grandpa Hank was a lawman, a Korean War vet, and the last of the Old Guard. He was "equal parts Andy Griffith and John Wayne." He was an old-school lawman who never used his firearm and rarely made an arrest. He would solve disputes with reason and common sense.

Jon's father was a bit of a scoundrel. He was a union agitator. He was buddies with teamsters and gangsters. He knew that the future of California was in grifting taxpayers through union extortion. Since Jon's family was divided so strongly between the Old Guard and the new face of corrupt unionization, this led to some interesting conversations that Jon was privy to. For example, his grandfather warned that if police unionized, they could devise financial incentives to make arrests and they would less accountable for corruption because the union would protect their jobs. The prisons would fill up. Unions would suck the money from the treasury and it wouldn't make the state safer. Public service unions would not be a check on "capitalist exploitation" like in the coal mines of West Virginia, they would be *gangs* that protected government interests and reduce accountability. They would turn the Golden State into a cesspool of corruption. Jon's father said to get with the times. You can make a lot of money. Everyone else was.

Jon agreed with his grandfather more than his father on these issues, but he was a young man and needed to find his own way in life. While he was still in school he worked as a ranch hand, "tendin' animals, buckin' hay, and mendin' fences." "I'd spend my days with the animals, namely one pet billy goat that I could pat, tug on and wrestle until he head butted me. This was our game… he seemed to be better at the head butt than I was… but it'd get up, dust myself off, and get right back to playin'." He did one traumatizing stint in the "gladiator school" called the California Youth Authority for destroying property, but after his release, he restarted his life on a promising path.

As an adult Jon went to cosmetology school, and later attended Shasta College in Northern California, trained as an E.M.T. first responder, was certified in CPR and basic life support, tended a bar at a club, worked as a mortgage organizer for a major corporation, and helped local rock bands find their way into clubs and concert venues. He was a singer himself in a punk rock band called "Nation of Idiots." That's how he got the tattoo of the microphone on his neck. He played the Northern California punk scene alongside groups like Guttermouth, Union 13, Pressure Point, The Whiskey Rebels, The Crawlers, and The Vibrators (U.K.). No recordings of his music are available to the public, but some concert posters show them playing at "On The Y" in Sacramento several times.

Jon liked to challenge people's stereotypes during his punk days. He wrote: "When you look "punk" people make a lot of assumptions, and then they realize they've got the bloody wolf by the ears when they engage you in conversation, and that you're a buzz saw of teeth!" He believes that he owed a lot of his generation's music to Lars Fredericksen (of Rancid) just like the previous generations owed a lot to Johnny Cash. Underneath the noise and defiant symbolism was a threat of patriotism. He used to wear a T-shirt that read "Kill Your Local Drug Dealer."

Despite their political disagreements, Jon admired his father's ability to get along with anyone. He found his father drinking on a front porch one day with a members of a hardcore rock band. He was a lovable old scoundrel, and he seemed to think that Jon and these other musicians were taking the wrong path in life. Jon reminisced on this saying "He no doubt thought 'You boys need to pull up a piece of porch and enjoy a quiet Northern California Sunset. We'll learn you about animals and old trucks… Life shouldn't be a Johnny Cash song.' Though I seemed to turn mine into one."

One day, Jon took his fiancé to dinner at Ruby Tuesdays in Shasta County. As he enjoyed his meal and his company, he noticed a familiar face at the table next to him. It was Merle

Haggard, one of his mother's favorite musicians. Jon worshiped "Old Merle," especially for his song "Fightin' Side of Me" which he referred to as "Commie-punchin' music." He believed that Merle Haggard was the most punk rock man of all time. As he looked at his hero in the restaurant, he noticed the "thousand-yard stare" in Merle's eyes. "It was terrifying. He has the measure of you in a second flat. And you also knew just how dangerous you are not, as he dismisses your threat level as quickly as he had put you in his sights. I wouldn't see that glare again until I came to prison, and then, only on the oldest of CDC-R numbers, the A+B numbers did I see it (Merle was #A-45200 I believe). Those men are gone now, and their stories are lost… except for Merle's songs. If you can listen to Merle Haggard with dry eyes, then you have a lot to learn about this world. Merle deserves sainthood among the weary."

Somewhere along the way, Jon and a man named Jason Leon Belles were arrested for murder. A 27-year-old man named Garrett Benson was killed in a home invasion and robbery. According to the police, the shooting was over a large amount of marijuana that was found in the home, but if that was true, why didn't they take the marijuana? Jon committed a crime that day, but he does not have sympathy for the victim. He wrote "I wasn't forced, I *chose* to smoke a drug dealer." Jon himself hated drugs. He smoked pot once and didn't like it (as hard as it is to believe that a punk rock singer does not use drugs, I have spoken to friends of his who support this statement). Some people call themselves punk and wear "Kill Your Local Drug Dealer" T-shirts, but Jon felt it would be hypocritical not to walk the walk.

After he was arrested, Jon pled guilty to murder with a firearm enhancement. Belles received a better deal after pleading guilty to voluntary manslaughter (3). Jon tried to withdrawal his guilty plea at the last minute, claiming that he had been under the influence of medication at the time of his plea and he did not understand what he was agreeing to (4). His own attorney argued against his claim saying that she had asked him if he felt okay to make decisions. He told her several times that he didn't understand what was going on, but she interpreted this as him not understanding why he was being offered a plea deal *for fifty years in prison* (5). The court took his attorney's word over his and sentenced him to fifty years for the homicide (6).

When he was transferred to the custody of the California Department of Correction and Rehabilitation, he instantly understood how inefficient and poorly managed the prison system really was. "I can really recall what it was like when I was bright-eyed and skeptical at age 30 coming into this… I was *not* prepared… I did *not* believe that humans nor their institutions by extension could be so slimy or cruel. It was a hell of a learning curve."

Jon was transferred so often it was like being an embedded journalist traveling from battlefield to battlefield, absorbing information, and accumulating thirty years' worth of prison experience in less than a decade, what he calls "accelerated exposure." He moved between San Quentin, Mule Creek, Salinas Valley, High Desert, Corcoran, Folsom, and Kern. A whirlwind tour of the CDC-R archipelago.

Jon sees the gangs as a tool of the custody staff. "The soldiers answer to the shot callers. The shot callers answer to the cops. The cops have the drugs. So the shot callers get 'first taste' before the product is 'stepped on' (cut), and as a quid pro quo they keep a blanket of silence over mistreatment." He asks how the prisons are full of drugs after Covid restrictions have stopped all face-to-face visits with family for a year and a half? Clearly the staff are bringing the drugs. "D.R.E.A.M. – Drugs Rule Everything Around Me," he writes.

Jon tried to adapt to the prison paradigm in California. He kept his nose clean, worked hard, and tried to help others. When he was fresh to prison he was "still trying to fumble through my tool belt and trying to deploy reason, diplomacy, and bending to satisfy my new masters. I was a housing-clerk then and spent my days trouble-shooting situations." He felt like Alice in Wonderland trying to talk reason to insane people with twisted logic and inverted social values.

The lessons were all around me and I could only see two pathways forward. Grovel for favor and make much ado of kissing the ring of custody like so many sycophants do, or f★ck shit up.

The Fightin' Side of Me

Jon grew up speaking his mind, playing hardcore bands, and dealing with hostile people. "Sortin' stuff out is literally what I do best." The staff started using him to deal with prisoners they didn't like. They would send them to "Ol' Watson" to straighten out. He felt like a privateer on the high seas. If you commit a crime against someone the staff liked, you get in trouble. If you target someone who sails under an unfavorable flag, then the staff reward you. Not exactly a pro-social environment.

Prisoners who want to have a little privacy in a single cell had to do favors for the staff. A system of "quid pro quo" was established. If a prisoner performed a violent action on behalf of the correctional officers they were "fully-vested" and would be given a private cell. "Are you going to earn your single cell this year?" the staff would ask Jon. Sometimes they would tell him who they wanted him to sort out. Other times they just transferred him to share a cell with an undesirable person and hope he got the message. He played along for a while, but even a privateer has some moral qualms. He was placed in a cell with an alleged child sex abuser and told in no uncertain terms to "pay [his] dues."

The cops put me in a cell with a molester, (a big fat thing that was mostly bed ridden and I often likened him to the fat helpless vampire in the first Blade movie), and for some reason I'll never understand, I sat down to talk to him and look him in his eyes before I made clear that it was his time, and *only* then did I realize that the guy was disabled mentally. Stone cold retarded. Did the cops just try to get me to kill a fucking retard? Seriously? A *fucking retard*? Yes. Yes they did.

Needless to say, I did not do what I was tasked with. The next year of my life was one of absolute punishment for being "That Guy." I was behind the Green Wall at Salinas… the Watson that emerged from this "Year of Punishment" is the Watson that can walk into a room and beat two pedophiles to death.

He followed the formal and informal prison rules as long as he possibly could, but realized that being sensible doesn't work in a behemoth prison system. "You cannot reason with tyrants. Both inmates and custody. And when I lost, at least I lost on *my* terms, and I'm actually doing SHU and Hole time for something I *did* rather than some invented story by custody." His behavior changed. He bucked the system. He refused to kiss the ring anymore.

Jon decided he would rather live in isolation than have to tolerate the chaos of the general population. He repeatedly told his mental health counselors not to house him in a cell with another prisoner. "These cells are built for one man. Not two. Do not put their lives in danger by putting them in here with me." When a man says "I'm going to kill someone if you put them in a cell with me, I'm already serving life, I don't care what you do to me" that is a clear warning that the person is dangerous. To house them with another prisoner after they documented this threat would constitute deliberate indifference. But the counselors just wrote down whatever the custody staff told them to write down. If they wanted to put Jon in a dorm full of sex offenders, no mental health professional was going to tell them otherwise.

In 2020, Jon was moved to a medium security dorm with several known child sex traffickers. Jon had been introduced to a prisoner, and he felt the gooseflesh rise on his spine and run across his shoulders and down his arms and legs. He calls this spine-tingling sensation "the Howling." He believes this instinct is 80%–90% accurate in identifying pedophiles. He refused to shake the man's hand, and instead said "You don't want to know me bud, I'm an asshole." The man simply shrugged and engaged the next man in conversation. At that moment, Jon knew, "I'm going to kill this dude… I know it. The Howling is never wrong." Jon asked a correctional officer about this man, and the officer told him this child sex trafficker was going to be released from prison soon. That sealed the deal.

Later, Jon saw this man watching PBS Kids. He was leering at the child actors in the show *Odd Squad*. He put his hand down the front of his pants and looked around with a smirk on his face "*as if to say 'Yeah, I'm a cho-mo, you ain't goin' to do anything about it.*'" Jon had tolerated enough. He looked around to see if anyone else was going to do something to put a stop to this. The other prisoners looked at him blankly. So, Jon grabbed a walking cane from another prisoner and beat the child sex abuser to death.

Jon walked toward the correctional officer's desk to turn himself in but he spotted another sex offender standing in the hallway. Jon said "In for a penny, in for a pound" and beat him to death too. He dragged the bloody, dying man by his foot and challenged the other prisoners. He pointed at them and said "*You were eating with this pedo yesterday! You were buddies with him!*" Apparently the legend of convict justice is greatly exaggerated. Few men ever do what Jon Watson did. He killed two child sex abusers faster than anyone could react. Both of the dead men had been serving sentences for aggravated sexual assaults of children under 14 years old.

What's Done in the Dark

He tried to warn them. He left a paper trail too. They knew Jon was dangerous. He mailed letters to the C.C.I, the C.C.II, the psychiatric division, the administrators in Sacramento, and even Governor Gavin Newsome (whose office declined to get involved in CDC-R matters). He attached a letter from his mental health provider that is reproduced below:

To All concerned,

(CCA, CCII, Warden, Director Review Board and All Counselors)\

I would like an information chrono (128G) placed in the file of inmate Jonathan Watson, CDC-R# AA 4712, Stating that I have worked with Inmate Watson for the better part of five years, and that it is my opinion as a mental health professional that inmate Watson should remain on single cell status for the duration if [sic] his stay in the CDC-R.

Additionally, to force inmate Watson to double house would constitute an immediate threat to the safety and security of both himself and any/all inmates forced to house in a cell or dorm with him. It would be both negligent disregard and deliberate indifference to the safety of all concerned should inmate Watson single-cell status be revoked.

This letter is extremely interesting. It uses very clear language, including the phrase "deliberate indifference." This phrase was used by the Supreme Court in their ruling on *Farmer v. Brennan* that said any correctional officer or prison employee could be in violation of prisoner's Eighth Amendment rights prohibiting cruel and unusual punishment if the prisoner suffered physical harm due to the "deliberate indifference" of officers who knew of a credible threat and failed to reasonably respond to keep the victim safe. It has been the basis of many lawsuits and civil suits against prisons when an individual is harmed due to deliberate negligence of staff. The written policies of most prisons require that a safety list be kept and strictly adhered to. If a prisoner poses a threat to a specific person, race, gender, sexual orientation, gang affiliation, or the general population they should not be allowed to have contact with them. Prisons have no problem using this case law to defend their use of long-term administrative segregation policies (much to the chagrin of activists who want to abolish solitary confinement), but they are usually very careful to avoid the accusation of being "deliberately indifferent" to a prisoner's safety. When a mental health professional says that Watson should *not* be allowed to bunk with another person and should *not* be allowed to live in a dorm because it poses "an immediate threat to the safety and security of both himself and any/all inmates forced" to live with him, and that it would be *deliberate indifference…* we have a paper trail. The staff allegedly disregarded this letter as unofficial. Only CDC-R specialists can make housing recommendations. You may ask why they do not have a policy of being safe rather than sorry in cases where a prisoner threatens to murder people around him, but they didn't take him seriously.

One day Jon was escorted to a mental health conference where his counselors and the custody staff were waiting for him. Jon stood outside the open door and heard the counselors talk about his personal and private matters. They told the custody staff they could "Do whatever you want with him" because Jon's family members were all dead so nobody would go to bat for him or cause any trouble. They failed to consider that having no family ties would also give him even less to worry about if he did start killing people.

Jon decided that they needed everything to be spelled out for them in explicit detail. He sent out a warning to the authorities in his detailed "letter from a concerned citizen" that was an unambiguous threat of violence.

LETTER FROM A CONCERNED CITIZEN

By Jon Henry Watson

Well, if someone is reading this, then all has went bad. Charles Bronson bad. In a world surrounded by pimps, drug dealers and baby rapists, the only surprise is that it took this long, but I get ahead of myself.

First things first, I warned C.C.I Lomeli and C.C.II Costa that if my single cell was removed, that people would die. I put it on CDC-R Form 22s, and there is no plausible deniability as both signed and responded to the 22 forms (attached along with 602 Log# MCSP-B-19-04238, in which I requested that C.C.II Costa recommend taking my single cell so that I can help the CDC-R get the violence statistics it needs to battle Prop 57 and get more funds for staffing and overtime. So long as I was issued single cell again after the kill, and housed in close custody for the remainder of my life in the CDC-R as a quid pro quo for my services to this union).

So again, if you are reading this, then I have given you at least one dead body. If it happened in the cell, then it is likely that I made it to the yard to kill more. In for a penny, in for a pound right? But what is important is what got me to this point. For a decade I have exhausted every tool a human being can fathom trying to negotiate a reasonable and diplomatic course through the bureaucratic shit-show that constitutes your administrations in this Orwellian quasi-commie prison industry, but reason and diplomacy are not the currency of prison. So it is clear to me that despite my greatest efforts (I've begged your staff and so-called "mental health" clinicians ad nauseum to help me with this one thing, see Health Care Services 602# MCSP-HC-19001394, more on this later, additionally I have written the wardens, the DRB, and even Governor Newsom) what you need from me is plain old fashion murder. The more horrific the better the odds that it will raise the questions that deserve answers. Why are murderous lifers being forced into medium custody dorms living with low-level offenders which we will no doubt kill should the situation turn to violence? Are you forcing integrated housing (G.P. w/ SNY) to get statistics to support your desire to reconstitute indeterminant SHUs, more funding for staffing, to battle Prop 57, and to throw against Newsom's hiatus on the death penalty? I believe so. And you are using the mental health workers to sweep the pleas of the mentally disabled under the rug while you weaponize and utilize these people as cannon fodder.

The mental health workers of the CDC-R are a sham. I told clinician sanders that I would kill a celly if I were to be double housed, yet still she facilitated the needs of custody over the safety of inmates. Keep in mind that no sooner than Dr. Dreiss recommended single cell for myself and three other inmates, you had him shipped to a dorm living yard (D+E) and as-signed Sanders to our caseload who worked as Costa's henchman and immediately gunned for our single cell. (I can only hope that of the dead bodies that litter this coming crime scene, her favorite pet inmates and the sycophants that bend the knee and kiss the rings of custody are among them, for though I currently have not changed my R.O.E.s to attack and harm your free staff, I can at least murder them in effigy. For now; this is a proxy war.) Also I told Clinician Robinson that I feared I would harm or kill a D.D.P. should I be cleared to live among them, still in the interest of custody, she recommended that I be D.D.P. cleared. I do hope that no retarded persons die in the wake of Costa's situation here with me as that is not my M.O. (I should've never been housed with them).

Keep in mind that this is all simply just your chickens coming home to roost. For years I have allowed your C/Os to use me as a weapon, housing shit-bag after shit-bag with me, know that Ol'Watson would "take out the trash." You know it and I know it. So cut the shit. *You* want to pick who I harm. *You* want to be the architect of violence in prison. And *you* want to control the narrative. Well. I am no longer compliant. Should I ever have to disclose the violence I have rendered unto these shit-bag inmates on behalf of custody we'll all be in court for the next decade. So that is also not my M.O., *but*, should I somehow survive the upcoming storm, know this: I will never double-cell and bow down to your manufactured housing crisis. These cells are designed for one man, and while I do deserve to be in prison for the rest of my life, I do not intend to let my 8th Amendment be trodden upon. *Sic Semper Tyrannis.*

So I propose this: Should I live, I am willing to go back to the original agreement I struck with the warden at High Desert. If you leave me single cell, I will stay in my cell and I will not make weapons, not bother inmates or staff, I will not politic, check paperwork, etc. It was a good agreement, and it worked. Costa broke the treaty. Additionally, and more importantly, I hope that this violence is enough to finally get someone's attention, and force someone to look into how mental health is only serving the needs of custody, and making negligent recommendations with deliberate indifference to the well-being of the inmates they should be helping, all to facilitate and co-sign on the desire of administration to do as they will with the inmates. The same with medical staff... they are paid gross sums of money just to facilitate custody's needs, and to hell with the pain and needs of inmates. I'm done with this construct... I can no longer passively sit and be a cog in this machine. So once more I'll jump on this grenade with hopes that my end, whatever it may be, can serve the greater good.

If I shall miss some of the child rapists in my violence I then apologize to their victims as this is a missed opportunity to bring them closure, but with the continued antagonizing and manufacturing of dangerous living situations, specifically in-cell and dorm housing, my R.O.E.s have changed to prioritize the sycophants and yes-men that serve custody by throwing their fellow prisoners under the bus. The construct needs to change, so that's the grenade I'm jumping on. M.A.C. reps that do not serve the interests of the population are just as bad as these doctors and mental health clinicians that ignore our health needs to facilitate the needs of custody.

One news report stated that Watson had "killed his fellow inmates." He doesn't think there was any "fellowship" between him and two child sex traffickers. He killed them, but he was not a traditional vigilante who might be thought of as seeking justice through violence. He was waging a "proxy war" on prison bureaucracy that pushed human beings to their absolute limit and then told them to obey the rules. Jon was tired of following their rules so he gave them two dead bodies. He believes this will help inflate their homicide statistics so they can justify expansions of their correctional budget, and Jon's "reward" will be serving the rest of his sentence in solitary confinement so he doesn't have to associate with "degenerate" prisoners anymore.

"My Best Me"

Nate Gartrell is a journalist at the *Mercury News*. He sent a letter to Jon Watson to ask for a phone interview so he could learn more about the double homicide. Jon wasn't allowed to use the phone because the CDC-R finally decided he was a security risk. Jon replied to Nate by mail and filled him in on all the lurid details of the homicides.

Being a lifer, I'm in a unique position where I sometimes have access to these people and I have so little to lose… And trust me, we get it, these people are every parents' worst nightmare. These families spend years carefully and articulately planning how to give their children every opportunity that they never had, and one monster comes along and changes that child's trajectory forever.

Nate wrote up the article for the *Mercury News* and posted a link on Twitter. He added that Jon was grateful beyond words for the letters of encouragement and donations to his commissary fund he received from random civilians. Jon also said he hoped to be an inspiration to others to kill their own local pedos. Jon didn't directly encourage anyone to risk their freedom by killing someone in prison, but in his own case, he was serving life. He had "so little to lose" that a double-homicide afternoon was not a problem. Robert Hood, a former supervisor of the federal supermax prison, ADX Florence, commented on Jon's case. He told the *Mercury News* that it's no secret that child sex abusers are targeted in prison (7). They are only put in the general population because there are *so many of them* that they can't keep them safe all the time.

With the division that occurs between white collar criminals, drug addicts, different gangs and all that, the one magnet that pulls them all together truly is the sex offender," Hood said.

He added: "I'm not trying to sound like a bleeding heart here, but the chemistry we put people into in certain prison environments is not healthy for anyone – especially the person at the bottom of the totem pole, which is the sex offender."

I spoke to Nate Gartrell, the journalist who published Jon's story, and asked him how he reacted when he received Jon's letter. He said a feeling of numbness overcame him and he had to process it all, but he also had a story to run so he kicked into journalistic high-gear and posted the article. It went viral. Almost all of the responses to his article were supportive of Watson, but he did get criticism from one anonymous person. This person accused Gartrell of publishing Jon's words in order to provoke violence against pedophiles. This person also criticized Gartrell because he didn't write graphic details about child sexual abuse acts (Gartrell has a hunch that the guy might have been a pedophile).

Nate was grateful that Jon had written to him in a frank and honest manner. Journalists usually have to chase a story and piece together the events. The CDC-R refused to comment, as usual, so Nate had very little to go on before Jon wrote him. He tried to thank Jon with a return letter but it was blocked by the CDC-R. They sent it back to the *Mercury News* as being undeliverable. They also stopped Jon from receiving funds in his commissary account, a restriction that is scarcely used, even for shot callers who used their prison bank accounts to launder drug money (see *The Black Hand* by Chris Blatchford).

The CDC-R conducted an investigation into their classification procedures to determine if any employees had overlooked any reasonable threats to prisoner safety. The internal review found "insufficient evidence" of any oversights in the prison system. The state Inspector General also found that the CDC-R's review was "satisfactory." The watchers never see the watchmen making a mistake.

Jon didn't plan on spending his time in prison waging war on sex offenders. He just wanted to be left alone. He saw this double-slaying as an opportunity to expose the CDC-R for their failures. He could expose their incompetence if he could get a message in a bottle outside the prison walls. He could speak for the other 115,000 prisoners in California. Killing child abusers was a bonus. As he wrote to me, "I feel as though I speak for those who can't. Just as when I strike at a predator, I've done so on behalf of those who couldn't." After he killed them he used his notoriety to tell the world what he thought about the prison system in California.

I am always surprised by Jon's letters. He describes the events of that day as his opportunity to "make it rain pedos!" I offered to make his participation in this book anonymous and he said "I would prefer *not* to be anonymous as I really do want to have these conversations with people and be accountable for my words and opinions, and more importantly to leave a record of the truth for the sake of posterity." I did not censor his curse words. He does that himself. I think this fits well with his belief that patriotism, conservativism, and decency are the most "punk" things imaginable in the California prison system. That belief in decency does not extend to prohibiting homicide.

He is a man who is extremely frustrated by the prison system. He already had nothing to lose when he was given a 50-year prison sentence, but he couldn't adapt to the rules in a prison system he considers to be fundamentally dysfunctional. When he realized that it was never going to improve no matter how polite and rational he was, he decided to force the issue. He killed two sex offenders because had access to them and he despised them. He also got himself placed in the Secure Housing Unit where he wouldn't have to worry about other people anymore. Given the choice between irrational corruption and total isolation, he chose isolation. The lesser of two evils.

I had some questions for Jon. If he hates the staff so much, why did he target child sex abusers instead of them? The answer is simple. Jon *really* hates pedophiles.

It was plain old gunslinger justice... Sex offenders *always* recommit... it's a type of sickness with no real cure and we all know it. They (offenders) act smug and entitled... they think they're smarter than all of us. Surprisingly, for bein' a guy that's rather blasé about dispatching human adults, I *love* kids. I mean absolutely *love* kids... and a lot of people feel this way... so while we have a committee in over our heads deliberating what to do about pimps, dope pushers, gang bangers, etc.... and we can burn calories weighing out the value of these souls... for child traffickers, there's no debate. So again, I'm just in the position where I can absorb the consequences for doing what needs done before the CDC-R weaponizes these turds and launches them back into our communities to teach voters how much they *need* this whole prison industry sh*t show.

There was nothing in Jon's past that would have indicated he was on a path that would end in targeted violence toward child abusers, and yet, Jon's decision to kill those two men was not taken merely out of convenience. He had an almost supernatural reason for choosing *those* types of offenders. He wrote to me with this remarkable story about a dream he had where he was tasked with protecting children, and it stayed in his mind in the period leading up to his crimes.

In the run up to 2020 I had a re-occurring dream that almost certainly was viewed as a premonition by me in the clutch moment when I was feeling "the Howling" in that form, and after the event I had a different re-occurring dream. I dreamt that I paroled and that I really was intent on going to find a new job, but people kept leaving their kids with me! Every time I turned around there was a new kid!? Mostly 7- to 10-years old... I'd say "Who's kid are you!?... and they'd answer in various hood, Ebonics, slang, "My daddy say that the safest spot for me is with you." So I'd have these little ragamuffins around tracking down their parents and no sooner than I gave one back, another would appear... It re-occurred for about 10 or 12 months.

What about that "Howling" instinct that he mentioned? Jon said he can sense a pedophile by the blood-boiling sensation he feels when he looks at one. He said this is a call to arms. He knows that this semi-supernatural sensation will not fit well into a scientific theory that predicts his behavior, but he believes it was an instinct that justified his homicides.

The failing to me, when so-called intellectuals try to extrapolate and quantify people's processes, especially people like me, they try to use some "Western" model where A+B with C catalyst creates Identity Type F... they look for indicators in history, genetic patterns... It's the dogma of academia, the pressure of peer reviewed papers. They use confirmation bias to find supporting facts. It's all so Freudian... so "Western" and "Scientific"... This is because *they* have never felt the Howling... They never looked evil dead in its eye and thought "It is my civic obligation to my fellow man to *destroy* you!" or "A divine calling" that is not answerable to the laws of man, so they think, if I don't experience these things without some sort of pre-existing circumstances, then neither can persons X, Y, or Z. And that is why they fail.

People try to take away from this divine call-to-arms by saying "He or she was raised by... or attacked by..." but as you've seen, I was raised by Christians, Atheists, cops, criminals, Republicans, Democrats, and everything in between... I am welcomed at Islamic services, Native

American sweat lodges, and Odinist Grounds... no specific creed has informed my ideology any more than another... So where does this calling have its origin? Can everyone hear it? Edger Cayce said so... he called it the Akashic Record.

But I do know that when I am in harmony with this Howling, when I am only a vessel of truth, I am my best me. And I am entirely more dangerous and stronger than I would be if I were serving my own interests. And those are the facts.

When I asked if he killed sex offenders to curry favor among other prisoners, he said there is no real honor code in California prisons anymore. Gang members with "Supreme White Power" tattoos play checkers with sex offenders. They will do anything for drugs or money. He thinks that living in crowded dorms lowers the prisoners' sense of right and wrong to match the average of the group, and that is quite low. Jon has no love for his "fellow prisoners" and thinks that only 2% of them are tolerable for any length of time.

Jon told me that on the day he killed those two child abusers he was exhausted. He thought that he would be shot by the correctional officers. This is another lesson we can learn from this case. Lifers have so little to lose. They rarely commit homicide, and double homicide is even more rare, but maybe if these men had a light at the end of the tunnel they would be much less likely to act on their impulses. The slight incentive of a few years of freedom at the end of his life might work wonders on a man like Jon, but the state wanted to send a message that would deter future crime. His response was to commit twice as many murders.

Jon Watson does not fit the profile of a traditional vigilante because he was not abused as a child and he did not follow a path to ideological radicalization. He seems to have exploded with frustration at the prison system, but he had enough self-control to direct his energy toward two people who were almost universally reviled rather than attack a staff member.

Redemptive Justice

Vigilantes who hunt down and kill sex offenders in the community choose to throw away their freedom before they act, but Jon had already lost his freedom. The prison environment in California is often characterized by violence, fear, and control. The pressure was too much, and Jon lashed out at a specific target. The dynamics of "convict justice" are explained in the next chapter, as we look into the dark and disturbing world of America's prisons, but Jon's case stands out as a unique double homicide that might easily be confused with run of the mill vigilantism. His burst of violence has more to do with the pressure of the environment than the desire to "get justice."

I have spoken to some people who know Jon Watson personally. They do not consider him to be a threat to decent people (excluding sex offenders, of course). They would gladly trust him to supervise their children, knowing that Jon would never let anyone hurt them. These supporters know the State of California will never let Jon walk outside the barrier of concrete walls and razor wire, lest he kill again, but it seems possible that in a more rational prison setting he might have used his intelligence and energy to "make good" in a pro-social way that would have prepared him for an early and successful release, back to the community. But in California, serving a life sentence surrounded by "corrupt" staff and "degenerate" prisoners, the only way he thought he could "make good" was to bludgeon two people to death to earn some measure of cosmic justice through retributive violence.

Vigilantes and the practitioners of "convict justice" against child abusers are uniquely associated with child protection virtues that are taken to a level that some people find quite heroic.

Are these child protection virtues enough to convince people that he is really a "good" person, and not just a triple murderer?

Winston Churchill once said of prisoners "There is a treasure, if only you can find it, in the heart of every man." Many people write letters to Jon Henry Watson because they believe they have found his one redeeming characteristic: he protects children. He has passed through a redemption arc. Perhaps the enforcers of "convict justice" are attempting to achieve salvation through violence. As Jon wrote to me:

> We look for redemption and we are throwin' Hail Marys with '12 seconds on the clock. Also, guys like me believe in Cosmic Justice or Karma or Viking Örlög, so it's a bit of a universal offset.
>
> Perhaps some "Wisdom" is watching and I can gain favor when I destroy the monsters who prey on children.
>
> I'm a piss poor Viking, but my desire to correct Cosmic Örlög is what makes me entirely different than my "peers" and not answerable to the laws of man. Not anymore.

In the minds of prisoners, killing a sex offender might be the equivalent to the plenary indulgences of soldiers who were forgiven for their sins during the Crusades. Sinners were required to do penance for their misdeeds, but they could have their punishments remitted if they participated in a "just war" fought in the defense of innocents. Some crusaders fought for personal profit or pleasure, but most fought for their souls.

Using the same logic, American penitentiaries are a type of earthly purgatory. Our prisons were designed to coerce prisoners to live virtuous lives through suffering. The worse your sins, the more time you needed to be reformed. Maybe some prisoners like Jon Watson believe they can be spiritually restored more effectively through violent actions than they can by sitting in a concrete cell for decades. They kill child sex abusers because they believe they are fighting a "just war" for innocents. They might not believe in metaphysical redemption, but their "good deeds" may restore their moral self-esteem. If this description of their motivations is accurate, it begs the question of why these people cannot find a better path to redemption in our prisons that are meant to "correct" and "rehabilitate" them, so they feel they must resort to homicide.

Fierce Magic Beyond Withstanding

By "A Son of Solitude"

It doesn't matter to me if you support my actions or not. I was never trying to impress you or garner your accolades. I wanted to live up to those who were like me when I was young, so I chose to throw myself at the machine and relieve myself of this burden. It is a fierce sort of magic, beyond understanding, this cursed life, which arrives at the hand of an abuser. I am neither a Republican nor Democrat, progressive or liberal, for my right to vote was stripped from me as soon as I plead guilty to my crime. Thus, I cannot belong to any political party. I cannot bear arms. These fundamental rights, no longer mine, I am something sub-American. Through my own choices I have not rendered up the last vestiges of my intrinsic value as a citizen of this country. I am not angry. I don't resent anyone. I will not allow myself to live as a victim, therefore I accept my lot as being further manifestation of a life path which I found myself on, long before I had the capacity to fully reason on my own accord. My life has been laid bare for others to judge. I was a thief and a liar for many years along the way. I was unstable and unhappy, untrustworthy and often unkind. There was no one I trusted, for in my world, no one, no one, could be trusted.

Isn't it interesting how our modern society operates? If a child who was viciously abused for years grows up maladjusted, flawed, imperfect, and sets about to relieve himself and others of the sort of pain he experienced as a child, everyone is shocked. The courts are outraged. Many rush in to microanalyze his past to determine why. "He must be a self-serving bully. An opportunistic criminal." Others want to raise him up as a hero, and use their words to laud the violent expressions of his agony. I've listened to them call for the murder of these child abusers. I've seen them write odes to the torture and assault of pedophiles. But you see, those things, they are all words, and words are easy for anyone to produce. Our society today produces endless words. They are convinced, have convinced themselves and each other, that their words have the same value... for the most part, they do not.

I wish for you to support the righting of wrongs. I wish for you to do this... through action. I wish for you to support the sanctity and surety of a child's peace while they grow up. And I wish for you to do this... through your actions. I wish for you to contribute alongside myself and others, to the deterrence of child abuse, of all types, and I'm asking you to do this... through action. I would never ask you to break the law, and while I have enjoyed our time together very much, I would never, ever, want you to end up here with me, but you must take action, and there is much work to be done. Those of you who can vote and participate in political action, you <u>must</u> do so. The disparity in sentencing guidelines and the ongoing misuse of judicial discretion is glaring. These things can only continue on, through inaction.

Child abuse and molestation are our problem. They have thrived and ran rampant in our communities under our control. All of the laws which have facilitated this sort of crime were written and enacted during our lifetimes, therefore, all of us are responsible. Children are assaulted and abused in our country, in spite of us they are abused. <u>Because of us</u>. I know you are busy. I know that your own family unit is the most important focus of your energy. But I can assure you, your daughter has a little friend who is being abused. Your son knows somebody who is being molested. But if we don't take the time to notice those things, or take action on behalf of others, then nothing will ever change.

When I was a young boy I needed you. I was at your church, and when I came in to the service on many nights, I was walking stiffly. I was visibly injured, but you looked right through me, busy with your religion. I was near to you, at the grocery store, the bruises on my legs quite visible in my little summertime attire. I looked right into your eyes, pleading silently with all my might, but you looked right past me, didn't even notice my pain. My stepfather said no, I couldn't come over and play with your son. Didn't that seem strange to you, time and time again, how a man you knew was isolating his children? I needed you to notice and ask questions, but you did not. You just rolled your eyes and extended the invitation to someone else. Summer camp was only three days, but on that last day I climbed in the canoe and rowed it out onto the lake, and when you found me, I cried and begged you not to send me home, but you laughed, didn't recognize my genuine terror and fear. There was my stepfather, obviously upset at having had to wait. You handed me over to him, with no second thought whatsoever.

I stood there, shaking, on the sidelines of the soccer practice. I was the only kid on the team who didn't run on the field that day. What you didn't know was that I couldn't run that day. My legs were beaten and in pain. None of you ever asked if I was alright. Not a single adult even approached me. But the coach did mention that next week I needed to show a little hustle if I wanted to play on this team...

Seeing my world as I do through a lens fashioned by my experiences as a child, my first ride through the Alaskan prison system was quite enlightening. Up here, the child abusers are heavily segregated. They are almost all housed in totally separate areas. However, I learned quite quickly that the gangs in our system made a commodity of the other sex offenders and divvied them up, like property, depending on their race or financial ability. These prison groups had developed a system which I actually thought was a bit of simple genius, and I began to envision its real-world application. They would basically allow "their" sex offenders to go to work, go to the store, and that's it. They were then required to stay in their room and be grateful that they were still sucking our air. No hanging out in the dayroom, no walks on the yard, no TV time, just room restriction. Full time, if not at work. And the taxation, they paid heavily. This was a big part of the process. They had to contribute monetarily, monthly, to the "community" which managed them. In return, no one was allowed to bother them, smash them out, whatever. They were basically left alone.

I had these puzzle pieces in my mind. This never-ending river of tattooed gang members flowing out the doors of the prison, a readymade structure, a hierarchy with some controls or a value system of sorts. Seemed as though for the most part they would all get released and then begin selling dope, shoplifting, stealing cars, costing taxpayers and regular customers untold sums of money. But they would completely forget about their offender economy as soon as they were released. On the street, none of the child abusers were managed, watched, or taxed. I then thought of that app I downloaded on my phone which pinpointed the addresses of the endless thousands of sex offenders in my state. I wondered to myself, what would it be like if these groups divvied up neighborhoods, and introduced themselves to each one of the sex offenders in that area. Really let each one of them know that there were some tough guys watching. Offered them the opportunity to make donations monthly. Advised them to go to work, go to the store, then just be a homebody. "Don't be hanging around neighborhoods." "Best not to be out and about." I wondered how great it would be to give these tough guys a noble task, manage and tax pedophiles, make yourselves known, keep an eye on your own neighborhood. I remembered that in one of my interactions with a State Trooper up here, regarding a registered sex offender who had given a completely nonexistent address as his location, the trooper told me that the state simply did not have the manpower to supervise them. They could arrest if warrants were issued. Only then. If the offender was caught through a happenstance encounter. Our children deserve so much more than this weak line of protection.

So maybe some of the prison gangs are onto something. Maybe there is a positive application for the barbaric fraternities they've developed in isolation. I personally like the idea of these gangs using their group mentality and structure for the purpose of adding idyllic value to their group, while also adding to the safety of our communities. There is so much manpower available, it's absolutely incredible, as our prisons have basically become large, organized gang recruitment centers. These groups need direction and purpose once they hit the street, and it seemed like a perfect match of skill set versus need to me.

If this sort of idea seems outrageous to your sensibilities, then just imagine how it could have changed my life, if, as a young man, my adoptive father had been accountable to some scary badasses. If he had known that they would be coming through to check on my brother and I, keeping him in line through a very rough sort of support system. Also, you must factor in the enormity of the prison/human warehousing system that has been built, and much like colleges or the military, it is the breeding ground for gangs and fraternities. The government has been eminently aware of this for well over a hundred years. These gangs are never going away. It would be best to give them real purpose. Remember, these various gang members are every bit as much a part of the community as you are. If they were respected and acknowledged, and further, given purpose and direction, believe me, they would all love to be seen in a good light, and all of them claim a concern for women and children. In the context of this particular subject matter it's a great idea.

References

1. Burris, J., Harkness, R., Lent, D., & Weyrauch, C. (1976). Inside San Quentin. https://www.youtube.com/watch?v=YrSAJLRZ1bo.
2. Mumola, C. J. (2005). *Suicide and homicide in state prisons and local jails.* U.S. Department of Justice, Office of Justice Programs. https://bjs.ojp.gov/content/pub/pdf/shsplj.pdf
3. The Times-Standard. (2009, August 11). Gunman pleads guilty to Cutten murder. https://www.times-standard.com/2009/08/11/gunman-pleads-guilty-to-cutten-murder/
4. White, A. (2009, August 29). Second man sentenced in Cutten murder case. *The Times-Standard.* https://www.times-standard.com/2009/08/29/second-man-sentenced-in-cutten-murder-case/
5. *People v. Watson*, A126276 (Cal. Ct. App. Oct. 26, 2010). https://casetext.com/case/people-v-watson-973
6. White, A. (2009, August 29). One man sentenced for Cutten man's death, other contests his plea. *The Times-Standard.* https://www.times-standard.com/2009/08/22/one-man-sentenced-for-cutten-mans-death-other-contests-his-plea/
7. Gartrell, N. (2020). Exclusive: Convicted killer confesses to murdering two child molesters in California prison, says his warnings to guards fell on deaf ears. *The Mercury News.* https://www.mercurynews.com/2020/02/20/exclusive-convicted-killer-confesses-to-murdering-two-child-molesters-in-ca-prison-says-his-warnings-to-guards-fell-on-deaf-ears/

7

CONVICT JUSTICE

In November 2002, Jonathan Kyle Binney was convicted of murder and first-degree burglary after he shot a woman to death inside her home (1). Binney did not have a traditional motive for this crime. He didn't have a grudge against the woman and he wasn't trying to steal anything. He just wanted to go to prison for murder instead of the *other* crime he was awaiting trial for. He had raped his 3-month-old daughter and the physical evidence was damning. He wasn't worried about how he would be treated as a murderer in prison, but he was terrified of being labeled a "baby raper." That is because he knew about the prison hierarchy, and he knew his place was at the very bottom (2, 3).

In American prisons, cop killers are at the top of the pyramid of respect. Bank robbers, desperados, and armed robbers have a high position. Successful drug dealers and professional thieves have some respect. Trashy lowlifes who sell drugs to kids or beat their wives are not respected. White-collar offenders are extorted for protection money or ignored. Seriously mentally ill prisoners are not tolerated if they are too annoying. Former law enforcement officers, child killers, and snitches are targeted for violence. If prisoners find out that you're a "Mo" (molester) or a "Cho-Mo" (child molester) you go to the bottom of the hierarchy. There are regional differences in the terminology (e.g., "skinners," "chesters," and "rapos") but the hierarchy holds true across the country. Men who rape adult women might be openly despised in some prisons or tolerated in others, but anyone who sexually abuses a child can expect their time in prison to be a living hell. It is open season on "Cho-Mos" all year long in America's prisons. The prisoner subculture is proud to endorse vigilante violence against "Cho-Mos." They consider "smashing" a sex offender to be the ultimate sign of virtue.

Perhaps this extrajudicial violence is meant to restore the attacker's self-esteem and social standing. Maybe this is their way of making up for their own misdeeds. Prisoners think they are doing "community service" and should get time off for good behavior when they commit these violent acts. Some might even think they are correcting the court's lenient oversight by getting true justice in the form of the death penalty. A more cynical appraisal is that these violent prisoners merely see "Cho-Mos" as weak targets to be preyed on: a friendless and socially ostracized group of people they can hurt with impunity. But maybe some prisoners have personal motives for attacking a child sex abuser.

Those who were the victims of child abuse and turned to drugs to cope with their trauma might have spiraled into a horrifying life of desperate behavior and crime. They find themselves sharing a prison cell with the type of person who lives in their nightmares. They resent having

DOI: 10.4324/9781003393849-8

to wear the same uniform as the child sex abuser. They eat the same food. They are all lumped together as "inmates" in a correctional facility without distinction on the severity of their crimes. And then the traumatized prisoner learns that the sex offender is serving a shorter sentence and will be back on the street, while he serves years and years on drug charges. How do you think the prisoner feels about the "justice" system in a case like that?

Prisoner attacks on sex offenders happen with enough regularity that we can find plenty of examples without much difficulty (4). The most famous attack is probably the beating administered to "the Subway Guy" Jared Fogel by a prisoner named Jimmy Nigg. In that case, Fogel was serving 15 years for crimes related to the sexual exploitation of children. Nigg was serving the same amount of time for possessing a firearm as a convicted felon. It goes without saying that Nigg resents any comparison of his crime to those committed by "the Subway Guy." He punched Fogel repeatedly and caused minor injuries. The news media picked up the story and Nigg received fan mail from across the country (5). One of Nigg's supporters even coded a wrestling video game where players can reenact Nigg's beating of Fogel on their computers.

Beatings and harassment can lead to lawsuits against the prison. Sometimes a sex offender gets a broken nose. Sometimes broken ribs. One was beaten and drowned in his toilet. Another was convicted by a "kangaroo court" of prisoners who shouted out his guilt and condemned him to be tortured to death. He was beaten for four nights. His teeth were knocked out against the toilet and he was stomped on his groin until the bruises reached his waistline. The correctional officers didn't hear a thing (6–8).

In one case a young man named Shane Goldsby was placed in a cell with a 70-year-old sex offender named Robert Munger. In a twist of fate, it turned out that Munger had raped Goldsby's little sister a few years before. Goldsby beat Munger to death. Goldsby considered this very unlikely coincidence to be like "winning the jackpot in the casino seven times." How did he end up in the same prison, the same unit, the same pod, and the same cell as the man who raped his sister? I know some family members of victims would love to have this opportunity. "Just a few minutes alone with him" is sometimes wished for between clenched teeth. Goldsby had that chance, but he didn't want it. He asked for a transfer to another cell after he discovered the truth, but the officers denied him that opportunity. After he killed Munger, Goldsby was given a life sentence (9).

Jeremy Moody told me when he first arrived in prison for killing a sex offender in 2013, he wasn't sure how he would be received by the prison community. A leader of a Black prison gang was eying Jeremy's "White Power" tattoos. He told Jeremy to follow him into his cell. A dangerous blind spot. For some reason Jeremy agreed. Inside, he saw a pile of commissary snacks on the shot-caller's bottom bunk. The Black gang leader told Jeremy he appreciated his act of community service. "Killing a child molester is something that Black and White prisoners can all agree is a good deed." He told Jeremy to help himself to the grocery store whenever he wanted. When Jeremy politely declined, the shot-caller told him it would be a sign of disrespect to turn down his generous offer. He even let Jeremy use his contraband cell phone any time he wanted. As Jeremy was selecting a few candy bars, the shot-caller told him that his girlfriend on the outside had told him all about Jeremy's case. She sent her gratitude as well. The shot-caller took a selfie of himself with his arm around Jeremy, and texted it to his girlfriend. Can you imagine this scene? A Skinhead and a Black gang shot-caller taking selfies together inside a prison cell? Jeremy joked that he was "Bringing people together, one murder at a time."

A common medium for newly released prisoners to share stories of their prison experience is YouTube. Returning citizens will record vlogs and tell stories about memorable events that happened throughout their incarceration. One of the most popular topics of these videos is "what happens to pedophiles in prison?" Some describe stabbings or beatings, but it is more common to find stories about the psychological torture and harassment of child sex abusers. This abuse is meant to scare the "Cho-Mo" into "rolling up" their belongings and requesting a transfer to protective custody.

Unfortunately, it is difficult to confirm or refute anecdotal stories. While I cannot know for sure if these events happened, they form part of the prison lore that shapes our understanding of prison life. I have compiled some accounts told by former prisoners who publish their work on YouTube to introduce you to this popular form of storytelling:

Uso Ron (30 to Life): (10)

So, I'm in San Quentin prison, 1999, one of my homies, his sister was sexually assaulted, and Karma would have it they sent this dude who did this to my homie's sister to San Quentin, straight to Badger's section, to the fifth fucking tier, right in the middle of all of us. Talk about Fate, right? So, it was able to be set up to where my homie was able to catch this one-on-one fade in the middle of the tier with this dude right before we went to chow, and as the homie was whooping him when the police came up to break it up, the police started mace-ing the old boy that had the case and didn't my homie. It was cool, you know what I'm saying. That was kind of a respect thing from the C.O.s, you know. Can't be in there with that type of crime. Period.

Larry Lawton: (11)

What happens in prison … if you're my cellie in prison and I pull your paperwork and I find out that you're a child molester- that level- fucking with a under 12-year old, it's my duty as a convict to fuck you up. So, the cellmate of a dude who mighta thought he was cool, mighta gave him soup, hung out with him, didn't know that the dude was either a snitch or a child molester for sure, would fuck that dude up. So, we pull paperwork on this fat dumpy white dude in his 40's, looked like – I hate to say the typical look – but I'll never forget this fucking guy's look. He's fucking short and fucking dumpy fat, he just looked like a fucking pedophile. Sure enough, I pull his paperwork, has his charge, had sex with a girl that was 10. Never forget that. 10 years old. So I bring the paperwork to the dudes … I said man this is it. It's your cellie motherfucker. It's your job. Your day. We wait a minute, give him a day or two to solve the problem. Sure enough the fat dumpy guy is sitting in the TV room looking up at the TV … this dude comes up from behind – BAM – fucking slams this fucking guy right in the head, knocks him down, this dude had steel boots on I'll never forget the boots … we're all standing there watching it up against the wall, and blood is flying, blood is flying, blood is flying, he's kicking this fucking dude in the head. Dude is fucking *out*. We get out of there. There's no cameras in TV rooms, so sure enough the guy's laying there, pool of blood, we all go, just leave. Sure enough a guard makes a round … hits the alarms … this guy is dragged out of there, literally on a stretcher. He was fucked up royally, and that was taken care of. The dude who did it, good dude, gotta give him a lotta respect. He did what he had to do in the joint. If you're a child molester, they're worse than rats.

Outside Looking In: (12)

How are sex offenders and child molesters treated in prison? Well, when I was first locked up, I was first incarcerated they got treated *bad*. I ain't know what was going on. I ain't even think nothing about that I just know that it was like every 15 to 20 minutes that went past, guys was going past this one cell it be like, there's three of them …. The did this like every 20 to 30 minutes, like clockwork. This one would yank the door open the other two on this side had cups. Cups full of urine and boo boo, so when he yanked the door open they just throw the cups of boo boo in there on him and then boom close the door, lock it on him …. So I asked someone what's up with that, what's going on over there, I seen them do it like three times, and they say 'Oh, he's a pedophile.' Some was getting jumped on, some was getting slapped, extorted, some was having to do sexual favors for inmates, turning they self out, but over the years it started to getting watered down so that nothing was happening to them. The staff was basically taking up for them and you could get penalized severely for taking up with one of those, a pedophile or sex offender.

Big Herc: (13)

So if you're out there touching on kids or you're a child molester or you got busted for having sex with an underage teenagers whatever the case may be, you go to prison, somebody's going to find out about what you're locked up for whether it's a guard who don't like you and tells someone else what you're in there for or somebody has a person on the street to go online and check your paperwork, but one way or the other they're going to find out you're a child molester and you're going to get your wig split. So, if you find that the guy is a child molester you might as well just slap him upside the head and split his wig yourself so you don't get *your* wig split. So that's what happens to child molesters. They get their head busted. So, the Subway boy? You're gonna get your head busted when you get in prison.

Wrong to Strong: (14)

All I know is they told me 'You and two other guys have to go over there and take care of business.' I was like alright man. I put my boots on … come around the corner, sure enough the dude is sitting there watching TV and I walk up to him and go 'If you don't leave here in two minutes I'm gonna fuck you up.' And I walked away. Went to the bathroom. Got my shit right. When I come back the guard is already walking him to the segregation … I ended up doing my last month there and I ended up coming home …. If I woulda fucked that dude up, what would have happened is I would have caught new charges, probably 3 or 4 years on my case, and I woulda got shipped up to a higher security prison.

Besides the personal interest of getting YouTube views, these stories might have a moral purpose: it might serve as a deterrent to sex offenders who hear the horror stories of life in prison, and therefore scare them straight. Also, it helps challenge society's assumptions about the other prisoners. It is essentially saying "We're not as bad as you think we are. We love children, and we believe in justice." This is a redemption story as much as it is bragging about violent crimes.

Perhaps the allure of the vigilante archetype compels ex-prisoners to describe some virtuous moral system they hold that makes them superior to the "free world" that rejected them. It is a way to out-do the justice system they resent. A man who regrets their earlier crimes might want to balance the scales of Karma. They want to do a good deed for society and regain their self-esteem in the process. They might never be able to make up for the felonies that sent them to prison in the first place, but maybe they can use their unique criminal skill sets to find another way. They can innovate a new way to earn the world's respect. But it begs the question why so many sex offenders survive their prison sentences at all. Maybe some non-sex offenders leave them alone because they don't want additional time added to their own sentences. They are deterred. One

YouTuber, Jay Williams, explained this on his channel. Everyone hated child sex abusers, but they weren't willing to lose their release date over some "piece of shit Cho-Mo."

Jay Williams: (15)

But in my opinion you can never, ever, ever pay for that type of crime. At the moment you decide to take somebody's innocence, violate somebody like that, hurt somebody like that, there is no saving you. You gonna have your day in front of God and have to explain yourself. A lot of them guys walk around untouched. A lot of them guys walk around undetected …. Everybody says, why don't you all kill 'em? You come in with five, ten years, fifteen years, you have a release date. At the moment that you kill another inmate they're going to give you life. They're gonna take you back to court and resentence you. From there they're going to send you to a prison so far away they're gonna pump the sunlight in. The atmosphere you're breathing changes because of how high up you are in the mountains. If you think that this is some movie, that when nobody's looking you're going to pull somebody over into the broom closet and kill them and nobody's gonna tell on you … you don't realize what day and age we're living in. Somebody's always watching and somebody always want to go home … You're going to throw it all away for that piece of shit? Not many men are doing that. And the ones that are the ones who are crazy in the head and the ones that aren't never ever going home.

Let's be honest though … if child sex offenders were truly hunted down and killed on a daily basis there wouldn't be many left alive. Maybe this is another one of those jailhouse legends that come to us from popular culture and former prisoners who want to exaggerate their jailhouse experience. Do you want to make a YouTube channel where you talk about how *boring* prison was? Maybe they heard about a sex offender who was smashed in the prison a few years ago … or maybe it was in another state …. These stories spice up their narrative a little and give them an air of dangerousness.

We need better information. Do eyewitness accounts of violence against child sex abusers support one another? How often does violence against these people occur in America's prisons? Why are they put in the general population? How many are assaulted? How many are raped? How many are killed? Where do these events happen? Do classification and protective custody policies reduce this type of violence? Is violence endemic to our system for all prisoners, not just child sex abusers? What role does race and gang affiliation play in the culture of prison violence? This chapter will explore these questions by bringing together first-hand accounts, social science research, and original data analysis to determine how much of the Convict Code is bluster and how much is deadly serious.

Hard Time

Shaun Attwood was arrested in Arizona for trafficking ecstasy and was held in pre-trial detention. Unfortunately for him, he was arrested in Maricopa County, Arizona where "America's Toughest Sheriff" Joe Arpaio prided himself on his bare-bones correctional facilities. Miserable jails were supposed to deter lawbreakers. "If you don't like it, don't come back" was his motto. The living conditions in the jail were so terrible that Shaun began writing them down on paper and passing them off to a visiting relative who would post the messages on the internet, like a modern-day Boethius. "Jon's Jail Journal" exposed the inhumane conditions including cockroach infestation, deadly spider bites, lack of medical care, dead rats in the food, and excessive heat. These deprivations were bad enough on their own, but the fear of prison violence trumped all other considerations.

When Shaun first arrived, he was clearly out of place in the prisoner subculture. He tried not to show fear. On his first day, members of the Aryan Brotherhood decided to "check his papers." They took him into an empty cell and asked him what his charges were. Shaun didn't even know at that point what his charges implied because they involved a lot of technical information about the conspiracy to traffic drugs, so he hesitated. The gang members became aggressive and asked him if he was a Cho-Mo. The following excerpt is taken with permission from Shaun's book *Hard Time*: (16)

. . . .

"You need to come inside the cell, dog, so we can have a little chat."

"OK," I say.

"Go in there."

I walk into the cell, stop by the window and turn around. Gazing at them, I notice my left eyelid is twitching. One of them blocks the doorway. Another leans an arm adorned with a Valknut – three interconnected triangles found in early-medieval Germanic inscriptions – against the wall, forming a barrier.

"Where you from?"

"England."

"What the fuck you doing out here?"

"I was a stockbroker who threw raves."

"So what they arrest you doing?"

"I'm not quite sure. They didn't actually arrest me doing anything. I was just-"

Raising his forearms, the biggest steps forward, fists clenched. "What the fuck you mean, you're not quite sure?"

All of my muscles tighten.

"How the fuck don't you know your charges?"

I'll try to push my way though them and escape.

"I do but-"

"Every motherfucker knows his charges! What're you hiding from us?"

Got to push through them. If I fight against the wall they'll just close in on me.

He's bullshitting us!" The third closes the door to almost locked.

I'm screwed. Charge and hope for the best.

"If you've got sex offences, you'd better tell us now 'cause we will find out!"

"I don't have sex offences. What I mean is, I don't understand my charges: conspiracy, crime syndicate. I'm new to this. The cops just raided me and nobody's explained what evidence they have. I thought they'd let me go when they didn't find any drugs. I don't know what's going on."

"Where's your paperwork?"

"Right here." I fish it out of my top pocked.

"Let me see." The biggest skinhead snatches the charge sheet. "Goddam, dog! $750,000 cash-only bond! You some kind of Mafia dude or what?"

"No I threw raves. We did drugs. Everyone had a good time." *Are my charges acceptable to them?*

. . . .

Shaun was relieved that the gang members left him alone. If he had been a mo (molester) or a Cho-Mo (child molester) he would have been "KOS" "Killed-On-Sight." Gang members were searching for people to attack so they could gain respect in the jail and earn new tattoos. "The most serious acts of violence earn the highest-ranking tattoos. To be a full gang member requires murder." But Shaun was not out of danger yet. He was assigned to a cell with another newly arrived prisoner. This man was suspected to be a child molester. One of the gang members told Shaun "You can get smashed in here for having a celly who's a Cho-Mo … usually, we'd tell you to tell him to roll up [request a transfer to protective custody], but we're gonna handle it for you." Shaun was grateful that they would take care of the problem for him. Shortly after this he saw a crowd of prisoners heading toward the showers where a man was laying naked on the ground.

………

The naked man raises his head. *It's David.* There is a plea for help in his eyes as they meet mine – a look that freezes me against the wall ….

"Die, you sick child molester!" Rob yells, dropping his heel on David's temple.

"Arghhhhhhhhhhhh …."

The skinheads vie for stomping room. David arches his back in agony …. The blows silence David. Blood streams from his nose …. A skinhead jumps up and down on David. I think I hear his ribs snap. I scrunch my face in revulsion of the cracking sound …. The spectators have adopted the safety-in-numbers strategy of the wildebeest. None of them dare venture from the herd. Mesmerized by the violence, they watch from a safe distance. Gripped by the same instinct, I join the back of the herd.

As if they've exhausted their supply of aggression on David, the skinheads stop the beating and march away. David is a whimpering heaving mound of flesh, blood pooling around his head.

What kind of world am I in? This stuff really happens. It could have been me last night. How will I survive?

Just when the violence seems to be over, a rhinoceros of a man with spider webs tattooed on his thick neck approaches the skinheads. "How come we can still hear the little bitch?"

"We fucked the chomo up good," Rob says.

"Not good enough." The man approaches the shower with the causal gait of someone going to the shop to buy a bottle of milk, grabs David's neck and starts slamming David's skull against the concrete as if he's trying to break open a coconut. *Crack-crack-crack ….*

I'm revolted but compelled to watch. The big man has increased the stakes. The code of these people probably includes killing anyone who interferes or flags down a guard. Even walking away will be a show of disapproval, and invitation to be attacked next. I'm too scared to move.

David's body convulses. His eyes close. Stillness. Silence. *Is he dead?* He remains on the floor while the prisoners resume their activity as if nothing happened. Eager to distance myself from what looks like a corpse, I return to my cell.

Ten minutes later, a guard enters the pod to do a security walk. When he arrives at the shower, he yells. "Everybody lockdown! Lockdown right now!" shouted the guard. The prisoners return to their cells, slamming doors behind them. Guards rush into the day room. Having never seen violence at this level before, I press myself to the cell door to assess David. I watch them remove him on a stretcher. There is fluid other than blood leaking from his head. A yellowish fluid.

…….

By the time Shaun was sentenced and transferred from the jail to state prison he knew how to handle threats of violence. When one established prisoner asked him his charges and he replied that he was throwing raves, he was accused of partying with underage girls. Shaun immediately responded "Hey, I'm not child molester, and I'd prefer you didn't say shit like that!" and offered to show him his paperwork. "Checking papers" and "heart checks" are an initiation ritual that must be navigated quickly and forceful or a new prisoner will get a reputation as an easy target. Expressing extreme disgust and hatred toward "dirty" offenses sends a message. Hesitation implies you have something to hide. What is it about prison life that results in this hierarchical structure within the society of captives?

Anecdotal accounts may not be easy to confirm, but their plausibility can be supported by similar events occurring elsewhere. A nearly identical story to Shaun's happened in Orange County California around the same time as the events recorded in *Hard Time*. A man named John Chamberlain was held in the county jail on charges of downloading child sex exploitation material. The prisoners wanted to check his paperwork. He refused (17). Allegedly, a sheriff's deputy told a White gang shot-caller "There was a child molester in Cubicle J., Bunk 7." A group of 12–20 prisoners took turns beating Chamberlain and yelling "baby raper!" They stomped him to death. The three sheriff's deputies on duty didn't hear anything. They were watching television. The killers went to the shower and washed the blood off their shoes. They forced all non-involved prisoners to wet their own shoes so they wouldn't stand out. After an investigation, the jail spokesman said "We stand by our record, and we stand by the professionalism of the men and women who operate our jails each and every day." Several convictions were made in this case, but how many more "Cho-Mos" are smashed in American's jails and prisons that are never reported to the public?

The Convict Code

Prisons have been called America's sewage disposal system. We flush away the people we do not want in our society. These people are not gone, just out of the sight of most of us. They congregate together inside the prison system. If the environment is tightly controlled then the institutional culture will influence their behavior in profound ways. If it is loosely controlled then the prisoners develop their own internal structure. They filter and sift themselves into different strata to create a social order amongst themselves. This "society of captives" has changed over the years. Excessive crowding, legislative changes, and social movements from the wider society have altered how prisoners behave. The formation of race-based gangs in the 1960's and 1970's had a tremendous impact on the social order inside prisons, but there is a persistent legend that underneath all the tattoos and slang there exists a foundational law of the prisoner's social order: the Convict Code.

The most frequently cited "convict criminologist" was John Irwin, who served five-years in the California prison system during the 1950's. He later earned his doctoral degree in sociology and published several books about the changing landscape of prisoner subcultures [these were *The Felon* (1970), *Prisons in Turmoil* (1980), *The Jail* (1985), *It's About Time* (with James Austin, 1994), *The Warehouse Prison* (2005), and *Lifers* (2012)]. Irwin's description of prisoner subcultures in men's prisons differed in some ways from those observed by outsider sociologists, but mostly in terms of detailed nuances in the prisoner hierarchy.

Rather than focus on a prisoner's "role" like previous scholars, Irwin emphasized a prisoner's adherence to the "Convict Code." The basic rules of this code were: (1) do not inform, (2) do not openly interact or cooperate with the guards or the administration, and (3) do your own time. Simple enough for even a fresh fish to understand. Mind your own business and keep your mouth shut. Irwin found that some prisoners were unable to fulfill their part of the code and they often found themselves socially ostracized, vulnerable to victimization, or even targeted for violence because of their place in the prison hierarchy.

Irwin made a clear distinction for one type of offender he called "rapos" (those convicted of rape). These were sex offenders who were "repulsive to most prisoners" and therefore were relegated to "the very bottom of the pile" (*The Warehouse Prison*, 2005, p. 34). Men's prisons are extremely hierarchical, but their caste system is upheld by the threat of violence. Rapos stay at the bottom, and they are always in danger.

Anecdotal evidence supports the hierarchy in prisons across America. When Clark Fredericks went to prison in New Jersey for killing the man who sexually assaulted him as a child, he was asked by his cellmate what his conviction charges were. The man said "I have to ask because older white guys are usually child molesters, and if you're one I have to take care of you." Clark said "I'm the opposite of a child molester" and he showed the man a newspaper clipping describing the homicide of Dennis Pegg. Instant respect.

In a way, prison subcultures are prime examples of what society would look like if everyone was expected to take the law into their own hands for self-protection (18, 19). When you are the victim of a crime, you can call the police. In parts of America where the public have a profound lack of confidence in the police, they get revenge themselves. In prison you would think that prisoner behavior is continually monitored and rule infractions are instantly suppressed by watchful correctional officers, but in reality, omniscient supervision has only ever existed in the imagination of philosophers like Jeremy Bentham. C.O.s might be more likely to turn a blind eye to a prisoner beat-down if it helps them maintain order among the other 200 men in the dorm. Even if the C.O.s would help you, you have to ask them for protection, and "snitches get stitches."

Prisoners are truly on their own. Those who cannot make themselves valuable to a gang or clique have to pay for protection. Money, drugs, and sexual favors might be enough to keep them from being preyed upon. Within this extremely anti-social society, we might have a perfect example of a vigilante culture. It is a social system built on the expectation of retaliation and deterrence through fear. As one prisoner said to me "Humpty Dumpty Cho-Mos don't stand a fucking chance in here. They got no friends and they can't stand up for themselves. Even the cops won't protect them."

Socially unacceptable crimes are punished severely, even in women's prisons. There are anecdotal reports of women ganging up on "baby killers" and "baby rapers" in the shower and sodomizing the offender with a broomstick. Whether these stories are proof of systematic torture has not been established, but the persistence of the *legend* shows what prisoners prioritize in their culture. It is more likely that women prisoners will socially isolate a child abuser, but violence does happen. As one woman is reported to have said "If you're a pedophile no one really does want to hang out with them. Some are hurt. Particularly people who attack child case convicts. [It's] like a police force in here because most of us were abused" (20).

The most in-depth discussion of violence against child sex abusers in prison comes from research conducted by Rebecca Trammel (at the Metropolitan State University of Denver). Professor Trammel went into the homes of recently released prisoners who were members of White Power prison gangs to interview them – a courageous way to conduct research. She asked them about life in prison and the convict code in California. Once she accidentally called them her "informants" and was quickly reminded that they were not snitches. She was careful not to use that word again.

The results of Trammels' work were published in peer reviewed academic articles and comprises some of the only scholarly work on the phenomenon of prison violence targeting child sex abusers. Her 2009 article entitled "We have to take these guys out: Motivations for assaulting incarcerated child molesters" (published with co-author Scott Chenault) explains the prisoners' animosity toward child molesters in graphic detail (21). It must first be understood that the average California prisoner finds it strange that anyone needs to hear an explanation for why they hate child sex abusers. They are surprised when anyone asks them to explain. They do not need a justification because "everyone is on board," "there is no debate on this issue" and even the CO's "hate these guys too." Here is a quote from Trammel's interviews (borrowed with permission):

> If they are too stupid to go to the PC yard, then we have to do them. There is no debate on this issue. Everyone knows what we do, and it's very simple. We all work together on this issue, trust me, no one is arguing their case for them, we all know what needs to be done. I took a guy out once, he raped his own kid, can you believe that? What the hell is wrong with the world? He raped his kid, and I showed him what happens to the assholes who do that kind of thing.

Child sex abusers are different than other prisoners. They tend to be physically weak, older, out of shape, and even if they come to prison in decent physical condition, they tend to stay in their cells to avoid trouble. They don't go into the yard. Eventually they get fat. Their uniforms don't fit anymore. They're always depressed or anxious. There are many obvious signs of a Cho-Mo in prison. Some might "lose" their paperwork or refuse to show their conviction charges when they arrive in prison. This is a sign that they have something to hide. Sometimes a prisoner arrives with missing teeth or a black eye. This is a sign that some other prisoner already targeted them for violence, and where there's smoke there's fire. Prisoners will "take him out back" to a blind spot and administer convict justice. If the Cho-Mo is too stupid to go into protective custody they will teach him a lesson. When he leaves the cellblock, the other prisoners no longer have to share space with them. They exile these undesirables from the society of captives.

Trammel found that some prisoners do not merely attack child sex abusers because they are disgusted by them, they have a true vigilante motive. Vengeance and deterrence. They want to finish the job that the justice system was too weak to perform. They want retribution.

> They raped a kid. They deserve much worse than just going to prison. They should know how that kid felt to be alone and vulnerable. They should know real terror.

> Child molesters are really sick and can't be cured. We just need to get rid of them. Rapists, you know someone that rapes a woman or something, they just need to learn a lesson. They're sick too but, um I guess it's all the same. You don't force people to have sex, that's just wrong.

> Baby killers or people that mess with kids. They can't be cured or anything, so we're just trying to remove them from the picture.

> To hell with those guys, they are going to hell and I don't mind sending them there early.

One prisoner called Jimmy mentioned that killing a child molester would finally achieve justice for the victims and their families (not unlike the interrogation responses of Steven Sandison in Chapter One). Here is the exchange he had with the interviewer.

Jimmy: If someone raped your kid, you'd want me to kill him right?
Interviewer: I don't know if I'd want them killed.
Jimmy: Don't pull that PC shit with me, you'd want him dead. We all would. We are doing a favor to the family. That's why we put people to death and stuff, we do it for the family. Think of the mom and dad or the brother and sister and stuff, don't they deserve some revenge? I think they do. I'd sleep at night if I knew that anyone that raped my kid is killed in prison.

There is also a strong sense of resentment that these prisoners who were convicted of stealing cars, selling drugs, or even for violent crimes should be mixed with "dirty" perverts. They resent the relatively short sentences these offenders receive. They resent wearing the same uniform as them. They resent sharing the same space as them.

Mike: I committed a crime, I got caught, I did my time, but shit, I never hurt anyone. I've never even hit anyone before I went to prison. I've never hit my girlfriends, I never hurt a kid. I wouldn't want to hurt a kid. I've only had sex with adults that wanted to have sex with me. So I get to hang out in the yard in prison with all the freaks? What's up with that? That's not right.

Question: What should we do with them?

Mike: Put them in the yard. Let nature take its course. I bet people rape kids and shit knowing that they get special treatment in prison, so they don't even worry about that if they do get caught. That's not protecting our kids.

In the absence of official governance, prisoners develop community responsibility systems-better known as gangs. In a life-or-death situation, prisoners cannot afford any weak links in their groups. According to prison gang expert David Skarbek, the prison social order is precariously balanced according to in-group loyalties. In California, for example, gangs want members who *can't* betray them. Race-based membership means that someone can't simply leave one gang for another. They have to stay in the group. An interesting finding in Trammel's work is that prisoners did not attack child sex abusers who were of a different race. They did not want to spark conflict, but they did expect the other races to "take care" of their own child molesters.

Other accounts by prisoners have revealed how important a gang's reputation can be, and how the walls of the prison can be porous enough to export violence to the streets. When a Mexican Mafia member was implicated in a drive-by shooting that killed two children in 1992, leaders inside California's prison system were enraged. They didn't want their unique honor-code to be stained by the blood of children. The shooting might have been an accident, but they wouldn't stand for one of their own hurting a baby. They had the shooter killed and declared a moratorium on all drive-by shootings in the state. This truce lasted for several months and helped reinforce the gang's semi-honorable image (22).

A more pragmatic reason for gang members to attack child sex abusers is because they are more likely to snitch. Just as gangs fall along racial lines to keep members from defecting, "Cho-Mos" are a weak link that can be exploited by the prison officials. The "do not inform" rule is not a suggestion. As we all know, snitches get stitches, so why would anyone break this rule? A child sex abuser might be the most likely type of prisoner to snitch in order to gain protection. They are terrified that someone will find out they are a "Cho-Mo." If they can avoid having their papers checked they might be exposed by the staff at any time. If a correctional officer needs information they know who to call on. The "Cho-Mo" will snitch in order to keep their conviction charges a secret. It is the ultimate leverage.

Prisoners hate the people who go into protective custody. It is a major stigma for someone if other prisoners know they had to ask "the cops" for help. They often accuse prisoners of racking up drug debts and then requesting a transfer to P.C. so they don't have to pay up. But the real stigma is the possibility that a P.C. inmate is secretly a child sex abuser. After all, why would someone in P.C. want to come back to the general population at all? The most likely explanation is that they are a spy for the prison staff. They made a deal with the officers to find some juicy secrets in gen-pop, like an escape attempt or a hooch distillery. They give this intel to the officers in exchange for privileges and protection.

Pete Earley's book *The Hot House: Life Inside Leavenworth Prison* explains how federal prisoners identify snitches and child sex abusers. The first red flag occurs if the new arrival refuses to explain their conviction charges, implying they have something to hide. If a prisoner transfers from a state prison to the federal system, they are suspected of being extreme troublemakers or they are being transferred for their own protection. Notorious offenders might be killed in their own states, but in the federal system they can be transferred thousands of miles away. That explains why a state might want to get rid of a "dirty" offender, but not why the federal system would accept them. One prisoner interviewed by Earley said "I know exactly what happened .... Some hack from Michigan called up a lieutenant here and said, 'Hey, I got a prisoner and I got to get him out of my state institution before someone kills him.' Now, a lieutenant here says, 'Well why should we take him? Does he cooperate?' and the guy in Michigan says, 'Fuck yes, he'll cooperate, because if he don't we'll tell everyone he's a baby-raper and they'll kill his ass.'" Child sex abusers need protection, and if they become informants for the staff they might be protected.

I have interviewed correctional officers in several U.S. states, and most of them laugh at these allegations. They think most officers don't care about playing politics with prisoners at all. They lump sex offenders in with all the other "inmates" as manipulative threats, and the best way to avoid trouble is to stay professional and distant. They deny "hanging a jacket," coercing snitches, or turning a blind eye to violence. Most C.O.s don't want anyone to get hurt because they'd have to fill out paperwork and tolerate an investigation. I am presenting both sides of the issue here, but we should keep in mind that the cultural context varies between states, facilities, and even shifts of officers, so anything can happen.

Fleisher and Krienert's research on prisoner beliefs about sex and rape uncovered some interesting information that is pertinent to this discussion. They were repeatedly told that rapists (whether their crimes occurred outside or inside the prison) were repellent. Rapists were socially marginalized by other prisoners because "Nobody wants them in the group. They are pushed away." They have no allies because mainstream prisoners do not want to hurt their own reputations. "Inmates abhor rape and rapists" write Fleisher and Krienert. "Rapists are negatively stigmatized and may be targets of violent or nonviolent aggression within prison walls." Among the prisoners they interviewed, 25% of men who had served more than ten years claimed to know about a rapist who was killed in prison, and just under 5% of women said the same. "Street rapists and Cho-Mos are pieces of shit, in everybody's eyes. Rapist [inside] is no better than a rapo outside" one prisoner said.

However, there is another variable that we have not considered yet, and that is money. Money and drugs are synonymous in prison, because they both bring power and influence (D.R.E.A.M. = Drugs Rule Everything Around Me). Money can bribe the staff or pay a debt. Sometimes it can even buy respect for a "Cho-Mo." Jon Watson and a few other prisoners told me that child sex abusers are like pets for the gangs. They pay for protection. The gang members let them leave their cell to get food and buy things from the commissary. Then they take a percentage of their property and hustle them back into their cells. Like letting your dog out before kenneling them. Everyone has their price, and for some gangs, a few bags of potato chips might be enough to prevent violence against child sex abusers.

One example from Fleisher and Krienert's research might illustrate this point quite well. Not only can child sex abusers pay for protection, but they can also pay for sex with young baby-faced teenagers. Fleisher and Krienert interviewed a man they called "Country" who was a "sex entrepreneur." He procured punks, bitches, and penitentiary turn-outs for prisoners who could pay for their services.

> $1.50 for some sex, a bag of coffee, it just depends, each case is different. I might find a child mo-
> lester who wants a real young cute 18-year-old boy and he might send me $100 cause he doesn't
> want anyone to know he's involved …. All kids would be about the same age, 18 or so. If they're
> a little older, they can be spotters, and can go out and bring me new people. I'll tell them "Hey,
> keep an eye out and get me new people" they'd get rewarded with extra tobacco or marijuana.

Where does this type of activity rank inside the prisoner hierarchy? Rapists are supposed to be "abhorred" and child molesters are "reviled," and yet a rapist is able to coerce a young man to have sex with a child molester for $100? Where is the honor code of the noble convict in this case? It should be remembered that despite some improvements in recent years, juveniles can be sent to adult prisons in some states. Rodney Hulin was 16-years-old in 1995 when he was sent to an adult prison for arson-related crimes. He was unfortunate enough to be sentenced in Texas when the slogan *Do Adult Crime, Do Adult Time* was in vogue. He was 5'2 and weighed 125lbs. He didn't stand a chance. He was repeatedly raped by the adult prisoners. He begged to be transferred to protective custody, but in the days prior to the Prison Rape Elimination Act, the officers did nothing to help him. After all, prison "ain't the Holiday Inn" as we are so often reminded. Rod-ney finally discovered that the best way to be put in isolation was to break a rule, so he did, and the officers quickly responded by throwing him in the Hole. Rodney was finally alone in solitary confinement, and he used this opportunity to hang himself. He did not die immediately. He fell into a coma and was transferred to a prison hospital. They did not want to send him to a private hospital because his unconscious body might escape, so they kept him until he turned 18-years-old and he was paroled. He never regained consciousness. He died shortly thereafter (23).

The Texas Department of Criminal Justice repeatedly failed to protect this 16-year-old from his torment, but maybe that was part of their plan. They want prisons to be nightmarish hellholes in order to amplify the public's fear of punishment. Prison rape is an added deterrent. Maybe they wanted his case to scare the rest of Texas' teenagers into obedience. But this nightmarish scenario begs another question: if the officials couldn't protect this kid from being raped, where were the brave convict vigilantes who do not tolerate "rapos" and "Cho-Mos"? Which of the rules in the convict code permit the rape of teenagers?

Fleisher and Krienert's research provide us with a potential answer. Some prisoners do not believe that prison rape is "really rape." At least in men's prisons, if a prisoner is sexually assaulted then they are deemed too weak to protect themselves, so they deserved it, or they actually wanted it to happen. This is a classic "blame the victim" technique. One that complicit prisoners share with the "Cho-Mos" they claim to despise.

As we have seen in this book, some prisoners *do* attack child sex abusers. But if it is not because of a moral code pervasive in the inmate subculture, *why* do they do it? It may not be such a noble cause after all. Maybe they just pick on "Cho-Mos" because they are weak and friendless. Andrew Vachss had no faith in the so-called "Convict Code." He wrote a fictional story explaining this fraudulent virtue (24).

> You know why cons always target baby rapers? Because they're usually such sorry bastards –
> old, sick, weak, with no crew outside. Or young and fucked up in the brain, you know? The
> kind that can't protect themselves. And this bullshit that the cons fuck them up because they

love kids, or 'cause they 'got kids of their own'? Crap! They kill them and they rip them off because they are fucking weak .... That's the only rule in here. There's no 'code.'

Gangs aren't in the business of securing real justice against child sex abusers any more than they are in the business of protecting weak members of their own race. They are in the business of using violence to extort weaker prisoners and retain their monopoly over the prison drug market. One "good deed" of "smashing a Cho-Mo" doesn't wash away their criminal careers, even among people who consider this behavior to be noble. It's a free pass for violence and extortion. Like jack-rolling, mugging drug dealers, or robbing adulterous Johns, child sex abusers are targeted because they are unlikely to call for help (25, 26). Who would help them?

Tall Tales and Virtue Signaling

The famous undercover journalist, Ted Conover, worked in Sing Sing prison for almost a year to get stories for his book *NewJack*, and even though he tended to be on the prisoner's side on most issues related to incarceration, even he admitted they were shameless liars. A joke he heard in prison was "How do you know when a prisoner is lying? When he opens his mouth." He acknowledged that there were good reasons to lie in a place where appearing tough can keep you safe. He also wrote that child sex abusers pretended to be murderers so others would leave them alone (27). Unfortunately, this culture of fraud makes it impossible to know if the information you receive has an ulterior motive. As Rebecca Trammel wrote in her book *Enforcing the Convict Code: Violence and Prison Culture*, the greatest limitation of qualitative research with prisoners is knowing whether they were actually telling the truth. She acknowledges this in the introduction of her book with the polite phrase "They may, by accident or deliberate action, have given me inaccurate statements."

Despite these concerns of inaccurate information, we should remember that truth is stranger than fiction in prison. There is no story so bizarre or extreme that hasn't actually happened at some point, but if child sex abusers were being brutally murdered every day in our prisons it should be obvious in the official statistics. In reality, prisons in America are not as dangerous as most people think.

Trammel and Chenault found that there were almost 1,300 prisoners admitted to prison in California for "lewd acts with a minor" and almost all of them stayed alive throughout their prison terms. Some are in protective custody, but most are simply allowed to live. After all, how many prisoners are willing to commit a murder in order to fulfill their part of the convict code? Jon Watson (Chapter Six) told me that "you can't throw a rock in a California prison without hitting a child molester." According to the California Death in Custody statistics, only 22 prisoners died by willful homicide in 2020, and most of these were not convicted of sex crimes (and remember that two of those were killed by Jon Watson).

I examined the California death in custody data with the assistance of James Bacigalupo, a doctoral candidate at the University of Massachusetts-Lowell. Of the 1,602 sex offenders who died in California prisons, 19 died of a drug overdose, 94 died by suicide, 1,369 died of unspecified "natural" causes, and 49 were killed by another person. Among these, 4 were killed by a blunt instrument, 18 were killed with hands, feet, or fists, 16 were strangled to death, 9 were stabbed to death, 2 were killed by unknown means, and one was killed by a staff member. The remaining number died of unknown causes or an investigation was still pending. The average age of murdered sex offenders was 50 (range = 26–73). There is a very real possibility that the cause of death is labeled inaccurately, and many of these homicides could have been motivated by drug debts, disrespect, or personal beefs that had nothing to do with vigilantism. Sex offenders were most likely to be killed in the California Substance Abuse Treatment Facility (6), High Desert State Prison (6), Salinas Valley State Prison (6), and Wasco State Prison (4). Future research should evaluate the role of protective custody in preventing sex offender homicides. Unfortunately, this data was not available for analysis at the time of this writing.

We found that in the period between 2005 and 2019, sex offenders were *not* more likely to be killed than most other prisoners, a finding that goes against the pecking order theory. We found that people incarcerated for drug offenses were the least likely to be killed, but every other type of offender had similar odds of dying at the hands of another prisoner. These findings held up even when we controlled for the effects of age, race, and gender (incidentally, all of the sex offenders who were killed in prison were male). The biggest limitation of this study is a lack of important individual-level data. For example, we could not control for "time at risk" so perhaps some of the unlucky homicide victims were serving longer sentences.

I also used the *National Corrections Reporting Program, 2000–2019* data to determine if sex offenders were more likely to die in custody than other prisoners. The data was not ideal for this analysis. Some states reported the cause of death, but most did not. Still, I was able to control for the prisoner's age and time at risk, so I could adjust my predictions for two of the most important causal factors in a natural death, thereby increasing the chances that I was measuring unnatural death. Using a binary logistic regression model, I was able to control for the individual's state, year of sentencing, gender, race, and ethnicity. Out of 8.9 million cases, 31,777 people were listed as dying in custody. People convicted of rape were 2.1 times more likely to die ($p < .001$), those convicted of lewd sexual acts with a child were 1.6 times more likely to die ($p < .001$), and those convicted of aggravated sexual assault of a child were 1.8 times more likely to die than other types of prisoners ($p < .001$). When I ran alternative models I found that violent offenders were also at a high likelihood of death (e.g., murderers and armed robbers), but sex offenders remained a high risk group for dying in prison. I can't say for sure if this increased mortality is due to homicide, suicide, accidents, or natural causes unexplained by age and time in prison, but it does support the idea that prison is a health hazard for sex offenders. I would not assume this is a completely reliable estimate, but it is a starting point that other researchers can use to justify further exploration with more detailed databases.

While "increased risk" of victimization is certainly worth measuring, we also have to acknowledge the extremely low base rate of homicides in US prisons. It's not like the movies. People are not killed every day, and when they are we cannot assume it was enforcement of the convict code that caused the crime. An article by Cunningham, Sorensen, Vigen, and Woods in 2010 examined official homicide records in prisons operated by the Texas Criminal Justice System. There were 35 total homicides between January 2000 and June 2008 (a remarkably low number considering that the average annual population of prisoners during this time period was around 150,000 prisoners). Interestingly, the offense status of the victim was only considered to be a contributing factor to the homicide in four cases (12.5% of the total number of homicides). All of these murder victims had been convicted of child molestation crimes. While this is a commonly reported motivation for homicide, it is still a rare event, and the desire to kill a child sex abuser was reported as being only one factor among others in each case. For example, one of the sex offenders who was killed had terrible hygiene. His cellmate killed him because he would not clean himself, and his child sex abuse crimes were not a primary motivation (28).

If the research on prisoner subcultures is accurately defining groups within a hierarchy, we would expect to see that prisoners designated as social outcasts would be more likely to experience victimization. The general consensus is that prisoners who are troublemakers (violent towards others), seriously mentally ill, dependent on drugs and alcohol, and who are incarcerated for sex offenses have the least respect in the prison hierarchy. Therefore, these prisoners are expected to be most vulnerable to victimization within the prison. Other factors certainly play a role, but despite the complexity of prison violence across facilities and over time, if the prison "pecking order" is a stable characteristic of prison subcultures then there should be some *evidence* of this in victimization data.

So we have a problem. How do we know for sure if these anecdotal accounts are really explaining a foundational component of the prison social order? The biggest confounding factor is that there are many *other* reasons why someone might be physically attacked in prison that have nothing to do with their sex offender status. I should explain what we know about the other factors that predict prison violence before we investigate violence against child sex abusers.

The Science of Prison Violence

You've seen the movies. You've read the stories. Prisons are dangerous places. Many people have an incentive to *minimize* reports of violence, but this is overcorrected by those who exaggerate the problem. American prisons are not as violent as they are portrayed by entertainment media or even the news media, but that doesn't mean they are safe. The Bureau of Justice Statistics has estimated there were 1,598 homicides in U.S. state and federal prisons and 469 homicides in U.S. jails between 2001 and 2019, which translates to about 109 homicides in our correctional facilities each year (29). We have seen an increase in prison homicides in recent years, with 2019 having the highest number of murders during this period (143). Prisoners have told me that the real number is much higher because deaths have been misclassified to make some prison staff "look good," but obviously I do not have any way of knowing that for sure. I can only use the official statistics to analyze these events.

Even if the number of deaths are lower than you might think if you watched *Shotcaller* and *Brawl in Cellblock-99*, we can all agree that prisons do not guarantee one's safety. Non-lethal violence is a real threat to any prisoner who isn't careful. For over a century, there have been reports of violence in men's prisons that range from personal beefs, organized gang warfare, collective uprisings, and seemingly senseless acts of cruelty. If you can take your eyes away from the blood stains you might notice that the majority of prisoners are peaceful (I always baffle my students when I say this). It's true. Most prisoners want to do their time and mind their own business. They want to "get their program on" and earn points for early release. They want to pass the time and might be willing to break a few rules to earn creature comforts, but they generally keep their hands to themselves. I met one prisoner who spent 38 years in prison in Michigan and he *never* had a single rule violation. I confirmed this with his official records.

Most people in prison don't want to start trouble with the staff or other prisoners. In 1976, a prison psychiatrist at San Quentin said:

> There's a different value system here in the prison whereby it's okay to kill someone in certain situations, such as if that person has killed a friend of yours or a member of your gang, you're supposed to retaliate by killing them. Or if that person owes you a debt, it may even be for just a few packs of cigarettes, it's okay in the inmate peer group to kill that person …. Only a small percentage of the inmates really espouse this different value system actively; maybe ten, fifteen percent of the population. The rest of the population are somewhat terrorized by the small percent at this time. They're afraid to speak up against it. They're afraid to try to control these inmates. The only way they could control them would probably to become violent themselves and they wish not to do that.

I analyzed official prison misconduct data with criminologists Matthew Logan (Texas State University), Matthew DeLisi (Iowa State University), and doctoral candidate Andrea Hazelwood (Penn State) to determine if this statement would hold up in a Midwestern state using more recent data (30). We were surprised to see that our final results were in line with the San Quentin psychiatrist's estimate that 10%–15% of prisoners were terrorizing the rest. We found that the top 10% of rule violators were responsible for 100% of violent misconduct. The top 1% of rule violators were responsible for 24% of violent infractions in men's prisons. This information is useful because it reminds us that not all prisoners are violent and out of control. Most (90%) never get in any trouble for violence. They just do their time. The other 10% are committing violent acts, but it is not always easy to understand why. We should keep in mind that Ohio is not as violent as California, so this kind of research should be investigated in other jurisdictions.

The reasons why someone might engage in violence in prison are as multitudinous as the reasons why they committed the crimes in the community. It might be the individual's personal characteristics, the environmental pressures they face, and the situational aspects that provoke or permit the violence to occur. It's complicated, and unlike the science of "criminology" that has attempted to name a theory for every imaginable causal influence, prison researchers are satisfied with a very short list of explanations: the person *imported* their violent tendencies with them into prison, the *deprivations* of the prison environment cause violent behavior, or the people in charge of the prison have failed to prevent violence through proper governance. When these three explanations are combined together we can see potential policy implications for reducing prison violence. If prisoners are bringing their violent beliefs with them into prison then we should give them aggression replacement training at the beginning of their sentences, not at the end. If the deprivations of prison life are causing violence we should alleviate those conditions with more safe and humane living environments. And finally, we should attempt to maintain a predictable and orderly prison environment where prisoners do not have to fear for their lives. We can do that through proper prison management and by training correctional officers in evidence-based violence reduction practices. Sounds easy, right?

Researchers have been studying prison violence for a long time. They want to identify the most predictive factors that can help make classification decisions to help restore prison order. We know that prisoners who had extensive childhood behavior problems, more extensive criminal histories, violent behaviors, gang involvement, and were diagnosed with serious behavioral disorders and psychopathy are most likely to engage in criminal conduct inside prison (31–38). A systematic review of all prison misconduct studies published between 1980 and 2013 found that although there were some inconsistent findings in the research, there was considerable evidence that supported certain risk factors. Younger prisoners, those with antisocial peers, those who used drugs prior to incarceration, those with mental health problems, prior criminal history, prior misconduct history, and higher security level placements were the most consistent predictors (39).

This information is useful, but difficult to conceptualize in practice. When I speak with prisoners about violence they never talk about the characteristics of the perpetrators or the victims. They talk about the *situation*. They talk about interpersonal conflicts, drug debts, aggressive looks, provocative statements, stress, and emotional frustrations. I think this highlights the main difference between outsiders attempts to study prisoners and the prisoners themselves. They see the situations in more human, personal terms. We tend to study them like a specimen under a microscope. We adjust the magnification to see the big picture (the prison environment) or zoom in to see the details (prisoner characteristics), but we rarely ask the microbes their opinion. Maybe if we did, we would learn something new.

Prison administrators have also been studying prison violence. Oftentimes they have to wait until violence happens before they can respond, but they also have classification procedures in place to assess individual prisoners for the risk of future violence. If they can identify a dangerous prisoner in advance, they can move them to a more restrictive setting. This doesn't prevent all violence (even in the restrictive settings), but it can be helpful. An alternative approach is to identify potential *targets* of violence in order to move them into protective custody. Just as a violent gang member might be moved directly to maximum security when they are admitted to prison, a vulnerable target might be sent straight to P.C (40). This includes former law enforcement officers, the seriously mentally ill (whose behaviors might provoke an assault), and sex offenders.

The people in charge of America's prisons could abdicate their duties and allow child sex abusers to be murdered with impunity. The fact that any child sex abusers survive prison at all is an indication that classification policies work to a certain extent. Some prison officials have decided to completely segregate sex offenders from other types of prisoners. In New Mexico there is a private prison where hundreds of sex offenders live together so they can focus on rehabilitation. Corrections Secretary Joe Booker says it is pure common sense to have separate facilities. The fear of violence keeps many people inside their cells, but if they stay in self-isolation 23 hours a day in another prison they will not be able to participate in reentry programming. A separate facility for sex offenders can alleviate those fears.

The majority of prison violence research looks at one side of the coin: the characteristics of the alleged perpetrator. Fewer researchers bother to study the characteristics of the victims. This is a major oversight because often the line is blurred. A man who successfully defends himself from an unprovoked attack might be listed as the offender, while the guy who started the fight ends up labeled as the victim. When you win, you lose. Still, we do have some research evidence that helps identify the prisoners who are at the highest risk of being the victims of physical harm. Nancy Wolff (Rutgers University) and her colleagues have given surveys to prisoners to ask them about their victimization experiences (41). The percentage of prisoners who answered her survey questions were often quite low (typically less than 50%), but this is common in most survey studies. In one analysis she found that 12.4% of prisoners had been threatened or actually harmed with Hollywood's favorite prison weapon, the "shank." About 10% were slapped, hit, kicked, or bitten. Only 4.5% had been beaten up. Prisoners felt safest in the prison chapel, and the least safe in the shower or while being transported. About twice as many prisoners reported being physically injured by staff than by other inmates. Another study by Blitz, Wolff, and Shi found that mentally ill prisoners were 1.2 times more likely to be assaulted by staff and 1.6 times more likely to be assaulted by other prisoners (42).

Few studies have specifically examined victimization rates for sex offenders (43). When researchers have included offense characteristics in their models, they have found a significant and substantial increase in the risk of violence for sex offenders compared to non-sex offenders. Wolff, Shi, and Siegel (2009) used their survey of almost 7,000 prisoners to predict the likelihood of sex offenders being victimized. Sure enough, they found sex offenders were *1.53 times more likely* to be the victims of personal victimization by inmates, 1.25 times more likely to be victimized by staff (not statistically significant), but they were not more likely to be the victims of property theft victimization (44).

Wooldredge and Steiner (2016) used a different sample of prisoners (n = 6,997) but they found very similar results to those reported by Wolff et al. (45). After controlling for age, race, marital status, pre-incarceration characteristics, prior criminal history, and a bevy of confinement factors, they found a statistically significant relationship between sex offenses and victimization. They were *1.53 times more likely* to be victims of physical assault and *1.31 times more likely* to be victims of theft.

The most recent study to investigate sex offender victimization was conducted by Susan McNeeley at the Minnesota Department of Corrections. She examined the records of 7,326 prisoners over a six-month period (between January 2, 2021, and June 30, 2021) to find trends in violent victimization. She did not find that sex offenders were more likely to be victims of violence during this time period, but they were more *frequently* the victims of violence. In other words, those who were victimized were attacked repeatedly. When this sample of prisoners were broken down into racial categories another pattern emerged. White sex offenders were the only group who were significantly more likely to be victimized. Their risk was *two and a half times greater* than White offenders who were not incarcerated for a sex offense (46). Perhaps McNeeley's finding that sex offenders were more frequently victimized is a reflection of systemic harassment campaigns, rather than situational violence. Keep in mind that this victimization happened during the Covid-19 pandemic when prisoner movements were more restricted. And it also does not separate sex offenders who targeted adults ("Mos") from those who targeted children ("Cho-Mos"), so victimization rates may be higher than we can estimate with the best statistical models.

We see a pattern here. Even though these effect sizes differ depending on the study design and the target population, we can see that there is something to the legend of sex offender victimization. They are a targeted population in our prisons. Certainly, more research needs to be done. A study by Ellison, Steiner, and Wright (2018) of prisoner victimization in local jails did not find that sex offender status significantly predicted violent victimization (although the odds were slightly greater), so it is likely that environmental conditions matter (47). We need research that examines the value of protective custody placements. We should also consider that some of these victims might have been targeted for other reasons that were not included in these statistical analyses (e.g., sex offenders might be easier targets because they look weaker, not because their offense status was known). But I think we should also consider the fact that non-sex offenders have many reasons to fight each other, such as drug debts, gang affiliations, and rude looks. Yet within that maelstrom of violence we still see sex offenders standing out in the crowd as especially vulnerable victims in our prisons, even if they are not being "smashed on sight" or "killed on sight" as it is popularly believed.

I would like to turn our focus back to the prisoners who attack sex offenders- the "jailhouse vigilantes." In most of the cases of "convict justice" against child sex abusers that I examined, the perpetrators were serving life sentences. I wondered if the real problem was hopelessness. If so, the solution is obvious. If you want to reduce violence in prison, you should give people serving long sentences a reason to live. If they had a parole date on the horizon they might obey the law, but when they have *nothing to lose* they are expected to be difficult to control because they cannot be deterred with threats of longer sentences.

While Steven Sandison, Jon Watson, Joseph Druce, and several other prison murderers were serving life sentences when they killed child sex abusers, it is not necessarily true that lifers are more dangerous than others. In 2020, America had 203,865 people serving a life sentence in our prisons (48). That comprises one-seventh of the entire US prison population. That sounds like a recipe for disaster: taking away everyone's incentives for good behavior by cutting off all hope of being free. So why aren't they killing with reckless abandon? John Irwin's qualitative work challenged the myth that lifers are hopeless, and some quantitative analyses by Sorensen and Reidy have found that people serving life without parole are only more likely to commit misconduct in prison during the first 18 months of their sentence, and after that they match the misconduct rates of people serving life with the possibility of parole (49, 50). Lifers *live* in prison, and they often follow the rules because they want to make that life as comfortable as possible. If they went around breaking every rule they would do hard time, the whole time. Although it is counter-intuitive, misconduct is more common among people serving shorter sentences. Specific studies on *homicide* have not differentiated lifers from short-timers.

We should also remember that the vigilantes who killed child sex abusers outside of a prison were sacrificing their freedom to achieve their goals. They had freedom and gave it up because they believed so strongly in the righteousness of their cause. Is it possible that a prisoner with a release date would give up their chance of freedom to kill another prisoner? I do know of one case that meets this criterion. I spoke with a man in the Florida Department of Corrections who has an amazing story to tell. Among all of the cases of "vigilantism" presented in this book, his is the most remarkable.

From Hell's Heart

Scottie "Gypsie" Allen was 25 years old when he murdered a woman in 2003. The details of the case are murky. He befriended the woman and strangled her to death so he could steal her car. He was arrested, pled guilty, and was sentenced to serve 25 years in prison. A quarter of a century in prison is not easy, but he was a young man at the time. He could have been released in 2028 at the age of 50 and enjoyed a few quiet decades of life on the outside. But in 2017, Allen decided to kill a child sex abuser in prison.

One day, Allen learned that his cellmate was an attempted child sex abuser. Ryan Mason had been convicted of arranging to meet with a 12-year-old girl for a sexual encounter, but it was actually a police sting operation (much like the *To Catch A Predator* operations) (51, 52). Immediately after Mason was paired with Allen, the murder was being planned. On October 2, 2017, Allen put a sheet over the door so officers could not see inside. Then he strangled Mason to death with a t-shirt while telling him "Say hello to the devil for me." Allen then made himself a coffee and ate a honeybun. He did not tell the staff right away. He exited the cell and went about his business, but when he returned a few hours later the smell bothered him. He told a correctional officer "Hate to ruin your day, but I killed my bunkmate." It should be noted that this homicide reportedly occurred inside the "protective management unit" at the Wakulla Correctional Institute (53).

The district attorney was perplexed. Why would a man who had 11 years left to serve kill someone in such a brutal fashion? He could only conclude that Allen wanted the death penalty. He was tried for the murder and found guilty. A jury sentenced him to death. Allen did not want an attorney to represent him, and he did not represent himself. He made no defense. His case was so baffling that the Florida Supreme Court argued whether they could overturn the death penalty on the grounds that Allen did not have adequate representation. They concluded that the Constitution and state law only require him to be offered representation. He waived that privilege so many times that it was causing him "distress" because it felt like nobody was listening to him (54, 55). He was transferred to Florida's death row.

Why did he do it? Maybe he was not entirely rational and there was no "good" reason that would make sense to us. Maybe he is so mentally ill that he did not care about the consequences of his actions. I mailed a letter to Scottie Allen to ask him directly. This is what he said:

> The short answer to your question is NO I did not kill Ryan mason specifically to come to death row. When this happened I had an outdate which was 5/4/2028. Committing this crime was for a very specific reason. Now, whether I was justified in the eyes of law or men is something else entirely, but when I look at myself in the mirror I can look myself in the eye and respect the man I am and the decision I made.

I would like to share with you though, a life history of sorts in future correspondence if for nothing else than context of who I am as an individual. Joshua, (may I call you Joshua?) I'm not a heartless monster! I am capable of sympathy and empathy and experience both normally. In a lot of the local media I was made out to be some sort of psychopath, Nothing could be further from the truth! I hope as this correspondence progresses that that will become more than evident.

Josh, I've never been a saint. I was born into a criminal family where crime was really the basis for regular income, or the outlet of entertainment. I learned how to steal cars from my father at the age of eight, and was introduced to drugs and alcohol at the age of nine by my mother. She gave me my first drink and my first joint. I never really did get into the alcohol, but reefer became a daily thing for me from then on. Being beaten was a regular thing for the most minor of incidences, and affection was nothing more than a myth.

I started being molested by my grandfather at the age of nine. And for some reason that seemed to open a floodgate of molesters into my life. I was repeatedly molested by four men and two women by the time I was twelve. I'm not talking about just some fondling and touching either. I'm talking full on rape. Now 5 of these ppl were family and one was a family friend. I would tell my mom and be beaten for lying so I just stopped telling. I would run away from home just to be brought back and be dropped off for days at the very persons house that was the most brutal …. my grandfather. I can't prove it but I think he paid my mom's bills on many occasions because she was "dropping me off". I finally ended up at the juvenile home and was able to tell a counselor there, my grandfather got six months in the county jail with daily work release for his years of raping me. My grandmother stayed with him. Nothing ever happened to the other ppl. At the age of 14 I tried to kill my grandfather. I took one of the high-powered rifles from home and went thru the woods (we lived in the country) and came to a spot where I had to cross a road, several police were there waiting for me …my mom had called the cops. She somehow figured out what I was up to. To say I have a deep seeded hatred for child molesters is the understatement of the eons!

So here we have it. A motive beyond all other motives. A motive worth sacrificing his only opportunity of freedom. He would have been in his 50's when he was released. Plenty of time to enjoy life. Many prisoners would kill to have that opportunity, but Allen was willing to sacrifice that opportunity so he could kill.

Scottie had an intense hatred of child molesters because of his own childhood experiences of chronic and severe sexual abuse. He was raped by his grandfather, Vernon Mulkey, who was convicted of sexually abusing children three times (with a total of six known victims). In prison he has been officially diagnosed with post-traumatic stress disorder. He once told a prison counselor that the happiest time in his childhood was when he was in a state juvenile institution. Like Steven Sandison, Scottie Allen was a bomb built in hell. His anti-social personality was forged in his abusive childhood and refined in our institutional schools for crime. When he had a child sex abuser at his mercy in the concrete cell that comprised his universe, he did what he always wanted to do: get revenge. The laws of man were of no concern inside that prison cell.

How would he have turned out if he had enjoyed a protective and loving childhood? What if he had been given therapy instead of incarceration for his juvenile crimes? What he had served his adult prison sentence in a humane and well-managed facility? When traumatized men are housed together in an uncaring and unsafe prison environment, violence happens. And sometimes it is personal.

Scottie mailed a letter to the Wakulla County State Attorney's Office that included the following logical explanation of why the death penalty was an appropriate response to his murder:

… I made it very clear that I planned Ryan Mason's murder. I made it very clear that I made him suffer physically, mentally, and emotionally in the days leading up to his murder. I also made it very clear that in Ryan Mason's last moments on Earth I made sure he knew he was going to die. That early morning of October 2nd 2017, he struggled valiantly in those last moments. Begging me with his eyes as I sat on his chest with my hands around his throat. The last words Ryan Mason heard in his last moment before he succumbed to unconsciousness was "Tell the Devil I said hello." I do not regret nor do I feel the least bit of remorse for killing Ryan Mason. I believe I've made that abundantly clear ….

With the information I have given I find it hard to believe that you won't seek the death penalty. But stranger things have happened.

So with that I ask you the following questions. 1.) If you don't seek the death penalty are you in essence saying I have a license to do it again? 2.) If you don't seek the death penalty are you in essence saying Ryan M. Mason deserved his fate? 3.) If you don't seek the death penalty and I happen to kill again is that blood on your hands? *I believe it is!* Do the right thing and seek the death penalty in this case. It is a slam dunk!

At this point in my life I have nothing to lose, and think it in the best interest of all parties involved that you charge me with 1st Degree Murder, and seek the death penalty.

P.S. Let's get this over with ….

Scottie called me from Death Row one night. We talked for half an hour about various topics. I learned that he was given an IQ test as part of his death penalty eligibility hearings. He scored a 143. I believe it. He is an Odinist (Asatru), which is a pre-Christian nature religion that is often maligned as a racist prison gang. He says it has nothing to do with race, it is a belief system that encourages you to strive to better yourself, always. He has standards and morals. One of them is the belief that some crimes deserve the death penalty: child sexual abuse, and his own homicides. He is not a hypocrite about the death penalty. He doesn't think he deserves life and liberty. But he surely disagrees with the lenient "meatball" sentences that sex offenders get.

I asked Scottie what sparked the murder of Ryan Mason. If Scottie hated child sex abusers, there are plenty of them in Florida's prisons. He'd be working overtime if he were a dedicated vigilante. Scottie told me there were two primary reasons he acted against Mason. The first is betrayal. He asked Mason what his crime was, and Mason lied. Scottie was friendly with him until he learned the truth. He was more disgusted because he fell for his lies.

The second reason was a pure vigilante motive: to protect future child victims. Scottie went undercover to gauge Mason's risk of harming kids if he were released from prison. Scottie casually pretended to oppose age of consent laws. Mason nodded agreement, and like many pedophiles desperate for validation, he thought he found kinship. Mason started acting like a teenage boy obsessed with sex. He was bragging, fantasizing out loud. He told Scottie that he was going to find a new child victim as soon as he was released. Scottie related this event to me:

I pretended it was okay (pedophilia), and he divulged all his sick fantasies. I was raging internally, but I let him talk himself into his grave. He went on and on about raping little girls. I feel these pedophiles are defective. When you're a kid and you're normal, and you discover that you're attracted to girls, that's all your mind is focused on: sex, sex, sex. Pedophiles always have that fascination but it's with kids. Kids, kids, kids. Some are obsessed with the power differential. Just the fact that kids are smaller, less intelligent, weaker … that lets the pedophile feel dominant. They have faulty synapses. You can't turn a heterosexual male who is attracted to adults into a pedophile and you can't cure a pedophile. I knew that, but Mason proved it to me that night. He told me, and I'll never forget his exact words, "I can't wait to get out so I can get one that don't bleed yet." He had the nerve to tell me that.

Monsters do exist. They steal the innocence of children. I've been a piece of shit my whole life. I was born in a criminal family. It's all I've ever known, but if by killing that one Cho-Mo I saved one child from harm, I have no problem sacrificing my life for that. I'm a hardened criminal murderer, but I watch TV and I see kids singing on America's Got Talent or shows like that, and it brings tears to my eyes. I don't want anyone to hurt kids.

Scottie Allen is prepared to sit in the lethal injection chair and face his death. He may not have a clear conscience for everything in his life, but he will not apologize for killing Mason. He believes his one good deed of killing a child sex abuser has earned him some measure of cosmic favor.

Complicit Guardians

Prisoner-on-prisoner violence has received the most attention from scholars, but there is also the very real threat that correctional officers are directly targeting sex offenders for violence. In their book, *Shadow Vigilantes*, Paul and Sarah Robinson have said that police, prosecutors, and judges have many opportunities to subvert the justice system in order to give additional punishments to offenders they deem worthy of such treatment. A police officer might lie in court to circumvent the rules of search and seizure (called "testilying"). Perhaps they use more force than is necessary to detain a suspect. A prosecutor might overcharge the defendant or withhold evidence that diminishes their likelihood of securing a conviction. Judges might push or exceed the limits of sentencing guidelines for more severe punishments.

In the corrections system there are certainly many opportunities for prison staff to abuse their power and directly harm a particular prisoner, or they may simply allow convict justice to take place. The song "Penitentiary Blues" by The Convicts refers to correctional officers turning their heads and walking away when they see "baby-rapers" getting their comeuppance. I have personally spoken to dozens of prisoners who said the same thing. CO.s are alleged to be part of a conspiracy with the prisoners to punish Cho-Mos.

The "Pittsburgh Prison Guards" case is an example of how correctional officers might act more like a prison gang or vigilante group than custodial staff (56). In 2009, a group of officers in a Pittsburgh prison decided to give extra punishments to sex offenders. They would announce details of a newly admitted sex offender's crimes to the other prisoners. For example, a man had raped an 11-year-old girl and this information was immediately relayed to the general population of prisoners. Some officers ordered prison workers to defecate or urinate in the sex offenders' food. The officers themselves would administer "swirlies" by shoving the sex offenders' heads into toilets and flushing them.

The leader of the officer's group, Harry Nicoletti, was accused of sexually harassing and raping these prisoners. When the abuse finally went to court, Nicoletti was charged with 117 counts against 31 victims. He was convicted of 27 counts against 13 victims. The jury did not convict him of any rape charges. The judge could have sent Nicoletti to prison for many years … but decided to show him some mercy. "You were painted as an ogre," the judge said "you were painted as a sex fiend. You were painted as a villain who liked to torture and seek out sex offenders." However, the judge did not want to put him into a prison system where he would suffer the same fate. "I'm sparing you from the danger you imposed on the individuals you were in charge of. I hope you understand that." And with that, Nicoletti was given five years' probation and six months' house arrest. Perhaps the judge was not signaling pity for Nicoletti as much as his own disdain for his victims. The other officers also avoided jail time. One of them was given 12 years' probation and the others were never convicted of any crimes (57).

In 2020, abuse by Ohio correctional officers led to life-changing personal injuries for one prisoner, and a payout of $17.5 million dollars (58). Seth Fletcher was sent to prison for two years for "child sex offenses" when he was 18-years-old. His age is important because Fletcher filmed sex acts with his younger girlfriend who was technically underage, and he was convicted of making child sex exploitation material with her. This falls into a moral grey area that some activists and researchers have warned legislators about for some time: the so-called "Romeo and Juliet" clause that renders an act criminal only on someone's 18th birthday, but not the day before. Teenagers consensually "sexting" one another might be dangerous and should be addressed, but it does not approach the spirit of the law that child sex exploitation material laws were designed for. Still, Fletcher was sentenced to prison and his paperwork clearly stated that he was incarcerated for "child sex offenses." The prison staff decided that two years in prison wasn't enough, and he needed additional punishments.

While he was in prison Fletcher was tackled by correctional officers, handcuffed, then picked up and dropped him on his face. Fletcher complained about his injuries and begged for water. An officer poured water down his nose to "waterboard" him. He was left without medical treatment for hours. When he tried to move his legs he discovered he was paralyzed. He told the staff that he couldn't move, but no medical care was provided. The next day a psychologist visited him and decided to call for medical help. He was given emergency spinal surgery in a nearby hospital, but it was too late. He is now quadriplegic.

The correctional officers responsible for his injuries posted about their behavior on social media. One said:

> I broke a dudes nose today, yeah this was not reported, there was way too much blood so I mopped it up.

> The dude I broke his nose is now paralyzed with a broken neck, and they say his face looks like he had been dropped and dragged through concrete, LMAO.

> It feels good to know that I played a small part in paralyzing a cho, LMAO.

> We also water boarded him, LMAO.

The officer resigned his position and has not been charged with any crimes. The Ohio Department of Rehabilitation and Corrections paid a $17.5 million settlement to Fletcher, or rather, the citizens of Ohio paid with their tax dollars.

For anyone who has read this far in the book and holds the view that attacking child sex abusers is always justified, please consider how Seth Fletcher was treated by government employees and decide whether his case merits such harsh punishment. Should everyone convicted of a "child sex offense" be brutalized, left without medical care, and paralyzed for life, no matter what the circumstances of their crime happened to be? The entire purpose of our laws and the rules and regulations of our prisons are to ensure that punishments are not cruel, unusual, arbitrary, or capricious. Seth Fletcher might never walk again because he was sexting his underage girlfriend when he was 18-years-old. Is that justice? If you think so, perhaps elected officials should pass official laws to deliberately paralyze 18-year-olds convicted of these crimes so it would no longer be "unusual" or "arbitrary." Or would seeing it in print cross the line enough to shock the conscience?

Jon Watson has no compassion for child sex abusers (he killed two of them), but he knows a scam when he sees it. He claims there was a "quid pro quo" in some California prisons where the officers would tell him who they wanted to be attacked. In one case he refused to beat up a prisoner because he was "retarded." He also ignored officers who told him when a new arrival was a "weirdo" (aka pedo), because if he didn't see the paperwork it might be a false flag. He knew times when officers had mislabeled prisoners so they could get their own petty revenge. If a prisoner "602'd" a staff member (that means they filled out a CDCR 602 Inmate Appeal Form to file a complaint) the officer would spread word that the complaining inmate was a Cho-Mo, hoping that someone would kick their ass. They'd let the convicts do their dirty work. Maybe the officer would reward them with an extra roll of toilet paper for their efforts. After the C.O.'s cried wolf too many times, prisoners stopped listening to their murder requests. "That ruined it all," Jon said.

James Fairbanks, the vigilante in Omaha Nebraska (Chapter Three), told me that he was encouraged to continue his war on pedophiles in the county jail when he was awaiting his trial. He didn't want to hurt his chances of receiving a favorable outcome, but he felt compelled to play along with the C.O.s and other prisoners.

As was reported in one news article when I arrived at Douglas County I was treated as a "Jailhouse celebrity." This was not only from the inmates but by the correctional officers and support staff there. It felt every officer at some point initially let me know of their support and if I "needed anything" to let them know. Most meant legal things. Extra food tray, A move to a different cell, etc. etc .... After a while, as the story unfolded and court tv and other outlets were reporting it and as inmates kept coming in off the streets having been following the case the jail became very much hyper vigilante against pedophiles.

I can give you numerous incidents but basically it started when a few correctional officers started giving me info on incoming inmates and their charges. Also would read any news reports about their arrest. Depending on the C.O. on the unit, who was in booking assigning inmates and who the floor Sgt. was that day it progressed to numerous times where an officer would call me over, tell me John Doe was in booking and his charges were "this" and if I wanted a couple of moves could be made and the off-camera cells (usually two on every unite) could be freed for him .... They would then have the booking officer move them into the off-camera room, then tell me how far I could go (depending on floor Sgt. and who was in medical).

It was usually made clear not to hurt them to the point they needed outside treatment. They would then tell me when they were going upstairs to do a cell search on a top-tier room and let me know I'd have 10 minutes in their room. Usually me and another inmate would go in. Depending on their charges and their physical shape we would do anything from beat them, often with soap socks (soap bars in socks) and or humiliate them. Make them drink all the toilet water out of their toilet one cup at a time as an example .... Usually some kind of physical assault. After we were done we would threaten them and make sure they knew exactly who I was (they all knew the story locally) and let them know if they said anything other than they fell off their bunk to explain injuries they wouldn't make it out of the jail. Usually after we left they would try and get the guard on the floor to come to their cell anyways .... Usually that officer would advise them to stay quiet but if the inmate persisted he or she would call the floor Sgt. and then the floor Sgt. would usually say something like, we have no P.C. unit in county.

You've seen the news. He's a big deal and a lot of people in here support him. If you insist on making a report there's nowhere we can place you you'll be safe. They would usually say they would talk to me and make sure it doesn't happen again. Never once did I get charged or that I know of did an official report get filed or if it was it was thrown away. Usually after that we would just humiliate and charge rent for the rest of their stay but no more physical assaults ....

I could give you numerous examples and scenarios but you get the gist. When I was in there everyone was on board with getting some "long overdue punishment" which is how one Sgt. put it. But it amazed even me when I would be getting meds at night and the sweetest old lady nurse would be on the unit and say to me "I heard we stitched one up for you today Fairbanks, good job!"

There were many other things like bringing in stuff for me, like print outs of news articles about me, one let me use their cell phone to check in on my son's live high school football game and other stuff ....

Having said all that I want to point out that the mindset I got into when I decided to go kill Matteio and the very violent and troubling to even me behavior I partook in during that time in County has left me wondering what happened to me. How did I go there and how did I do all that? I stopped behaving violently to anyone shortly before leaving county jail and since coming to prison have not taken part in any of this type of stuff and have not even verbally chastised any inmates. I've spent almost a full year now trying to only focus on answering my own questions and not worrying about them.

It is difficult to estimate how often crimes like these occur because the C.O.'s are the ones who keep the records. We do not know how often C.O.s use force without a justifiable reason, and we certainly do not know how often they indirectly cause harm by letting prisoners attack each other. Despite the lack of hard evidence, I think it goes without saying that "not all" C.O.'s contribute to these crimes against prisoners. Pete Earley was interviewing correctional officers for his book *The Hot House* to learn more about the challenges of dealing with prisoners in a maximum-security prison every day. A Captain told a story about a prisoner who was convicted of kidnapping and raping two children, and who begged for a transfer to protective custody because his cellmate could sexually assault him. The Captain knew the prisoner was a child rapist and was disgusted by his crimes. He could have shown deliberate indifference to his imminent danger of sexual assault or death, but the Captain did not act on his impulses. He said:

> Now you tell me: how much sympathy do you think I'm going to have for some punk who does that to two innocent kids? I got children of my own, you know. How much would you have? And now this puke wants me to protect him from Slim. Can you imagine what it's like to be put in a position where you have to make decisions like this every day .... You have to have a lot of love in your heart to act professionally and do the right thing no matter what you feel.

Retired prison inspector Gary York has fought his entire life to ensure that Florida prisons operate according to the strict letter of the law. He has gathered evidence that has led to corrupt correctional officers being terminated, charged with crimes, and even imprisoned for their offenses. He has a highly refined sense of justice and fairness, and he condemns all acts of correctional officer misconduct. He thinks that bad apples are tarnishing the reputation of the hard-working officers who deserve more respect for tolerating the extremely difficult work environment of America's prison systems. He has written two books on the subject (*Inside the Inner Circle* and

Corruption Behind Bars). He also hosts a YouTube channel where he discusses his career and current events through a prison inspector's lens. His most popular video on YouTube is (you guessed it) "Pedophiles in Prison" (59).

> Your meanest cruelest inmate, way down inside that heart, most of the inmates actually have a care and concern for children and they don't like these pedophiles anymore than I do or you do. They will take care of the pedophiles in prison. … If I'm a correctional officer I treat all inmates the same. It's none of my concerns what the inmate is in prison for … pedophiles in prison don't have it easy. Any prisoner will tell you, you have to sleep with one eye open all the time, but pedophiles need to sleep with both eyes open and their butt turned to the wall, because these inmates got something for them.

In this conversation he does not endorse any act of "shadow vigilantism" by government employees. York argues that correctional officers should restrain their personal biases so they can perform their duties as required by law. York tells every correctional officer provide the three C's: Care, Custody, and Control. Reasonable actions to protect inmate safety are required of all officers. If an officer doesn't want to protect sex offenders from harm, they should seek employment somewhere else. They should not let their personal opinions about crime and punishment influence the execution of their duties. In other words, they should be capable guardians of all prisoners, and not allow themselves to be complicit in crimes against them.

Individual malefactors should always be held accountable for their behavior when the evidence clearly shows they broke the law. Sometimes correctional officers commit acts of misfeasance (doing their job poorly), but sometimes they can cause harm through malfeasance (deliberately causing harm), or nonfeasance (not performing their duties to keep prisoners safe). The latter term has been called "deliberate indifference" by the Supreme Court, and it is a serious accusation. One that might have led to the death of a defrocked Roman Catholic priest named John Geoghan (Chapter Eight).

It should always be noted that no group of people should be defined or categorized according to the behavior of individuals within the group, whether they are prisoners or correctional officers. The various case circumstances described throughout this book have differentiated different types of child sex abusers, different types of vigilantes, and I trust that you can differentiate corrupt correctional officers from those who perform their duties without resorting to criminal behavior. There are 462,300 correctional officers supervising 2.3 million prisoners in the United States (60, 61). If this behavior was endemic to our system it would be obvious in the data despite all of the research limitations and obfuscations we have to overcome.

Criminals' Justice

Why do people attack each other in prison? Do they import their violent tendencies with them? Do the deprivations of the prison environment cause them to lash out for their own safety? Do prison governance policies fail to control dangerous men, or do they turn them into rebels? These questions have fascinated prison researchers for decades, and while we have been able to answer some questions, we are often faced with bizarre outliers that defy our statistical models. Why did Steven Sandison strangle his cellmate with his shoelaces and then sleep peacefully with his corpse on the bunk below him? Why did Jon Watson kill two child molesters when he was surrounded by other potential targets? Why did Shaun Attwood witness a helpless man's skull crack open as gang members stomped him to death? Why do former prisoners all tell the same story that child molesters are "scum" who need to be terrorized and killed?

I hope the complexity of the issue was explained well enough in this chapter to encourage you to be cautious. Don't trust everything you read. I attempted to explain the possible reasons why this type of violence occurs while acknowledging that it happens within a maelstrom of other forces that contribute to overall rates of violence in prison. There is a lot going on inside our prisons. While overall trends of prison violence have decreased over time, and the murder rate was never as high as Hollywood portrays, we can all agree that prisons are a poor environment for people to learn how to be pro-social. We need to consider the impact that these "Schools for Crime," "Gladiator Pits," and "Thunderdomes" are having on the people who will return to our communities someday. Do you want your future neighbor to be a hyper-vigilant, traumatized, violent person?

We can't forget about the lifers either. They might never come back to our communities, but they are the ones shaping the prison environment for those who do. If we had truly therapeutic environments where people could be "rehabilitated" and "corrected" instead of being trained to fight for survival we might see better returns for our taxpayer money. It might also result in more incarceration offenses for sex crimes if judges didn't have to worry that they were sending sex abusers to a potentially deadly environment. If Convict Justice is supposed to compensate for lenient sentences, it may be backfiring by giving judges an excuse to divert sex abusers away from prison.

Until the utopian prison is finally invented, we will be forced to deal with these acts of violence. "Cho-Mos" and other "rapos" might be safer than the stories lead us to believe, but they can never be sure. Maybe their cellmate has a personal debt to settle that has been accruing interest since their childhood. If the classical view of deterrence holds any truth to it, "Cho-Mos" who can't afford protection should add these prison punishments into their calculations before they decide to commit a crime. "It's not the Holiday Inn," as they say.

Maybe the reason we allow our prisons to be dangerous and inhumane is that the American public are complicit in their own vigilante shadow war. They do not believe that child molestation and other serious crimes are punished harshly enough. If sex offenders were sent to nice, Norwegian-style prisons where they are treated with dignity, the American public would feel that their own desire for retribution was blunted. The prisoner would not be suffering enough for their crimes. So when they hear that child sex abusers are tortured and terrorized by the other prisoners they get to feel that a just measure of pain was inflicted. Sure, he might only get a two-year sentence, but those will be the longest two years of his life. This is merely speculation on my part, but I think this might be an intriguing line of study in the future. Winston Churchill once said "The mood and temper of the public in regard to the treatment of crime and criminals is one of the most unfailing tests of the civilisation of any country" (62). If this is true, then the American spirit of retribution is reflected in our prisons, and it is ugly.

Silent War

By "A Son of Solitude"

There's a war raging outside that no man or woman or child is safe from, and I am a soldier in that war. There are no monetary advantages from this sort of commission. No salary, no health insurance, and very few accolades. But there is a payment of a sort that cannot be found anywhere else, a reparation to the soul, a look in the eye of a child just like I was, the knowledge that tonight, at least one will sleep well, untouched. These small things are treasures I hold onto while I serve out the punishment for my services. If you are a pedophile, you are my enemy, and you should know that we are linked together and always will be, in a way that is beyond your evasion or control. I am connected to you and your kind. This powerful bond was forged in the furnace of my own abuse as a child. I was beaten and molested by someone just like you, so now, I can sense you. I can read your devilish nature in your eyes. Your stance. The way you speak. I. Know. You. I would give my life ten times over to stand in between you and the focus of your sick desires. And there are thousands just like me. It doesn't make any difference if you believe in a god or an afterlife or if you seek forgiveness or not. I know you didn't create yourself. I know your path hurts, and you should know that I and those like me are always waiting. Waiting for you to slip up. Waiting for you to expose your real nature. So conceal yourself. Bury your illness deep in a shell. Stay well away from the children. This is my advice for you. Those of us who have been molested, we dream of you. We carry you around in our thoughts. Your shadow follows us, and our lives are permanently altered by your vibration. This means you are well loathed. We will hurt you as a steppingstone to our own healing and will hang your head like a trophy on the mantel of our heart.

I have found you hiding in my churches, with your nose buried in a holy book of one type or another. I have exposed your true nature there. You cannot conceal yourselves with religion. What has worked in the past will no longer save you. I have encountered you in worship services and in choir practice. I've seen you at the youth fellowship services. You cannot hide. I've stood next to you in an evening service and have listened as you faithfully recited the requisite words of a believer. This is no shroud. I can see you plainly. I smell your disease as readily as a fresh cut lawn. I wish to diminish you and your kind to nothing. Less than nothing. I have encountered you in the parking lot at the mall. On the streets. In the cities and towns. I have seen you. Your house looks just like mine, but when I knock on your door, you hesitate. Then, when you open the door and our eyes meet, your guilt and shame overwhelms you. We both know why I have come. You should stay back. Stay humble. Your lot is in the shadows. Don't busy yourself in the streets of our neighborhoods. Our children deserve summer days without the threat of your kind lingering around. You must understand this and learn to respect it.

You will never win this war. For as the years go by, more and more of your victims mature and join the opposition. We, survivors of childhood abuse, are an army. We are many. We will never stop searching for you. Every child eventually speaks. Every child molester eventually slips. We will be close by, waiting for these moments. I also wish you were never born this way, but you were, and now you've become a burden for all of us to bear. You and your kind made me dangerous. You made those like me dangerous, by killing off our hope and happiness, by murdering us one piece at a time, every time you touched us or beat us. Now we are an army of living dead. Our souls torn and blackened, but we weren't born this way. This condition was imposed on us, by you, our enemy. I don't hate you, but I despise everything you love. All that brings you pleasure and joy disgusts me. Makes me sick. I cannot answer the question that you have asked me in so many of our encounters. Why? Why were you born like this? I don't know. Truthfully, I no longer care. My only concern is to meet you at every step and remind you that it cannot happen again. Not here, not ever.

I want each one of you to wake up scared. I want you to constantly check your locks and look over your shoulder. I want you to wonder why you feel a sensation of impending doom, frequently at the strangest times. And I want each one of you child abusers to wonder, every night, is it tonight? Is that noise you heard the sound of one of my soldiers coming through the window to hurt you? I wish for each one of you to live like this for many years, just to give yourself a hint, an idea of what its like to live as a survivor of your sort of debauchery.

You and I will always be connected. And throughout the course of my life I have been led great distances with seemingly divine guidance, to intercede on the lives of those just like you. Bury your sickness, bind your own desires, and stay away from children. This is the only thing I can offer you now. For there is a war going on outside, and you are my enemy. I will find you. Those like me will find you. You cannot hide. Take heed to these words, for they are not given lightly, and I will not offer them again.

References

1. State of South Carolina Supreme Court. (2004, May 28). The State v. Jonathan Kyle Binney.
2. Vaughn, M. S., & Sapp, A. D. (1989). Less than utopian: Sex offender treatment in a milieu of power struggles, status positioning, and inmate manipulation in state correctional institutions. *The Prison Journal, 69*, 73–89.
3. Akerstrom, M. (1986). Outcasts in prison: The cases of the informers and sex offenders. *Deviant Behavior, 7*(1), 1–20.
4. KRQE News. (2014, October 7). Video shows attacks on suspected child molester. https://www.youtube.com/watch?v=erC3S5fS_dQ&t=41s
5. Golgowski, N. (2017, January 4). Nephew of inmate who beat up Jared Fogle says he was seeking 'justice' for abused kids. *Huffpost.* https://www.huffpost.com/entry/jared-fogle-attacked-by-inmate_n_56eacc5fe4b0860f99dbbdd7
6. Ankney, D. (2019, August). Allegation that prisoner was beaten after guard outed him as sex offender stated Eighth Amendment claim. *Prison Legal News.* https://www.prisonlegalnews.org/news/2019/aug/6/allegation-prisoner-was-beaten-after-guard-outed-him-sex-offender-stated-eighth-amendment-claim/
7. Ravikumar, V. (2019). Convicted Florida child molester beaten by another inmate and drowned in jail toilet, report says. *USA Today.* https://www.usatoday.com/story/news/nation/2019/08/01/florida-convicted-child-molester-beaten-drowned-toilet/1896140001/
8. LaFraniere, S. (1992, February 21). In Maine, prison crowding leaves grisly legacy. *Washington Post.* https://www.washingtonpost.com/archive/politics/1992/02/21/in-maine-prison-crowding-leaves-grisly-legacy/c3780cdb-8010-44be-b48b-3e9cf0c444f2/
9. Elliot, J. K. (2021). Man gets 25 years for killing his underage sister's rapist in prison. *Global News.* https://globalnews.ca/news/8097258/child-rapist-killed-victim-brother-prison/
10. Uso Ron. (2022, February 2). Prison chomo on the tier. https://www.youtube.com/shorts/u3iSJomhyXE
11. Lawton, L. (2020, January 30). What happens to pedophiles in prison? Chapter 13: Episode 17. https://www.youtube.com/watch?v=zkGF_8SegT8
12. Outside Looking In. (2019, February 20). How are sex offenders and child molesters treated in prison? https://www.youtube.com/watch?v=i4UxFXmH7vk
13. Prison Talk. (2015, September 6). Child molesters in prison – Negotiating with guards. https://www.youtube.com/watch?v=zyAobTg4c54
14. Wrong to Strong. (2020, December 1). Pedophiles in low security prisons. https://www.youtube.com/watch?v=plc8ZvwwnjM

15. Williams, J. (2021, October 4). Let's Live Life. Child predators in prison. *The truth.* https://www.youtube.com/watch?v=SQ-NAZ-rlBU

16. Attwood, S. (2016). *Hard time: Locked up abroad.* Liverpool, UK: Gadfly Press.

17. Srisavasdi, R., & Saavedra, T. (2007, March 28). Death sentence: The deadly jail beating of John Chamberlain. *OC Register.* https://www.ocregister.com/2007/03/28/death-sentence-the-deadly-jail-beating-of-john-chamberlain/

18. McKorkle, L. W., & Korn, R. (1954). Resocialization within walls. *Annals of the American Academy of Political and Social Science, 293,* 88–98.

19. Skarbek, D. (2014). *The social order of the underworld: How prison gangs govern the American penal system.* New York, NY: Oxford University Press.

20. Fleischer, M. S., & Krienert, J. L. (2009). *The myth of prison rape: Sexual culture in American prisons.* Lanham, MD: Rowman & Littlefield Publishers.

21. Trammell, R., & Chenault, S. (2009). "We have to take these guys out": Motivations for assaulting incarcerated child molesters. *Symbolic Interaction, 32*(4), 334–350.

22. Blatchford, C. (2008). *The black hand: The story of Rene "Boxer" Enriquez and his life in the Mexican mafia.* Harper Collins.

23. Prison Legal News. (1999, October 15). Texas settles with hanged prisoner's family. https://www.prisonlegalnews.org/news/1999/oct/15/texas-settles-with-hanged-prisoners-family/

24. Vachss, A. (2012). *A bomb built in hell: Wesley's story.* New York, NY: Vintage Crime/Black Lizard.

25. Shaw, C. R. (1966). *The jack-roller: A delinquent boy's own story.* Chicago, IL: University of Chicago Press.

26. Wright, R., & Decker, S. H. (1997). *Armed robbers in action: Stickups and street culture.* Boston, MA: Northeastern University Press.

27. Conover, T. (2005). All prisoners lie. *The Moth.* https://themoth.org/story-transcripts/all-prisoners-lie-transcript

28. Cunningham, M. D., Sorensen, J. R., Vigen, M. P., & Woods, S. O. (2010). Inmate homicides: Killers, victims, motives, and circumstances. *Journal of Criminal Justice, 38,* 348–358.

29. Carson, E. A. (2021). Mortality in local jails, 2000-2019 – Statistical tables. *U.S. Department of Justice, Office of Justice Programs.* https://bjs.ojp.gov/library/publications/mortality-local-jails-2000-2019-statistical-tables

30. Logan, M. W., Long, J., DeLisi, M., & Hazelwood, A. R. (2022). Serious, violent, and chronic prison misconduct: Are the predictors the same for men and women? *The Prison Journal, 103*(1), 1–32.

31. Wooldredge, J. (2020). Prison culture, management, and in-prison violence. *Annual Review of Criminology, 3,* 165–188.

32. DeLisi, M., Berg, M. T., & Hochstetler, A. (2004). Gang members, career criminals and prison violence: Further specification of the importation model of inmate behavior. *Criminal Justice Studies, 17*(4), 369–383.

33. Drury, A. J., & DeLisi, M. (2011). Gangkill: An exploratory empirical assessment of gang membership, homicide offending, and prison misconduct. *Crime & Delinquency, 57*(1), 130–146.

34. Goetting, A., & Howsen, R. M. (1986). Correlates of prisoner misconduct. *Journal of Quantitative Criminology, 2*(1), 49–67.

35. Lahm, K. F. (2008). Inmate-on-inmate assault: A multilevel examination of prison violence. *Criminal Justice and Behavior, 35*(1), 120–137.

36. McCorkle, R. C. (1995). Gender, psychopathology, and institutional behavior: A comparison of male and female mentally ill prison inmates. *Journal of Criminal Justice, 23*(1), 53–61.

37. Myers, L. B., & Levy, G. W. (1978). Description and prediction of the intractable inmate. *Journal of Research in Crime and Delinquency, 15*(2), 214–228.

38. Schenk, A. M., & Fremouw, W. J. (2012). Individual characteristics related to prison violence: A critical review of the literature. *Aggression and Violent Behavior, 17*(5), 430–442.

39. Steiner, B., Butler, H. D., & Ellison, J. M. (2014). Causes and correlates of prison inmate misconduct: A systematic review of the evidence. *Journal of Criminal Justice, 42*(6), 462–470.

40. National Institute of Corrections. (1990). *Protective custody management in adult correctional facilities: A discussion of causes, conditions, attitudes, and alternatives.* Washington, DC: U.S. Department of Justice.

41. Wolff, N., & Shi, J. (2009a). Type, source, and patterns of physical victimization: A comparison of male and female inmates. *The Prison Journal*, 89(2), 172–191. https://doi.org/10.1177/0032885509334754

42. Blitz, C. L., Wolff, N., & Shi, J. (2008). Physical victimization in prison: The role of mental illness. *International Journal of Law and Psychiatry*, 31(5), 385–393.

43. Steiner, B., Ellison, J. M., Butler, D., & Cain, C. M. (2017). The impact of inmate and prison characteristics on prisoner victimization. *Trauma, Violence & Abuse*, 18(1), 17–36.

44. Wolff, N., Shi, J., & Siegel, J. A. (2009b). Understanding physical victimization inside prisons: Factors that predict risk. *Justice Quarterly*, 26(3), 445–475. https://doi.org/10.1080/07418820802427858

45. Wooldredge, J. D., & Steiner, B. (2016). Assessing the need for gender-specific explanations of prisoner victimization. *Justice Quarterly*, 33(2), 209–238. https://doi.org/10.1080/07418825.2014.897364

46. McNeeley, S. (2022). Reaffirming the relationship between routine activities and violent victimization in prison. *Journal of Criminal Justice*, 78, 101883.

47. Ellison, J. M., Steiner, B., & Wright, E. M. (2018). Examining the sources of violent victimization among jail inmates. *Criminal Justice and Behavior*, 45(11), 1723–1741. https://doi.org/10.1177/0093854818788590

48. Nellis, A. (2021, February 17). No end in sight: America's enduring reliance on life imprisonment. *The Sentencing Project*. https://www.sentencingproject.org/publications/no-end-in-sight-americas-enduring-reliance-on-life-imprisonment/

49. Reidy, T. J., & Sorensen, J. R. (2018). The influence of sentence length on the commission of serious and violent prison infractions by female inmates. *Criminal Justice and Behavior*, 45(9), 1420–1434.

50. Sorensen, J. R., & Reidy, T. J. (2019). Nothing to lose? An examination of prison misconduct among life-without parole inmates. *The Prison Journal*, 99(1), 46–65.

51. WFTV9. (2013, January 24). FDLE: Child sex sting suspects fought agents, broke Taser in escape attempt. https://www.wftv.com/news/local/man-arrested-underage-sex-sting/271360593/

52. Florida Supreme Court. (2020, May 7). Scottie D. Allen v. State of Florida. Filing # 107208221.

53. Etters, K. (2017, October 3). Wakulla Correctional Institute prisoner killed in 'inmate-on-inmate altercation'. *Tallahassee Democrat*. https://www.tallahassee.com/story/news/2017/10/03/wci-prisoner-killed-inmate-on-inmate-altercation/729255001/

54. Olmeda, R. (2021, June 3). Court upholds death sentence for Broward convict who murdered child molester. *South Florida Sun Sentinel*. https://www.sun-sentinel.com/news/florida/fl-ne-jailhouse-murder-death-penalty-20210603-qu4a475bdjcyfigqjlifer3gum-story.html

55. Florida Supreme Court. (2020, October 27). SC19-1313 Scottie D. Allen v. State of Florida. https://www.youtube.com/watch?v=vqPO634f00I

56. Pittsburgh's Action News 4. (2013, March 28). Guard at center of Pittsburgh inmate abuse gets probation. https://www.wtae.com/article/guard-at-center-of-pittsburgh-inmate-abuse-gets-probation/7460502#

57. Brandolph, A. (2013, March 28). Former SCI Pittsburgh prison guard to serve five years of probation in abuse of sex offenders. *Tribune Live*. https://archive.triblive.com/news/former-sci-pittsburgh-prison-guard-to-serve-five-years-of-probation-in-abuse-of-sex-offenders/

58. Dawson, B. (2021, November 7). Prisoner, 21, convicted of child sex offense wins $17.5 million lawsuit after being left paralyzed by guards who bragged about 'sadistic' attack. *Insider*. https://www.insider.com/ohio-sex-offender-wins-175m-after-prison-guards-left-him-paralyzed-2021-11

59. York, G. (2020, August 20). Pedophiles in prison. https://www.youtube.com/watch?v=EibFR_yWgVE

60. Kaeble, D., & Alper, M. (2020). *Probation and parole in the United States, 2017-2018*. Washington, DC: U.S. Department of Justice, Bureau of Justice Statistics.

61. Sawyer, W., & Wagner, P. (2020). "Mass Incarceration: The Whole Pie 2020." Prison Policy Initiative. https://www.prisonpolicy.org/reports/pie2020.html.

62. Churchill, W. S. (1910). House of Commons Debate, 20 July, 1910. Vol. 19, CC1326-1357. https://api.parliament.uk/historic-hansard/people/mr-winston-churchill/1910

8

MAXIMA CULPA

Father John Geoghan was ordained as a priest in the Catholic Church in 1962 and was made the assistant pastor of a parish in Saugus, Massachusetts. There he began his decades-long career of molesting children. Sometimes he was caught in the act. Many of these incidents and Geoghan's confessions were documented by the Church. Despite clear evidence that he was committing felonious sexual assaults he was never charged with a crime and was retained in his position in the Church. Several times he was referred to psychotherapists to treat his pedophilia. When new accusations became too troublesome to ignore, Geoghan was transferred to different parishes across the United States where the abuse was allowed to continue. Each transfer was followed by new accusations, confessions, and transfers. Despite this pattern of behavior, his supervisors in the Church placed him in positions of power over children, including installing him as a leader of youth groups. In 1984, Auxiliary Bishop John Michael D'Arcy submitted a formal complaint to Cardinal Bernard Francis Law stating his belief that it was dangerous to allow Geoghan to have contact with children, but the Archdiocese cited medical records to the contrary: a general practice physician and a psychiatrist declared that Geoghan was "fully recovered" from his pedophilia and there were "no restrictions on his work as a parish priest" (1, 2). These experts didn't have a clue.

It wasn't long before more accusations of sexual abuse were causing trouble, and Geoghan was again diagnosed with a pedophilic disorder. In 1989, Auxiliary Bishop Robert Banks attempted to remove Geoghan from Church leadership, but he was sent to another treatment center for a few months where he showed "moderate" improvement. The treatment center declared that "the probability he would act out again is quite low. However, we could not guarantee that it would not re-occur." The Archdiocese continued to move Geoghan from church to church and never told his parishoners that he had been abusing children. Perhaps this is the only experiment in complete destigmatization of child sex abuse crimes that has ever been attempted. No labeling. No restrictions. No criminal record. But the accusations did not stop. An estimated 150 different individuals came forward to report that Geoghan had sexually abused them during his tenure as an ordained priest. If not for a public crime he committed in 1991, he might never have faced justice. He had groped a child's buttocks in a public swimming pool and a formal police report was made (3).

DOI: 10.4324/9781003393849-9

It wasn't until 1998 that the accusations against John Geoghan became impossible to ignore, and the Catholic Church defrocked him. Geoghan's trial was front page news in 2002. His grown victims attended the trial or stood in the hallway of the courtroom to lawfully demonstrate their pain and defiance. Geoghan ignored the crowds as he walked by. One man stood near the court-room elevator and shouted "You're a pig! You're a filthy pig!" while most victims remained quiet. The Archdiocese of Boston paid 10 million dollars to 86 of his victims (after haggling down from an original agreement of $30 million).

It took 40 years, until February 2002, for Geoghan to be sentenced to any criminal punishments for his crimes. For his single incident of groping a child, he was sentenced to a minimum of nine years in prison and a maximum of ten years in prison. His lawyer asked for three years' probation instead, because Geoghan had "no criminal history." He was not charged with any other crimes because some victims were unwilling to testify or because the statute of limitations had been exhausted. Justice has an expiration date. After his conviction, the 67-year-old Geoghan asked "Where am I going now?" He was taken to prison, where his punishment was just beginning (4, 5).

Spotlight

The Clergy Sex Abuse scandal has inspired deep feelings of outrage among Catholics and non-Catholics alike, with many people calling for severe punishments for the perpetrators and their collaborators (6–10). The history of John Geoghan's criminal career was most thoroughly investigated by *The Boston Globe*'s Spotlight team. This Pulitzer Prize winning team of investigators sued to uncover documents that revealed the extraordinary lengths that the Diocese of Boston went in order to conceal abuse allegations. The Spotlight team destroyed the secrecy that had protected hundreds of priests from accountability and thereby facilitated their future acts of abuse. By the end of 2001, the Church had removed 450 priests from their positions as a direct result of *The Boston Globe*'s tenacious reporting (11).

The Roman Catholic sex abuse crisis can be assessed at the individual level by examining specific cases, but the numbers are so overwhelming it would be impossible to catalog them all. Statistical analysis helps us understand the scope of the problem, but this ignores the experiences of the individual victims. One productive way to examine the situation is to evaluate the policies and procedures of the Church to see how they contributed to more crimes against children. As late as 2001, a cardinal in the Vatican had written "I congratulate you for not denouncing a priest to the civil administration. You have acted well and I am pleased to have colleagues in the episcopate who, in the eyes of history and all other bishops in the world, preferred prison to denouncing his son and priest." This indicates that some Church leaders praised those who obstructed legal proceedings to protect child abusers (12, 13).

Under the intense pressure of this scandal, the Church now advocates for zero-tolerance policies, mandatory reporting of child abuse to authorities, and cooperation with law enforcement. Michael D'Antonio's book *Mortal Sins* explains how the scandal has taken a massive toll on the Church's reputation. A 2,000-year-old institution can probably survive this scandal, but it will never be the same. After all of the denials and obfuscations were dismantled, people began looking for explanations. What could have caused this crisis within the Catholic Church? Are the causes different than other religious and secular organizations that have been caught covering up their own abuse scandals?

The United States Conference of Catholic Bishops commissioned a report by John Jay College to identify the causes of child sexual abuse by Catholic priests (14). This report was published in 2011. The research team used qualitative assessments, surveys, and reports along with quantitative evaluations of clinical data retrieved from psychiatric treatment centers serving priests. The authors of this study did not find any single cause of child abuse within the Church. They suggested that crime rates within the Church followed the rising trend of crime in the United States at the time (late 1970s to 1985). However, the researchers did not find any statistically significant risk factors that differentiated abusive priests from non-abusive priests, except that those who went through seminary in the 1960s and early 1970s began abusing children soon after being ordained in comparison to other seminary cohorts. The authors concluded that there was a difference in training standards and regimentation during this period that may have contributed to abuse rates. Overall, the researchers estimated that 4% of priests had an accusation of abusing a child between 1950 and 2002. Even though most crimes are not reported, Catholics will be glad to know that the vast majority of priests (96%) have never been implicated in a sex crime. It really is a case of bad apples giving everyone else a bad name.

The report by John Jay did identify several organizational factors related to trends in abuse reports. By 1985, Catholic bishops had only received 6% of abuse reports that were recorded by the dioceses. If they had known the full scope of the problem perhaps they would have instituted different policies. As a matter of routine, victims were ignored. Reports made by the dioceses focused on the priests and their rehabilitation efforts, and little mention was made of the victims themselves. Diocesan leaders were not in the habit of meeting with victims or their families until 2002 when the pain and trauma of the abuse were made common knowledge in society. The report says that some bishops were "innovators" who tried to be proactive and solve problems in their organizations, but that the media focused mostly on the "laggards" who were slow to respond, thereby giving the Church a bad reputation.

John Geoghan was sent to prison during the most fervent period of public outrage over the clergy sex abuse scandal. With nearly 150 known victims, some of them expressed their relief at knowing he was being punished after so many years of disappointment. Perhaps his conviction and prison term sent a signal that there was hope in the legitimacy of the court system. For many, justice was served, but within the Massachusetts prison system, some people thought that justice needed a helping hand.

Puerile Cruelty

After being convicted of child molestation, John Geoghan was transferred to the Massachusetts Department of Corrections where he was formally processed. He was given a prison uniform, bedding, hygiene products, and a state-issued identification number. The prison intake process can be a dehumanizing initiation into a cold bureaucratic system. Prisoners are often distressed over the loss of their individuality. But Geoghan probably would have preferred to be an anonymous figure.

Sex offenders are not treated well in prison, especially not those who hurt children; especially not those who were prolific serial offenders with well over 100 victims; especially not those who have been front page news for years; especially not those who were in positions of authority and trust; especially not those who claimed to be Holy Men. The hypocrisy of the situation must have added to the universal scorn heaped on John Geoghan. Outsiders rarely get to see what happens behind the concrete walls and razor wire of our correctional facilities. We usually rely on first or second-hand accounts by prisoners who are willing to talk about their experiences, but in the case of John Geoghan, we have two sources to explain how he was treated.

The first source is a letter written by a fellow prisoner and was forwarded to the *Boston Globe*. This prisoner was a convicted child murderer who struck up a friendship with Geoghan. He described Geoghan as a target of abuse by prison staff, a process called "tuning up" the inmates. The letter described a dozen incidents of abuse in the Concord Correctional Facility. The prisoner wrote "As far as safety goes, there is none… [the guards] do whatever they see fit, and if they want to do something to you they will. And they have no problem letting someone else do it to you either." Prescient words. This concerned citizen of the prison claims to have written a formal complaint to the prison officials to intervene on Geoghan's behalf, and he offered to testify as a witness. Officers were accused of defecating on Geoghan's bed and destroying his personal property. They forced him to strip naked and stand for extended periods of time. His supportive relationship with his sister was mocked by the staff as an incestuous sexual relationship.

One officer was named in the *Boston Globe* as the most prolific abuser of Geoghan (15). This officer was never found guilty of any wrongdoing but was accused of torturing the defrocked priest. He was reported to have posted news articles about Geoghan's case near his desk. His nickname for Geoghan was "Lucifer." Geoghan's legal team spread the officer's name in news reports, but this approach backfired. The officer received a diagnosis of posttraumatic stress disorder caused by the public accusations and was awarded partial disability benefits. Whether this officer was actually harassing prisoners has not been proven in a court of law, but Geoghan's life in prison was "horrific." His attorney characterized his treatment as "gratuitous and puerile cruelty."

Geoghan wrote a letter to his attorney saying he was a "poster boy" for abuse by the staff (5). He believed his food was tampered with. Prison staff and prisoners commented that Geoghan was not adapting well to prison life because he expected to be first in line for food and wanted people to hold doors open for him. He called correctional officers "clowns" and "fools," pointed his finger in their faces and shouted at them. He was used to being in a position of power and authority and could not tolerate even the most common prison experiences, let alone the targeted harassment and abuse. He couldn't abide profanity and would visibly wince if someone said a bad word in his presence. "Die in Hell!" "Pedophile!" and "Skinner" (child molester) were shouted at him. "Bless me father, for I have skinned" the officers reportedly said to him (16). One prisoner described him as "highfalutin." Geoghan complained about not being allowed to put condiments on his food in his preferred way. He wrote, "I am amazed at the audacity of the institution!" He mocked the correctional officers' union's "Godly powers" and said the staff were "minions of Satan!" He never believed that a powerful organization would neglect its duty by failing to take allegations of abuse seriously and refusing to take meaningful steps to prevent further harm. It was shocking. Simply shocking.

Other witnesses claimed that when Geoghan was abused he would turn the other cheek and say "God bless you." Geoghan woke early each morning, prayed, and read his Bible. He attended Catholic services and tried to act like a priest. He would mutter the Mass along with the chaplain under his breath. He even tried to offer holy water to the Catholic prisoners who resented his presence. If his picture appeared on television he would deny the charges by saying "They're making up stories." His denials only made the other prisoners angry. It is a tenant of the old convict code that you "do your own time" and not talk about your crimes. Prisoners who spend too much time arguing their cases violate this rule and annoy everyone else. Like Theodore Dyer in Michigan, he "wouldn't shut up." One prisoner had to help the old man open his peanut butter jar and fold his laundry. He told Geoghan not to talk so much about his crimes because it was not "prison smart." Geoghan supposedly replied, "God is looking out for me."

Officials decided to transfer Geoghan to "protective custody" in the most secure maximum-security prison in Massachusetts – the Souza Baranowski Correctional Center, also called the "Shirley Max." In a counseling session, Geoghan told his therapist "I feel depressed, tired, and beaten – on the verge of death row. I feel condemned." He preferred the transfer to a Level 6 security facility. He told his attorney "It's worth trading liberty for security" (17). A maximum-security prison might sound like a good place to feel "secure," but that's the interesting thing about prison classification. The more secure the prison, the more violent the population.

Unrest, Confusion, Mystery

The second source we have for Geoghan's prison experiences is over ten hours of security camera footage recorded from different cameras in the protective custody wing of the Shirley Max prison (18). This footage was posted on the internet without the authorization of the prison authorities. It was uploaded to YouTube in 2007 in 68 short segments on a channel named "josephdruce." The date and time stamp in the footage indicates that it was recorded on August, 23rd, 2003. Some of the cameras are manually controlled, but others have a static position.

The footage revealed correctional officers talking near the control desk inside the cellblock before the crime occurred. Everything appeared to be a routine morning in the prison. Groups of prisoners were passing by the desk to return food trays. At 11:53 AM, most of the prisoners entered their cells and the doors were closed remotely. A prisoner later identified as Joseph Druce had entered a cell belonging to John Geoghan just before the doors closed. The cell was immediately adjacent to the control desk – a distance of fewer than 20 feet. The footage is not clear enough to show whether the officers saw Druce walk inside the wrong cell. An officer was staring at a computer before he walked into his office.

One prisoner was looking in the direction of Geoghan's cell as he opened trash bags. He appeared to be talking to another prisoner who was cleaning the area. For the next few minutes, these prisoners cleared trash and mopped the floor. At 11:58 AM both prisoners stood in the doorway of a room. A correctional officer exited with them and examined his computer. The two prisoners went back to their cells. At 11:59 AM the officer walked around the desk and headed toward Geoghan's cell. The officer quickly returned to his desk and radioed for assistance. Several officers entered the cellblock immediately and headed toward the cell door.

The camera pivoted to a front view of the cell. Six officers were shown leaning against the door and pulling the handle. From 12:00 PM to 12:04 PM they were unable to open it. Finally, they pulled the door open and threw Joseph Druce to the floor before restraining him and taking him off-camera. Geoghan remained inside the cell as officers entered and exited in small groups. Medical equipment was taken inside. One officer can be seen taking photographs from the door-way. Medical staff can be seen entering the cell at the 12:08 mark. At 12:31 PM a stretcher was brought to the cell. Geoghan was carried out and placed on the stretcher at 12:46 PM. Artificial respiration was attempted until 12:53 PM when the nurses pushed the stretcher out of the cell block. At the same time, an officer can be seen laying out stacks of paperwork on his desk before the recording cuts out.

The official disciplinary report of this homicide was rather dry and bureaucratic. It described how Druce entered Geoghan's cell as the doors were being remotely secured. "Inmate Druce entered this cell without being detected by staff" it explains. The report ends with the almost ludicrously sterile phrase: "Inmate Druce's actions greatly disrupted the orderly running of the facility." The Massachusetts Department of Corrections has always been a relatively safe prison system when compared to the gang wars in California, Texas, or most of the other states in this country. In the seven years between 1996 and 2003, there were no recorded homicides in any Massachusetts prison. That flawless record ended on August 23, 2003, inside John Geoghan's cell.

The subsequent investigation revealed more details of this event. When Druce was transferred to the special protective custody unit (J1) he was placed in a single cell next to Geoghan. According to some prisoners, Druce made threatening statements to the old man. "Why don't you kill yourself and save the state some money." "I'm glad I wasn't an altar boy." He would stand near the tables while Geoghan played rummy with the other prisoners, biding his time. Druce was sent into disciplinary confinement for fighting with another prisoner. When he returned to J1, Druce was transferred to a cell farther away from Geoghan. Prisoners in the cellblock said Druce's demeanor had changed. He was quiet and "stalked" Geoghan with his eyes. Joseph Druce told the investigators that he had planned his attack for longer than a month, and plotted the details during his time in segregation.

On August 23rd Druce was pacing near the control desk. Geoghan put his tray away and walked into his cell 20 feet away from the officer on duty. Druce followed. The doors automatically closed behind him. Druce had an extra T-shirt and stretched-out socks tied around his waist. Druce wedged a book in the top of the cell door to prevent any interruptions, then he tied a makeshift noose around Geoghan's neck and tightened it. Geoghan begged for his life saying "It doesn't have to happen like this." Druce replied "Your days are over. No more children for you, pal."

Two prisoners looked inside the window and saw what was happening. The witnesses were torn between two codes of behavior: ignore the murder and risk being punished as accomplices (they saw the cameras were pointed right at them), or tell the C.O. and be called a snitch. A dangerous choice in prison. They decided to tell the officer before running back to their own cells.

The responding officer observed Druce laying on top of Geoghan with a T-shirt-torniquet around his neck, tightened by using Geoghan's own shoe as a fulcrum. Druce also allegedly jumped up and down on Geoghan's chest to make sure he was dead. Authorities later found a razor in cell and considered the possibility that Druce was going to mutilate Geoghan's body if he had enough time (Druce wrote to me saying he intended to use the razor to castrate Geoghan).

When the officers were trying to open the door Druce told them "Don't hurt me, it's not against you." During his extraction, he offered no resistance, but told the officers to take their time administering medical care to Geoghan because "he's dead already." A prisoner asked a C.O. what happened and the officer reportedly said "Put it this way. The diddler's dead." The prisoners in the cellblock reportedly were upset by the murder. They didn't think it was fair for Druce to kill someone so old and frail as Geoghan. Some prisoners said, "John didn't really deserve it."

The Boston Globe had broken the story on Geoghan's abuse and the Church's cover-up, but they wrote that his death in prison made him "a kind of victim" (19). They said he was "failed by an institution that bungled its basic duty to keep him safe." Reverend Maurice Connolly, who had gone to seminary school with Geoghan, remarked that "John was a little old man at that point. He was kind of shriveled and frail, and he was not the type who could really stick up for himself."

The accusation of "deliberate indifference" is a serious concern for prison officials. It is relatively easy to identify "cruel and unusual" punishment in a prison setting if a correctional officer caused the death of a prisoner. It must be demonstrated that the officer acted unnecessarily, with malice, and their behavior was directly responsible for the prisoner's death (20). But how can you blame a correctional officer when one prisoner kills another? "Deliberate indifference" is a term used in Supreme Court rulings that mark the line where prison staff can be held criminally and civilly liable for the actions of prisoners if they do not take steps to respond to reasonable threats to a prisoner's wellbeing. The Court has said "the Constitution does not mandate comfortable prisons, but neither does it permit inhumane ones" (*Farmer v. Brennan, 1994*).

The staff might have had foreknowledge of a threat to Geoghan's life. A prisoner who was on good terms with Geoghan has said that he warned the staff two months before the murder that Druce had it out for the priest. A different prisoner claims to have witnessed this report. If the officer in the surveillance footage saw Joseph Druce enter Geoghan's cell, but he "jerked his head" as the video description states, then he showed deliberate indifference to Geoghan's safety. However, the footage is not clear and none of the officers were charged with any crimes for their actions that day.

Unlike the response to Steven Sandison's homicide described in Chapter 1, most people were not happy with John Geoghan's brutal death. The mother of one of the victims said "Oh, my God. How could that happen? He was supposed to be in a more secure place. What survivors wanted was justice. Not something like this." (19). An attorney representing 140 of Geoghan's victims said "My clients would rather have seen John Geoghan be punished in a way seen fit by society." Geoghan's family and friends attended his funeral and shared their sorrow. They remembered his meek personality and his desire to help others. Geoghan's former attorney remarked that the murder gave people permission to think kindly of him. When he was alive he was considered "one-dimensional and purely evil," but now that he was dead some people were allowed to pity him as the victim of a cruel and indifferent prison system.

On a Mission from God

With over 150 victims coming forward, and probably more remaining hidden, few people would have pity for the puerile harassment Geoghan suffered in prison. After all, the Supreme Court has said prisoners are not entitled to comfortable prisons. But strangling and stomping an old man to death in his prison cell is not usually a punishment that is endorsed by the general public. So why did Joseph Druce do it?

The historical record of Joseph Druce's life can be pieced together from news reports, court testimony, and a podcast he recorded through a prison phone call (21). He was born on April 15, 1965 (his given name was Darrin Ernest Smiledge, but Joseph Druce is used throughout the remainder of this chapter). One of his attorneys has claimed that Druce was a troubled child who used to bang his head against windows when he was a toddler. He has said that his childhood was pretty good and his mother did her best for him and his younger brother Dan, but when he went to the Lakeside School in West Peabody his life fell apart. This was a residential school run by seminary students at the nearby Gordon College in Wenham, Massachusetts. When Druce was in residence at this school there were 16 other boys and 6 girls. He would stay on the campus on weekdays and go home on the weekends. "That's where I was first abused by seminary priest who became a priest, named Edward Solomon." Druce claims that this seminary student abused him and at least two other children before he became an ordained minister, and later he and another priest named John Schmidt were charged with sexual abuse. An investigator would later say of this abuse that Druce "didn't have a chance in life from Jump Street" (22). Druce still remembers that quote decades later because it was so depressing to believe that he was set on a path of misery.

Druce completed the 10th grade before leaving school to work as a truck driver and a mechanic. He was addicted to many different types of drugs before he left his teenage years. He was charged with dozens of nonviolent crimes such as drug possession, larceny, and forgery.

In 1988, Druce and an acquaintance named Kenneth Tarantino were drinking with a stranger named George Rollo. Rollo was later found dead in the woods near Gloucester, Massachusetts. According to media accounts and courtroom testimony, Druce killed Rollo because the older man touched his groin. Druce is said to have been "homophobic" or triggered by the memory of his past abuse and so he beat Rollo, tied him up, and put him in the trunk of the car before driving him to a remote location. Then he is said to have strangled Rollo with a rope and stolen his car. This account was provided by Kenneth Tarantino who was offered immunity from prosecution if he testified against Druce (23). Druce was later characterized as having an intense hatred of homosexuals (his own father made this comment to the press), but he denied this. Druce's attorney said he had strong opinions about pedophiles and the psychological harm they do to child victims of abuse, but that he has no homophobic beliefs.

Druce reflects that this was the worst night of his entire life. He could have done so many other things, but instead, he went to prison at age 22 and has been there for 34 years. He had the opportunity to go to Alaska immediately before these incidents unfolded, and now he wonders what his life would have been like if he had gone there instead of Massachusetts. Still, he wondered if there was some other reason that fate put him in prison. Maybe he had some other destiny to achieve.

> Did God put me in this position and let me rot all those years prior to Geoghan being killed?? Was that my only mission in life??

In 1989, Druce was interviewed by a prison psychiatrist when he said he expected he would "go to Satan" and he would "die before I serve a life sentence" (24). He was characterized as being "angry, frustrated, blaming, remorseless, intense" and "determined." In 1999 he changed his name to the current "Joseph Lee Druce" for "safety" reasons. In 2001 he offered to provide details on the unsolved murder cases of two girls in Massachusetts in exchange for a commutation of his prison sentence, but his claims were not found to be credible. He is reported to have joined a neo-Nazi group around this time. This was the Aryan Nations Church of the Chosen Ones. The founder of this group was Richard Girnt Butler (1918–2004) whose "Church of Jesus Christ Christians" was connected to a variety of anti-Semitic hate groups and violent crimes across the United States (25). In prison, Druce was a "pastor" of this group and lead the Massachusetts branch, but there is no clear record of how involved he was in the group's activities or even how many members there were.

Druce was in the news again in 2002 for sending letters to attorneys across the United States that contained a white powder inside the envelopes. This "fake anthrax" scare was sensational during a time of intense fear of terrorism and weapons of mass destruction, but also because the attorneys who received letters had "Jewish-sounding names." He also is said to have mailed fake mail bombs from prison and sent a letter containing human feces to a public official. Despite his membership in the Aryan Nations, Druce denies targeting lawyers with Jewish names. He says this was simply a coincidence. He was sending harassing letters with fake bombs and anthrax to draw attention to his own attorney's poor representation of him in his appellate claims. Whatever his reasons were, this part of his biography is always mentioned and will remain a permanent part of how he is remembered (26, 27).

After killing Geoghan, Druce is said to have been "boastful" (28). One law enforcement official said that Druce was proud that even the Pope would know his name. When he was asked to sign a form indicating that he was waiving his Miranda rights he signed his name "Rev. Joseph Druce."

Druce wrote a letter to the Catholic Free Press of Worchester where he laid out his rationale for killing Geoghan:

> I'm the alleged murderer of Defrocked priest John J. Geoghan, and a victim of Sexual Abuse as a child… This wasn't a crime to committee (sic) a crime, but to let the world no that all child predators must be dealt with a more stringent hand, and to stop focusing on Catholicism as the mainstream. Let's look at the crime and not the Church. Joseph Druce says 'Leave the children alone… To stop these tragedy's (sic) and violence toward children we must come together and demand the house of legislators to re-enact stringent sentences and rehabilitations to cure this plague on our children.

This letter was characterized by criminologist Jack Levin as "extremely manipulative" because it attempts to improve Druce's image in the world. Rather than being characterized as an evil murderer he was trying to appear very rational. "He wants to save the children," said Levin. "Who can argue with saving children?" (29).

During his second murder trial, Druce came to court with a black eye one day. He claims that someone opened his cell door in the night and punched him in the face. The perpetrator was wearing "correctional officer pants" but was not identified. Druce believed he was targeted because he placed the Massachusetts Department of Corrections under scrutiny. Despite his attorney's arguments that Druce was not culpable for his behavior due to insanity, Joseph Druce was convicted of first-degree murder and was sentenced to life in prison without the possibility of parole.

Druce has shared his thoughts on Geoghan, saying "That perv will never again molest that many kids. 149 documented, then up to 320. That's crazy. He was the number one raper for sure." Druce has claimed that his motives for killing Geoghan stemmed from a conversation he overheard in the prison. Apparently, Geoghan was sitting at a table with three other sex offenders in the cellblock. They said, "No, no, no, you can't just fuck a kid you have to use your finger to break 'em in so you don't rip 'em open." Joseph Druce is the only source for this claim.

Druce claims that this conversation caused him to have a panic attack on the 19th, four days before the murder. He spent 45 minutes in the shower during this panic attack and the C.O. had to ask him to come out. He believed that he had to prevent this predator from hurting other children. When Joseph Druce approached Geoghan the priest made a comment that he was going to go to South America or Central America to open up a mission to help impoverished children.

> He was going to open up a mission to take in throw-away kids and have unlimited access to these kids because they couldn't complain to no one. As throw-away kids they are considered as peasants, and if they're picking through your trash and robbing your garden you can shoot and kill them and not go to jail. He had the perfect means and perfect plans to access these children. He'd be able to molest them whenever he wants at will and have no repercussions at all. They're just throwaway kids. He actually said this to me.
>
> At one point I said 'You cost the Archdiocese 10.8 million dollars in settlements' and he said 'I'm worth 20 million.' I said 'What about the 147 kids that they said you molested?' and he said 'I'm worth 287 kids.' So he was just an arrogant smug prick who just wasn't going to stop. He'd been molesting kids since 1962 ever since he was in the seminary process of becoming a priest he was introduced into other sexual misconduct and sexual abuse of children.

It just started there and bloomed from there. Him and many other priests who went to the same seminary college as all these other pedophile priests.

He also claims that official documents prove that the prison staff were complicit in the murder of Geoghan. His rationale for this is that the correctional officer on duty "allowed" him into Geoghan's cell before he closed the doors.

What happened is, I had talked to the correctional officer, and the correctional officer was going to let me go into the cell and let me beat him up. And you can see him on camera, earlier in the day I was talking to the correctional officer and he said "hey, go in there and do what you gotta do" but he was like "yo please don't kill him." I knew this cop, I knew this CO from the street so he was just, I don't know if he was serious or joking he's like "don't kill him Joe" and I'm like don't worry I'm just gonna beat him down, you know. So you can look at him on the YouTube and see the video of the CO watching me go into the cell and closing the door after watching me.

The officer may have jerked his head to avoid seeing Druce enter the cell that was a mere 20 feet away, but the surveillance footage makes this difficult to detect and an investigation ordered by Governor Mitt Romney found no wrongdoing by the staff.

I've been the only one to be prosecuted, the only one to be blamed for anything that went on that day. And that's because of the corrupt administration within MA who sent me here to a segregation unit in Arizona, to keep me away from my family and friends, who limits my phone calls keeps me with no visits and keeps me in a permanent state of lockdown, which is unconstitutional especially after I did 12.5 years in DDU in MA for killing John Geoghan, that was my punishment but now I'm being punished in AZ for no reason. And that's because the officer that was 100% responsible for letting me in that cell.

When Druce learned that I was writing a book about this topic he wanted to give me any information that would "correct the record." One thing that stood out to me in his correspondence is Druce's feeling that he was put in that cellblock with John Geoghan for a purpose. Not that the prison staff necessarily wanted him to kill Geoghan, but that *God Himself* wanted Druce to kill Geoghan. Druce has spent decades thinking about the events that led him to commit the crimes that put him in prison and the circumstances that lead to Geoghan's murder. From his perspective, it is not all coincidence or tragedy. There was a purpose. There was even a hint of foreshadowing in the title of the book he used to jam the cell door shut. It was called *The Cross and the Switch-Blade* by David Wilkerson and John and Elizabeth Sherrill. This book describes how a priest was confronted by gang members with knives in Brooklyn. For Druce this book was another sign that his mission was divinely inspired. How can a little paperback book prevent 11 correctional officers from opening a door unless it was the will of God? Druce would write letters to his supporters citing Bible verses to justify his crime.

Then said He unto the disciples, It is impossible but that offences will come: but woe unto him, through whom they come! It were better for him that a millstone were hanged about his neck, and he cast into the sea, than that he should offend one of these little ones.

Luke 17:1-2

But Joseph Druce's story did not end there. He didn't just kill Geoghan. He basked in the spotlight. A photograph appeared on the internet shortly after the murder of Geoghan. It depicted Joseph Druce in his prison uniform. Above and around his head were the hand-written words "The pedophiles must pay." This autographed piece of "murderabilia" was sold for $300 on a website called "Serial Killers Ink: The Premier True Crime Collectibles Website" (30, 31). The business owner, Eric Holler, sells artwork and memorabilia to the fans of famous murderers, then sends some of the funds to the prisoner. It is a controversial business model. One of Druce's drawings is called "Stop the Evil" and contains the line "Leave the children alone now." It is a long-haired prisoner holding a bloody knife in one hand, and a human head in the other. On the ground is a headless body with blood dripping down over a priest's collar onto the corpse's lap.

A final example of this type of murderabilia is illustrative of the disdain that Druce feels toward Geoghan: four color photographs of Geoghan's dead body in the hospital with his swollen purple face held up by a neck brace. These authentic crime-scene photographs were from Druce's legal paperwork. They are signed "A Dead Pervert Cannot Molest Innocent Children ANYMORE. -Joseph Druce." The website adds this description: "A very unique item as it is highly unusual for a killer to sign victim photographs. One of a kind item." These photographs apparently sold for $100 each and are no longer in stock. What kind of person buys crime scene photos of dead bodies signed by the murderer?

Andrew Vachss (who was always alert to these cases) weighed in Joseph Druce's case in his 2008 book *Another Life*, where he expressed his sarcastic disdain for the "creepy-crawly fans" who search the internet for *noir verité* examples of real-life murder, and who take a pornographic delight in seeing dead pedophiles (32).

> One endlessly recycled fave was the prison surveillance tapes of Father John Geoghan being strangled in his cell. The notorious "pedophile priest" had been murdered nine years ago. But the guy accused of doing it demanded a showcase trial… which meant the tapes were part of the discovery evidence the prosecution had to turn over. How that tape got so popular on the Internet is less of a mystery than why so many people keep insisting there's no such thing as snuff films.

In Chapter 1, I described how Steven Sandison's killing of Ted Dyer earned him a fanbase. Total strangers sent him money and wrote him heartbreaking letters about their own abuse. On the internet, he found thousands of supporters who shared his videos and commented with flippant jokes about "time off for good behavior." But Joseph Druce's murder of John Geoghan seems to have attracted a different kind of "fan." Ones who like to collect autographed crime scene photos. This behavior crosses a line that the average vigilante supporter would have a difficult time commiserating with.

We can speculate all day about Druce's real motives for killing Geoghan. Was he trying to protect children? Was he mentally unstable? Was he a sadist who liked hurting people? Did he do it for fame? But like a Rorschach test, your answer might tell us more about *you* than the case itself.

Perverted Justice

The case of John Geoghan and Joseph Druce brings together many of the themes found throughout this book. Geoghan was given an 8-year sentence for a single act of child molestation and he had no official criminal history. The judge was over-punishing him in order to "get justice" for the alleged 150 other crimes that were known to the Archdiocese but could not be proven in the courtroom. This was an even more severe sentence given Geoghan's advanced age. And yet, many people wished he had received a worse punishment. Their thirst for retribution was not satiated. The full scope of the Clergy Sex Abuse scandal was personified in this one elderly man.

Geoghan had been sent to a relatively safe and humane prison system. The Massachusetts DOC hadn't recorded a single homicide in the preceding seven years. But he was immediately targeted for harassment by the staff and prisoners. He was eventually transferred to a maximum-security prison for his own safety, but it was not a safe place for Geoghan.

When Joseph Druce decided to brutally kill John Geoghan he might have expected the other prisoners to praise him for his act of "community service," but instead they shunned him. The alleged victims of the priest did not respond with gratitude, they were horrified. The *Boston Globe* Spotlight team were appalled and wrote about how the Massachusetts Department of Corrections had failed in their basic duties to protect their wards. Druce wasn't given a pat on the back by the C.O.s either. He accused them of conspiring to help him kill Geoghan, so they allegedly retaliated against Druce by roughing him up and transferring him to a supermax prison in Arizona.

Let's tie some of these threads together. Many people wanted Geoghan to suffer, but when he died in that prison cell he was transformed from a monstrous caricature into a sad victim. Revenge is not always sweet, and Joseph Druce was reviled for being a vigilante who went too far.

And yet he still has fans. People who write him letters of support. People who send him money and birthday cards 20 years after his crime. He is still called as a guest on podcasts and his gruesome artwork is sold online for hundreds of dollars to collectors. If we think of "vigilante support" on a scale, members of the general public might fall anywhere along the continuum, but most people have a limit before they acknowledge that some crimes go too far. Stomping an old man to death and selling autographed pictures of his corpse on the gurney should serve as an extreme example of how far some vigilantes will go, and more surprisingly, how far other people will go along with them.

Shadow of an Angel

By "A Son of Solitude"

Have I now fallen under the dominion of an officiating angel? Does it lead me to dark places of necessity? You must agree by now, that as a child, I fell under the dominion of a tormenting demon, and you must also acknowledge that the human body is a container of sorts, capable of housing any number of energies. Ever been seized by fear? Overcome with laughter? So ran over by new love that even the oxytocin couldn't be completely to blame? We can approach this process and define it through the lens of any number of disciplines, but it is only the result, timely service, that validates the practice.

We choose to believe in guiding spirits and guardian angels because we have seen the devil and his demons in human form. We lean toward the invisible, the immaterial, because we were shown the great pain and misery that lies around us, in our homes, the places of surety and safety. We form relationships with that which we cannot see, because that which we do see, misrepresents itself, and cannot be trusted. Perhaps, these many generations, all generating the results of ordered entropy, mankind's only real specialty, have littered the atmosphere with beings, now animate, which can and at time do, guide those of us who have been attuned properly.

Or perhaps, this is all just some psychosis or disorder?

The origin of the divining rod is not known, it has been lost to antiquity. We know that in Germany, in the 16th Century, divining rods were used to find precious metals and treasure.

To survive repeated traumas and assaults, a child, now a man, must become like the willow. It is soft and malleable, is capable of surviving the most strenuous of storms, without breaking. It is also, the ancient magical implement of the Water Witch. Is it the willow itself? Or is it the entity that guides its movement that we credit with discovering the hidden well? In my experience, it is a combination of both. You must gain respect on the invisible plain, in the same manner, that it is done on the material plane. Become like the willow, and you will find, much as I have, that the hardest piece of wood in the room is easily snapped. I have walked out of a number of situations that were designed to take my life. These occasions I credit the entity whose hands were on the willow. I credit myself only for not caring if I lost my own life, for the willow is not easily broken.

This life has tempered me greatly, and the forces I contend with daily continue to do so – isolation, loneliness, separation, guilt. These are something of a pressing tide, always there, pushing, pushing. But I can assure of this, if you live in a mundane world, it is only because you haven't chosen to exercise your right, your power, as a "conscious co-creator." This mind is powerful and dynamic. It generates images and has the capability of seeking out, or even creating connections that seem divine. This nervous system is a powerful interface, a vibrating tuning fork which can draw us to many things, wealth, opportunity, sorrow, suffering. This is magic. The complexity of this existence is always reducible to simplicity and the terms we choose to populate our perception and will. How did this plain sheet of paper end up in your hands? Have you chosen to let the words I've selected populate your perception? This is conscious co-creation. We are here, together, practicing the oldest of magics. You cannot touch my hand, and yet, in this moment, my spirit has permeated your atmosphere. This is the evidence of that which so many have spoken of. Energies move, they inhabit our existence, we have only to increase our visual intelligence, learn to see them. In this way, I've been driven to strange and mysterious places. I've been privileged to arrive in the exact moment that I was needed. To participate and submit yourself to a process like this is a rare treasure. The rewards are few, but they are beyond compare. There is no procedure for outside validation of this. It must be lived.

How can I say what this life has in store for me now? What do I deserve? The same as the next man I suppose. The difference here is this. I am entitled to expect great things from the universe because she expected great things from me. Expected me to survive, to learn, to remain grateful, not bitter. To trust in that which could only be sensed, to follow a mere scent, wholeheartedly, and then be willing to throw myself into the fray, with abandon. Because of these things, I expect great things, for I have learned well that the gorgeous, reliable, faithful, Ms. Universe always, always, returns to us in kind that which we project to her. Thus, I have been faithful to her, and she…

… remains faithful to me.

References

1. Rezendes, M., & Carroll, M. (2002, Jan. 16). Doctors who OK'd Geoghan lacked expertise, review shows. *The Boston Globe.* https://archive.boston.com/globe/spotlight/abuse/stories/011602_doctors.htm

2. *The Boston Globe.* (2004). Geoghan's troubled history.http://archive.boston.com/globe/spotlight/abuse/stories/010702_history.htm

3. *The Boston Globe.* (2003). The Geoghan case. http://archive.boston.com/globe/spotlight/abuse/geoghan/

4. Farragher, T. (2003). A priest by turns demanding and timid trod prison's path. *The Boston Globe.* http://archive.boston.com/news/local/massachusetts/articles/2003/12/01/a_priest_by_turns_demanding_and_timid_trod_prisons_path/

5. Farragher, T. (2003, Nov. 30). John Geoghan: Abuser, inmate, victim. *The Boston Globe.* http://archive.boston.com/news/specials/geoghan/

6. Berry, J. (2013). *Lead us not into temptation: Catholic priests and the sexual abuse of children.* Champaign, IL: University of Illinois Press.

7. Baran, M. (2014, July, 21). Betrayed by silence. *Minnesota Public Radio.* https://minnesota.publicradio.org/collections/catholic-church/betrayed-by-silence/ch1/

8. Moore, E. (2013, Oct. 5). Church abuse case haunts lawyer who defunded priest. *Daily World.* https://www.usatoday.com/story/news/nation/2013/10/05/gilbert-gauthe-catholic-priest/2926325/

9. Gullage, P. (2019, Feb. 17). Mount Cashel: After 30 years, the pain still has not gone away. *CBC.* https://www.cbc.ca/news/canada/newfoundland-labrador/mount-cashel-anniversary-1.5017182

10. Osmond, J. (2020). *When you can't unearth the cover up: Archaeology and the memorialization of Mouth Cashel Orphanage.* Master's Degree Thesis. https://research.library.mun.ca/15013/1/thesis.pdf

11. Baron, M. (2003). To the judges of the Pulitzer Prize. *The Boston Globe.* https://www.pulitzer.org/cms/sites/default/files/content/2016/globespotlightletter.pdf

12. Thavis, J. (2010, Apr. 19). Cardinal: JP II OK'd letter on shielding priest abuser. *Catholic News Service.* https://www.ncronline.org/news/accountability/cardinal-jp-ii-okd-letter-shielding-priest-abuser

13. D'Antonio, M. (2013). *Mortal sins: Sex, crime, and the era of Catholic scandal.* Macmillan. https://www.youtube.com/watch?v=AK_eFaqfb6o&t=948s

14. Terry, K. J., Smith, M. L., Schuth, K., Kelly, J. R., Vollman, B., & Massey, C. (2011). The causes and context of sexual abuse of minors by Catholic priests in the United States, 1950–2010. *John Jay College.* https://www.bishop-accountability.org/reports/2011_05_18_John_Jay_Causes_and_Context_Report.pdf

15. Supreme Judicial Court of Massachusetts, Suffolk. (2008, Nov. 20). Bisazza case. https://caselaw.findlaw.com/ma-supreme-judicial-court/1194523.html

16. Farragher, T. (2003, Dec. 2). Behind walls, trouble built to a brutal end. *The Boston Globe.* http://archive.boston.com/news/local/massachusetts/articles/2003/12/02/behind_walls_trouble_built_to_a_brutal_end/

17. Farragher, T. (2003, Dec. 1). A priest by turns demanding and timid trod prison's path. *The Boston Globe.* http://archive.boston.com/news/local/massachusetts/articles/2003/12/01/a_priest_by_turns_demanding_and_timid_trod_prisons_path/

18. Daily News. (2007, July 8). Prison kill scene gets on YouTube. https://web.archive.org/web/20080918102451/http://www.nydailynews.com/news/ny_crime/2007/07/08/2007-07-08_prison_kill_scene_gets_on_youtube.html

19. Kilroy, I. (2003, Aug. 25). Victims dismayed by sex abuse priest's killing. *The Irish Times.* https://www.irishtimes.com/news/victims-dismayed-by-sex-abuse-priest-s-killing-1.370767

20. Whitley v. Albers, 475 U.S. 312 (1986). https://supreme.justia.com/cases/federal/us/475/312/

21. Criminal Perspective Podcast (2021, Sep. 11). DECLASSIFIED- Interview with murderer Joseph Druce. https://www.listennotes.com/podcasts/criminal-perspective/declassified-interview-with-kmQFD0vAj9n/

22. Murphy, S. P. (2003, Sep. 24). Druce beaten as child, inquiry finds. *The Boston Globe.* https://archive.boston.com/globe/spotlight/abuse/stories5/091303_druce.htm

23. Supreme Judicial Court of Massachusetts, Essex. (1994, Dec. 14). Commonwealth v. Smiledge. 643 N.E.2d 41 (Mass. 1994) https://www.casemine.com/judgement/us/5914bdb2add7b049347a3c83

24. McElhenny, J. (2003, Aug. 26). Alleged Geoghan killer led troubled life, records show. *The Boston Globe*. http://archive.boston.com/globe/spotlight/abuse/stories5/082603_suspect.htm

25. SPLC: Southern Poverty Law Center. (2004). Richard Butler. https://www.splcenter.org/fighting-hate/extremist-files/individual/richard-butler

26. Levin, J. (2004). *Why we hate*. Amherst, NY: Prometheus.

27. Guart, A. (2003, Aug. 31). Perv rev.'s strangler a hero in his own sick & evil mind. *New York Post*. https://nypost.com/2003/08/31/perv-rev-s-strangler-a-hero-in-his-own-sick-evil-mind/

28. Murray, G. V. (2005, Sep. 10). Officer says Druce boasted about killing. *Telegram & Gazette*. https://www.bishop-accountability.org/news2005_07_12/2005_09_10_Murray_OfficerSays.htm

29. Murphy, S. P. (2003, Sep. 13). Letter says Druce was abused as boy. *The Boston Globe*. https://archive.boston.com/globe/spotlight/abuse/stories5/091303_druce.htm

30. Serial Killers Ink. Retrieved from Web (2022, May 5), https://web.archive.org/web/20230513020600/https://serialkillersink.net/

31. Palin, M. (2017, May 13). Chilling drawings from sadistic serial killers in prison. *News.com.au*. https://www.news.com.au/world/north-america/chilling-drawings-from-sadistic-serial-killers-in-prison/news-story/e11a4c9c8d858e6ee0f4edc754b71e81

32. Vachss, A. (2008). *Another life*. New York, NY: Vintage Crime/Black Lizard.

9

A BOMB BUILT IN HELL

The Criminology of Vigilantism

In this chapter, I will summarize what I have learned through my research on these vigilantes (their motives, circumstances, thoughts, beliefs, attitudes, and behaviors), and I will try to explain their crimes using various theoretical models proposed by criminologists. I am working with a small number of cases, and they do not all fit together. Still, there are some important trends that should be acknowledged in order to help us properly define these crimes in the future. And maybe if we start thinking about these cases in a systematic way, we will eventually be able to design interventions.

The title of this chapter is borrowed from Andrew Vachss, the fiction author whose quotes have dotted this entire book. Vachss worked with violent juveniles and he knew that much of their destructive behavior was caused by childhood trauma and abuse. In 1973, he wrote a book called *A Bomb Built in Hell,* but it was considered to be too extreme to publish until 2012, although he said he was toning down realities not exaggerating them. He said this book was "meant to be a Ph.D. thesis in criminology without the footnotes, exploring such areas as the connection between child abuse and crime." Vachss argued that dangerous children were products of their environments. They were constructed, like a bomb, by outside forces. They might be born into abusive families without their consent, but he hoped that by drawing attention to their tragic humanity they would be accepted into a "family of choice" where they could develop social bonds, social support, and purposeful lives. This could defuse the bomb. He described this theory of criminology in his essay "Today's Victim Could Be Tomorrow's Predator": (1)

We make our own monsters. The formula is frighteningly simple: Take child abuse or neglect, especially at the hands of those constituted by the laws of man and nature to protect their own, and let the government either ignore or exacerbate the situation. Time will do the rest.

The maltreated child cries, "I hurt!" If we don't listen, and listen quickly, the same cry for help will turn prophetic: The unanswered plea for help will evolve into a deadly pattern. Only a tiny percentage of abused children actually die from their torture, but the survivors are the recruits for an ever–growing army of predatory criminals. Today's victim is tomorrow's predator.

Does this mean that every abused child will grow into a monster? No. But when the monster does emerge, the fallout is incalculable.

DOI: 10.4324/9781003393849-10

Out of respect for Andrew Vachss' work in this field, I am using his analogy of the bomb to frame my discussion of criminological theories of vigilantism. Therefore, this chapter investigates how a human bomb is manufactured, why some bombs explode and others do not, how to defuse a bomb, and how to clear the debris if we fail.

Hazardous Material

Common, everyday chemicals and substances can explode under the right circumstances, such as occurs when methane gas is under too much pressure. Safe storage protocols can prevent them from becoming dangerous. In a way, humans might be similar. We all have explosive potential, but we also have non-explosive outlets to keep us from hurting ourselves and others, like a pressure release valve. But some hazardous materials are naturally unstable, just as some people are prone to acts of violence to make their points. How do they get that way?

Sympathizing with Child Victims

I often think of Jeremy Moody's claim that a vigilante is "a person who is hyper-sensitive to moral injustices." If this is true, then we may be able to identify the characteristics of people who are more sensitive, more volatile, more explosive, than others. As I explained in Chapter Two, many vigilantes experienced traumatizing sexual abuse as children. The vast majority of child sex abuse victims do not grow up become career criminals, and even fewer take on the mantle of vigilantism, so this is not a sufficient explanation for vigilante conduct. It is also not a necessary condition. Jeremy Moody and Jon Watson have told me they were not victims of child abuse, but they care very much about the safety and happiness of children. Just as you can make a bomb out of fertilizer or uranium, vigilantes can have different life experiences that all bring them to the same deadly conclusion.

Steven Sandison was kidnapped and sexually tortured as a young child. He did not cope with this experience in an effective way. He had no family support. He ended up in juvenile detention centers, and eventually prison. Joseph Druce had a similar path in life stemming from his sexual abuse in a religious school. Lawrence Trant, Patrick Drum, Michael Allen Mullen, Scottie Allen, Donte Stokes, and Clark Fredericks were all sexually abused as children. Not all vigilantes were victims of sexual assault, but a disturbing proportion of the cases I reviewed shared this experience.

People who suffer from more Adverse Childhood Experiences (ACEs) suffer worse life outcomes across the board. Often the consequences of these ACEs are cumulative, and if protective experiences are not used to mitigate their effects, the results can be devastating (2). Medical, emotional, and psychiatric distress plague the "survivor," and some do not survive at all. A study of over 22,000 Canadians found that those who experienced sexual abuse as children were 4.4–5.5 times more likely to attempt suicide than those who did not experience sexual assault (depending on the number of control variables and mediator variables included in the model). Sometimes bombs explode and only destroy themselves (3).

Victims of child sexual abuse might cope with their trauma through drug and alcohol use. They may end up in the juvenile justice system and later find themselves in an adult prison. The abuse-to-prison pipeline is merciless. It is more likely that people who suffer these severe forms of abuse will become self-destructive, they will have damaged relationships, or they will commit commonplace crimes than they will become a vigilante. In that sense, we can think of the downward spiral of these victims as creating an unstable bomb that explodes without purpose or direction. They are hazardous materials.

Agnew's General Strain Theory might be the best single explanation for the behaviors of emotionally-driven vigilantes (4). This theory explains how people who are faced with high magnitude, inescapable, and clearly unjust strains in their lives might cope with criminal behavior. The chances that they will resort to crime increase if the person thinks crime is an appropriate response, if there are few non-criminal responses available, and if the person believes they will not be sanctioned for their actions. Clearly, childhood sexual abuse is a strain that meets the criteria outlined by Agnew as especially suited for a criminal response. The likelihood of a former victim picking up a knife and stabbing their abuser to death is greater if the person is a man who thinks violence is an appropriately masculine response, if they know the statute of limitations has run out and the courts can't help them, and they do not fear punishment, like Clark Fredericks. At the time of his crime, he was hopeless, reckless, and did not care what happened to him. There is no punishment that could have deterred him when he was prepared to die to escape the strain of his trauma.

Masculine Roles

Why do men think that violence is an appropriately masculine response to victimization? The nature versus nurture debate is beyond the scope of this book, but I can list some propositions. The first is that the brain development of boys follows a different trajectory than girls because of the androgen transfer of testosterone after eight weeks in the womb. This testosterone exposure slows boys' brain development. Boys have a larger and more active amygdala, which triggers aggression. Boys' amygdala also has more testosterone receptors, so they become angry quicker, and stay angry longer than girls. Women have faster development of their pre-frontal cortex than boys, which helps them to regulate their emotions and control their behavior. These biological risk factors contribute to male delinquency and violent crime, but there is a social component that cannot be ignored (5–7).

Men might have a biological predisposition for violence, but then why aren't all men violent brutes? Men can *learn* to be non-violent, and they can also learn to be more violent. Differential Association Theory by Edwin Sutherland and the Social Learning Theory of crime by Burgess and Akers propose that people are exposed to definitions of what is acceptable behavior. Their family, peers, and communities influence them by example. Children learn through observation and imitation, and their behavior may be reinforced or punished until they adopt these definitions as their own cherished beliefs (8, 9).

Men are under pressure to be "doing masculinity" at all times (10). If a man reports his attacker to the police and meekly accepts the legal system's response, he would not feel like a "real man." If he brutally slays his attacker, he has regained his honor even if he is punished. Every Father's Day people on the internet share pictures of Gary Plauché shooting his son's kidnapper and refer to him as a "real father." These beliefs might even be shaped by entertainment media portrayals of comic book vigilantes who use their muscles and guns to get "real justice." I wouldn't want to overstate the case that men are influenced by every form of entertainment media of our society. It is more likely that the intense, frequent, priority relationships formed in childhood matter more in shaping these ideas than any song or television show. Clearly this is a complex issue. Each human being's learning history is shaped and buffeted by forces throughout their lives that cannot be tracked and measured with enough precision to account for everything. But it does seem likely that male victims of childhood sexual assault feel a societal pressure to kill the things that hurt them.

Moral Injury

Different people respond to traumatic events in different ways. Some people may suffer "moral injury" by their exposure to especially stressful circumstances. Soldiers, law enforcement officers, medical professionals, and crime victims have experiences that alter their moral landscape (11–13). A child who grows up in an abusive household may have an attenuated sense of the moral rectitude of non-violence. A person who is thrown into a violent prison yard might learn that violence is not a rare or special event that ought to inspire shock. Violence is normalized.

Some people struggle with this injury to their moral compass. They might prefer to live in a world without violence, but they acknowledge that we live in a world where sometimes Might makes Right. They are more willing to use violence to solve their problems because their life experiences affirmed that, sometimes, violence is the answer.

This theory of human morality might be considered a hybrid of social-learning theories and strain/stress response theories, but it is perhaps most similar to the symptoms of post-traumatic stress disorder. Feelings of survivor's guilt, shame, loss of trust, and fear of harm are often seen in cases of PTSD. A list of criteria in the Moral Injury Events Scale asks the following questions: (14)

1 I saw things that were morally wrong.
2 I am troubled by having witnessed other's immoral acts.
3 I acted in ways that violated my own moral code or values.
4 I am troubled by having acted in ways that violated my own morals or values.
5 I violated my own morals by failing to do something that I felt I should have done.
6 I am troubled because I violated my morals by failing to do something that I felt I should have done.
7 I feel betrayed by leaders who I once trusted.
8 I feel betrayed by fellow service members (or other shared group) who I once trusted.
9 I feel betrayed by others outside the U.S. military (or other shared group) who I once trusted.
10 I trust my leaders and fellow service members (or other shared group) to always live up to their core values (reverse coded).
11 I trust myself to always live up to my own moral code (reverse coded).

As I read this list of questions that indicate the degree to which one's moral code might be injured, I am thinking of the men I interviewed for this book. Those who were sexually abused as children certainly experienced many immoral acts that were morally wrong. Those who went to prison saw horrible things done in the name of "justice." Those who felt they should have acted sooner to protect kids (e.g., James Fairbanks) felt guilt for not reporting their abuse. Those who coped with irresponsible behavior, drugs, and alcohol (e.g., Clark Fredericks) were ashamed of themselves. All of them felt betrayed by the justice system that gave lenient sentences to child sex abusers. Few of them trusted anyone. It is reasonable to assume that child abuse causes moral injury. The abuser sows the wind, and when violence erupts, society is reaping the whirlwind.

Neutralizing the Conscience

Sometimes a person's learned beliefs can be very general (e.g., "killing is wrong") and other times they are quite specific (e.g., "it is okay to kill pedophiles because they are dangerous and disgusting"). You can imagine how these beliefs might be shaped and reshaped by one's life experiences, and also how men in particular might suffer a different type of shame and humiliation from sexual assault that might be avenged through a masculine expression of violence.

The vigilantes I spoke to understand that anarchy is a bad thing. They do not want people to take the law into their own hands for every perceived insult. They thought that violence was appropriate in their own case under specific circumstances. These ideas can be compared to the "techniques of neutralization" outlined in Sykes and Matza's Neutralization Theory (15). They believed that people committed crimes when they could justify their behavior to themselves. This is certainly evident in vigilante excuses for their crimes, so much so that few vigilantes consider their acts to be crimes at all. They usually put the word "crime" in quotation marks when they write to me. Here are some examples:

Technique	Example
Denial of Responsibility	"If the courts weren't so lenient I wouldn't have needed to kill them."
Denial of Injury	"They deserved far worse than I gave them. It was merciful."
Denying the Victim	"I wanted him to feel how his victims felt. If he didn't want this to happen he shouldn't have hurt those kids."
Condemn the Condemner	"The so-called 'justice system' might condemn me, but they are the ones who let child rapists go free."
Appeal to Higher Loyalties	"I would gladly sacrifice my freedom to save children."

There are other cognitive distortions that might help vigilantes justify their crimes. There is the "claim of normality" ("this country was founded on vigilantism"), the "claim of entitlement" ("I deserve to get revenge"), and the "metaphor of the ledger" ("I might have killed a Cho-Mo, but at least I never hurt a child"). These thoughts, beliefs, and attitudes can be targeted with some forms of therapy, like cognitive behavioral interventions. This might help the vigilante to understand the link between their thoughts and their actions, and to recognize the inevitable consequences. A major component of cognitive behavioral therapy is the need to replace one line of action with a prosocial alternative. Perhaps some vigilantes could be directed to behaviors that address their problems through actions that do not result in a prison sentence, like seeking justice or helping children in other ways, such as Patrick Drum's quest to reform sentencing legislation.

Some researchers argue that widespread cultural attitudes help offenders to justify their victimization of others (16). As I mentioned in Chapter Three, there are subcultures of support for vigilante actions that may shape and reinforce attitudes favorable to violence against child sex abusers. Just as the sex offender might comfort themselves with "rape myths" that blame victims for their offenses, vigilantes might believe in "myths" about sex offenders. A common misperception is that all sex offenders reoffend. This belief might justify a swift death penalty as the only way to ensure that future potential victims are saved. This idea contributes to the feeling of necessity that pushes a vigilante to murder. I doubt that they would restrain themselves if they read recidivism statistics, but it is one more straw on the camel's back contributing to their final decision to engage in violence.

Obviously, the subcultures in prisons can inspire violence against sex offenders. "Cho-Mos, skinners, and rapos" are at the bottom of the prison hierarchy. Acts of violence toward sex offenders might be rewarded with gang tattoos and social reinforcement. Failure to act in an aggressive manner toward known child sex abusers can damage a prisoner's reputation and make them an outcast in the prison. This subculture of prison hierarchy is so intense and isolated from mainstream social interactions, that it can be considered a school for anti-pedophile radicalization, or maybe in a less dramatic sense it is simply a place where unhesitating violence is a preferred response. The intense cultural pressure reinforces ideas about how child sex abusers deserve extra-judicial punishments, often with deadly results.

Some people blame society's stigmatization of sex offenders for the "moral panics" and "punitive populism" around sex offender justice policies. It has been argued that the justice system punishes sex offenders so harshly that they thereby *encourage* vigilantes to attack them (16). The state is said to over-punish sex offenders by putting them on a registry and stigmatizing them in the community. This puts a target on their backs and gives tacit permission for citizens to harass, assault, and kill them. While this certainly appears to be the case in prison settings where correctional officers may be coordinating such violence, I should say that none of the community-based vigilantes I interviewed believed this was true. They all said their actions were influenced by their belief that the government was too lenient toward sex offenders. None said they felt emboldened by the government's hostility toward sex offenders.

Online memes are one form of communication that depict a culture of vigilante support for these crimes, but they are just the most recent variation of this theme. John Lawrence and Robert Jewett's book *The Myth of the American Superhero* summarizes examples of superheroes, cowboys, and antiheroes who comprise an American Monomyth that cut across all forms of media (17). American heroes tend to be loners who break the law to fix problems an incompetent or corrupt government can't. Batman is a prime example. These American heroes fight a crusade against evil, but Lawrence and Jewett consider them to be "pop fascists" because they do not follow democratic norms to achieve their goals, they simply impose their will on others through violence. Clint Eastwood frequently embodies this archetype in his many films, and I have no doubt that every one of the vigilantes I interviewed would be honored to be compared to Dirty Harry.

The film *Death Wish* starring Charles Bronson is described by Lawrence and Jewett as follows:

In Death Wish the vigilante actions of the modern superhero solve the knotty problem of urban crime. Mythical redemption works out in everyday life according to mythical expectation. Complex social problems are neatly solved with a single gesture; tangled human relations are sorted out and resolved; evil is eliminated with a single heroic stroke. In Death Wish the elements of mythic massage touch the fate of villains and vigilantes, the achievement of justice for the community, and the redemptive impact on the world.

So, what came first, the violent media or the violent crimes? It is possible that a reciprocal relationship exists between real-life vigilantism and fictional vigilantes. Films like *Joker* (2019) depict events similar to the Bernard Goetz Subway Vigilante case of 1984, but this event was preceded by the first *Death Wish* film (18). Academics often debate whether violent entertainment brutalizes society or provides a harmless outlet for anger. I am not qualified to test those claims here. Jon Watson was a fan of the *Death Wish* films, Michael Mullen was a fan of Andrew Vachss' fiction books, and Jeremy Moody watched the television show *Dexter*, but if everyone who hated child sex abusers *and* consumed those forms of entertainment became a vigilante, there would be widespread destruction of that community.

Patrick Drum read Greek myths about revenge. Was he trained to kill by Aesop? The rarity of these crimes and the prevalence of violent media indicate that the majority of people in our society are not brainwashed or propagandized into felonious conduct just because they watch *Dexter* on television or read superhero comic books as children. It is far more likely that these vigilantes have a deeply felt conviction that their behavior was justified and they would not need to cite fictional characters as role models. Their animosity has deeper roots than pop culture can explain. However, the "moral panic" over the harms of violent media has been embraced by many psychologists, politicians, and media organizations, so I mention it here as one potential cause among many others with greater importance (19). The relationship between media and vigilantism may be more a reflection of the general public's broad support for these crimes rather than a causal influence on vigilante behavior. If "the customer is always right," then the predominance of vigilante superheroes in American pop culture may be a way for members of the public to vent their frustrations with the formal justice system. Seeing "The Punisher" kill criminals without offering them a plea bargain can give momentary pleasure to citizens who dislike the due-process approach.

One cultural belief that may actually contribute to vigilante violence is the dehumanization of pedophiles by the wider society (20). "Pedos aren't human" is the most blatant rebuttal to calls for compassion, and many non-offending pedophiles live in fear that they will be victims of violent crimes if they admit they are sexually attracted to children. This may prevent them from seeking social support or professional advice about how to cope with their paraphilia (21). As mentioned previously, the feeling of *disgust* toward pedophilia is a common justification for vigilante violence (22). Every one of the men I interviewed used the word "disgust" without prompting by me. Scottie Allen said it most clearly:

> To me, they're like cockroaches. Killing that pedophile was like stepping on a cockroach. I felt no satisfaction or discomfort. It was like killing a disgusting cockroach. Not sorry you had to do it, but sorry it existed in the first place.

This disgust is so profound that it extends to anyone who is seen to be "on the side of the pedos." Jeremy Moody wanted to kill people who were *related* to sex offenders so he could purge their bloodline. How can you argue for due process if your opponent thinks you're a "filthy pedo-lover?" There is a cycle of reinforcement that encourages vigilantes to be proud of their actions, and this gives more material for their online supporters to spread memes about their heroism.

David Livingstone Smith's book *Less than Human* is rife with examples of dehumanization and its consequences (23). He explains how an antidote to dehumanization is to take a sentimentalist approach. To draw sympathy for the outsider by evoking pity and commiseration. This may have occurred in the case of John Geoghan. When he was alive, Geoghan was seen as a monstrous pervert. But after Joseph Druce strangled him to death and stomped on his chest, people began thinking of Geoghan as a frail old man who was too weak to defend himself. But as Smith argues in his book on dehumanization, the sentimentalist approach is a double-edged sword. Sentimentalism is exactly the same method used to vilify less-than-human targets. Vigilantes and their supporters can easily tell a sympathetic story about the children who were abused, how their innocent trust was used against them, and how the venal and sadistic predator received sexual pleasure from the child's pain. Maybe the sentimentalist approach is a risky strategy for people who want to defend pedophiles and sex abusers. Emotions can cut both ways, and this is a particularly emotional subject. Better stick to the due-process argument.

Vigilantes are sometimes quite angry when they commit their crimes. However, anger itself is not a necessary or sufficient motivator for vigilante violence. Many people are angry every day, but they do not resort to violence. Perhaps they have non-violent outlets for their anger, or they suppress their anger for one reason or another. It is also worth noting that violence can be committed without anger at all, including horrible atrocities perpetrated for banal reasons.

David Matsumoto and his colleagues have proposed the ANCODI model (Anger, Contempt, and Disgust) to explain how hatred and aggression are linked (24). Anger is an emotion that provides passion and energy to be aggressive, but it is not sufficient to produce violence. Anger might be displaced from a responsible individual to the circumstances or "the system." Contempt is a belief that a person deserves scorn, and therefore focuses one's anger to an individual deemed worthy of aggression. Still, a person can be angry and contemptuous and not resort to violence, because they do not want to "stoop to their level" or they hold prosocial attitudes that offset their aggressive desires. The third component, disgust, is a decisive ingredient that completes the dehumanization of the target. A disgusting person is placed at a distance, psychologically speaking. They are not empathized with because they inspire an instinctive sneer, a curling of the lip that marks them as revolting. When anger, contempt, and disgust are combined, they form a dangerous type of hatred that is particularly suitable for an aggressive response. Matsumoto and colleagues find some evidence that these emotions interact to produce intergroup hostility and aggressive cognitions. Certainly, the vigilantes in this book show strong evidence of all three emotions, and they are not ashamed to admit it. They would scoff if anyone tried to convince them to feel different emotions in response to child sex abuse. And yet, many people in our society are angry when they learn about child sex abuse crimes, they have contempt for the abusers, and they are disgusted to the point of dehumanizing pedophiles. Why do so few people take the law into their own hands? The vigilante mindset with its neutralized conscience can only be a partial explanation for targeted violence.

Antisocial Personalities

Some people do not need to sanitize their conscience in order to commit a violent crime. They do not have a strong capacity for empathy to begin with. A person with psychopathic traits of shallow affect, lack of remorse or guilt, callous lack of empathy, and failure to accept responsibility might be eligible for any number of official mental health diagnoses (such as Conduct Disorder or Anti-Social Personality Disorder) if they meet other clinical criteria, but if they meet the full range of factors necessary to be assessed as a psychopath, they would be at a dramatically increased risk of engaging in violent crimes. The Hare Psychopathy Checklist (PCL-R) lists twenty factors that range from manipulative behaviors and pathological lying to irresponsible behavior and criminal versatility. It is possible that some of the vigilantes I interviewed are psychopathic or have the less severe form of Anti-Social Personality Disorder.

When Steven Sandison said, "I just don't have empathy for people," he might have been expressing a psychopathic trait. He claims to have empathy for "good" people, especially children, but this may be a ploy for compassion. Scottie Allen has been accused of being a psychopath because of the way he killed his victim and casually ate a snack afterward, but he tells me that he is not a monster. He feels emotions acutely, but he does not consider child sex abusers as worthy of empathy. Joseph Druce has been labeled a homophobic Nazi for his behaviors, but a variety of competing mental illnesses might confound the assessment of a personality disorder in his case. Despite their histories of homicidal behavior and their callous lack of empathy toward their victims, these men all scored less than 23 on the PCL-R (where a score of 30 is the standard threshold for a designation of psychopathy). It takes quite a lot to be assessed as a psychopath. Anti-Social Personality Disorder appears to be a better fit for these men, but they have not been assessed for this personality disorder by mental health professionals.

Jeremy Moody might be a candidate for a psychopath assessment because of his callous disregard for an innocent bystander during his crime, but he does not believe he is a psychopath. He feels emotions just like anyone else. He even thinks he is hyper-sensitive and overly empathetic, that is why he kills to protect children. His shallow affect may be social awkwardness symptomatic of his Autism Spectrum Disorder, a common confounder in psychopathy assessments (25). Killing a child sex abuser and his wife seemed appropriate to him, and he feels no guilt, although he does regret minor crimes he committed in his youth. Why the difference? He wonders if he is like the Nazi soldiers who were able to compartmentalize their war crimes by justifying their behavior as necessary. Ultimately, he is well below the threshold for a psychopath designation using the PCL-R despite the prominent factors he exhibits.

I am trained to assess people with the PCL-R for research purposes, and I have attempted to see which factors are present in the lives of these men. Criminal versatility and irresponsibility are present. So are lack of realistic, long-term goals. But one important factor that encourages me to think these men are not traditional psychopaths is their brutal honesty. Psychopaths often engage in *pathological* lying. They enjoy duping others. I worried about this during my conversations with these men. Are they just using me to paint them in the best possible light? I can't prove that everything they said was true, but if there is one overarching characteristic of a vigilante, it is their unrestrained honesty about their crimes. It is possible that this honesty is actually a post-hoc form of manipulation, (e.g., they tell the truth in one domain while concealing it in others), but the layers of subterfuge make this difficult to determine. I will leave it up to readers to apply their own skeptical filters when reading the vigilante's statements throughout this book. You may choose how many grains of salt you take them with.

These vigilantes have some characteristics of Anti-Social Personality Disorder, and if they are psychopathic, they would align with Factor 2 Psychopathy (less callous and more impulsive), but these men are complex. There is no singular vigilante personality, but some symptoms of ASPD can be seen in each of these men.

Wounded Narcissism

Psychiatrist James Knoll has written about the psychology of revenge with a focus on "pseudocommando" mass murderers (26). These are the people who decide to go out with a bang. They plot and plan to kill as many people as possible, often choosing innocent and vulnerable people in order to draw the most attention to themselves posthumously. He traces this destructive murder-suicide logic back to a core feeling of wounded narcissism. Many school shooters, workplace shooters, and supposedly random acts of senseless violence appear to be a last desperate act of revenge by narcissistic people who want to punish "society" for slights and insults. They brood over their revenge plans, communicate their intentions to the media, and try to kill as many people as possible.

I do not think this theory fits very well with the vigilantes I studied because they truly felt that their actions were a public benefit. However, there is a trace of suicidality and wounded narcissism in their justifications. For those who were abused as children, their "narcissism" may be overcompensation for a lifetime of shame and self-loathing occasioned by their abuse.

I will leave the official diagnoses to the psychiatric experts, but future researchers should keep in mind that these vigilantes did not choose to kill random citizens to get attention. They had a laser-like focus on a specific enemy. They are "collectors of injustice" who brood over lenient court decisions like the DuPont heir and Jeffrey Epstein cases, but unlike the delusional sense of entitlement and oppression that other mass killers itemize, these are situations that provoke general outrage from non-offending citizens. It doesn't take a fragile or damaged ego to be upset by those incidents. Knoll's work in this field is useful for identifying some risk factors for vigilante violence such as revenge fantasies, pride of being on the side of justice, and a desire to restore their sense of control, but the connection to pseudocommando forms of revenge appears to be different. For one thing, vigilantes are not complete nihilists. They do not want to destroy the world or kill random civilians. They wanted to sacrifice themselves in order to protect children.

One example might help illustrate this point. In May 2022, Jeremy Moody called me after the school shooting in Uvalde, Texas to share his grief that little children were killed by a callous narcissist. He wonders "Why don't suicidal people do something good for society like kill child molesters before they kill themselves?" He believes that vigilantes are fundamentally different from reckless and random killers because mass killers are delusional about their own self-importance. Jeremy said: "Killing and dying for a cause may be noble depending on the cause but killing and dying for your ego is just sick. Someone should have killed that school shooter a lot sooner. Then those little kids would still be alive. It's like our society has given up on protecting children."

Relational Poverty

So here we have the explosive components of a violent vigilante. They are often the adult victims of childhood sex abuse. They have lived reckless lives of drug and alcohol dependence. They have been in-and-out of the justice system. They often have nothing to lose and do not fear punishment for their crimes. They are hyper-sensitive to issues they consider to be important (such as protecting children) and they hold beliefs that are favorable to violence against sex offenders. They are almost always men, who generally believe that violence is an appropriately masculine way to resolve their anger. Altogether, we have a volatile concoction of ingredients that are primed and ready to explode at any time. And yet, if everyone who shared these characteristics became a vigilante, our legal system would be overwhelmed by the number of cases where people with similar backgrounds killed for their beliefs. When you have explosive materials sitting around, they might go off at any time. But if you store them safely, you might be able to prevent them from exploding.

Travis Hirschi's Control Theory describes the prosocial effects of social bonds in the lives of potential offenders (27). At its most basic level, this theory argues that people are less likely to commit a crime when they have strong attachment to their parents, peers, and role models, if they are invested or committed to their futures, if they are involved in activities that bond them to their community, and they hold conventional beliefs about the wrongness of criminal behavior. When someone has a bond with others, they are less likely to risk losing it. This theory was expanded by Robert Sampson and John Laub in their Age-Graded Theory of Informal Social Control (28). This updated model accounted for changes in one's social bonds over time, such as through marriage, divorce, caring for children, and ties to the community. Again, if someone has a strong personal bond to other people, they will not risk losing them to commit a crime.

Researchers like Bruce Perry at the Child Trauma Academy have dedicated their lives to studying the mechanisms by which early childhood abuse can lead to a range of undesirable outcomes in adulthood, including violent behavior (29). It would not be possible to summarize the work of his research lab in this book, let alone summarize the entirety of research that has been conducted in this field, but it should suffice to say that bonding and attachment are of vital importance in the neurological development of every child. Early, severe, and chronic abuse can make it difficult for a child to develop the capacity for empathetic bonding with others. However, if the child is protected, given a loving, predictable environment to grow in, and they develop a sense of control over themselves and their circumstances, it might be possible for them to leave their antisocial trajectory and develop strong bonds with others. We should remember that child abuse and neglect increase the risk of undesirable adult outcomes, but they are not determinants. Some children are resilient, and the most likely cause of this resiliency are their connections to people who support them.

If we think of these social bonds as something protecting the explosive material from detonating, we can see a path to preventing violence. Social support might have saved these men from disastrous decisions (30). Unfortunately, in most of the cases of vigilantism I have examined, the individuals were hopeless and alone. Maybe if we help volatile people form bonds and find purpose in their lives, their violent tendencies might be suppressed.

I believe this isolation from mainstream society and the lack of loving interpersonal relationships was a major risk factor for everyone described in this book, even Jeremy Moody who committed his crime with his wife helping him. Jeremy was isolated in a small group of fringe Skinhead extremists. "Mainstream values" were lost to him. When I think about Patrick Drum or Clark Fredericks, who committed their crimes in the community, I am struck by their inability to form strong bonds that would stabilize their behavior and give them something to live for. James Fairbanks had a wonderful, loving family, but after his divorce he was so distraught he considered suicide.

Steven Sandison might be the most isolated human being I have ever met. Not just because he has lived in solitary confinement for the past eight years, but because he *never* had any social bonds between him and other people. The instant he was born his fanatically religious parents *screamed* because he was born "en caul," which occurs when a newborn has a thin membrane of skin around their face. They thought he was a demon. His mother flew to another country to escape her demon child. His father refused to care for him, or even pray for his soul. As a small child, he wandered the streets of Detroit, until he was kidnapped and raped by strangers. He lived in juvenile detention centers, jails, and prisons where he was raped by the other detainees. When he had a chance at freedom, a woman he met through correspondence picked him up from prison. He immediately strangled her to death and was sentenced to life in prison. Steven's life is a nightmare so horrifying that he prefers to dissociate from reality and live in the "dark woods" of his mind. He wonders why people ask him his motives for killing a sex offender in prison, as if he had anything to lose by doing so.

If these men had strong social bonds, perhaps their self-destructive lifestyles would have been suppressed. They would have been insulated from the sparks that set them off, but often the abuse they suffered as children destroyed their capacity to trust others. Each of these vigilantes were outcasts at the time they committed murder, especially those who were in prison. These men were exiled from our society entirely.

How to Construct a Bomb

To continue our bomb-making analogy, we have to understand that explosive materials can detonate randomly, but a bomb has a purpose – to destroy a specific target. The difference between a child sex abuse victim who commits a random crime and a vigilante who targets specific people is the difference between a defective appliance exploding and a claymore mine pointed toward an enemy. When I speak to vigilantes, they always have a reason – a motivation – for *why* they killed a child sex abuser, so we have to assess their motives and try to understand how they were derived.

In 1996, Les Johnston attempted to define "vigilantism" in order to have a standardized method of measuring trends over time (31). He identified six characteristics that should be met in order for a case to be considered a vigilante crime. First, the crime should involve premeditation and planning. It cannot be spontaneous. Secondly, the participants should be private citizens (not legal authorities) and their participation should be voluntary. Third, the act is part of a "social movement" of some kind and not selfish. It should also involve the use of force or the threat of force. The victim of the vigilante crime should be alleged to pose a threat to "an established order" in society. And finally, it should aim to control crime or other social infractions. Many cases that are labeled "vigilante" crimes fall far short of meeting these criteria.

Vigilante Typologies

Some people are called vigilantes because they killed in self-defense or to escape from a dangerous environment. Prosecutors and news reporters often lump them in with vigilantes because they took the law into their own hands without trusting government agencies to solve their problems, but this is a blurry category that must be evaluated on a case-by-case basis. I label these cases ***pseudo-vigilantes*** because their crimes occur with little thought for vigilante goals. Sometimes they occur as part of a citizen's arrest when a crime is in progress (e.g., the Texas father who beat his daughter's kidnapper). Sometimes they involve the victims of sex trafficking or people trapped in abusive relationships who kill in order to escape danger. Often these homicides could be deemed justifiable by a jury depending on the evidence available, and vigilante labels should be limited to criminal overreach. Some of these cases are simply misclassified because not every act of violence against a sex offender is related to their sex offense. Some so-called "vigilantes" were enraged by a sex offender's immediate behavior (such as a father who discovered a naked peeping tom outside his child's bedroom window), but violence under these circumstances do not embody the spirit of vigilantism. Unfortunately, "vigilante" is a word that makes for good headlines, so there are many unjustifiable labels thrown around. I would include cases like Sara Kruzan in this category because she was trying to escape from a dangerous sex abuser who posed a threat to her life.

Some vigilantes do not try to help the justice system. They kill child sex abusers for their own selfish benefit, and often did not know they were killing a sex offender. A man named Kenneth Stancil was called a vigilante because he murdered a suspected pedophile, but Stancil himself said, "I'm just attracted to killing and hurting people." He killed for the mere thrill of the act. He would have killed someone else if his victim had been unreachable (32). Others might adhere to a subculture that respects this type of violence for its own sake. Shaun Attwood described how gang members would get new tattoos if they "smashed a Cho-Mo" in prison. They collect tattoos like merit badges and killing a child molester might give them full membership in a powerful prison gang. This, too, should be classified as pseudo-vigilantism.

Other vigilantes are not in immediate danger, but they lashed out because of unresolved trauma they experienced as children or they were avenging the abuse of a loved one. These are ***retaliatory vigilantes***, whether they targeted people who harmed them specifically, or just chose a random child sex abuser as a substitute. Their violence was extremely personal and they were not primarily motivated to "change the world." I would include Clark Fredericks, Gary Plauché, and Ellie Nesler in this category, and I would extend this definition to include prisoners like Steven Sandison and Scottie Allen. These men were the victims of childhood sex abuse and "got revenge" against child sex abusers in prison, even if it wasn't a person who harmed them. They may have felt they were doing a good deed for society, or that they would accrue some social benefit from their actions, but they were primarily driven by hatred of sex offenders and a desire to get revenge.

Among my list of vigilantes, there are people who wanted to challenge the criminal justice system and draw attention to lenient punishments for sex offenders. These people had a pure vigilante motive: taking the law into their own hands because of lack of faith in the government. They engaged in targeted, predatory, ideologically-motivated violence. These may be referred to as ***ideological vigilantes.*** They believe they can help society by acting as the judge, jury, and executioner of a dangerous person. Society passes laws against child sex offenders because they wish to incapacitate them from doing more harm, to deter them from committing the same crimes again, and for the purposes of retribution. Rehabilitation is an afterthought, punishment comes first. When vigilantes attack people who did not hurt them or their loved ones, they are acting as a substitute for the justice system. They want to incapacitate criminals (through death) and deter other potential sex offenders. They see themselves as helping the justice system achieve its own stated goals, but more efficiently than the government can do on its own. These vigilantes consider their motives to be utilitarian efforts to reduce future crimes and say things like "*A dead pedophile can't hurt anymore kids.*" They are willing to sacrifice their lives or their freedom to purge a dangerous predator from society.

These classifications of vigilante motivations are not set in stone. They certainly overlap. Just as a workplace shooter or a terrorist might have an impulsive desire to commit a violent act, they can also wait until they have an opportunity to strike most effectively. As psychologists Stephen White and Reid Meloy have said, affective and predatory violence share a bimodal distribution. The point at which they overlap is where we find the most difficulty in classification. The affective/impulsive offender is dangerous, but the man who can plot, and plan, and wait before he acts poses the greater threat. This escalation along the pathway to violence can also be *de-escalated* under the right conditions (33, 34).

Social Control

This brings us back to the motivational context. Why don't vigilantes write a letter to their congressional representative if they don't like sentencing practices? Because they feel a sense of urgency to solve the problem and believe the government is unable to secure real justice. The sociologist Donald Black has described vigilante justice (and most forms of homicide) as "self-help" crime control (35). In his 1983 article in the American Sociological Review, he wrote:

> There is a sense in which conduct regarded as criminal is often quite the opposite. Far from being an intentional violation of a prohibition, much crime is moralistic and involves the pursuit of justice. It is a mode of conflict management, possibly a form of punishment, even capital punishment. Viewed in relation to law, it is self-help. To the degree that it defines or responds to the conduct of someone else – the victim – as deviant, crime is social control.

In other words, most people do not wallow in blood and delight in causing the death of another. They do it reluctantly, because they believe they are doing a good thing for society or to punish offenses they deem worthy of death. Your definition of what "deserves" death might differ from the person sitting next to you, so we tend to rely on the justice system to proffer unbiased "blind" judgments on who should be punished and to what degree. However, if you felt that the system could not deliver justice, you might take the law into your own hands. It is "self-help" crime control. Retributive punishments are often dismissed by academics as non-utilitarian from a crime control perspective, but they are utilitarian from the actor's perspective if it makes them feel as though they performed their duty to the greater good. Injustice leaves a hole that violence is meant to fill.

Perhaps we can learn something from research on crime and community-level factors. One of the most widely studied phenomena in the field of criminology is "collective efficacy," a term originating in the psychological work of Albert Bandura and applied to studies of crime within neighborhoods by Sampson, Raudenbush, and Earles (36). This theory proposes that people will use informal social controls to reduce crime when there is social cohesion between community members. When the formal and informal social controls break down, people will take the law into their own hands and use violence to solve their problems. This is most clearly explained in the book *Code of the Street* by Elijah Anderson (37), who found that citizens prefer to get revenge rather than call the police in high-crime neighborhoods. The profound lack of trust in the police and fear of appearing weak in front of the other members of the community lead to a massive spike in violence in the 1980s and early 1990s in Philadelphia. In some places, such as Mantua (a region of Philadelphia), groups of citizens would march to protest drug dealers outside of crack houses to signal that they had social cohesion and would use informal social controls to reclaim their neighborhoods. This is also a type of vigilantism in the original "vigilance committee" sense of the term (38).

This logic may apply to vigilantism against child abusers as well. If the victim (or their family members) trust that formal social controls can produce safety and justice, they will make a report. If they do not trust law enforcement or the courts, they might still be able to trust informal social controls – their family, friends, and community leaders to protect them and secure some degree of imperfect justice. However, without these options or lacking the requisite degree of social cohesion, an individual might take the law into their own hands. The previously mentioned case of Dontee Stokes seems to fit these circumstances. Dontee was sexually abused by a priest in 1993. He reported his abuse to the police and the church leadership. Both organizations dropped their investigations after deciding that there was not enough evidence to support Stokes' claims, revealing that neither formal nor informal social controls would give him the protection and justice he felt was necessary. Stokes struggled with his trauma and helplessness for the next nine years, but when he heard that abuse throughout the Catholic Church was being exposed he "snapped," took a gun to the church, and tried to murder his abuser. The failure of formal controls and informal controls left Stokes to seek justice himself, but not for lack of trying alternative methods first.

Criminologist Jack Katz argued in *Seductions of Crime* that murder is often justified by a belief that one's actions are normal, necessary, and morally justified (39). Murderers consider a meek acceptance of law-abiding behavior to be cowardice. The individual feels humiliated by their circumstances and they seek to destroy a symbol of their humiliation. At the same time, they seek to become greater in self-worth by demonstrating that they have some purposive control over their lives. A "senseless" murder is perceived as "righteous slaughter." This seductive logic justifies crime in the mind of the offender, but it can also convince outsiders that the person's actions were justified. People who read about vigilante crimes might feel a slight tinge of commiseration with the vigilante's moral justifications. Some people proudly support vigilante actions for this reason, while others suppress their revenge instincts.

Perhaps in the end, what we find so repulsive about studying the reality of crime – the reason we so insistently refuse to look closely at how street criminals destroy others and bungle their way into confinement to save their sense of purposive control over their lives – is the piercing reflection we catch when we steady our glance at those evil men.

Innovation and Rebellion

One of the most influential theories of criminology is Anomie/Strain theory, first proposed by Robert Merton in 1938. This theory argued that people commit crimes for a reason. They want to achieve a goal, but they cannot do so through socially acceptable ways. Most people want to achieve the American Dream and achieve economic prosperity. Some attain this goal through established pathways (conformists). Some fail but keep trying (ritualists). Some innovate illegal ways to achieve the same goals (innovators). Some give up entirely (retreatists). And still, there is another group that might reject the goal and replace it with something else they value (rebels) (40).

If I apply Merton's five modes of strain adaptation to vigilantes, I can perceive them as people responding differently to the same blocked goal. Instead of the American Dream, they are striving to live in a safe and just society. We do not live in a perfectly safe or just society, so we have to go through the criminal justice system process in order to address crimes like child sex abuse. Some people are satisfied with the justice system response. These conformists believe that law enforcement and the courts gave them the best possible outcome in their case. Another group trusts the system, but they are disappointed in the outcome. These ritualists do not attempt to go outside the normal justice system to achieve safety and justice. They might try to file a claim in civil court, but they do not take the law into their own hands.

We might think of the victims of child sex abuse who embark on a self-destructive career of drug and alcohol abuse as "retreatists" who have given up on achieving justice, and really given up on everything. Suicide is the worst-case scenario for these people, but like Robert Merton said of those who have given up on economic goals, these people are "*in* the society, but not *of* it." He described these tragic people as aliens, outcasts, vagabonds, tramps, chronic drunkards, and drug addicts. "These have relinquished, in certain spheres of activity, the culturally defined goals, involving complete aim-inhibition in the polar case, and their adjustments are not in accord with institutional norms." They live among us, but do not feel as though they really are members of society. They are completely isolated. I can say that many of the Children of the Secret and the Sons of Solitude who suffered sex abuse as children feel this intense loneliness and hopelessness. Some transition out of this pit of despair and join the conformists. Others decide to get revenge by becoming innovators.

Innovators attempt to circumvent the legal system to achieve the same goal: safety and justice. They do not necessarily commit a crime to do so, but they innovate a new method that is not legally proscribed. The #MeToo movement decided to publicly call out powerful people who sexually abused them. The TV show *To Catch a Predator* exposed people who were seeking illegal sexual relationships with children. Viral-vigilantes film similar encounters on the streets to shame and humiliate pedophiles. And some people take this desire to help the justice system even farther. Maybe they burn down a sex offender's house so he can't move in next door. Maybe they harass them or threaten to kill them. And occasionally they take a gun and shoot them to death.

The purpose of these actions is to secure justice and keep children safe. *Ideological vigilantes* think of themselves as heroes doing what the system is incapable of doing. They innovate new ways to achieve justice, and they break the law in order to do so.

The final mode of adaptation is rebellion. When people have given up the goals and reigning standards of achieving them, they might try to create their own social order. These rebels tend to have an extremist position. They think the current model can never keep people safe and never achieve justice. They want to reject those ideals and replace them with something more realistic, and perhaps better in the long run. Maybe prison abolitionists who think child rape victims can sit in a restorative justice circle with their abuser are rebels. Some vigilantes (like Jeremy Moody) had strong ideological beliefs about overthrowing the current world order and replacing it with brutal retaliation against sex offenders. He even wanted to kill their family members to purge their bloodlines. Many of the practitioners of convict justice in prison have been thrust into a social order with its own rules: "KOS all Cho-Mos." These social movements are the ultimate expression of frustration with the ineffective justice system they believe exists.

Given these findings, Merton's typology of responses to strain appears to be quite useful in categorizing people's responses to a failed justice system.

Radicalization

When I was researching Jeremy Moody's case, I read two of his books (*Yesterday, Today, and Forever*, and *The Jewish Scourge*). His manifestos explained how he developed his racist world-views. He is a fan of the *Turner Diaries* and other extremist publications. While he never killed any racial or ethnic minorities, he was deeply involved in Skinhead groups that talked about the need to save the white race from an international Jewish conspiracy. He was the only vigilante I interviewed who held these extreme beliefs, but I found myself thinking about how an *ideological vigilante* might be explained in the same terms as a lone-wolf terrorist. The radicalization process happens in stages and the extremist's beliefs are refined until they are ready to strike with purpose. Just as some bombs are manufactured according to a specific formula rather than haphazardly thrown together, I think some vigilantes follow a well-known pattern of radicalization that culminates in vigilante violence.

In the strictest sense of the term, a vigilante is not a "terrorist" because most of them do not want to inspire fear. They think they are helping society, not terrorizing the public. But in other respects, an *ideological vigilante* can share characteristics of a terrorist. They tend to be men searching for significance. They want to be a hero, but they may find it difficult to care about the same values held by mainstream society. They choose to be champions for innocent and helpless children (an unambiguously virtuous cause). The vigilante might not be able to help children through other means (such as being a police officer or social worker) so they desperately look for a way to help children while simultaneously condemning the system. They are trying to reform the criminal justice system from a position of absolute weakness. Nobody will listen to them, so they will make them listen.

Through a process of social-learning radicalization, they are isolated from mainstream social support (especially those who spend time in prison), and they seek personal significance through great deeds. They fantasize about their actions and often broadcast them to the world (e.g., Jeremy Moody's books and other vigilantes' letters to the media). They might receive some reinforcement from online communities who praise their statements. When they are ignored by the authorities, they decide to get attention. They train and plan their vigilante actions. They read about similar cases and try to out-do their role models. They might go to great lengths to plan their crimes (like Patrick Drum) or confidently throw themselves at a specific target regardless of the danger (James Fairbanks). And then one day, they act. It usually doesn't go as smoothly as they planned. Murder is messy.

After they are apprehended, they use this opportunity to become champions for their cause. They proudly proclaim the righteousness of their behavior. They become media stars. Memes lionize their behavior and spread across the internet. They receive letters from supporters and former victims of child abuse from across the world. They might be spending the rest of their lives in prison, but their doubts are put to rest. They became significant through an act of heroic self-sacrifice. The corrections system does not bother to rehabilitate them or convince them that their crimes were wrong, they simply punish them, so their sense of righteousness is solidified. And the cycle repeats.

The "Quest for Significance" model of radicalization has been used to explain acts of terrorism across the globe since it was proposed by Dugas and Kruglanski in 2014 (41). This theory combines the motivational, ideological, and social theories of crime to follow an extremist's progress through stages. Their desire to be "significant" is a motivating force. Ideology gives them a path to achieve significance. And there is a process of social reinforcement that launches them into action. While this model was based on cases of religion-motivated terrorist acts, it can easily be conceptualized to fit the circumstances of *ideological vigilante* crimes.

Prison Radicalization

We might also be able to adapt the significance quest theory to fit a prison environment. If "convict justice" is an attempt to draw attention to lenient sentences for sex offenders, then we can easily imagine that Joseph Druce fits this profile. He had a desire to perform some public benefit to society, but as a prisoner serving a life sentence would never have the opportunity. He may have been radicalized by the convict culture that places Cho-Mos at the bottom of the prisoner hierarchy. A prison redemption significance quest is certainly plausible. Dugas and Kruglanski worried that the radicalization process would be made worse in prison environments because deradicalization efforts are not employed, and the shared suffering with likeminded violent men will push them to adopt more extreme views.

This is perfectly exemplified by Patrick Drum's association with Michael Mullen. When Drum was serving time for burglary, he met Mullen who had just pled guilty to two murders of child sex abusers. When Drum was released, he followed in Mullen's footsteps and killed two registered sex offenders. Radicalization is not entirely caused by internet misinformation. It can spread more effectively inside prisons during a chess game.

Dugas and Kruglanski note how extremists might be more willing to sacrifice themselves for a cause if they have personally experienced a "significance loss" during a moment of social exclusion. Can you think of anything more isolating or devastating to the loss of one's personal significance than suffering extreme child sexual abuse? Perhaps the only thing more isolating and depriving of significance is a prison sentence. Combining these nightmarish experiences together and we can see that many of the cases related in this book meet these criteria. Andrew Vachss coined his "Bomb Built in Hell" analogy in 1973 when he was the superintendent of a juvenile detention center for violent youth. He witnessed the shortsightedness of policies that placed traumatized youth together in a school for crime. These kids were ticking time bombs. When they were released, they wouldn't care about themselves or anyone else, but they would try to go out with a bang.

What about the elusive motivations of Jon Watson? He was extremely frustrated with the prison system in California, and he was no fan of pedophiles. Was he fighting a proxy war against the administration and pedophiles were a convenient target? Or was he doing a favor to society? He told me it was a combination of the two. I would suggest that he is not fighting a war against pedophiles as part of a personal quest for significance. He fits better into the frustration-aggression hypothesis first proposed by John Dollard and his colleagues in 1939 (42, 43). This theory claims that when a person has a blocked goal in life, they become emotionally frustrated. When the individual finds a group that they can express their frustration toward, they might be aggressive toward them. Sometimes this group is chosen for convenience and not because they are closely tied to the source of the individual's frustration. The severity of their response depends on the situation and the punishments they might receive for their actions, but they tend to pick a scapegoat that is marginalized in the community rather than an authority figure. Prison "Cho-Mos" fit the bill.

Therefore, the frustration-aggression hypothesis would predict that someone frustrated by the deprivations of the prison environment would find a convenient target to unload their aggression upon. This fits well with Jon Watson's particular circumstances, but I don't think his actions were determined by his frustration threshold. He was deliberately planning to attack child sex abusers. He wanted to punish them specifically because of their behavior in prison (watching PBS Kids), and he had been encouraged to assault child sex abusers throughout his time in prison. This was not a "snap" decision caused by low emotional thresholds. With that said, frustration-aggression hypothesis is a better fit than the quest for significance hypothesis in this case. I might add Lawrence Sherman's Defiance Theory as a supplemental explanation (44). This theory suggests that when an offender is punished, they must accept the legitimacy and moral authority of the punishment or they might convert deterrence into a source of defiant pride. They lash out at the punishing agent so they can demonstrate they are not cowed by unfair or excessive punishments. I think that fits Jon Watson's war against the CDC-R quite well. In that sense, he is not a true *ideological vigilante*, even if he shares their sentiments toward child sex abusers.

Child Protection Extremists

Pure vigilantes might have any number of factors relevant to explaining why they began the radicalization process, but at a certain point, they continued to radicalize themselves. Of all the explanations for vigilantism, this one is the most likely to offend the vigilantes themselves. The stereotype of terrorists is that they are brainwashed religious cult members indifferent to collateral damage and delusional about their own heroism. Vigilantes would never see themselves as "terrorists."

Vigilantes might be proud of being called "Child Protection Extremists." Defending children is an unassailable motive, and they see themselves at war with *criminals* not civilians. They are attacking child sex abusers, not blowing up random buildings. These vigilantes do not even fight back against the police. Sometimes they turn themselves in. They see themselves as *helping* the police (or at least out-doing them). The terrorist label will not be accepted by vigilantes, but they may comfort themselves with the saying that "one man's terrorist is another man's hero." They would agree with the famous statement by Barry Goldwater "moderation in the pursuit of justice is no virtue."

None of the men I interviewed considered themselves to be anything like a terrorist. They saw themselves as performing a necessary task for humanity, but the quest for significance might be applicable if we drop the terrorism label and think of them as lone wolves fighting for a cause. Perhaps Jeremy Moody fits into this model better than any others, because he was not abused as a child so he did not have personal motives for his actions like Patrick Drum or Michael Allen

Mullen, but there is some evidence of the radicalization process in those cases as well. Cases like James Fairbanks (Nebraska) or Steven Marshall (Maine) have a few elements of the significance quest, but the resemblance is shallow. There are not enough cases of pure vigilantes for me to draw trustworthy conclusions. It is certainly possible that a man searching for significance might latch onto vigilante justice as a cause worth killing and dying for.

If I could summarize these assessments into a simple blueprint for how to make a vigilante-bomb, I would say this is the basic formula:

$$\textit{Child abuse experiences} + \textit{Desire to protect children} + \textit{Lack of alternatives}$$
$$+ \textit{Nothing to lose} + \textit{Potential reward} = \textit{Vigilantism}$$

None of these motivations/ingredients are sufficient to cause an explosion on their own, and they do not all need to be mixed together for the explosion to be possible, but if they were combined, they would be more likely to combust. Still, a pile of explosive material is not going to just randomly explode. Dynamite can be stored safely for years. The explosion doesn't happen unless someone lights the fuse.

Tick, Tick, Tick ...

The hazardous materials have been combined. The safety restraints have been removed. The detonator has been primed. How do you stop a bomb at this point? The threat of punishment is unlikely to deter a dedicated vigilante from achieving their goals. Many of them have nothing to live for. Their goals of achieving a safe and just society, avenging themselves on child sex abusers, and earning significance can only be achieved through self-sacrifice. The bomb doesn't expect it will survive the explosion. They just want to take out as many of their targets as possible. They wait until the best opportunity presents itself, and then they strike. The vigilantes in this book never thought they would "get away with it" and escape punishment for their crimes. Patrick Drum left a calling card with his name. Michael Mullen called 911. James Fairbanks confessed on Facebook. They just didn't care what happened to them. This is important because it means we cannot deter these crimes with the threat of severe punishments.

I believe the only thing that would deter a dedicated vigilante is the possibility that they will be defused before the crime occurs. They do not want to go to prison for *attempted* murder. That wouldn't serve their purposes at all. The sex offender would still be free, and they would be in prison. A man named Jorge Porto-Sierra was arrested for trying to "barbecue" child sex abusers by setting their motel rooms on fire. Nobody died. He failed in his mission (45). These failed attempts are more terrifying to the vigilante than any punishment that might come after their crime. It is a humiliating defeat. Deterrence doesn't work on those who have nothing to lose, but an aspiring vigilante still has one last thing they want to achieve. For some, it is the culminating purpose of their life. A chance to go out with a bang.

Addressing Opportunities

Criminologists spend most of their time discussing motivational and control theories of crime, but they all recognize that for a crime to happen there must be an opportunity. Deprive the individual of the opportunity, and you can prevent the crime. Routine Activities Theory identifies three necessary elements for any crime to happen: a motivated offender who has access to a suitable target in the absence of a capable guardian (46). If these vigilantes didn't have access to child sex abusers, the crimes could not happen.

The online sex offender registry made it easy to find suitable targets for some of these men. It is not just the stigma of online registration that puts sex offenders in danger. It is listing their home addresses. Will we ever manage to abolish the sex offender registry because it puts people's lives in danger? I can't speculate, but I do know that my sample of vigilantes believes it will not stop a dedicated individual from finding their targets. Clark Frederick's victim was not on a registry, Patrick Drum knew both of his victims and lived with one of them. But vigilantes like Lawrence Trant, Michael Allen Mullen, Stephen Marshall, and Jeremy Moody surfed the registry to find suitable targets. Would they have taken the time to search court databases then track their victims down in the phone book?

For the vigilantes who were in prison, having the sex offenders segregated from the rest of the population would have eliminated all opportunities for violence against them. However, there are many cases where the supposed "capable guardians" are actually motivated offenders themselves, resulting in targeted violence. The sex offenders don't want to be killed, and the other prisoners don't want to be housed with sex offenders. Why not split them up? Prison administrator excuses are unconvincing. If they want child sex abusers to survive, they should house them in separate facilities.

Addressing Motivations

It is a daunting task to address all potential vigilante motivations. It is unlikely that we can meet the vigilantes' high standard for a "just" punishment because they want a swift death penalty. It is also not advisable that we increase mandatory minimum sentencing laws for sex offenders because this may dissuade these offenders from making a plea deal, thereby resulting in fewer convictions. Prosecutors and judges have the most important role in assigning appropriate sentences, but as I explained in Chapter Four, there are many factors that decrease the predictability of sentences in America's courtrooms. Although the "leniency" question is of vital importance to vigilantes, it is not something that can be easily corrected, especially not on a national scale that would satisfy everyone who is dissatisfied with "the System."

If we cannot make vigilantes happy by punishing sex offenders to their satisfaction, perhaps we can recalibrate the sentencing guidelines for less serious crimes. This might help address the injustice gap often used as a justification for violence against sex offenders. Perhaps we can stop the failed War on Drugs or at least reimagine it in a medical/therapeutic sense to treat substance abusing offenders with basic human dignity. We can give them therapy instead of prison. We can divert them from the downward spiral of criminality and slow their accumulation of prior criminal history points. This may resolve the gap between lenient sex offender punishments and harsh penalties for drug-involved offenders. Helping substance-dependent people is a noble goal in and of itself, so regardless of your opinions about vigilante perceptions of the legal system, this is a policy worth developing.

We might also try to deconstruct their motivations by altering their perceptions. This will require intensive cognitive behavioral and mental health therapy. Each of the vigilante's cherished techniques of neutralization would have to be addressed. We might be able to deradicalize some of them. We could convince them to think of the counterfinality. Ask them to consider that even if their vigilante violence is instrumental in achieving their personal goals (gaining significance or exposing the justice system) those actions are in conflict with other valued goals (a fair justice system and due process). However, this type of intervention usually comes after the crime has been committed, and vigilantes who receive a life sentence in prison are not eligible for expensive evidence-based therapies.

As we disassemble these living bombs, there are two opposing criminological theories that might fool us into cutting the wrong wire. If vigilantes commit their crimes because they were encouraged by social reinforcement (public praise, memes, and tacit approval by authority figures), the remedy is to strongly condemn their actions. This will extinguish the positive reinforcement they receive and send a message to their supporters that they are morally wrong. On the other hand, if vigilantes are marginalized from mainstream society and see violence as their only path to significance, we should not push them further into extremist territory with high-and-mighty condemnation. Perhaps a dual solution is to re-direct their community-service mentality into non-criminal activities. We should be glad when they start a Facebook page and use democracy to fight for children's rights. These activities may be an outlet for their strongly held child protection beliefs, and by "fixing the system" they can relieve the pressure that might explode into vigilante violence if left unchecked. Democracy is a pressure release valve that gives people hope that things can change.

We should also treat the victims of child sex abuse differently when they find themselves wrapped up in legal trouble stemming from their adverse childhoods. The justice system seems content to watch these troubled young men and women cycle through their courtrooms as they accumulate longer and longer rap sheets. They assume that America's signature crime control method, deterrence, will eventually scare these miscreants on the straight and narrow path of obedience to the law. And if it doesn't, they have a solution. Bury the bomb deep inside one of our prisons and never let them out. This solution might place the vigilante out of sight, but they won't be out of mind for long. I am waiting on the next viral confession video to be published online. Maybe a new generation of prisoners will follow in Steven Sandison's footsteps and start killing "Cho-Mos" for sport. Landmines explode underground, and so do people buried in prison.

Retrospectives

If I could choose one or two theories of crime to fit with each of this book's primary case studies, I would choose the following:

> *Steven Sandison (retaliatory vigilante)*
> General Strain Theory and Moral Injury Theory
> *James Fairbanks (ideological vigilante)*
> General Strain Theory and Quest for Significance Hypothesis
> *Patrick Drum (ideological vigilante)*
> Anomie/Strain Theory and Social Learning Theory
> *Clark Fredericks (retaliatory vigilante)*
> General Strain Theory and Moral Injury Theory
> *Jeremy Moody (ideological vigilante)*
> Anomie/Strain Theory and Quest for Significance Hypothesis
> *Jon Henry Watson (ideological/pseudo-vigilante)*
> Frustration-Aggression Hypothesis and Defiance Theory
> *Scottie Allen (retaliatory vigilante)*
> Anomie/Strain Theory and Moral Injury Theory
> *Joseph Druce (retaliatory/pseudo-vigilante)*
> General Strain Theory and Quest for Significance Hypothesis

My eight primary case studies provided me with enough information to assess each vigilante using various risk assessment tools. The Level of Service/Case Management Inventory measures the risk for recidivism (subsequent arrest), the Violence Risk Appraisal Guide-Revised measures the risk of violent offending, and the Terrorist Radicalization Assessment Protocol organizes information to understand pathways to lone actor terrorist violence. The TRAP-18 assessments are represented by the number of risk factors that were prominent in the lives of each individual before their offense. It does not measure an actuarial level of risk. It is a method of organizing information that indicates a threat is present. I assessed each vigilante retrospectively, that is, I assessed them using information that was relevant at the time of their offenses rather than trying to assess their current risk levels, but I used information we have today that may not have been available at that time of the incident offense. Not all information was known for each individual, and not all statements could be confirmed for accuracy, but most of these men gave me access to their official classification assessments, pre-sentence investigation reports, and conduct reports that did not contradict their claims.

Name	Setting	LS/CMI	VRAG-R	TRAP-18
James Fairbanks	Community	Low	.12	2/18
Patrick Drum	Community	Medium	.34	10/18
Clark Fredericks	Community	Medium	.12	2/18
Jeremy Moody	Community	Medium	.45	10/18
Steven Sandison	Prison	Very High	.76	5/18
Jon Watson*	Prison	Medium	.45	7/18
Scottie Allen	Prison	Very High	.76	7/18
Joseph Druce	Prison	Very High	.58	7/18

Note: Jon Watson was officially ranked "Low risk" with the COMPAS tool but this CDC-R assessment omitted his unreported violent misconduct which I have included in my LS/CMI assessment.

The LS/CMI scores measure the likelihood of general criminal recidivism. Those who were living in the community at the time of their vigilante offenses would have ranked lower than those who were incarcerated at the time of their crimes, with the exception of Jon Watson who scored Medium risk. The VRAG-R is described in terms of the proportion meeting criteria for violent recidivism within five years. Once again, those who committed their crimes in the community were at a lower risk for reoffending than those who were incarcerated at the time of their offenses. An interesting trend revealed itself during the TRAP-18 assessment. The risk of crime and violence was not associated with terrorist-style radicalization. Steven Sandison ranked Very High for general recidivism and in the highest category for violent recidivism, but there was little evidence that he had proximate warning behaviors or distal characteristics that would have signaled a threat of violence. That is because his murder of Ted Dyer was largely spontaneous, not ideologically driven.

Only Patrick Drum and Jeremy Moody showed a clear pathway toward ideologically motivated, targeted violence that was somewhat comparable to lone actor terrorists, but even their cases were distinct from ideologically driven pseudocommandos seeking glory. Both scored positively on only 10 of the 18 potential risk factors that predict targeted violence. Taken as a whole, this indicates that vigilantes in the community differ from the average offender in terms of our likelihood of predicting their future outcomes. They are simply outliers who are difficult to predict. Prison violence is more predictable, but even so, there are no reliable assessment tools that predict *homicide* in prison, only rule violations and general "violence."

I do not believe any of these theories are sufficient to explain vigilantism. The problem is that each person is different. If we were examining car thieves, we might have a sample size of 10,000 people so individual differences would converge around averages and we might detect patterns in the data. We might even be able to design interventions that would prove to be useful in preventing large numbers of those crimes. But with a small sample of vigilantes, some of whom cannot even be called a vigilante at all, we see how individual differences thwart our attempts to invent a science of vigilantism. Rare events grab our attention and give us a false sense of understanding that is not generalizable to future events.

Jon Watson was never abused as a child, but he was under immense pressure inside the CDC-R. The overbearing influence of that *one* factor, prison deprivation, applied so much pressure that he became one of the most successful individual vigilantes in American history, with two completed deaths. But he thinks this scientific approach is missing the point. He doesn't think there is a combination of factors that cause an individual to make a choice. He said he felt a call-to-arms that he refers to as "the Howling." Some primal instinct meant to keep society safe from child abusing "freaks." Most of the other men I interviewed had similar compulsions, but they thought of themselves as hearing a spiritual calling. Jon summarized his feelings this way:

> We look for redemption and we are throwin' Hail Marys with '12 seconds on the clock. Also, guys like me believe in Cosmic Justice or Karma or Viking Örlög, so it's a bit of a universal offset.
>
> Perhaps some "Wisdom" is watching and I can gain favor when I destroy the monsters who prey on children.
>
> I'm a piss poor Viking, but my desire to correct Cosmic Örlög is what makes me entirely different than my "peers" and not answerable to the laws of man. Not anymore.

I do not know if these feelings come from nature, the supernatural, or if they can be explained in psychological terms as rationalizations. I mention these explanations here because it demonstrates just how difficult criminology can be. Sometimes you find the things that supposedly "cause" violence hold great personal meaning for the offender, but they cannot be easily observed or measured by outsiders. How can social scientists measure the effects of Karma or Örlög?

Maybe we can take away an important lesson by reviewing one last theory of crime: Redemption Scripts. This is best explained by Shadd Maruna in his book *Making Good*, a discussion of how criminal offenders follow a script in their lives, as if they are living in a movie and they are a star. If they believe the narrative is doomed no matter what they do, they persist in their criminal behavior. If they believe they can change, they will desist from crime and "make good." These life stories helped the offenders to understand themselves and their place in the world. Those who felt condemned to a life of crime were hopeless, and those who were optimistic about overcoming their past had invented a script that would lead them to success. They invented self-fulfilling prophecies. Their cognitive landscapes were no doubt constrained by their environments. Those who were condemned by social prejudice and lack of opportunity knew they would fail, so they didn't bother to desist from crime.

If we think about the vigilantes in this book, at the time of their crimes four of them were incarcerated, and three of those knew they would never be released from prison. The others might have had opportunities to live in the free world, but their prospects for happiness were bleak. Although doomed to a life of unhappiness, they chose to write their own redemption scripts where they could "make good" by killing people who cause unambiguous harm to society. They could sacrifice themselves to save children. They truly believed their actions were necessary and alternative responses were insufficient. We might read this script as a slasher movie. They thought it was heroic.

As White and Meloy found with their suicidal workplace shooters and lone actor terrorists, they tended to have a preoccupation with self-identity. *Who am I, really? What can I be?* For the men who killed child sex abusers in prison, they ask *Am I just another anonymous inmate? A dangerous felon rejected by society? Maybe I can be a hero.* Which one would you choose?

Post-Blast Investigation

Let's examine other cases of vigilantism to determine if there are any observable trends in a larger sample than my case studies. I have said that it is important to divide vigilantes into groups based on their primary motivations (*retaliatory vigilantes, ideological vigilantes,* and *pseudo-vigilantes*). We can also divide these cases by other categorization criteria. Those who committed their crimes inside a jail or prison should differ from those who broke the law in the community. While the major focus of this book is on murderers, there are cases of vigilante violence used against sex offenders that did not result in a death. Therefore, we should divide our cases according to the crime committed by the vigilante.

Remember that these crimes are rare even though they may persist in our memories longer than other violent crimes. I have conducted a thorough search for cases of vigilantism using internet searches, library archives, and targeted searches. I have limited my investigation to crimes that occurred between the years 2000 and 2022 in order to maximize the likelihood that I will find information on the internet, and I limited my search to cases where serious violence occurred, even if it did not result in a death. Although I have not discussed women vigilantes very much in this book, I have retained their cases in this section for the sake of being thorough. I have excluded any cases that were not a severe assault, aggravated assault, or a homicide.

It is often difficult to separate cases of vigilantism that targeted child sex abusers from those targeting any type of sex offender. Most vigilantes make a distinction, but news reports might omit this information. I have decided to err on the side of caution here and only include cases where the vigilante was targeting a child sex abuser because that is more germane to my focus, but this analysis could easily be expanded to include a broader definition.

Since government agencies do not track these crimes, I am particularly reliant on news media reports which might be expected to misclassify and therefore over-report these crimes. On the other hand, acts of violence toward sex offenders inside a prison are probably under-reported because an inmate-on-inmate homicide might not be reported in detail in the press (see Chapter Seven). Therefore, I have decided to separate prison violence cases from community cases unless I am comparing the two environments.

I do not assume that I have discovered *every* case of vigilante violence that has occurred. I have reviewed most of those that are available, detailed, and influential, and this may skew my results toward the newsworthy cases. I did not include unsolved crimes or vague news briefs because those stories do not provide enough information to examine the motives of the alleged vigilante. I am indebted to Douglas Evans at the Research and Evaluation Center at the John Jay College of Criminal Justice for sharing his list of cases to cross-check my own list. With his help, I was able to identify an additional 20 cases that would otherwise have been left out of this chapter.

Between January 2000 and March 2022, I identified 116 alleged child sex abusers who were the victims of serious violence. Of those cases, 48 assaults resulted in death. On average that translates to slightly more than two murders each year. Even if this is an underestimation, the murder of a sex offender for "vigilante" reasons is a rare crime. The number of homicides were not equally distributed across years. The highest number of murders occurred in 2005 and 2020 (both with six homicides), and the highest number of assaults that did not result in death occurred in 2012 and 2013 (with nine incidents in each year).

I reviewed each of these cases through media reports and court records. My overall impression is that most of these cases do not fit the traditional vigilante stereotype. Many were simply violent crimes that could have happened to anyone. The sex offender status of the victims were coincidental. This should not be surprising. Why should sex offenders be immune from victimization? The baseline of comparison is not *zero* crimes, it is the same as any other citizen. The fact that news agencies reported their sex offender status might simply be a matter of convenience. When a crime occurs, one of the first things a journalist will do is search for more information on the people involved. Sex offender registries offer a wealth of information that they can include in their story, even if it is irrelevant for deciphering motives.

In cases where more than one offender was involved, not everyone bore an equal claim to the title "vigilante." In 2014, Daniel Narron tried to kill a sex offender by running him over with his car. His three passengers supported his decision, but they were not behind the wheel of the car. Should this story count as one vigilante or four? Brian Young was a correctional officer convicted of opening a door to let four prisoners attack a child sex abuser in the county jail. Is *he* the vigilante for opening the door, or were the prisoners who administered the beating the real vigilantes? Real-life cases are messy. It's not easy to fit them into boxes, and media reports often lack the ideal amount of information to make such determinations.

The most common murder weapons were firearms (13) followed by hands/feet (12). The remaining homicides were caused by knives (9), strangulation (6), blunt weapons (4), arson (1), and a combination beating and drowning (1). In the community, there were 30 homicides and 35 non-fatal assaults. In prisons and jails, there were 18 homicides and 18 assaults. Keep in mind that these cases were derived from news sources and the majority of assaults in prison were not reported. Also keep in mind that many of these cases have dubious relations to vigilantism. I judged 33 of the total number of cases to have retributive or revenge-based motives, and I could only determine that 42 cases had an ideological motive that aligns with popular perceptions of vigilantism. The remaining incidents were misclassified, self-defense, or there was not enough information to draw a conclusion.

In cases where the offender was targeted, 33 were "retribution" style offenses where the vigilantes were avenging themselves, a family member, or a friend. Often, the vigilantes were under the influence of drugs, alcohol, or a passionate rage at the time of their attack. A typical story is of a male attacking someone who allegedly sexually abused their family member. While this does capture some of the vigilante mindset we discussed in this book, it may not be unique to avenging sex offenses (fathers get in fights over their children's sports games too), but those cases do not make for a good news story, so again we are left with these marginal cases of sex abuse vigilantism.

There were more vigilantes than victims in these cases. It's a stretch to call them "angry mobs" but there were more than two perpetrators in 13 incidents. There were 16 cases where two people worked together, and there were 81 solo actors. Few vigilantes attacked more than one victim. Jon Watson, Patrick Drum, Michael Mullen, and Steven Marshall were the only vigilantes who killed two victims. None killed more (Jeremy Moody killed one sex offender and his wife, who was not a sex offender). There are some failed attempts at homicide as well. Lawrence Trant tried to burn down two buildings housing seven sex offenders, and he tried to stab another man to death, but none of his targets died.

Of the 169 separate participants in these vigilante crimes, only 14 were women, and 8 of those acted without the involvement of at least one man. The average age for a woman at the time of the crime was 30 (range = 16 to 42). For men, the average age was 31 (range = 16 to 69). The alleged child sex abusers were all men, and their average age was 47 (range = 15–82).

An unexpected discovery in these news reports was the relatively lenient sentences some vigilantes received for their crimes. To be sure, homicide was usually punished with very long prison sentences, but some attempted homicides and brutal beatings were handled delicately. I found cases where people who stabbed a sex offender or beat them with a baseball bat were given probation. In one case, two brothers beat a sex offender and whipped him with an electrical cord and were given two to three years in prison. Correctional officers who permitted violence against sex offenders were often terminated from employment but not charged with crimes.

I excluded one case from this review because it was too absurd. I will relate it here in order to demonstrate how a simple threat of violence can be exaggerated into a threat to society. A disabled man who was paralyzed from the waist down called the police on a relative who was accused of sexually abusing a child. The disabled man told the alleged sex offender to wait until the police arrived. When the suspect tried to leave, the disabled man hit him on the arm with a child-sized baseball bat. There were no injuries, but the prosecutor charged the disabled man with aggravated assault with a deadly weapon. They offered him one year in jail with a suspended sentence if he pled guilty. The case was dropped, but it drew national attention back in 2011 for being yet another example of the legal system overextending themselves to protect "the rule of law," even if it means putting disabled citizens in jail to preserve the government's monopoly on violence (47). I can't, in good conscience, call this man a vigilante.

Unfortunately, not much can be learned from these cases because their circumstances differ so much. A young woman who convinces her boyfriend to help her kill her abuser is different than four teenagers who try to run over a stranger with their car. Two men who set a house on fire to kill a registered sex offender have nothing in common with a father who punches a naked man peeping in his daughter's window. "Vigilante" has become a meaningless term.

News reports fail to explain the true motives of many of these perpetrators. They rarely discover if the person had been sexually abused as a child. Few describe the vigilante's history with the criminal justice system, drugs and alcohol, or family situations. The crimes that took place inside jails and prisons were the most confusing because they failed to consider alternative explanations for each crime. I personally reached out to three incarcerated "vigilantes" from this list to ask if they had vigilante motives. They all denied those claims. One murderer wanted to be transferred to another prison so he killed someone who happened to be a sex offender. Another killed for revenge because the victim had gotten him fired from his prison industry job. The third said he was an accomplice to a murder and he was just helping his friend collect a debt. All three declined to be identified for this book. Only true vigilantes want the spotlight.

The "bomb built in hell" theory does not seem to be an appropriate explanation for the generic cases of vigilantism that end up in the newspapers. It doesn't fit well with concerned fathers apprehending a naked peeping tom, a young woman killing her own abuser, or the obviously mislabeled cases that turn every physical altercation with a sex offender into a hate crime lamented by pedophile activist groups. The bomb analogy seems to work best for the rare and especially dangerous cases described in detail throughout this book. Steven Sandison, Joseph Druce, Patrick Drum, Michael Mullen, Scottie Allen, and Jeremy Moody seem to be the best examples of intentional, premeditated, ideologically-driven vigilantism precipitated by trauma and failed justice system interventions. The rarity of these events makes it unlikely that we can predict or intervene to defuse these human bombs in the future, even if we took the time to ask them their life stories to discover if they were explosive in the first place. We are inhibited by a lack of information to draw better conclusions.

One case stood out to me as especially perplexing. A 20-year-old man named Stephen Marshall hunted down two registered sex offenders in Maine. He killed them, and then killed himself. You might think he would have a case history similar to Patrick Drum, Michael Mullen, or Jeremy Moody, but the truth is, we have no idea what his motives were. He had been arrested as a juvenile for threatening a young man with an AR-15, but had no convictions. He tried to join the Canadian military, but was rejected for having asthma. He had a small group of friends who considered themselves to be outcasts at school. He took college classes. One day, for apparently no reason, he took a bus to Maine and killed two strangers before killing himself. This act of desperation could be considered "going out with a bang" or trying to end his life with a significant act of "community service," but we will never know. He took his explanations with him (48).

Civilized Justice

Maybe the analogy of the bomb builder is inappropriate. Perhaps we should use a different explanation proposed by Andrew Vachss. He once wrote that failure to protect children was a sign of our species' regressive evolution. While every species on the planet protects its offspring, humans seem to be the only ones who prey on theirs (49). He explained this in his essay "Our Endangered Species" which is quoted below:

> We cannot continue to tolerate those who prey upon our children – the future of our species. Evolution is a race, a relay race, with the baton passed from generation to generation. The competition is between those who value children as the seedlings of our species and those who value them as vassals and victims.
>
> We are not winning this race. And we cannot, unless and until we change our priorities and our conduct. All the pious rhetoric on the planet will not save one child. And while we endlessly debate the "right" of pedophiles to post kiddie porn on the Internet, our species moves farther away from its biological roots.
>
> We must take the abuse of a child as an offense against (and threat to) our survival. And we must replicate the conduct of our animal ancestors and respond as they did – or fail to do so and vanish as some of them did. Forever.

Vachss was not suggesting that people resort to animalistic violence to protect children. He was encouraging people to re-direct their protective instincts (their "righteous rage") to get involved in the child welfare and justice systems. The vigilantes I interviewed took a less civilized approach to this subject. One vigilante had an interesting take on the role of violence in the survival of the human species. This individual said our society has become so "civilized" in terms of bureaucratizing punishment that we have strayed from the behaviors that kept our species alive.

> Killing seems immoral always, but corporal punishment and physical pain as a deterrent not necessarily so. We are really discussing ways to prevent animalistic urges from being expressed in our society. Many times the snapping of the jaws and the tear of the claw is the only thing

which restrains the other beasts. Victimizing children is beastlike, it's prehistoric, the notion that this vein of dysfunction still penetrates our society so heavily is disturbing at best. Predators don't need protection, they need evolutionary adaptation. Stop stalking children, stay alive and happy. Humanity must allow this process to take place. It's how we survive as a species. Eventually, those who carry these maladaptive traits are weaned out of the species.

If a group of chimpanzees attacked a member of the community because they were harming infants, any expert on National Geographic would conclude this was an evolved response that benefited chimps by preserving the long-term survival of the species. As Patrick Drum observed, even scorpions fight to the death to protect their young. These ideas might appear similar to the eugenics beliefs of early criminologists: that child abusers are a threat to the future of humanity so they should be castrated or killed (a position that Jeremy Moody endorses wholeheartedly). Vigilantes long for the days when "snapping of the jaws and the tear of the claw" were appropriate safeguards for children.

Those who oppose vigilantism might be able to turn the tables. Many experts scold moral panickers and punitive populists for their uncivilized desire for retribution. They believe the revenge instinct is atavistic, so they endorse sentencing departures to protect child sex abusers from the "unrelenting harshness" of emotional voters (50). For them, the progress of civilization depends on being merciful to the perpetrators of crimes, even serious crimes against children. They believe that stigma, punishment, and violence are vestiges of our animalistic past, better left behind. They are glad they live in a civilization that has evolved to such a refined level that we invented the plea bargain.

This is an ancient battle of ideas. Should we violently retaliate against sex offenders to strengthen our society? Or is society stronger when we replace emotion with a bureaucratic justice system? Retribution can be seen as good or evil depending on your answer (51).

Vigilantes believe violence is an appropriate reaction to sex abuse crimes. For both the chimpanzee and the vigilante, the goal is to satisfy their primal emotional desire to cause pain to those who cause pain. These instincts have been labeled and re-labeled until we can no longer tell the difference between an animalistic fitness benefit (52, 53), settling a score, retribution, and revenge. Dismissing these goals as emotional and non-utilitarian misses the point. These goals serve a purpose if they help the vigilante sleep at night, knowing they tried to balance the scales of justice. For some of them, violence was their method of earning a *clean* conscience.

Fateful Choices

By "A Son of Solitude"

If you live to seek revenge,
Dig a grave for two.
Ancient Jewish Proverb

Retribution and Revenge were brothers, brought into this world by parents who true names have been buried in the sands of time. Their story has been told a number of times, most recognizably as Cain and Abel in the Bible, whose inherent characteristics were transmitted to them through the crooked tree of their parent's lineage. One could never have existed without the other, for they gave each other life as they grew and matured. Both of them must be recognized and acknowledged for their mighty influence and powerful impact on our world, while they may appear at first glance to be similar they are quite unique in many aspects.

Revenge was the firstborn, the eldest of the two brothers. He has always been a hunter, who stalks and slays for personal gain. He has many tactics and methods, yet only one impetus drives him … hunger. The hunger to take that which he feels, so strongly, belongs to him. Revenge's hunger is legendary, the king of myths. His all-consuming drive to travel any distance, traverse any hostile terrain, and potentially suffer any loss for the sake of satisfying his own internal desire is fearsome in its scope and intensity. Revenge is short-tempered and keeps few genuine friends, but he prefers to practice in public, thriving on the thrill of the hunt, and the subsequent joy of taking the kill while being observed. To stand in the presence of Revenge and feel his glowing visage and electrifying power can be overwhelming to the senses. He has an energy which cannot be denied, and any of his methods are valid, for truly his only real guiding principle is the necessity of a successful hunt. He simply does not allow himself to be distracted by paltry moral or overtly ethical considerations. For that would only lessen his focus on his current prey, that which is in season, and his avid calculation toward its capture. Remember, this was the brother, this Cain, Revenge, whose sacrifices were much pleasing to the Deity, the slaughter at Revenge's hand was acceptable to the Lord, which our forefathers worshipped and bowed down to.

Though much like his older brother in so many ways, Retribution, our young Abel, was a farmer. An agriculturalist of a sort. His existence was centered around planning fields and plotting the placement of the seeds he sowed, careful to always consider their eventual influence on the other crops. Retribution has tough hands, leather and rough from a lifetime of hard use. But his hands have as often blessed and comforted as they have performed the difficult tastes of honor. When he walks in his proper form, his character polished, devoid of superiority or selfishness, Retribution radiates the aura of a loyal and benevolent friend. He has the power to reinstill your own intrinsic worth, and within his altruistic gaze you will feel abundant comfort and solace. The fields of Retribution are vast and ancient, and their beauty is something to behold. Many individuals and families have been sustained, validated, and have feasted upon the fruits of Retribution's finest, well-wrought labors. Many of them never knowing the true depth of his sacrifice or his supreme diligence to his responsibilities. Throughout history, endless rivers of humanity were serenaded to one of his many fields for the generous bounty of Retribution was made available to all, but many of them became intoxicated and were compromised in those same fields. If he is allowed to be what he truly is, Retribution is sincere and well respected. If misunderstood and casually entertained, he is much like his brother and cannot be trusted.

These two brothers, Revenge and Retribution, so very much alike, yet, so very much different at their core, but this tale has been told and was then memorized and retold for countless thousands of years. For Retribution had the honorable promise of a birthright, and for this, he would be murdered. Revenge, the hunter, was born to dominate and kill, and thus, in the midst of one of the beautiful fields of Retribution, a most hideous act took place. Having lured his brother into the peaceful solace of one of his own gardens, Revenge destroyed Retribution with his own hands, leaving only a memory of his existence. And now, we all live, each one of us, under the shade and influence of this crooked branch of humanity. Though we call him by many names, Justice, Penitence, The Debt, his name, his true name, is Revenge, and his lust for the hunt, and the glory of the capture and kill, remains as strong, if not stronger, now, that it ever was.

With proper Retribution having been buried many centuries ago, legend has it, that his remaining brother, Revenge, became the father of all humanity. You can readily see the truth of this tale, surrounding us and our everyday lives. His character traits are powerfully dormant and they seed our gentle core, becoming the instructional urges that guide many of the decisions we make, the laws we pass, fundamentally, the way we view and treat each other. At the root of these things and so many more, lies the influence of our true progenitor, Revenge, and his never-ending thirst for vengeance and blood.

The story of Cain and Abel is the key to understanding the inherent nature of our society today. We continue to try to evolve ourselves and each other away from the roots of our distant past. And yet these roots still entangle our motives and facilitate actions which seem beyond our control, but we can awaken and shake off the bondage of our past. Retribution and Revenge have had their time. We can now move on and allow the next generation to flourish and establish a new path forward. Remuneration and Restoration lead to peace and progress, while these ancient relics of humanities past ignorance should be buried, standing in the time and place where they belong … far behind us.

Revenge and Retribution have a proper home, and they prosper in their appropriate setting, but it is not here, not now, with any of us. May they always rest in peace, in their place ….

…. *In the* distant past.

References

1. Vachss, A. (1990, June 3). Today's victim could be tomorrow's predator. *Parade Magazine*. http://www.vachss.com/av_dispatches/disp_9006_a.html
2. Hays-Grudo, J., & Morris, A. (2020). *Adverse and protective childhood experiences: A developmental perspective*. Washington, DC: American Psychological Association.
3. Fuller-Thomson, E., Baird, S. L., Dhrodia, R., & Brennenstuhl, S. (2016). The association between adverse childhood experiences (ACEs) and suicide attempts in a population-based study. *Child: Care, Health and Development*, 42(5), 725–734. https://doi.org/10.1111/cch.12351
4. Agnew, R. (2005). *Pressured into crime: An overview of general strain theory*. New York, NY: Oxford University Press.
5. Brizendine, L. (2006). *The female brain*. New York, NY: Penguin Random House.
6. Moffitt, T. E., Caspi, A., Rutter, M., & Silva, P. A. (2001). *Sex differences in antisocial behaviour: Conduct disorder, delinquency, and violence in the Dunedin longitudinal study*. Cambridge University Press. https://doi.org/10.1017/CBO9780511490057
7. Adler, F. (1975). *Sisters in crime: The rise of the new female criminal*. New York, NY: McGraw-Hill.
8. Sutherland, E. H., Cressey, D. R., & Luckenbill, D. F. (1992) *Principles of criminology* (11th ed.). New York, NY: Rowman & Littlefield Publishers, Inc.
9. Akers, R. L. (1998). *Social learning and social structure: A general theory of crime and deviance*. Boston, MA: Northeastern University Press.
10. DeKeseredy, W. S., & Schwartz, M. D. (2016). Thinking sociologically about image-based sexual abuse: The contribution of male peer support theory. *Sexualization, Media, & Society*. https://doi.org/10.1177/2374623816684692

11. Bryan, C. J., Bryan, A. O., Roberge, E., Leifker, F. R., & Rozek, D. C. (2018). Moral injury, post-traumatic stress disorder, and suicidal behavior among national guard personnel. *Psychological Trauma: Theory, Research, Practice, and Policy, 10*(1), 36–45. https://doi.org/10.1037/tra0000290

12. Litz, B. T., Stein, N., Delaney, E., Lebowitz, L., Nash, W. P., Silva, C., & Maguen, S. (2009). Moral injury and moral repair in war veterans: A preliminary model and intervention strategy. *Clinical Psychology Review, 29*(8), 695–706. http://doi.org/10.1016/j.cpr.2009.07.003

13. Griffin, B. J., Purcell, N., Burkman, K., Litz, B. T., Bryan, C. J., Schmitz, M., Villierme, C., Walsh, J., & Maguen, S. (2019). Moral injury: An integrative review. *Journal of Traumatic Stress, 32*(3), 350–362. https://doi.org/10.1002/jts.22362

14. Nash, W. P., Marino Carper, T. L., Mills, M. A., Au, T., Goldsmith, A., & Litz, B. T. (2013). Psychometric evaluation of the Moral Injury Events Scale. *Military Medicine, 178*(6), 646–652. https://doi.org/10.7205/MILMED-D-13-00017

15. Sykes, G. & Matza. D. (1957). Techniques of neutralization: A theory of delinquency. *American Sociological Review, 22*, 664–670.

16. Cubellis, M. A., Evans, D. N., & Fera, G. (2019). Sex offender stigma: An exploration of vigilantism against sex offenders, *Deviant Behavior, 40*:2, 225–239. https://doi.org/10.1080/01639625.2017.1420459

17. Lawrence, J., & Jewett, R. (2002). *The myth of the American superhero*. Dulles, VA: Wm. B. Eerdmans-Lightning Source.

18. McCombs, P. (1985, Jan. 17). The vigilante Mystique. *Washington Post*. https://www.washingtonpost.com/archive/lifestyle/1985/01/17/the-vigilante-mystique/c1887806-d4f6-4032-a5a0-a569fb19b227/

19. Markey, P. M., Ferguson, C. J., & Moral Combat (2017). *Why the war on violent video games is wrong.* Dallas, TX: BenBella Books.

20. Viki, G. T., Fullerton, I., Raggett, H., Tait, F., & Wiltshire, S. (2012). The role of dehumanization in attitudes toward the social exclusion and rehabilitation of sex offenders. *Journal of Applied Social Psychology, 42*, 2349–2367.

21. Walker, A. (2021). *Long dark shadow: Minor-attracted people and their pursuit of dignity*. Oakland, CA: University of California Press.

22. Stevenson, M. C., Malik, S. E., Totton, R. R., & Reeves, R. D. (2014). Disgust sensitivity predicts punitive treatment of juvenile sex offenders: The role of empathy, dehumanization, and fear. *Analyses of Social Issues and Public Policy, 15*(1), 177–197.

23. Smith, D. L. (2011). *Less than human*. New York, NY: St. Martin's Press.

24. Matsumoto, D., Hwang, H. C., & Frank, M. G. (2017). Emotion and aggressive intergroup cognitions: The ANCODI hypothesis. *Aggressive Behavior, 43*, 93–107.

25. White, S. G., Meloy, J. R., Mohandie, K., & Kienlen, K. K. (2017). Autism spectrum disorder and violence: Threat assessment issues. *Journal of Threat Assessment and Management, 4*(3), 144–163.

26. Knoll, J. L. (2010). The "pseudocommando" mass murderer: Part I, the psychology of revenge and obliteration. *The Journal of the American Academy of Psychiatry and the Law, 38*(1), 87–94.

27. Hirschi, T. (1969). *Causes of delinquency*. Berkeley, CA: University of California Press.

28. Sampson, R. J., & Laub, J. (1993). *Crime in the making: Pathways and turning points through life*. Cambridge, MA: Harvard University Press.

29. Perry, B. D. (2009). *Maltreated children: Experience, brain development, and the next generation*. New York, NY: W. W. Norton & Co.

30. Cullen, F. T. (1994). Social support as an organizing concept for criminology: Presidential address to the Academy of Criminal Justice Sciences. *Justice Quarterly, 11*(4), 527–560.

31. Johnston, L. (1996). What is vigilantism? *The British Journal of Criminology, 36*(2), 220–236.

32. Strong, T. (2017, May 2). Stancil guilty in Wayne Community College murder trial. *CBS17*. https://www.cbs17.com/news/stancil-guilty-in-wayne-community-college-murder-trial/

33. Meloy, J. R. (2017). *The TRAP-18 manual version 1.0*. Washington, DC: Global Institute of Forensic Research.

34. White, S. G., & Meloy, J. R. (2016). *The WAVR-21: Workplace assessment of violence risk including campus and student contexts* (3rd ed.). San Diego, CA: Specialized Training.

35. Black, D. (1983). Crime as social control. *American Sociological Review, 48*(1), 34–45. https://doi.org/10.2307/2095143

36. Sampson, R. J., Raudenbush, S. W., & Earls, F. (1997). Neighborhoods and violent crime: A multilevel study of collective efficacy. *Science*, *277*(5328), 918–924. http://www.jstor.org/stable/2892902

37. Anderson, E. (1999). *Code of the Street: Decency, violence, and the moral life of the inner City*. New York, NY: W. W. Norton & Company, Inc.

38. Dimsdale, T. J. (1866|2003). *The vigilantes of Montana*. Guilford, CT: Morris Book Publishing, LLC.

39. Katz, J. (1988). *Seductions of crime: A chilling exploration of the criminal mind- from juvenile delinquency to cold-blooded murder*. New York, NY: Basic Books.

40. Merton, R. (1938). Social structure and anomie. *American Sociological Review*, *3*(5), 672–682.

41. Dugas, M., & Kruglanski, A. W. (2014). The quest for significance model of radicalization: Implication for the management of terrorist detainees. *Behavioral Sciences and the Law*, *32*(3), 423–439.

42. Dollard, J., Miller, N. E., Doob, L. W., Mowrer, O. H., & Sears, R. R. (1939). *Frustration and aggression*. New Haven, CT: Yale University Press.

43. Cohen, A. R. (1955). Social norms, arbitrariness of frustration, and status of the agent of frustration in the frustration-aggression hypothesis. *The Journal of Abnormal and Social Psychology*, *51*(2): 222–226. https://doi.org/10.1037/h0039947

44. Sherman, L. W. (1993). Defiance, deterrence, and irrelevance: A theory of the criminal sanction. *Journal of Crime and Delinquency*, *30*, 445–473.

45. ABC7. (2018, May 7). 'Barbecue all the child molesters': Man accused of trying to set multiple people on fire. https://abc7news.com/barbecue-sex-offenders-child-molester-set-people- on-fire/3439065/

46. Cohen, L. E., & Felson, M. (1979). Social change and crime rate trends: A routine activity approach. *American Sociological Review*, *44*, 588–608.

47. Sigelman, N. (2011, July 27). Frank Herbert, charged with assault on child molester, nixes deal. *MV Times*. https://www.mvtimes.com/2011/07/27/frank-hebert-charged-assault-child-molester-nixes-deal-6871/

48. Sharp, D. (2006, November 4). Police documents shed light on Maine sex offender killer. *Associated Press*. https://www.timesargus.com/news/police-documents-shed-light-on-maine-sex-offender-killer/article_8df32109-7d40-5bdd-81cb-20f9d0ce9239.html

49. Vachss, A. (1998, March 29). Our endangered species: A hard look at how we treat children. *Parade Magazine*. http://www.vachss.com/av_dispatches/disp_9803_a.html

50. Pfaff, J. F. (2017). *Locked in: The true causes of mass incarceration – And how to achieve real reform*. New York, NY: Basic Books.

51. Tonry, M. (2012). *Retributivism has a past: Has it a future?* New York, NY: Oxford University Press.

52. Wiegman, I. (2019) Payback without bookkeeping: The origins of revenge and retaliation, *Philosophical Psychology*, *32*(7), 1100–1128. https://doi.org/10.1080/09515089.2019.1646896

53. Robinson, P. H., Kurzban, R., & Jones, O. (2007). The origins of shared intuitions of justice. *Vanderbilt Law Review*, *60*(6), 1631–1688.

10

AVENGING ANGEL

Jason Vukovich was born in June 1975, in Alaska. He was raised in a very religious household, but by anyone's standard, it was not very Christian. His stepfather, Larry Lee Fulton, terrorized Jason throughout his childhood. He beat him mercilessly with belts and wooden boards. He also sexually assaulted him during nightly "prayer" sessions. Jason's brother, Joel, also suffered the same fate. Both boys shared this nightmarish experience, taking beatings for each other. Joel would go first to help spare Jason from their stepfather's worst wrath. Every day was the same. Church, beatings, prayer, and sexual assault.

The abuse was so terrible that Larry Fulton was taken before a judge in 1989. He was charged with second-degree abuse of a minor and might have served 3 years in prison for his crime, but the judge suspended the sentence and let him go back home. This demonstration of mercy had a profound impact on Jason's opinion of the justice system thereafter.

Jason's parents pulled him out of public school and he was trapped in the same abusive household, cut off from any help from the outside (1). No one from the state ever came back to check on Jason to see if the abuse was continuing. When Jason turned 16 years old, he ran away from his abusive household. Jason struck out alone and turned to petty theft to survive. He did odd jobs and traveled from state to state, but supplemented his meager income with stolen credit cards and theft. He started accumulating those "prior criminal history" points that factor into a judge's sentencing guidelines. They rack up quickly.

Jason hated himself. He hated the abuse he suffered. He hated the fact that the court system had failed to protect him. He thought about other children like himself who were out there somewhere, helpless, just waiting for an adult to save them from abuse (2). He saw himself in their position, and he didn't want to let his younger self down. In 2016, when Jason was 40 years old, he decided to do something that he could be proud of. Something to make up for the cosmic injustice of an adult sexually assaulting a child with impunity. Jason searched Alaska's sex offender registry website and found the names and addresses of men who had sexually assaulted children. Three of these men were Charles Albee, Andres Barbosa, and Wesley Demarest.

Jason went to Albee's home and told the 68-year-old man to sit on his bed. He slapped Albee several times in the face, told him he knew he had sexually abused children, and then Jason robbed him. He left Albee's home without causing serious injuries to the man.

DOI: 10.4324/9781003393849-11

Two days later, Jason went to Barbosa's home with a hammer and two female accomplices. The women used their phones to film the altercation that followed. Barbosa was 25 years old and had been convicted of child sex exploitation material crimes just 2 years before. Jason entered the home and punched Barbosa in the face, then threatened to "bash his dome in" with the hammer if he didn't comply. While Jason confronted Barbosa, the women robbed the house and stole Barbosa's truck.

Later, Jason went to Demarest's house and forced his way in. He asked if Demarest was on the sex offender registry and Demarest said "Yes." Jason asked if he thought he'd paid for his crime. Demarest had served 9 months in jail for attempting to sexually abuse a kindergartner. Demarest said "Yes." Jason said, "No, you didn't pay for it enough." Jason told Demarest to sit down, but Demarest refused. He rushed towards Jason. At this moment, Jason felt that the man resembled his abusive stepfather. Jason reached inside his backpack and pulled out his hammer. He struck Demarest in the head and said "I'm an avenging angel. I'm going to mete out justice for the people you hurt" (3). Demarest's roommate called 911 and Demarest received medical attention. All three of the men that Jason targeted survived, but Demarest suffered the most severe injuries. He complained of ongoing headaches, brain injury, and an inability to go back to work. He was also unable to continue volunteering at his local church after the attack.

Jason was arrested nearby with items stolen from the men, his hammer, and a list of names and addresses from the sex offender registry. Apparently, he had more targets in mind. He was charged with assault, robbery, burglary, and theft (4). He later accepted a plea deal that included pleading guilty to first-degree attempted assault and first-degree robbery.

Unlike the sweetheart plea deals that some sex offenders orchestrate, Jason was not permitted to negotiate for any specific sentence. After all, he was not a DuPont. He wanted to speak with the District Attorney but was denied an audience. He asked "How can any District Attorney perceive a man's heart if he or she has never spoken to the accused? How does the state determine the intention of a man's heart if they literally never spend even one moment in conversation or the contemplation of his motives or mindset?"

Jason argued that his childhood trauma was a serious mitigating circumstance that the court should consider before they decided his fate. "Grown men who suffer physical wounds will heal, children who are maligned physically, spiritually, and emotionally, grow up but never become what they could have been. A molested or beaten child automatically receives a life sentence, there is no release date."

Jason decided to write a letter to the *Anchorage Daily News* to draw attention to his case. He offered to serve the prison sentences of four convicted child abusers, back-to-back-to-back-to-back, and mathematically showed that this was less than half the sentence he faced for armed robbery.

I will plead guilty to any combination of charges you wish, with the following caveat – my sentence is equal to in length, what each one of the pedophiles served for assaulting children." One of the men was convicted of raping his own daughter- he served approximately 3 years. One was convicted of molesting his own 10-month-old granddaughter – 1 year. The third was a child pornographer who served 2 years, 8 months... I offered to serve *their* time back-to-back-to-back: 6 years 9 months. "Run that. I'll sign the deal today." I also offered, as an added incentive, to serve the three years that the monster who "made" me never served. "Let's go 9 years, 9 months starting now!"

Jason's attorney said "He's already been punished. This whole thing started out as the punishment of a child who didn't deserve to be treated this way." Jason made one final statement before his sentencing:

I would first like to apologize to this court for my choice to break the law and for taking matters into my own hands. I'm sorry. I shouldn't have behaved like this. I'm now also going to apologize to Mr. D. for the injuries that I caused him. It was never my intention for anybody to be seriously hurt. You weren't even aware of it, but in my mind I was a kid again, standing there facing Larry Fulton. You look just like him. I went instantly into panic mode and things went completely out of control. So I'm sorry. I shouldn't have assaulted you.

To the best of my understanding, I'll relay what contributed to my flawed perspective and the mindset that led to my actions. There are many things that I have never spoke about, things that I saw as a child and things that were done to me, and the experiences that I did not want to burden other people with, memories that I constantly tried to prevent from overwhelming my brain and nervous system, but that I can still to this very day feel crawling beneath my skin, the movies that my mind still privately screens on the inside of my eyelids. These are the things that I could never put into words.

I didn't consciously recognize that I was a tormented individual or that I had placed myself on the pathway to where someone would be seriously hurt until it was too late. It was just that I had so much pain built up that I didn't know what to do with it all. I felt like I had to get rid of some of it. It felt like I had to finally act and try to make things right or else I would burst.

At the time, I didn't want to acknowledge that I had a mental health disorder. I thought counseling or therapy meant that I was weak, and I always wanted to be strong. My attorney has here letters from all over the country – Minnesota, Wisconsin, Oklahoma, Alaska, Oregon, and more – letters from people just like me, lives who were broken or ruined as kids, and now they're all in jail or, if they are fortunate, they're in therapy or counseling as adults. And I thought I was alone in this all throughout my life.

So let me state here plainly that I realize now that I had no business assaulting these individuals or taking the law into my own hands. I should have sought mental health counseling before I exploded. Therapy is not weakness, and I see this now. I will never conduct myself in this manner again. More importantly to anybody that's listening, this type of conduct is never justifiable.

I remember being hauled into this same courthouse as a child for an onslaught of condescending questioning related to the man who adopted, then systematically beat and molested my brother and I. And I'm ashamed to say that even though he was convicted, the state sent him right back into our home with no jail time to serve for his abuses.

This is also when I received my lifetime sentence and it formed the foundations of my inner feelings about the legal system which I have battled with ever since. As a young man, these feelings, combined with the years of sexual and physical abuse, reinforced my belief of just how ugly, how poor, and what a scrap of muddied cloth my life really was. As the years passed, the feelings dampened, but it never disappeared, and it continues to live on me like a thin scum of dark mold. It has infected all of my attempts at success. The course of my life demonstrates this clearly.

And so now here I sit again in this exact courthouse, facing the penalty for lashing out at child molestors – at people just like the man who molested me. The cycle of abuse could not be more clearly demonstrated. I was raised here in Alaska, and after those years I felt like the trash that blows in the wind around the ankles of normal citizens as they lived their lives. I had been condemned to feel constant anxiety and watchfulness around everyone because, obviously, to me, no one could be trusted – not the church, not even the law.

This type of vigilance is exhausting, but eventually it became just another part of my life. Now it's a habit, just like good posture. Silence also became a habit since I had been taught in the cruelest possible way that expressing the hurt just leads to more suffering. No one to this very day, except for my own brother most recently, ever told me I had a right to be angry, that I shouldn't have to be ashamed and hide it. So I just blamed myself again and again, and I buried my anger in pain.

A long time ago, I made a silent promise to myself that I would never ever speak again to anyone about what happened to me. So of course, therapy or counseling all through the years was never really an option for me up until recently. This is when the accumulation of my poor life choices and conduct spoke so loudly of something broken inside of me that I had to say something. All of this led to a doctor who diagnosed me with PTSD after just barely scratching the surface of a very deep set of emotional traumas.

At the time, I was unable to continue any therapy because I unconsciously sabotaged the process by breaking a rule, and I ended up back in jail. And unfortunately, jails and prisons in Alaska do not offer options to address mental health issues. They simply reinforce the separation from society that was already ingrained in me. So Your Honor, I ask you to please consider all of the aspects of this case and issue and alternate form of sentencing that can restore me to humanity.

Today, I take full responsibility for my actions and I do not seek to place the blame on anyone else. I should have done something, anything, other than acting out in this manner. So Your Honor, I ask you to please hand down a sentence that focuses less on shame and stigma and isolation, and more on rehabilitation, restoration, and compassion, one that allows for therapy and healing.

Please help me Your Honor. Take the time to craft a judgment that's appropriate to this particular set of circumstances, not only in its logic but in its understanding and expression. An act of merciful justice from this court would speak loudly to a heart that was long ago judged to be worthless. Thank you, Your Honor.

The judge did not show any mercy. He declared "*Vigilantism won't be accepted in our society.*" Jason was sentenced to 28 years in prison with 5 years suspended. He will also have to serve 5 years on probation when he is released in 2041. He will be 66 years old. One of his victims told the court that he would not be satisfied with any prison sentence that allowed Jason to be "walking around" while he is still alive because he would not feel safe. He said the assault ruined his life. When the judge sentenced Jason to such a long sentence, he used the language of deterrence, incapacitation, and retribution to justify his decision. Jason's punishment would "send a message" to anyone else who was considering taking the law into their own hands. His decades in prison would prevent him from hurting others in the community. And, notably, his suffering would demonstrate that the court system recognized the seriousness of his offense. All of these concerns had been waived for the "lesser offenses" of child sex abuse in the related cases.

Seward's Follies

Jason's case has sparked a fury among the citizens of Alaska. At this point in the book, it is probably not a surprise to learn that many vocal critics of the justice system endorse Jason's actions. In fact, thousands of people from across the United States have donated money to Jason's legal defense fund and offered to pay for this PTSD counseling. I have spoken to some of his most passionate supporters, and they have compiled a list of grievances against the court system in Alaska that they find relevant to this case. I have summarized their arguments below with references to state reports.

Alaskan Priorities

There are only 5,100 people in Alaskan jails and prisons, but the total population of the state is 731,000, so the incarceration rate is almost 700 per 100,000 (5). That places it well above the average incarceration rate of the United States, which is the #1 incarceration country on Earth. They also have 6,500 people on probation and another 1,700 on parole. The state spends $15 million every year on prisons, which may seem low, but since there are 5,100 incarcerated people, they spend about $60,000 per year for each prisoner. At this rate (which will not stay the same over the next 23 years), the State of Alaska will spend $1,380,000 to incapacitate Jason Vukovich. However, their decision to divert sex offenders from incarceration sentences seems to disclose a controversial flaw with their punishment priorities. Many people would prefer for Jason to serve a shorter sentence if those resources could be used to incapacitate child sex abusers instead.

Alaskan law enforcement agencies fail to test rape kits, often citing a lack of financial resources. They stored the DNA evidence taken from thousands of rape crimes but did not test them for decades. They recently spent $1.5 million dollars to test 568 archived rape kits, and they were able to convict a man who raped a woman in the year 2000 but was not convicted until 2019. There were 2,400 rape kits left to be tested, as of December 2020, and the backlog of kits dating to the 1990s were not tested until December 2021. Former Alaskan Governor Bill Walker said that testing the kits sent a message that every report mattered and no evidence would be ignored. Jason's supporters wonder, did waiting decades to test them send the message that reports *didn't matter*? They only mattered after the *#MeToo* movement drew attention to the flawed priorities of America's criminal justice system.

Jason's supporters argue that the money to test rape kits would have been available if the state was not paying 1.4. million dollars to incarcerate Jason for the next two and a half decades. The impression given is that the state of Alaska will pay any price to keep registered sex offenders safe from vigilante violence. But that same amount of money could have been used to test backlogged rape kits and potentially lead to justice for hundreds of victims of sexual assault. A system that routinely blames "lack of resources" for their decisions has chosen to prioritize one type of victim over another.

Alaska's Failure to Deter Crime

Alaska has a higher recidivism rate than any other state in this country. While other states might struggle with recidivism rates near 60% (e.g., California), or work to give effective rehabilitation programming to keep rates at a respectable 32% (e.g., Massachusetts), Alaska has the worst recidivism rate in the nation. After prisoners are released from Alaska's Department of "Corrections," 66.41% of them will return to prison within 3 years. In fact, two thirds of those recidivists return within 6 months. (If you would like to learn more about why this may be, you should read Jason Vukovich's letter in the Appendix of this book where he explains how the Alaska DOC forbids prisoners to prepare for reentry to their communities in his essay entitled "Mad Doctors").

According to FBI crime statistics in the Uniform Crime Report, while the United States saw a fairly steady decrease in violent crime from a high of 758 violent crimes per 100,000 people in 1991 to a low of 361 per 100,000 in 2014, Alaska's violent crime rate never went below 565 per 100,000 during the same time period. Between 2014 and 2019, the United States' violent crime rate never reached 400 per 100,000, but Alaska's shot up to a high of 891 per 100,000 in 2018. In other words, Alaska is one of the most violent states in the Union. In 2019 the homicide rate in Alaska was nearly double the United States average (9.4 and 5.1 per 100k, respectively).

Where Alaska truly distinguishes itself is in the crime of rape. Since 1985, Alaska has *never* had a rate of rape that was equal to or lower than the rest of the United States (6). This holds true no matter how "rape" has been defined by the Bureau of Justice Statistics or the state of Alaska. In 2018, 164.9 Alaskans out of every 100,000 reported being raped, while for the rest of the United States, the number was 44 out of every 100,000. The rate of rape is *3.75 times greater in Alaska than in the rest of the United States.* When you disaggregate the national statistics into each individual state, Alaska has the highest rate of rape in the entire country The runner-up is Arkansas, with 73.5 per 100,000; half the rate in Alaska.

Alaska's Leniency Toward Sex Offenders

In 2019, a report by the Alaska Criminal Justice Commission revealed that 46% of rape victims were Alaskan natives, 89% were women, 97% knew their assailant, and 47% were under the age of 18. The report also found that only 62.4% of reported rapes in Anchorage resulted in an arrest. Only 41% of all reports are accepted for prosecution. One study of arrest data found that 68.9% of cases resulted in a conviction, but only 28% of charges resulted in a conviction, usually due to plea bargaining (a "routine practice" in Alaska according to the Alaska Criminal Justice Commission Report of 2019, p. 19). Their explanation for using plea bargains in these cases is lack of evidence.

According to the Alaskan felony sentencing pattern report (2012–2013), the mean active time that Class A sex offenders spent in prison (for crimes like rape and sexual abuse of a minor) was 19.3 years, which seems like a long sentence even if it is shorter than the time Jason Vukovich was sentenced to prison. However, due to plea bargaining, if a defendant was initially charged with 1st Degree Sexual Abuse of a Minor, only *2.6% of cases* were disposed of at that level. 52.3% were reduced to a Sexual Abuse of a Minor-2, and their average prison sentence was 8.75 years. In addition, Class A sex offenses receive 34% of their sentence length suspended, and Class B sex offenses receive 48% of their sentence length suspended.

Outlier cases of excessive leniency are easy to locate in Alaska. Consider the 2018 scandal where Alaskan Superior Court Judge Michael Corey sentenced 24-year-old Justin Scott Schneider to serve *no jail time* after he pled guilty to kidnapping a Native American woman, choking her until she was unconscious, and masturbating on her body (7). This violent sex crime was "punished" with a residential treatment program instead of jail. After all, he had "no criminal history." ("It's not like he robbed a bank or anything" a sarcastic Alaskan resident told me). The prosecutor in this case, Andrew Grannik, said:

> I would like the gentleman to be on notice that this is his one pass. It's not really a pass, but given the conduct, one might consider that it is.

Just look at the language the court used and compare it to the public shaming and condemnation used to excoriate other offenders in the Alaskan justice system. How many defendants are called "gentleman" and given a "pass" by the prosecutor? The Alaskan Department of Law supported the judge. They said his ruling was "consistent with, and reasonable, under current sentencing laws in Alaska." The Judicial Council's executive director, Susanne DiPietro, is quoted as saying that the Judge Cory should not be condemned merely on one questionable decision, but that his entire 6-year performance as a judge should be taken into account. "When we think about our own job performances, would we like to be judged on one thing that we did on one day, or would we feel that it might be a little more fair or relevant to be judged on our complete performance?" (8). The Council stood by Cory's decision, having found that his ruling was well within the standards of Alaskan jurisprudence. Unlike vigilantism, which is an intolerable crime, strangling women and masturbating on their unconscious bodies is deemed worthy of a "pass" once in a while.

Judge Corey was up for reelection that same year, apparently unconcerned that his leniency toward violent sex offenders would hurt his chances of retaining his job, but he was wrong. An Alaskan social worker named Elizabeth Williams went to Facebook where she organized a petition to have the judge removed from office. Williams wrote: "If you are horrified by Judge Corey's brazen disregard for the victim in this case, then commit to voting NO on Judge Corey's retention."

Williams wasn't alone. Residents of Anchorage were furious. One woman said "I'm so mad, I can't see straight. I'm so angry." These angry voters might be condemned by academics for their "moral panic" and "punitive populism," but until the government finds a way to abolish democracy to protect their experiments in leniency, they will have to deal with the reality that angry Americans are motivated to vote. If court actors insist on using retributive language to justify sentencing non-sex offenders to long terms in prison they should not offer "passes" to people who commit violent sex crimes against indigenous Alaskan women.

Judge Corey lost his reelection campaign and joined a law firm as a private attorney, but he is not listed as an employee on the firm's website. Apparently, even judges can be judged "on one thing that we did on one day" just like the defendants they preside over.

This episode may serve as a warning to people who want to reform America's criminal justice systems to reduce mass incarceration. Excessive leniency to crimes that shock the conscience of society may set back the reform agenda. The outraged citizens who lacked faith in Judge Corey protested legally, through the democratic process. They shared the outrage and the lack of faith in the system that a vigilante holds, but they didn't take the law into their own hands. They just wanted a representative government that cared about their safety. Without a democratic pressure release valve, can we expect the outraged citizens to simply accept these decisions? Would they meekly accept a new moral paradigm where violent sex offenders get probation because high-information, low-salience academics want to end mass incarceration (9)? We may never be able to reduce the number of vigilante acts in our society, but we might be able to *increase* them if we eliminate democratic alternatives to violence. And, if we abolish all prisons as many academics desire, where will you send the vigilantes?

Selective Harshness

I had an interesting conversation with an anonymous supporter of Jason. She asked me "Why is the judge willing to spend over a million dollars to lock Jason up until he is too old to hit someone with a hammer, but they are not willing to lock up sex offenders until they are too old to rape children?" I wasn't sure if this was a rhetorical question because she knew I could not speak for the

Alaskan court system, but I offered a possible explanation for this perceived inconsistency. Perhaps the purpose of Jason's 28-year prison sentence was not incapacitation at all. His punishment was meant to deter other aspiring vigilantes from engaging in violence. The judge said "We do not tolerate vigilantism" and the long prison sentence was meant to scare Alaskan citizens away from similar crimes. Jason's supporter replied, "If that's true, why don't they send a message to rapists? Why do they get a second chance?"

I didn't have an answer for her, and maybe there isn't a good explanation. When prosecutors, judges, and lawmakers speak the language of retribution and deterrence they are justifying their sentencing decisions within a logical framework. "If you do *this* crime you will do *this* time. If you do a *worse* crime you will do *more* time." This is the language of an economist or a businessman. Some things cost more than others. Some crimes cost more than others. It is the foundation of sentencing guidelines and decisions based on precedent. It is supposed to tell the public what they can expect. If judges were making decisions on the basis of just deserts the sentence would be proportionate and fairly applied to everyone. The citizens of Alaska have accepted this logic and use it themselves to question why the courts make decisions that violate the rank order severity of offenses. So why do court representatives act surprised when they are criticized for violating their own logic?

This disconnect between the courts and the will of the people is important to understand because we live in a democracy where citizens can vote to recall judges, elect populist officials, and they can protest government decisions. Anyone concerned about reforming the justice system so it is more effective and humane should be wary that crimes like the sexual abuse of a child will undermine their entire reform agenda unless they address this problem up-front. Prison abolitionists and radical reformers tend to shirk these topics altogether, lest their audience panic. It doesn't seem convincing to the voters.

Thousands of Alaskan citizens and people from other states believe Jason exposed a legal system that is #1 in the rate of rape, and #1 in recidivism. They were convinced by his letter to the media offering to serve the prison sentences of four convicted child abusers, back-to-back-to-back-to-back, and mathematically showed that this was less than half the sentence he faced for armed robbery. But it wasn't just armed robbery. It was *motivated* violence. The state didn't like his motives, so they made an example out of him. They sent a message: *Do not take the law into your own hands. Trust the state… or else.*

Jason's Letters

Are these supporters wrong? Are they misunderstanding the nuances of a delicate subject that is best left to government experts? Should the system listen to "outraged" people, if they are endorsing violent crimes? I do not have any answers to these questions, but I see Jason Vukovich's case as a prime example of what we can expect in the future if we do not communicate with outraged citizens and marginalized victims of child abuse. If we want to restore faith in the legitimacy of the justice system we have a lot of work to do.

Some people will call Jason a hero without even reading the news articles. The headline is enough (10). Some people will demonize him as a violent thug who wanted to be the judge, jury, and executioner of people who had already paid their debt to society. These groups will never agree. But to you, the reader who has made it this far, you know a little about Jason Vukovich already. You've read his deepest thoughts at the end of each chapter in this book. He is the "Son of Solitude" who wrote about the brothers "Revenge and Retribution" and told his story of abuse at the hands of his stepfather. He wakes early each day in his Alaskan prison cell, drinks a cup of instant coffee (made with water from his stainless-steel sink, and one artificial sweetener), and pours his creative spirit onto the prison commissary paper that lays on his writing desk. His words are his artform, and he has a lot to say.

DISILLUSIONED BY THE ACTUAL

By Jason Vukovich

> She tore a page from the book and ripped it in half.
> Then a chapter.
> Soon, there was nothing but scraps of words littered
> between her legs and all around her...
> What good were the words?
> She said it audibly now, to the orange-lit room.
> "What good are the words?"
>
> Marcus Zusak, *The Book Thief*

> I really believe that languages are the best mirror of the human mind, and...
> a precise analysis of the significations of words would tell us more than
> anything else about the operations of our understanding.
>
> Gottfied Leibniz, *New Essays*

The power of words themselves, should be understood and revered by everyone. Words, and how we define them, literally are the blocks that make up the foundation of our reality.

It would seem quite simple to me, to design a community-oriented system of remuneration for criminal acts, with an additional focus on education, behavior advancement and healing. When aberrant behavior is displayed by someone in a community, they should embrace the individual and through a process requiring the individual to contribute directly to the community they damaged, healing and progress could begin. It seems the "penitentiaries" were rooted in religious beliefs and practices. These priests believed that sitting in a monastery, austere and isolated, being "penitent" in the presence of a Lord, was the best path to redemption. At least this is what was delivered to the masses as the means required to gain "forgiveness." However, while requiring this of the parishioners, what they knew amongst themselves, the "secret" invocation they privately utilized, was – "Laborare est Orare" – "To Work... Is to Pray..." And so, the masses continued to huddle inside cathedrals, churches, and yes- penitentiaries- and asked Invisible Guy for redemption, while the priests knew the entire time, if you wish for success, happiness, healing, progress... *you must work.*

The seeds of this old practice of redefining words, partially veiling truth, conditioning the group mind for various purposes, has led to where I sit today, in the half-light of the early morning, in an eclectic and isolated monastery of sorts, sentenced to contemplation. I should have been asked to contribute to the community I allegedly damaged. Myself, and the others I am warehoused with here, should be making daily trips to our community to build homes for the homeless, sweep sidewalks, fix roofs, shovel sidewalks, we should be gaining work skills and be exposed to humanity in its proper form. This is how we teach children... through demonstration, and by example... this is how we teach animals, through repetition and reward... and yet... we cannot bring ourselves to teach adults who need it the most, in a similar fashion.

It's interesting because in my own case, I was convicted of assault and robbery for injuring three convicted pedophiles. I was born and raised here in Alaska, and as a child, I was adopted by the monster who married my mother. I recall, after years of physical and sexual abuse, standing in a courtroom in Anchorage, this man having just plead guilty to child abuse, I was probably 12 years old... the judge sentenced him to a suspended jail sentence. 3 years specifically – *suspended* – no actual jail time to serve. My brother and I having been beaten with 2 × 4's and molested for years... Move forward 25 years or so, and I found myself in the *exact same courtroom*, being sentenced to 23 years in prison for having the audacity to assault child molesters. Now, I am a rational man, and I think in a rather linear fashion, so, prior to my case reaching sentencing, I telegraphed an offer, through the newspaper, to the prosecutor's office as follows:

"I will plead guilty to any combination of charges you wish, with the following caveat – my sentence is equal to in length, what each one of the pedophiles served for assaulting children." One of the men was convicted of raping his own daughter- he served approximately 3 years. One was convicted of molesting his own 10-month-old granddaughter – 1 year. The third was a child pornographer who served 2 years, 8 months... I offered to serve their time back-to-back-to-back: 6 years 9 months. "Run that. I'll sign the deal today." I also offered, as an added incentive, to serve the three years that the monster who "made" me never served. "Let's go 9 years, 9 months starting now!" (This offer became front page news by the way in the *Anchorage Daily News,* September 29, 2016).

Needless to point out, the prosecutor was furious. Again, how could I have the audacity to think that "justice" is meted out like that in our state? Ultimately, they disregarded all evidence related to the psychological damage resulting from my years being abused, disregarded the PTSD diagnoses related to that same abuse, and I was sentenced to nearly three times longer than all of the child abusers, *combined*! The court made it clear, that they wanted to "Send a message" to the community about vigilantism – as I stood there silently, being sentenced, the message from the court was loud and clear – and I'm certain it was to many others as well – sadly. In this state, if you abuse or molest children, we'll give you a slap on the wrist, however, if you dare to think that you can assault those who assault children... even if you are a product of that deviant behavior... we will punish you *severely*. No considerations whatsoever. This message reverberates in my life to this very day, as the D.O.C. blocks all my attempts at PTSD therapy, canceled all rehabilitation programs, and has denied us any access to higher education online.

Which brings me back to the "thought-form" that I opened this letter with – "What good are the words?"

Therapeutic Justice

My correspondence with Jason Vukovich has explored the tragic process of how childhood trauma impacted every facet of his adult life, and how our prisons and jails perpetuate that trauma with deliberate malice. He committed a serious crime and an incarceration sentence might not have been inappropriate, but a 28-year sentence would be highly questionable in any country except the United States, where "lock them up and throw away the key" has become a national anthem. His case brings together reform-minded liberals and outraged conservatives, for entirely different reasons, but still, he brought them to the same place to discuss the problem with America's obsession with retribution. I find it difficult to believe that our society could not find a better way to harness his intellect and insights for our own benefit, so instead, we buried him alive in a concrete box.

Jason wrote to me and shared these insights on vigilante motivations:

Commitment to an ideology or a cause can provide an overriding justification for unlawful acts. Punishing those who assault children is the most seductive of those causes. It places the children as a value so transcendent, that anything done on their behalf is noble, virtuous, and acceptable. This creates the wide discrepancy between 'moral order' and the regulated order of law. In this, a man comes to recognize that his belief in what is right and wrong cannot be fully reconciled with the laws of the society in which he lives. This contradictory mental state leads to costly choices with very real consequences for all of us. Each of us, ultimately will decide which of those consequences we are willing to bear.

Jason Vukovich is doing time in Alaska's prisons alongside men who shared his childhood experiences marked by abuse, neglect, or sexual assault. These broken men comprise a unique fellowship of outcasts. He calls these men "Sons of Solitude" and he knows there are many more across the world. He has written a book by that name where he tells his story in full detail, and where he encourages the victims of childhood sexual abuse to love themselves and take care of themselves. I have read a manuscript version of this book and I highly recommend it to anyone who studies the consequences of adverse childhood experiences.

Jason co-hosted a podcast within the prison called "Cliqued-Up." He and another prisoner named Anthony Garcia have interviewed the former Commissioner of the Alaska Department of Corrections, the superintendent of Spring Creek, and many of the prisoners who passed through the "Morals and Ethics" therapy program. Rather than seeing prisoners get "cliqued-up" in a gang, Jason hopes this podcast and ethics program will help prisoners plan for their return to society. This program takes listeners through the stages of grief that characterize their incarceration experience, passing from loss, to hate, to indifference, to acceptance, to learning, to teaching, and finally, to peace. At the beginning of each episode, Jason tells pieces of his own story:

Loss

Sometimes my life feels unreal. What have I done. How did I end up here. My own life now is the result of a long series of poor choices, lost opportunities, and unresolved pain. My name is Jason Vukovich. People call me Lucky.

Hate

People always say hate is a strong word, but I know what it is to hate, and really it makes you weak. It tears down everything you love, and in the end it disappears and leaves you behind to deal with the wreck you've made of your world... I came to know hate in a profound way when I was a young man. I never said it, but I hated the man who adopted me. And every time he molested or beat me with a 2 × 4 or a belt, the poison was placed deep inside of me.

It took a long time for it to develop, but when it was ready my hate came forth as violence. The funny thing is I was never a violent man. I was always a peacemaker for much of my life, but this hateful energy is so powerful and so toxic that it overrode all of my natural mannerisms, and when I gave myself over completely I ruined everything in sight.

Indifference

The best way to show you don't give a fuck is to break the law. If you don't care about yourself or anyone else, then the laws that are in place to maintain order and safety in this world go right out the window. How did we end up here? Does it matter if I care or not? This state of indifference is dangerous. It removes all responsibility. It makes me unstable, unpredictable.

Acceptance

It's not really about forgiveness. It doesn't really matter if anybody forgives me. And it doesn't matter if I forgive the ones who participated in fucking up my childhood. It's really all about acceptance. This is really the turning point. Accepting who you are. Accepting what you've become, what you've done.

Learning

When you live in a concrete shoebox and your movement is restricted to within a couple of hundred square yards, you had better be open to learning. Learning how real the results of your behavior is, is just the beginning. You're going to learn a lot of things coming through prison. This life is either a series of opportunities or a devastating lack of them. It's all up to you.

Teaching

Sharing life lessons and insight with the youngsters around here is the only thing that gives my life value. I don't wish this life for anybody. If I could go back and teach myself the hard lessons before I started hurting others and being destructive I certainly would. It's been a long winding path of poor choices and foolish behavior on my part, but I've learned a lot. So now I teach others in an informal fashion. Maybe some quick conversation while we work, maybe being a good example throughout the day. In an environment like this it's the little things that speak loudly. You can preach at somebody all day, but show him the way and he might learn something. I always say the best teachers leave footprints, easy to follow. It's never too late to change direction and leave people a track to better themselves. If I can arrive at the place where I teach others things that matter through my words and deeds, then and only then will I have achieved something.

Peace

It's hard for me to talk about a state of peace, because I've only experienced it in short moments. These times nowadays are early in the morning before work when most of the prison still sleeps. I focus on my studies and I continue to advance myself in spiritual things. It's pretty much my primary source of peace in here, and without these moments I would be lost… Peace is a state of being and I find it through spirituality. I find it by helping others, and eventually I hope to live it each day. Will I find peace? I don't know, but I see glimpses of it each day, and this is what keeps me going. Not on my own, but with my peers and fellow travelers. I may see peace.

Jason has turned his tragic life story into an opportunity to help others. He wants to help his family on the outside, his fellow prisoners on the inside, and his brothers and sisters across the world who suffered childhood sexual abuse. These are lofty goals for anyone, but Jason has a real chance of making it happen. He sits in his prison cell studying, meditating, and writing. He can make a difference. Despite everything, Jason considers himself lucky.

The Truth About Secret Captivity

By "A Son of Solitude"

I am Jason C. Vukovich, and I am the "Son of Solitude" credited for writing a number of chapters in this book. I started using that moniker some time ago, in reference to myself and other abused kids like me, because even when I am surrounded by a thousand other people, I felt alone, like a solitary tree in the desert. Sons and daughters of a painful solitude, each one of us, strong, capable of great things, yet it is so difficult for us to recognize this. Throughout the course of this book, I've peeled the planks one by one, which I had used to construct the walls around my heart, and I've laid them bare for you to see. It hasn't been any easy process for either one of us, has it? If you're holding this book, reading my words, then you must have a connection to this world. If you are a survivor of child abuse, then my spirit is standing beside you through these words, and my heart is always there for you. I will never leave you alone. Some mornings as I sat in complete isolation from the world, the tears would stream down my face as I wrote, as they are now. This is my gift to you, and in this way I honor each one of you by revealing my truth, and I wish for you to begin to nurture a new hope within you, because you are seen, and you shall have it, because nothing should stand in your way any longer. The truth about our secret captivity is that only we can now set ourselves free. All of the chains of shame and guilt and confusion and the endless sorrow must be worked free, one at a time. These things that bind us away from the world were forcibly imposed upon our consciousness, they were wrapped around our spirits, long ago. You must communicate your pain, and release your sorrow. This is very important, for even if they have never seen you, there are lights all around you. There are many who would help or intercede, there are certainly many who seek to understand our experience, but sadly, it is up to each one of us to speak, to speak loudly, and with clarity, for this world is a madhouse of distraction, and without our voices, loud and strong, all of this continues to remain beneath the surface, things continue as they always have. The Sons of Solitude remain as ghosts.

My personal experience shows that religious institutions and the legal systems currently in place, strangely, seemingly in spite of their own implied mission statements, do much to cover and suppress those who are being molested. This means that you must tell someone outside your family unit, your normal sphere of contact, about what's going on. People are not trained to see us. They have never been shown what an abused child looks like, acts like. And these religious groups, of all types, are formulated to conceal aberrant behavior. If this offends you, get over it, because it is consistently true. I and many others have lived it. I assure you, those of you with religious natures, God will never forgive that which a man does not recompense.

Stand up for a moment and reach your hand down towards your waist. Now, make your palm parallel with the floor. All of the little ones you encounter that have not yet reached that height are the future leaders and innovators of this world. And yet, sadly, those are also the little ones we unconsciously credit with being so resilient that we have allowed them to be assaulted, en masse, for many, many generations. Tools of sexual deviancy, targets for pent-up rage, byproducts of lives lived selfishly- children, the only hope for all of us, seemingly forgotten in many cases. *This. Must. End.* This is an individual responsibility, though we are all trained to summon strangers for help in every emergency situation.

We must all resolve to become first responders, certainly first reporters in a sense. Again, in my experience as a child, none of my families' friends or fellow parishioners at the church ever asked me a single question. Was I alright? Do I need help? Am I safe? These are simple, simple questions. Had they been asked, even once, I could've had a much, much different life. Instead, each day I delved deeper and deeper into myself, constantly reminded that the outside world didn't care for me, or my suffering, I wasn't wanted here. That's a lot for a growing kid to process, isn't it? These thoughts are occurring in the minds of children all around us, every day, take the time to see others outside of your circle. They deserve it. We deserve it.

As to the healing process, for those of you like me, the quickest route to healing yourself is to be found through service to others. In this way, we translate our pain into the hope that someone else so desperately needs. Find a cause that is dear to your heart, and then devote your available free time to it. This may seem a simple thing, but it is so powerful, so transformative, that I cannot recommend this strongly enough. I live in a concrete shoebox, a prison cell, and the worst of my daily torment is that the days continue to slip by and I cannot use my hands or my breath to help others. If I could only be allowed, each day, to reach out and encourage one of you, or to hug one affected child, or to speak life to one abuse survivor, I would. I would give anything to have that opportunity. Let me remind you of the value of freedom and fresh air. No matter what you feel compelled to do, you must value your own life and ability to move about and help others above all else. Use me as a lesson. For in some ways, I walked right back into the captivity I should have been freed from a long time ago, and I don't wish this on any of you.

> We are now well acquainted with Hope and Honor,
> We are finding Love and Truth.
> We are ascending the ladder, rung by rung,
> And the measure of our strength is the measure of our understanding.
> We help each other, for we know the best is yet to come!

> From My Heart
>
> To Yours,
>
> Jason Vukovich

References

1. Saha, M. (2021, Oct. 20). Hero or villain? Man used internet registry to track down and beat up pedophiles. *Truth Theory.* https://truththeory.com/jason-vukovich-used-internet-to-beat-up-pedophiles/
2. Margaritoff, M. (2021, Jan. 17). Jason Vukovich: The hammer-wielding pedophile-hunter known as the 'Alaskan Avenger.' *All That's Interesting.* https://allthatsinteresting.com/jason-vukovich-alaskan-avenger
3. Hanlon, T. (2016, Sep. 29). Anchorage man says an attacker who called himself the 'avenging angel' broke into his home and assaulted him with a hammer. *Anchorage Daily News.* https://www.adn.com/alaska-news/crime-courts/2016/07/15/anchorage-man-says-an-attacker-who-called-himself-the-avenging-angel-broke-into-his-home-and-assaulted-him-with-a-hammer/
4. Matthews, C. (2020, Oct. 30). Anchorage man who attacked sex offenders loses appeal that PTSD factored into his crimes. *Alaska's News Source.* https://www.alaskasnewssource.com/2020/10/31/anchorage-man-who-attacked-sex-offenders-loses-appeal-that-ptsd-factored-into-his-crimes/
5. Prison Policy Initiative. (2015). *Alaska profile.* https://www.prisonpolicy.org/profiles/AK.html
6. The Alaska Criminal Justice Commission. (2019, April 5). *Sex offenses: A report to the Alaska State Legislature.* https://www.ajc.state.ak.us/acjc/docs/ar/2019ACJCSexOffensesReport.pdf
7. Grove, C. (2018, Oct. 2). In Alaska, 'righteous rage' over sexual assault. *NPR.* https://www.npr.org/2018/10/02/652825497/in-alaska-righteous-rage-over-sexual-assault
8. CBS News. (2018, Sep. 24). Outrage in Alaska after judge sentences no jail time to man who pleaded guilty to felony assault. https://www.cbsnews.com/news/anchorage-alaska-justin-schneider-sentence-judge-michael-corey-recall-campaign/
9. Cordova, G. (2019, Jun. 27). Former judge Michael Corey is back practicing law, now as an attorney. *Alaska News Source.* https://www.alaskasnewssource.com/content/news/Controversial-former-judge-gets-a-new-job-as-a-lawyer-in-Anchorage-511907812.html
10. Hanlon, T. (2016, Sep. 29). Anchorage man charged with attacking sex offenders seeks plea deal. *Anchorage Daily News.* https://www.adn.com/alaska-news/crime-courts/2016/09/28/alaska-man-charged-with-assaulting-3-registered-sex-offenders-proposes-plea-deal-in-letter-from-jail/

CONCLUDING THOUGHTS

Justice or Revenge?

While I was putting the finishing touches on this book, a new "vigilante" crime made the headlines. This case is still being investigated, so the information is alleged and no convictions have been determined in a court of law. A man was arrested for lewd and lascivious acts against a child. He was released from jail and placed on supervision in the community. The victim's family was outraged. One of these relatives was a former UFC fighter named Cain Velasquez. Allegedly, Velasquez tracked down the alleged sex abuser and shot at him with a handgun, hitting another man instead. Velasquez is facing attempted murder charges. Some members of the public immediately responded with proclamations of support for Velasquez, saying they would have done worse if they had the chance (1). The immensely popular podcaster, Joe Rogan, weighed in saying "You could only imagine the rage, the fucking rage that must have been going through that man's mind. I mean, my only wish is that he did it with his hands. My only wish is that he just ran that car off the road, pulled that guy out of the fucking car, and beat him to death. Fuck you" (2). I couldn't have summarized the phenomenon of vigilante support more succinctly than that. *Why? Fuck you. That's why.*

These cultural attitudes are not limited to the United States. It was beyond the scope of this book to make international comparisons. News stories out of Mexico report organized vigilante groups who fight back against drug cartels, but occasionally these citizen "self-defense" groups police their neighborhoods for other crimes. Video recordings have been posted to the internet that depict brutal beatings, immolations, and crucifixions of suspected child sex abusers. These crimes are not committed in the dark. They happen in broad daylight in the middle of crowded streets. This is not a new phenomenon either. A famous case in 2002 involved an accused child sex abuser who fled the United States to Mexico for safety, but three years later he was found beaten into a coma and impaled on a cactus in the desert (3–5).

A study of anti-pedophile vigilantism/activism in the United Kingdom would be worthy of its own book. Massive scandals in government and the media have created a firestorm of activism in that country, including the recent vandalism of a statue at the BBC headquarters that was designed by a notorious pedophile named Eric Gill. The statue is of a man touching a naked child. In another case, a British prisoner named Richard Huckle was tortured and brutally murdered by another prisoner named Paul Fitzgerald. Huckle was called "Britain's worst pedophile" because

DOI: 10.4324/9781003393849-12

he traveled to Cambodia and Malaysia to sexually abuse hundreds of children and produce child sex exploitation material that he sold on the Dark Web. When he was finally apprehended and sent to prison in England, he was killed by Fitzgerald for reasons that will sound familiar: "poetic justice" to make him "feel what all those children felt."

Occasionally there are murders in the community as well. A mother named Sarah Sands learned that her son had been molested by a 77-year-old neighbor who had been convicted of 24 sex offenses over the previous three decades. She went to the perpetrator's house and stabbed him to death. She said "I'd never kill again. I don't see myself as a murderer, but I don't regret what I did. I was a mom desperate to protect my children." Time will tell if this growing lack of faith in national institutions will result in an increasing number of UK citizens taking the law into their own hands, but there is certainly enough material for researchers to explore (6–8).

The vigilante spirit might exist across the world and reside deep in our offspring-preserving genetic roots, but the number of people who take the law into their own hands are a miniscule proportion of the population. These cases are more interesting than other types of crime, so they appear to be more common than they really are. There are over 900,000 people on sex offender registries in the United States, and if my estimate of 2 homicides per year is accurate, they are actually safer from homicide than non-sex offenders in American society. Andrew Vachss rightly scoffed when his fictional characters were called vigilantes. He wrote "If I went around snuffing baby-rapers, I'd be on overtime- the city's full of them" (9).

I had several assumptions about vigilante behavior and their motives when I began this research project. I was mostly wrong. Sure, there are people who target and kill child sex abusers for readily understood reasons, but there are many situational factors that were not so obvious. The headlines and news articles barely scratch the surface. Hours of interrogation and surveillance footage were unable to reveal the true thoughts and motives of these vigilantes. It took months of correspondence, phone calls, and visits with open-ended questions to sound the depths of their personalities and rationale.

Perhaps this investigation into the "mind of a vigilante" was actually a Rorschach test for the rest of us. We can't draw inferences about vigilantism from such a small sample of different men, but we can learn a lot about the moral values and priorities of the rest of our society when we exhibit differential responses to their crimes. When Steven Sandison told the detectives "You arrest people all the time for stuff you wish you could shoot them in the face," one of them responded by chuckling and nodding his head. Child sex abuse crimes seem to be activating an override switch that changes people's normal responses to violent behavior.

We like to believe that we have invented bureaucratic systems and procedures that have eliminated the need for primal revenge fantasies, but we are fooling ourselves. Retribution is still a desire that persists in the emotional instincts of human beings, and sometimes that desire will be strong enough to motivate an aggrieved person to commit a violent crime no matter what the consequences are. Perhaps these stories of child sex abuse are awakening some ancient memory in our species' distant past, when primates lashed out at perceived threats to their offspring - before mankind evolved to such a refined level of civilization that they invented the plea bargain. Reformers may have a naïve optimism that they can re-educate the American public into abandoning these revenge-fantasies, but they are correct in a limited sense. Our affection should be overruled by reason. If we want to prevent child sex abuse crimes we should direct our energy toward the most effective interventions, not necessarily the methods that are most emotionally satisfying. That means each person needs to examine their thoughts, beliefs, and attitudes critically before they trust their own judgment.

Vigilante violence hurts our society in many ways. It certainly hurts the victim, but many people can write them off as deserving their fate. It hurts the vigilante as well, but their official punishments are the consequences for their crimes. If the dangers stopped there, we might be able to call it a wash, but this kind of violence has many other consequences beyond the vigilante and his victim. Falsely accused and convicted people may be killed. Bystanders (such as Gretchen Parker) are in danger. The family members of both the vigilante and child abuser may suffer emotional distress. Society pays a cost through emergency services and criminal justice system expenses. Vigilante objectives might also be set back. If they really want to ostracize sex offenders, their violence may inadvertently inspire compassion and protection. There is no surer way to abolish sex offender registries than the argument that these systems place the registrants in danger (certainly nobody seems to care about registries lack of effectiveness) (10). There is also the ongoing cost to the reputation of the justice system. Vigilante messages amplify outrage against a legal system that is rife with examples of absurd leniency. This focus distracts us from the preponderance of cases that were unfair because they were too harsh. Vigilante actions may also re-direct people's righteous rage into unhelpful avenues and dissuade them from the hard work of democratic legislative reform: the only reform that will have long-lasting impacts for victims. The only people who seem to "win" after a vigilante crime are a few victims who feel as though their anger was validated. My heart goes out to those people who wrote letters of support to Steven Sandison, telling him that his homicidal behavior was a comfort to them in their grief. It is sad to think that no other methods of validation were available to these neglected people.

We will probably never eliminate these problems in our society. Child sex abuse crimes will continue to happen, the justice system will fail to punish the perpetrators in a manner that satisfies everyone, and very rarely, someone will take the law into their own hands to make up the difference. It seems inevitable. But perhaps I can offer some recommendations that would help improve outcomes for specific individuals along this path. I am not naïve about these recommendations. It's easy to say "fix the system." It is much more difficult to map out a real plan for change.

Helping Victims

Prevention is the key. The more child sex abuse crimes we can prevent, the better off everyone will be. This means a continuation of the good work that has happened over the past few decades in this regard. David Finkelhor at the University of New Hampshire studies trends in child sex abuse crimes, and he sees plenty of room for optimism. There was a 62% decrease in the rate of child sexual abuse crimes reported between 1990 and 2018 (11). There were still an estimated 62,000 child sex abuse crimes reported to children's services agencies, and these reports are only a fraction of the true number of cases that occur, but this is evidence of a decline. Perhaps mandatory abuse reporting systems, education, social movements, and trauma-informed care has helped move us in the right direction. This is something to be proud of. Is it enough? No. We still need to do more, but we should acknowledge that the landscape of child sex abuse attitudes and official resources in our society has improved substantially since the days when Steven Sandison, Clark Fredericks, Patrick Drum, Joseph Druce, Scottie Allen, and Jason Vukovich were children. There is more work to do, but there are people who are stepping up to the plate to continue this important work.

When these crimes do occur, we need to focus our attention on the child victim. They need support. They need legal representation in court. Not volunteers or legal substitutes. A vulnerable population who cannot represent themselves, cannot pay for assistance, and cannot vote should not be without paid legal counsel. Offenders are entitled to legal aid. Why not their victims? We shouldn't have to rely on amateur volunteers to provide these services. As noble as their intentions are, saving children should be the highest priority of our *government* and not left to part-time volunteers. You can learn more about this need at LDICP.org (Legislative Drafting Institute for Child Protection).

Child Advocacy Centers can help present recorded testimony in court so the child does not have to suffer the humiliation and terror of a cross-examination. Therapy resources are available, and many ineffective treatment modalities are being replaced with evidence-based models of care. There has also been an increase in the availability of financial and legal resources through state and federal funds. Again, we have a positive trend. One that will help victims cope, overcome, and thrive instead of falling into the worst pits of despair.

The vigilantes profiled in this book who were free at the time of their crimes believed their lives had little meaning. Suicidal, reckless, aimless lives. Clark Fredericks said "I didn't care if I lived or died." Maybe giving victims of sexual abuse *something* to live for would direct their energies away from violence. Whose responsibility is this? I don't believe "Society" can solve every individual problem, but we can increase the probability that they will succeed if we tear down obstacles and make the resources available. At the very least our system should *do no harm*.

Worst-case scenarios will happen. When children are abused and they turn to drugs, alcohol, and risky lifestyles to escape their nightmarish lives they can end up in the juvenile justice system or the adult justice system. This is where a lot of work needs to be done. Therapeutic jurisprudence must be the cornerstone of justice system reforms. With so many incarcerated people suffering from PTSD, mental illness, and substance abuse issues related to their childhood sexual abuse, we need to stop thinking we can merely punish traumatized people into law-abiding behavior. They accumulate "prior criminal history" points and end up serving longer sentences than the people who abused them. This is the moment when a vigilante looks like a hero and the criminal justice system looks like the bad guys. We have to stop processing people through an ineffective and cruel justice system just because "it's what we've always done."

In 1982, Andrew Vachss gave a speech for the Office of Juvenile Justice and Delinquency Prevention that described his experiences working with serious, violent, habitual offenders. He said: "I have never seen one of these kids that hasn't been within our child protective and child–caring system for years and years before the juvenile justice profession is asked to 'intervene.' We have to create the beast. It cannot be born whole" (12). His scathing critique of the compartmentalized justice system focused on how failed child protection agencies led to failed social services programs, which led to failed juvenile justice intervention, which predictably led to adult prisons. A path that left enormous collateral damage down the line. A "rape-to-prison pipeline" if you will. You may dismiss this 40-year-old criticism as out of date. Surely our modern systems are much improved. But we are reaping a slow harvest. The adults who commit violent crime today passed through the systems that Vachss was describing.

What about the institutions that are meant to "rehabilitate" troubled youth? Like Jon Watson's upbringing in the gladiator school called the California Youth Authority, Steven Sandison's repeated stints in Michigan's juvenile detention centers, and Joseph Druce's boarding school where the seminary instructors raped children. The "happiest days" of Scottie Allen's life were in Florida's boarding schools, where he learned how to be an effective killer. Despite the euphemistic labels of "training centers" rather than prisons, it was obvious why those kids were locked up. They weren't there for their own good. They saw through that lie immediately. They were being punished for their bad behavior. They were there to suffer.

These delinquents didn't learn how to be pro-social members of society in those institutions, but they did learn the true religion of America's justice system: *Retribution.* The blood-lust of our retributive system demands that crimes be certainly and severely punished, even if that punishment is ineffective as a deterrent. *Vandalizing cars? You need to suffer. Using drugs to cope with trauma? You need to suffer. Shoplifting from a mega-corporation? You need to suffer.* The currency by which people "pay their debt to society" is punishment, and when some people pay more for one crime than another it says something about the priorities of the punisher. When those kids left their respective institutions, they decided to live by the code of their oppressors. They may not follow the laws of man, but they are true believers in the ancient law of revenge. The villainy we teach them, they will execute, and they will better the instruction. If you do not want people to think in terms of retribution and the rank order severity of offenses, then you should not use that rationale as the foundation of a "just" society. As Andrew Vachss and Yitzhak Bakal wrote:

> Ironically, when punishment is seen as nothing more than revenge, it finds its strongest endorsement among those who are most likely to suffer from it (13).

Recalibrating Just Deserts

What should be done with the child sex abusers who started all of this? Certainly, there are differing opinions on the subject. Sex offender punishments have increased over the past few decades, so it would appear that the pro-punishment activists are having an impact (14). On the other hand, evidence shows that re-arrest rates for sex offenders are low, and increasing supervision, residency requirements, and registries may increase their involvement in non-sex crimes. Reformers are advocating for a softer and gentler approach. Some want to replace punishment with restorative justice circles where the child can receive an apology from their abuser, instead of retribution (15). While these issues are debated in ivory towers, the legal system continues to use community supervision and incarceration as their primary correctional responses. Increasing the severity of punishment might not have a good long-term effect on crime from a cost-benefit perspective, but it is the currency of our retributive system. As long as drug offenders and property offenders lose their liberty in order to "teach them a lesson," the public will probably use that same logic to demand that sex offenders pay in the same coin. Reformers might have to put sex offenders at the back of the line when it comes to implementing merciful policies; otherwise, they risk alienating a large proportion of society who fear for their children's safety. Scolding them as "moral panickers" or "puritans" hasn't changed their minds yet. I encourage academic reformers to show respect for abuse victims and concerned members of the public rather than condemning them en masse as low-information, high-salience rubes.

I understand why people want sex offenders to be incapacitated for long periods of time "just to make sure," but that is unfeasible from a logistic standpoint. Even the toughest law enforcement officials recognize that we need plea bargains to overcome evidence problems and to stop the courts from being clogged up. A conviction with a relatively short sentence is preferable to an acquittal because it allows us to protect the victim and require treatment and supervision for the offender. The key here is making sure that the rank order of severity in punishment is not violated. If someone gets 5 years for drug possession and a sex offender gets 2 years for traumatizing a child it is going to breed resentment. You may not be able to increase the punishment level for sex crimes to where you want it, but you could reduce the drug possession sentence to a reasonable punishment that properly acknowledges the rank severity of harm inflicted by each crime.

Sex offenses are serious crimes and should be taken seriously, even within the context of a broad and ambitious reform agenda (16, 17).

Egregiously lenient sentences for sex offenders cast a long shadow on the entire justice system. On the other hand, tough, inflexible, mandatory-minimum laws have ruined the lives of tens of thousands of people unnecessarily. If you really want to prevent those devastating laws from being adopted you should endorse sensible legislation for sex offenses. There should no longer be any "passes" for sex offenders that are not available for less serious crimes, especially if these generous offers are based on the height, wealth, demeanor, or political connections of the offender. Judges and District Attorneys who endorse lenient sentences might be setting themselves up for a democratic revolt. While some people would like nothing more than to shield government employees from the public's wrath, we currently live in a democracy and the people can still vote on these issues. I recommend that court actors start thinking about the consequences of their experiments in leniency. Not all outraged citizens become vigilantes. Some gather signatures on petitions, and that may be the only thing that truly scares government employees. I predict that these sweetheart deals for sex offenders will utterly ruin liberal reform efforts for other crimes by eroding the public's faith in the legal system. The false alarms over "penal populism" may turn into real populism someday if the people are forced to endure another Jeffrey Epstein scandal.

Correcting Corrections

Even if sex offenders are sent to prison, we do not need to harass and torture them to get revenge. Our prisons do not need to be dungeons. Even sex offenders should be given a basic standard of living in a secure environment with human dignity and a safe opportunity for rehabilitation. If they spend all of their time in their cells because they fear being assaulted they cannot participate in rehabilitative programming, and will therefore return to society at a higher risk of reoffending. Those who want to reduce future incidents of child sex abuse should consider the impact that prison violence has on program participation.

If you have complete contempt for the suffering of child sex abusers, then at least consider that the danger they face is a consideration in judicial sentencing. How many sex offenders received probation sentences because the judge didn't want them to be tortured in prison? Maybe the judge who gave a lenient sentence to "the Du Pont heir" knew about the convict justice phenomenon, and she did not want to be party to a gruesome slaying. Lenient sentences may be an unintended consequence, and not the cause, of vigilante violence.

There are several practical ways to stop prisoners from killing "Cho-Mos." The first would be to separate sex offenders from the rest of the prison population. Not just by putting them in protective custody, but by sending them to entirely separate facilities where they can seek specialized treatment away from the men who despise them. At this point, anything less is deliberate indifference. The sex offenders would be safer, and the other prisoners would not have to tolerate them. Gangs could not exploit them for power and resources. Everyone wins.

Another necessary improvement would be changing the behaviors of custodial staff to ensure that they do not aid or facilitate these attacks as part of their own shadow vigilantism. A third option is to actually make our prisons humane institutions where rehabilitation and a hope for a better life are possible. If prisoners had something constructive to do with their time, they might not need an anti-social prison subculture to give them meaning. Our warehouse prisons are a waste of time and money, and they brutalize prisoners who already have enough problems.

We have more people serving life sentences in America today than the total number of prisoners in the entire system in 1970 (18). Most of the prisoners in this book who killed child sex abusers in correctional facilities were serving life sentences or very long sentences. They had nothing to lose. If there was a glimmer of hope they might live a few years of freedom in their old age they might have an incentive to refrain from murder. When men have nothing to lose, how can you deter them into good behavior? The only punishment is a loss of privileges or placement in restrictive housing. Cages within cages within cages. Prison officials are presiding over hopeless men, and they threaten to take away their books and art supplies. It is a bleak view of human nature for people who supposedly believe they can "correct" someone.

Maybe people serving life sentences should have some path to redemption and freedom: something to look forward to and strive toward. But that is not how our prisons operate. These men will "live" in a concrete box until they are 80, 90, or whenever. They have *nothing to lose and nothing to gain*. But maybe if they kill another "Cho-Mo" they can get a viral YouTube video and some fan mail. It is a perverse incentive structure.

What should the punishment be for vigilantes who committed their crimes in the community? The current judicial response is typical: arrest them and give them life in prison to "send a message that vigilantism won't be tolerated." Of course, murder, attempted murder, aggravated assault, and simple assault crimes will be given their due consideration in court and punished accordingly, but if prison reformers can find it in their heart to sympathize with child sex abusers, maybe traumatized vigilantes are worth considering as well.

Reforming Justice

I suggest that we try to determine how these men can serve some public good related to their offenses. Clark Fredericks is a free man. Look at how he has succeeded beyond any reasonable expectation. He has written a book about his life and travels the country helping others. He advises state legislators on how to help victims report their abuse. He is an enormous asset to society. If he were rotting in prison he would just be costing taxpayers millions of dollars in lifetime custody expenses.

Jason Vukovich is making the most of his time in prison with extremely limited resources. He gives hope to the hopeless by leading prisoners through morals and ethics training. He even teaches men how to wear a necktie so they can get a job when they are released. He will not see freedom for a long time, but he wants to help other people on their way out the door. Maybe men like Clark and Jason can be the best advocates for non-violent behavior and therapeutic growth.

Jason Vukovich is serving a 28-year sentence and will probably live to see freedom, perhaps sooner than his expected release date of 2041. He is seen as a hero among anti-pedophile vigilante supporters, so his message can have a profound impact on this group of people and draw attention to the elephant in the room- the traumatic childhoods of America's prisoners. Jason has a lot to offer the world, and his sentencing statement from 2021 is the perfect conclusion to this book:

I began my life sentence many, many years ago, it was handed down to me by an ignorant, hateful, poor substitute for a father. I now face losing most of the rest of my life due to a decision to lash out at people like him. To all those who have suffered like I have, love yourself and those around you, this is truly the only way forward.

Jason Vukovich, January 17, 2021

References

1. Gaydos, R. (2022, March 2). Ex-UFC star Cain Velasquez shot at man who allegedly abused fighter's relative, police say. *Fox News*. https://www.foxnews.com/sports/ufc-cain-velasquez-shot-man-allegedly-abused-relative-police

2. MMA Fighting Newswire. (2022, March 6). Joe Rogan, Colby Covington declare support for Cain Velasquez: 'You could only imagine the rage.' https://www.mmafighting.com/2022/3/6/22963941/joe-rogan-colby-covington-declare-support-for-cain-velasquez-you-could-only-imagine-the-rage

3. Ibbetson, R. (2020, January 13). Lynch mob burns 'paedophile' alive after he was accused of raping and killing a six-year-old girl in Mexico. *Daily Mail*. https://www.dailymail.co.uk/video/mexico/video-2087194/Video-Mexican-paedophile-tied-beaten-set-fire.html

4. Nsubuga, J. (2016, June 12). Alleged paedophile kicked to death by group of vigilantes. *Metro*. https://metro.co.uk/2016/06/12/alleged-paedophile-kicked-to-death-by-group-of-vigilantes-5939067/

5. Biggs, P. (2020, July 2). Accused child molester impaled on a cactus. *The Arizona Republic*.

6. Waterson, J. (2022, January 12). Man uses hammer to attack statue on front of BBC Broadcasting House. *The Guardian*. https://www.theguardian.com/media/2022/jan/12/man-uses-hammer-to-attack-statue-on-front-of-bbc-broadcasting-house

7. Bruno, G. (2020, November 19). 'Poetic justice': Jury hears Richard Huckle, the man named 'Britain's worst paedophile', tortured and killed in prison. *7 News*. https://7news.com.au/news/crime/poetic-justice-jury-hears-richard-huckle-the-man-named-britains-worst-pedophile-tortured-and-killed-in-prison-c-1616114

8. Steinbuch, Y. (2021, July 26). UK mom says she killed pedophile neighbor because he preyed on her son. *New York Post*. https://nypost.com/2021/07/26/uk-mom-reveals-real-reason-she-killed-pedophile-neighbor/

9. Vachss, A. (1991). *Sacrifice*. New York, NY: Vintage Crime/Black Lizard.

10. Rydberg, J., Dum, C. P., & Socia, K. (2018). Nobody gives a #%&!: A factorial survey examining the effect of criminological evidence on opposition to sex offender residence restrictions. *Journal of Experimental Criminology, 14*(4), 541–550.

11. Finkelhor, D., Saito, K., & Jones, L. (2020, February). *Updating trends in child maltreatment, 2018*. Crimes Against Children Research Center. https://www.unh.edu/ccrc/resource-category/2019

12. Vachss, A. H. (1983). Who is the serious, violent, habitual offender? *New Designs*. http://www.vachss.com/av_dispatches/lifestyle.html

13. Vachss, A. H., & Bakal, Y. (1979). *The life-style violent juvenile*. Lexington, MA: Lexington Books.

14. Cochran, J. C., Toman, E. L., Shields, R. T., & Mears, D. P. (2021). A uniquely punitive turn? Sex offenders and the persistence of punitive sanctioning. *Journal of Research in Crime and Delinquency, 58*(1), 74–118. https://doi.org/10.1177/0022427820941172.

15. McAlinden, A. M. (2017). Restorative justice and sex offending. In T. Sanders (Ed.), *The Oxford handbook of sex offences and sex offenders*. New York, NY: Oxford Handbooks, pp. 437–460.

16. Petersilia, J., & Cullen, F. T. (2014). Liberal but not stupid: Meeting the promise of downsizing prisons. *Stanford Journal of Criminal Law and Policy, 2*(1), 1–43.

17. Austin, D., Eisen, L.-B., Cullen, J., & Frank, J. (2016). *How many Americans are unnecessarily incarcerated?* New York, NY: Brennan Center for Justice: Twenty Years.

18. McGhee, J. (2021, February 25). Over 200,000 people are serving life in U.S. prisons. These are the consequences. *Injustice Watch*. https://www.injusticewatch.org/news/prisons-and-jails/2021/sentencing-project-report-life-imprisonment/

APPENDIX A

The Interrogation of Steven D. Sandison

Detective: Okay, like I said, we're investigating the incident that happened last night that you were involved in. Why don't you just go ahead and tell us what happened.

Sandison: Alright. I've been locking with Ted for about two months. Never asked him what his crime was. Never really cared. We got along okay. I never had any real problems, and then, like two days ago, somebody said that he was in prison for CSC, so I asked him about it, and he kind of never answered me. Then last night about nine o'clock at night I guess he decided to clear his conscience or something, but you know he told me what he was in prison for, that he had you know, was accused of raping an 11-year-old girl, and he got 25 to life for it, and you know I told him that's enough. I don't want to hear anymore, but he just for some reason kept talking and kept talking, and then I really don't have any patience for that kind of thing. I asked him three or four times just let it go, I don't want to hear about it. He didn't, so about eleven or twelve o'clock, somewhere around there I first, you know, punched him a couple of times. Still wouldn't shut up. Still kept telling me he wanted to explain that he didn't do it, that he was being set up and all this stuff. I don't know I just got mad and then hit him, and then I killed him. When I knocked, I hit him and knocked him out and then I took the shoelaces out of his shoes, tied them together, wrapped it around his neck, and strangled him. Then after I was done … I mean I was aware of what I was doing. You know and then I just put him on his bed and covered him up and climbed in my bed and went to sleep.

Detective: How did this come to the point of being reported? How did the staff become aware?

Sandison: Um. I mean I was gonna do it that night. Say something to the officers making their rounds, but I don't know. I was kinda tired and I didn't want to have to go through all the B.S. so I figured I'd wait 'til morning shift came in because I got along better with a few of the officers there. So that's what I did. I wanted 'til morning shift and the first time that they came on they broke our door for chow and I went down and told mister _____ what I had done and he put me in the room and then here I am.

Detective: Okay. Now evidently you and Ted had been bunkies for several months. Have you had any other kind of disagreements? You got along good? He was a good bunkie?

Sandison: Yeah.

Detective: You've been in the system for a while.

Sandison: Most of my life.

Detective: Obviously you've had bunkies that were not good.

Sandison: Actually, he's like my first bunkie.

Detective: Okay.

Sandison: I've never, you know, I made it clear that I didn't like locking with bunkies so usually in the past so they kind of kept me to a cell by myself.

Detective: So, this was kind of a new experience for you, having a bunkie. And in your opinion it was going okay.

Sandison: Sure. Yeah.

Detective: And then for whatever reason Ted felt it was necessary to declare his heart and you happened to the pair of ears that he decided to confess to or try to clear his mind.

Sandison: Yes.

Detective: Okay. So, he keeps going on about his personal business: what brought him there, what he did, like you say, he's alleging that it didn't happen and he's been framed and all of that. And I'm sure that having been in this system as long as you have you hear that all the time. You know, and to be honest I'm kind of a firm believer that if you're here and you've gone through the legal system, it's been proven beyond a reasonable doubt that the crime was committed and you're here.

Sandison: Yes. And I also know that you know getting 25 years for something like that it must have been extremely bad. Because most of the time people with CSC get really easy cases. You guys know that. There's no reason for us to talk about it. I was going to try to get moved tomorrow because I said I had heard about it, and you know, if I don't see it I don't believe it. Because everybody spreads rumors about everybody else in prison. So I confronted him about it and at first he said no. Then I left it at that. Then like I said last night, I don't know, out of the blue said he wanted to talk to me and you know told me everything. "I got 25-to-life," "11-years old" just a bunch ….

Detective: Things that you just didn't want to hear.

Sandison: Yeah. And I kept asking him you know, I don't want to hear it. And it just I don't know it just seemed to irritate me more and more, even when he didn't say anything. I think him denying it is what irritated me the most.

Detective: Okay. Now you mentioned that you punched him a couple of times yeah. Where did you strike him at?

Sandison: Just in the jaw. He's a little bit bigger than me. He's talking about he had all this military background and so you know, I was a little intimidated, but ….

Detective: Okay. Did you injure yourself? Do you have any kind of marks on your hands?

Sandison: Not really.

Detective: Okay. So you struck him in the face area. Okay. Did you see if there was any kind of injury? Did you give him a fat lip? A black eye? A nosebleed?

Sandison: I didn't really pay attention.

Detective:	So that didn't seem to stop him from continuing on?
Sandison:	No. It's just. I mean at that point he just became kind of ... I don't know I mean, I don't know if you'd say passive, but he just started trying to explain more that you know what had happened and what didn't happen, and the more he just tried to explain himself out of it the more mad I got.
Detective:	And I would have thought that you getting physical, punching him, he would have probably gotten the idea that you really didn't want to talk about this.
Sandison:	Yeah.
Detective:	And he continued?
Sandison:	Yeah, he continued.
Detective:	Okay. How many times do you think that you punched him?
Sandison:	Maybe once. Twice.
Detective:	Maybe once or twice. And at some point, evidently, you hit him hard enough to knock him down or knock him out. Where do you think that you struck him that time?
Sandison:	Probably caught him on a good shot on the chin.
Detective:	On the chin. So he went down and now he's on the floor. Do you recall how he was laying on the floor? Side? Back? Face up? Face Down?
Sandison:	No. I don't recall.
Detective:	And then you said that you choked him. Choked him out. I believe is that.
Sandison:	I didn't choke him out ... I took the shoe laces out of his shoes and I made a decision that this was gonna end now, so ....
Detective:	So I guess then I must have just misunderstood you. I thought you said that after you punched him he was down that you choked him prior to using his shoe laces.
Sandison:	No. I just took the shoe laces out ....
Detective:	They were out of his shoes?
Sandison:	Mm-hmm.
Detective:	Okay. So you took the shoe laces out. Um. Obviously you wrapped them around his neck. Just once?
Sandison:	Wrapped them around my hands, tied the two together. There were two shoelaces together. I tied the ends together. Wrapped it around a hand put it around his neck and held it.
Detective:	How long do you think you had to hold it before you were confident that he was ....
Sandison:	Actually, a long time.
Detective:	Long time being two minutes? Five minutes?
Sandison:	I don't know. But it just seemed like a long time.
Detective:	Okay. I imagine that probably your time recollection would probably not be accurate because I'm sure ....
Sandison:	They feel like a long time.
Detective:	... you know, a little little tense a little hyped, had the adrenaline going, so ... you will end up you're confident that he is now deceased. You pick him up and you said you put him back in his bunk.
Sandison:	Put him in the bed and faced him toward the wall so that it looked like he was sleeping.
Detective:	So he was sleeping. Covered him up.
Sandison:	Covered him up.

Detective: Okay. Do you recall what he was wearing?

Sandison: Not really. It was around bedtime so either probably long-johns and a t-shirt, that's usually what we sleep in, or pajamas, might then, I don't particularly remember.

Detective: Now you can recall like what time do you think this happened?

Sandison: I don't know. It wasn't that late. At first I thought it was around two, but now the more I thought about, earlier I said like two, right? Then the more I thought about it it was probably more like around, I don't know, I know it was past ten because they had made their last, their first round, third shift.

Detective: They being the third shift?

Sandison: Yeah so I know it was there so I don't know, between 10 and 12. Somewhere around there.

Detective: Now it's my understanding that at two they go through and do their count.

Sandison: Mm-hmm.

Detective: How elaborate is the count? What do they do? Do they open the cell, poke you say "how are you doing?"

Sandison: No, they just look in and walk by. Turn on the count light. Look in and walk by.

Detective: Do you remember that occurring or were you sleeping?

Sandison: No, I remember. I was up.

Detective: And by this time Ted was already ….

Sandison: Yeah, he was dead.

Detective: He was dead. Okay. So … you mentioned that you know, you realized that if you call the staff right then we're gonna swat that beehive. So you made that determination to ….

Sandison: Wait 'til the morning so I went to sleep.

Detective: I know, we obviously we've been in your cell that it appears that all of your belongings you ….

Sandison: Packed up.

Detective: Okay, well when did you do that?

Sandison: Mmmm … right after I knew he was dead.

Detective: Right after you knew. So the reason for doing that would be …?

Sandison: Because when you go to the hole that's usually what the police do. They pack it up, and I figured they're gonna tear my shit up so, might as well do it myself.

Detective: So ultimately you knew that there were some rough times coming for you here and you were probably going to be moved from that cell, segregation or whatever.

Sandison: Yeah.

Detective: So you packed up your belongings. Went to sleep that night. Got up. What time did they do breakfast chow?

Sandison: Early in the morning. Little after, between six and seven. Shift change at six so between six and seven.

Detective: Six and seven. So you were allowed out of your cell.

Sandison: Yeah, in fact I woke up right when they opened my door.

Detective: Okay. And you got up and you went to chow.

Sandison: Yes. I walked down to the chow hall. I went in. Um … said my goodbyes to a few people. And then went to Officer _____ and told him that I killed my bunkie. And he kinda laughed and, cause I didn't have I never had any problems with anybody.

So I guess he thought I was playing or something and I said well no, I'm serious, and then he put me in that room.

Detective: Okay. Now it wouldn't be unusual, would the staff think it odd that Ted didn't get up for breakfast?

Sandison: Not really. Not really a lot of people you know he usually goes to breakfast every morning so I mean, gotta remember that I'm on a rock that … let me see … what, what is it kind of like kind of like the troublemaker's rock, so people are always yelling a lot at night, and you know saying, the sometimes you know he's missed one or two times before.

Detective: But it wouldn't be something that in your opinion would alarm the staff to make them come and find out why Ted didn't come to breakfast.

Sandison: No.

Detective: So they wouldn't have on their own, found him until probably later.

Sandison: I mean … I mean I think they probably would noticed that he wasn't up and about, cause morning shift is pretty, you know, when they take their counts they gotta see movement so ….

Detective: So, when they do their count they would have realized.

Sandison: They want movement.

Detective: And you're aware of that. It wasn't like you're gonna be able to keep him hidden.

Sandison: No.

Detective: So you came right out went right out to Mr. _____, announced to him I killed by bunkie.

Sandison: Yeah.

Detective: First, obviously I think most anybody would look at you and say "yeah right."

Sandison: Yeah.

Detective: But you were persistent enough that he then did what?

Sandison: I told him I really did this and he looked at me, and he said okay, well I'm gonna have to put you in this cell. He put me in the observation cell. He went to the bubble, then he went and checked, then they locked the unit down.

Detective: Now it's my understanding that at some point you gave somebody some shoe laces?

Sandison: Yeah, I was in the observation cell and my shoelaces were in and I'm thinking Jesus Christ they're probably gonna kick my ass for having these, you know, I didn't want to sometimes because an officer just got stabbed a little while ago too, so pretty bad, so they're all one edge, you know, so I was kinda worried I better take these out real quick before they think I'm using it on them or something.

Detective: But normally you're allowed to have shoelaces?

Sandison: Yeah.

Detective: But because under the circumstances you're put in the bubble, or not in the bubble the observation cell, you took your shoelaces out of your shoes, I noticed you do not have shoelaces on now, and those are the shoelaces that you provided to the staff.

Sandison: Yes.

Detective: What happened to the shoelaces ….

Sandison: Flushed 'em down the toilet.

Detective: Okay. Now those laces came out of Ted's shoes.

Sandison: Mm-hmm. Yep.

Detective:	And then when you were done you flushed 'em down the toilet.
Sandison:	Mm-mmm.
Detective:	And why would you do that?
Sandison:	Because I'm an idiot. I don't know. I mean, obviously I don't think right. I'm in prison for most of my life. My thinking isn't really rational. I don't know I just kind of ….
Detective:	Thought that that was the appropriate thing to do at that time?
Sandison:	Yeah. I guess, I don't know, I just ….
Detective:	Like you've already said, you knew at this point that Ted was deceased ….
Sandison:	I knew it.
Detective:	Yeah. You know. I guess … you're, never having been in that kind of a situation myself I mean you know and sort of not gonna make judgment to why you did certain things, but you know yeah, I'm you thought so far out it was best to wash, flush the shoelaces and that's where they went. Okay. So Mr. _____ checks. Says okay yes ….
Sandison:	I don't know what he did after that. He's out of my sight.
Detective:	Out of your sight. And then you went into lockdown.
Sandison:	Right.
Detective:	Since then, who else have you spoken to that you may have relayed this ….
Sandison:	Some clown, some sergeant that wanted to play detective or something. I don't know if you guys know, but we went they asked me a bunch of questions and stuff and at first I told him he asked me what I strangled him with and I said I braided my pubic hair together, and because he was just being a dick about it. You know? And you know, I know murdering somebody's not a good thing, but I mean Jesus man, if, the things this guy did, the things *he* said he did … I wouldn't want someone like that out on the street.
Detective:	So I mean you obviously you've been in the system long enough to know that something as serious as what you just did it could be investigated, but it's not going to be investigated by a sergeant that works on the ….
Sandison:	No, and that's why it, is kind of fuckin' threw anything out there so he'd just leave me alone, you know.
Detective:	Now do you know Mr. _____?
Sandison:	Yes I do.
Detective:	Did you have a conversation with him?
Sandison:	Hmmm …. Yeah briefly.
Detective:	Briefly. And during that conversation you recall what you related to him?
Sandison:	Not really I just I told him "Man, I'm sorry that I did it" but the guy wouldn't shut up, and he was telling me about his case and he just wouldn't shut the fuck up. I think I told him, I like Mr. _____ so I told him that I punched him, knocked him out, and strangled him. Something of that nature.
Detective:	Okay. So, you just mentioned that you made reference to that you were sorry. I mean obviously not ….
Sandison:	No. Not sorry. I'm not sorry for killing him. Oh no.
Detective:	Oh okay.
Sandison:	Oh no. I was sorry that I caused them problems.
Detective:	Oh I see. Okay, alright. I'm glad to clarify that.
Sandison:	Yeah, no, I'm not sorry at all for killing him.

Detective: Okay, it's my understanding that you are serving a life sentence right now for homicide.

Sandison: Yeah.

Detective: Here again, I guess, it's neither here nor there, the details of that. I guess my question is that the kind of thing that … it appears to me that what you did was because of the crime that Ted committed.

Sandison: I do what's necessary. I do what some people won't. I mean you guys are cops. You arrest people all the time for stuff you wish you could shoot them in the face. I already know that. I'm not stupid. You know? I mean ….

Detective: I understand ….

Sandison: There's crimes that shouldn't be committed. I don't know. I just don't have any empathy for people so ….

Detective: So basically, what you did, you figure Ted got what he deserved.

Sandison: Ted got what he deserved. I believe that with all my heart.

Detective: Okay. And like you say you said you were sorry, and was not sorry for the act of actually killing Ted ….

Sandison: Oh no for causing the officers problems. For having you guys to come down here and go through all this bull crap over a piece of shit, so ….

Detective: I mean, Steve at this point we've put together our report. It's gonna go to the second prosecuting attorney. He will make a decision if charges will be authorized. You're here for life as it is.

Sandison: He'll waste everybody's money and time, and make things more difficult for everybody else. Yeah, I know that.

Detective: But you're still afforded your rights, I mean you're afforded the opportunity for a trial, give an explanation of why you did what you did.

Sandison: Yeah, I mean I don't want to put his family through anything. I'm quite sure they didn't do anything. I was gonna plead guilty and then get it over with, so … no sense in wasting people's time.

Detective: Okay. Did you ever tell anybody else outside of the corrections officers that are here. You said you said goodbye to a couple of people.

Sandison: Yeah, just one person. I'm not gonna bring his name into it, but one inmate that you know I was good friends with. I told him what I did, wanted him to understand what I did, cause like I said I didn't want to bother people. I would get into little fights here and there but nothing, but I wasn't bothering nobody. I just I told him what I did before I told _____ so that I wanted him to understand why, and I guess everybody knew that he was in here for that but me, so he said he already knew that so I was kind of ….

Detective: Is that why you're so open with us tonight is you just want us to understand why? That this is you know, just a problem that with this guy ….

Sandison: It's the truth. I mean if I do something I don't know why be ashamed or lie about something that I do. It just makes it more difficult for everybody.

Detective: A couple of times you said that he was trying to deny his charges with you?

Sandison: Well yeah, cause he was saying well, because it got me mad you know. First off, 25-to-life. They don't give you 25-to-life. He said it was his first offense. And then I'm thinking "Dude, 25-to-life on your first offense" and then he said um, well it was just touching, and dude, 25-to-life, I'm not a fool. That's penetration. That's bad, bad penetration. Well then he said the mother set him up, and then he said … now he was just a dick man.

Detective: I guess what I'm wondering you said he's denying it but then he's also going into details with you about what had occurred.

Sandison: Yeah.

Detective: So that kinda contradicts what he ….

Sandison: Yeah.

Detective: And it's getting you frustrated 'cause you know that he's lying.

Sandison: Yeah. And I'm telling him this. And you know, he' always been lying about crazy shit before, but nothing like this it was usually just bragging old man or something, you know? I don't know, just ….

Detective: There's no, no chance of him harming himself, killing himself, hanging himself.

Sandison: No. I did it. I did it.

APPENDIX B

Mad Doctors by Jason Vukovich

Not everything that counts can be counted,
And not everything that can be counted counts.

(Sign in Albert Einstein's office at Princeton University)

In a political/sociological sense, what is truly striking and cannot be avoided, is this undercurrent throughout the entire storyline of prisons, their inception, any iterations, and ongoing reformations, THAT THEY NEVER WORKED!! EVER!! All of these advanced thinkers and egotistical seats of judgment, discussing the most abstruse concepts of suffering and deprivation and solitude and labor and attainment of morality, and yet … all of this discussion and labor centered around an archaic process which has always been patently ineffective, the smartest folks on the planet, but blatant in their revenge-driven policies of stupidity. As I moved along with the various reformers, I felt as if I was sitting in a room full of mad doctors, discussing where and how, and in what manner or dosage, they should be draining the "poisoned" blood from children and adults, to fix any number of maladies. For a long period of our medical history, these insane priests of medicine and "healing" would drain pint after pint of allegedly tainted blood from patients of all types, killing untold numbers along the way, this ignorant medical procedure was eventually discontinued due to its utter lack of efficacy, and more specifically, its deathly results, and yet, these prisons … these insane priests of justice … their deathly practice … the bloodletting continues … unchecked. So foolish in their total lack of clarity, so power mad in their bloated sense of virtue, while the patient – society – continues to suffer, more and more pallid as each year passes … these self-absorbed cowards cannot see their own shadow … it's deflating. A moment of self-awareness and humility could lead to an effective solution to this part of our lives. Is it time?? I hope you can see why my little story of the two brothers is so important here, these two progenitors of humanity are the cause, through their genetic, instinctual impact, of our flawed perspective on those who disobey the law … MUST PUNISH … MUST CAUSE PAIN … MUST HAVE AUTHORITY OVER OTHERS … these are the echoes of Revenge and Retribution, in spite of our notions of refined intelligence, the greatest leaders of society throughout time, still debating the proper amount of blood to drain, how often, what gauge the device's aperture should be, completely blind to the Everest of evidence proving it to be a fool's errand.

They are so stuck, as a whole, on making sure that criminals suffer with as little as possible. "Kicking the puppy" feels so good, that they fail to see that all of these men are coming out to live in their backyards. I recall when they shut down the re-entry mod we had created, at ZERO cost to the State of Alaska, we, the inmates, had partnered with outside agencies to provide shoes, clothes, backpacks, and so on, to each person being released. We gave interview classes and got people back on a "get-up-early" and go work-type schedule. I personally crafted hundreds of resumes for mostly guys who had never even seen one before. We had bus vouchers and cell phone applications, so that when an inmate walked out the gate, he was at least given a small chance of success. This mod, mostly ran by inmates, had the lowest instance of write-ups and infractions, and it was probably the most effective tool in reducing re-offending upon release that has ever been conceived. The new administrator shut it down with a quickness. They were so worried that inmates were empowered, they were so horrified that we had a few suits and ties in the mod (most guys needed to be taught how to tie a tie for an interview). They were so shocked and disgusted that we had access to a computer and a printer (no online access, completely independent of any communication network). Point being, they stripped everything out, shut it all the way down. No thank you, no looking back. It absolutely melted my brain, because after my initial resistance I thought to myself, "Okay, yeah, you people would really prefer to have all of these tattooed-up convicts being released, coming to your neighborhoods with no clothes, phones, or resumes? You'd really rather have them dumped off, chasing your daughters, robbing your homes, stealing your cars, because it was too empowering for us to provide them with interview skills and bus passes?" Pardon my language, but – FUCK IT!!! What level of idiocy are we really looking at here? These guys aren't getting released to live with me, they're coming out to live with you!!!

All of our labor was ultimately to assist the people who keep us captive. We were trying to make their world better! And fundamentally, let's process for a moment, shall we? Can you imagine, building a nationwide system of isolation and human warehousing, and yet, not one of these behavior modification geniuses realized that every person should have a "re-entry" and reintegration mod and a formal mechanism leading to release? There isn't a single prison I'm aware of that has a re-entry section that an inmate is moved to for the last portion of his sentence where housing is more like the free world. Dump someone straight out of a prison like this, into a halfway house, see what happens … recidivism … re-offense … crime ….

What I'm getting at here, is that the way to meaningful change is through appealing to their selfishness. They need to be reminded that really you're not doing anything for those worthless convicts, you're helping yourself! Think of your property values! Educated and prepared inmates, lead lives more likely to be successful. Why throw them out of the plane, one after another and continue to watch them fall, when you could give each one a proper landing? Which leads me to my next shocking revelation. As I was sitting in my cell one Sunday evening, watching 60 minutes, a segment came on showing maximum-security inmates in Kenya, trudging up a dusty footpath to the concrete education building where they were all pursuing law degrees online, in the company of a few correctional officers, also attaining law degrees. They were all remotely attending classes at the University of London … Juxtapose this story with my own ongoing battle here, in the United States, where I literally cannot receive any hard back books from any college, no used textbooks, and they absolutely refuse to allow any access to online college courses. I've been attempting to attend college for years here in America, DENIED, but if I was in a third-world country, I could've already had a law degree. My only option is to pay cash for mail-order courses, from a marginally accredited school, Adams State, and I can only take the very few classes which offer a soft-back textbook available from Barnes and Noble. You are aware of the cost prohibitive nature of these obstacles. Inmates are not wealthy. Point being, they have "rules and regulated" us into a dark corner. Let me restate this again, the inmates in Kenya are allowed to educate themselves, probably mostly for the communities sake, and yet here in America it is prohibited, and to quote a recent response from the education department here "That request is way above my pay grade. Access to online education would require a legislative action, so sorry, request denied." Sigh … Never thought I'd pine away for the ability to do my time in Africa, instead of here, but damn, I'd love the opportunity to use my time wisely … but then again, what do I know? Clearly I'm just a lowly miscreant, properly segregated and housed here in the Land of the Free, Home of the Brilliant.

APPENDIX C

Distillation of the "Moral Vigilante" by Jason Vukovich

I must admit, I laughed to myself when I initially read that a law professor had written rules for a moral vigilante. I had this reaction initially, because a genuine "vigilante" is moved by a spirit, an energy of sorts – similar to the "spirit of volunteerism" or the "spirit of service." He should be altruistic in his motive, and the only qualification is *sincerity*. This is what truly matters. He must be sincere. A person who acts on behalf of others in an unorthodox manner must be centered and calm, selfless, and sincere. That is all. Nothing more. Now, if we were creating a new system of community-based policing and order, and we chose to refer to it as "vigilantism" we could then start applying these principles as enumerated by our law professor – thus it is no longer vigilantism.

1 *Don't act unless there is a serious failure of justice.*
   Justice is an intangible ideal which has never been defined or achieved; therefore, a "moral vigilante" should only act when it is necessary for the sake of another, never for his own satisfaction. "Justice" itself has already failed because we haven't agreed what it truly is.
2 *Don't cause more harm than is necessary and just, and avoid injury to innocent bystanders.*
   Sometimes deterring future heinous acts requires speaking in the language of a predator. This is the only thing they understand. This is how a lion keeps his pride in order. Exerting force on another should only done with purpose and sober responsibility. Also, vigilantism doesn't necessarily always include "harming" an "unpunished" animal. It can have many forms. In those cases, when necessary, never harm an innocent … period.
3 *Don't act unless there is no lawful way to solve the problem.*
   Our current system of arrest, detain, and incarcerate has never "solved" any of our problems. It has only satisfied our deep-set thirst for revenge. THERE IS NO LAWFUL WAY TO SOLVE SOCIETY'S PROBLEMS. If there were, we would no longer contend with them. So we must then say – Do not act unless the law of love demands it, and seek only to solve the problem, never to exact revenge or "punish."
4 *Don't act alone.*
   A vigilante must have a well-tuned moral compass, and yes, be in tune with what his countrymen have agreed is proper and improper conduct – generally. More specifically, a vigilante will

tend to always act alone, for the general lack of any courage in our fellow citizens in this regard, also to not indemnify others who could also be punished by the government for their actions. Accountability is beneficial.

5 *Before acting be sure of the facts, and take full account of all relevant mitigations and excuses.*
Excuses? Why he included that particular word here, I am not sure. "Mitigations and motivations" would be much more appropriate. When acting on behalf of another, you must seek to understand why the person committed the damaging acts, never focusing on only the acts themselves. This leads to temperance of action. In my case, I was able to thoroughly vet each one through the sex offender database, and collect information from the community regarding their ongoing behaviors. This allowed me to speak to each one with confidence.

6 *Show restraint and temperance, not arrogance or vindictiveness*
His commentary related to this vigilante principle interested me greatly, for in my case, I was *only* moved by the "Wrath of God" or the spirit of myself as a child. I didn't want to let my younger self down. I was completely unconcerned with the state government or its reach. That system had already allowed me to be destroyed as a child, and it was continuing to do so to other children. (Consider the same month I was given 23 years for assaulting three pedophiles, a school teacher in the village, given 6 years for sexually assaulting three children). However, the veracity of the state government's discourse related to my offense, and the wrath and stern anger displayed by the prosecutor and judge throughout, revealed to me that they had been shamed. Their authority checked. It was clear they were seeking retribution for that, in equal measure. And yes, they did everything in their power to dismiss my PTSD diagnosis and destroy my credibility. It was vicious. As to the principle itself – there is no quarter for vindictiveness, or a violent nature in a true vigilante. He absolutely must take no joy in harming another. It should never be an expression of his sickness, only an expression of love – a sacrifice. For me, that is exactly what it was!

Remember, heroes are made by popular demand. They are created only by public opinion, never really by the actions of any single man. No true vigilante, or community service-oriented individual, has any care of concern for this designation and all of the judgment it entails. Most of these folks love the awards and the ribbons and the medals and the accolades, but truly, they hate the labor. A real master has his hands in the dirt, and his eyes on the stars.

7 *Warn the government that it is in breach of its social contract with its citizens and give it an opportunity to fix the problem unless it is clear that such a warning would be useless.*
Sadly, we've been here for some time, and in my personal experience, there is no "government" who actually cares. Your value as a citizen is determined by your ability to contribute to the tax base, or to draw in additional voters through their self-interested association with you … nothing more. Through a vigilante's action, he is inherently "warning" the government that they have failed, however, as we've known for some time, once they defiled our system of government, it became beyond reproach in a sense, and no amount of "warning" makes any difference. This principle hinges upon there existing a government who is responsive and concerned. Where does that exist? Not in America. Not for me.

8 *Publicly report what you've done and why.*
To whom? And in what manner? I was accountable only to the families of the children on whose behalf I acted …. After the fact, I have publicly spoken, for better or worse, and I do agree that transparency is critical. In relation to the prior principle, the government dismissed offhand any notion that my actions had any positive motive, but the public reporting that occurred certainly gave my actions context.

Interlude

There's a heaviness in the atmosphere this morning which is palpable. It's difficult to convey in words the true nature of a "vigilante." – such a brisk and casual term. In my case, it was a calling. Nothing less. A painful sacrifice of sorts. I am not a violent man by any means. To invoke and channel that spirit was unpleasant and required much effort. The only exception was at that moment, late at night, facing this very large, 6'4" pedophile, who refused to obey my commands to sit down on the bed. He was a striking image of my stepfather. The man who systematically molested me for years – uncanny. And when he chose to attack me and started swinging, I was nine years old, looking at my stepfather. It was not a fight I could lose. So, I reached into my small backpack, and I swung the hammer hard, first striking his collarbone, then hitting him in the head, at least three times. This was a man who was convicted of molesting his granddaughter, had children in his home, coming and going. He was the "youth music leader" for some church. Why parents couldn't prove to police his activities, I cannot say. How you prove or disprove a child's accusations, I also cannot say. But I can tell you that I was there that night, and I never intended for that level of violence to be displayed. I am grateful he didn't die. It was surreal later on to have him stand next to me in the courtroom, and to listen to him complain to the judge about how awful his life was now. Couldn't sleep, had to constantly check the locks, had headaches, ongoing nightmares. Strange what a dramatic amount of force was required for him to understand the nature of his victim's lives ... but sadly, he still didn't see it. Each one of his current issues I could relate to, for they had been impressed into my soul as a child victim of a predator.

There's a heaviness in the atmosphere this morning, so I ask you, please remember this conversation has real pain, real loss, and genuine sorrow behind it. This wisdom was hard learned. It's not mere conjecture.

9 *Respect the full society's norms of what is condemnable conduct.*
   As a group, in this country, we have evolved what is acceptable or unacceptable conduct. It's changing. Therefore, a vigilante would have to be well informed and in line with modern society's codes of conduct. But this is what's most critical in this particular principle. It has become the norm for communities *not* to act, therefore a moral vigilante must be willing to break away from the repressive societal norm to avoid conflict, avoid service, he must be willing to do that which others will not do, and have deemed "condemnable." If nothing else, through their ongoing lack of action, acting outside of our current "system of justice" requires a peculiar world view. I can assure you, thus, in a fashion, this principle negates itself.
10 *If it becomes clear that the problem cannot be fixed through vigilante action, then withdraw from further action.*
   Vigilante action only occurs *after* the criminal justice system has failed .... His definition here also misappropriates the motive for action to being "to change the system." Vigilantes act on behalf of victims, not to change systems. I am however, living proof that the further evolution of a "moral vigilante" should eventually be to change the system. And certainly, yes, there should be a limit to ongoing action, but again, acting for the sake of another is a distinct difference from acting to change systems – two completely separate actions, typically calling for totally different actions.
   Now, having muscled through all that, let me tell you, I am absolutely enamored with the idea of creating and applying principles to future vigilante action. This of course is dangerous territory, for I can only imagine the shockwave of horror that would recoil if I personally, or others, were to be perceived as having encouraged "moral vigilantism." If we are then creating a "community policing" model, this is something else entirely. Are we deterring? Or punishing?

Are we concerned for others? Or ourselves? I think we need to first begin quickly, by defining justice, step one. Determine why we have decided that we should "punish" each other. Step two. Finally move forward, quickly, to deterrence, education, and properly directed application of maladaptive person's qualities …. Where do they fit in? Where do they belong? Certainly somewhere. Step three ….

We cannot allow ourselves to continue to worship the old structures of imprisonment and arrest, these cathedrals built in honor of dead notions and failed ideas, need simply, to be razed completely. In lieu of that devastating process and the vacuum left in its wake (for policing and isolation are the wafer and the wine of this religion), a new fervor must rise up. One steeped in individual responsibility, and volunteerism. No community need look elsewhere for its peace and its orderly existence, all of those resources lie within. For tens of thousands of years we looked to one another for assistance and education, for security and accountability. Now, a cowardly laziness has seeped in, and we wish to press a button, or call an outsider to make "problems" go away. We question our own desire to act and label each other as "vigilante" for having the courage and heart to do so. It's now become a derogatory term to take up on behalf of another. *Vigilance*, now *vigilante*: the spite of that word on our tongues, has become bitter, what was once hallowed.

I can speak on these things, and many others, with surety and confidence, for my hand was placed to the plowshare many, many years ago. I've taken up the shovel and toiled in the ditches. I've listened and learned, practiced and failed, I've sat in the most rarified of air, and breathed it in with those whose humility was shattering. I've stood on the cliffs and traversed the jagged trails with those most ancient of white robed monks, for I am a goatherd, and here in this isolated atmosphere is where I have stored many things. How much acclaim and fanfare to the shepherd, and yet his footfalls will never be tested in this manner. In the center of the tempest, blizzard raging around us, this is where I make my table, a crossed leg, a pen, my thoughts, engraved in this stone for all of you. For I am a goatherd, and you are well advised to never walk my trail ….

APPENDIX D

Letter to the Students by Jason Vukovich

Joshua,

Thank you for your letter. It must be difficult to teach a course on jails and prisons having never lived in, or survived one. Thus, I respect your willingness and desire to reach out to those of us who are, in order to facilitate a genuine understanding of what's occurring within our so-called "system of justice" in America. I would like you to share our conversation with your class in its entirety, whether you read or show it to them, is up to you, whatever is most convenient. I also have no issue with you using my name related to this process. I am a flawed and imperfect individual like most anyone, therefore my faults as well as my successes are my own. I accept this. Making the class privy to our conversation will give them a great sense of the gestalt of the concrete shoebox, that I currently reside in, within this most eclectic monastery of sorts.

A little insight about how my mind works: I consider myself to be a "student of the universe" and I have learned how to reduce complexity to its simplest elements. This is how I approach complicated fields of information. I prefer to take unnecessarily complex series of "knots" – untie them – and then observe the simple truths which underly the subject matter. To me, simple is genius, there is no paradigm in this world which cannot be understood in simple terms.

Let's address one of your questions at a time and see where we end up ....

What do you wish people and students on the outside knew about prison life?

I wish to begin answering this question with an allegory of sorts. If you ever visited California, and you encounter a giant factory, series and series of huge warehouse-like buildings, and you wonder to yourself, "Why did Elon Musk build this incredible monstrosity?" Using our "simple is genius" method, let us simply move to the end of this factory process and observe what is produced – Ah, shiny new Teslas .... This, very quicky, we can extrapolate that clearly, this factory and series of warehouse-like structures was clearly, purpose-built to facilitate the production of Teslas ... no question ... no accident. In similar fashion, it is *very* important for people to observe the prison and jail system, and simply recognize the finished product that has been rolling off of the conveyor, for a very, very long time. Tattooed, broken, homeless people, primed for reoffending, stripped of their right to vote, bear arms, under an additional structure of "rules" which allows for their re-arrest at any time, without breaking any laws, an ocean of mostly men, the largest fraternity system in America – the Sacred Order of Felons constantly being fed and growing. Let's remember our allegory, because simple genius reveals to us that complex factories and their resulting products are not built by accident, they are built with *purpose*, for the intended result. More criminals, more crime, this has been the evidence of our purpose-built prisons for a very long time. Who would want more criminals? More crime? Strange and sick, indeed ….

We have all known that isolating a person and forcing them to live apart from society for long periods of time is not an effective form of behavior modification …. It simply doesn't work. It *never* has. However, it is most clear to those of us who rationally observe our society, that we have developed and propagated a "system of revenge." This prison system has nothing to do with correction. We want to exact suffering on anyone who has violated one of societies rules. We are all still packing Roman coliseums to watch criminals suffer torture and pain. We love how it feels when we read about some criminal getting a long sentence … Aaaahhhh, that feels so good …. Sick, isn't it? Don't be fooled, our society hasn't even evolved to the place where we can properly define "justice." We are still Neanderthals, confusing justice with revenge. All of us are guilty.

Prison "life" is a version of existence that is most akin to being awake inside of a coffin. You are able to breathe, and move, just a little, but you cannot experience most of what constitutes life. This is most properly defined as torture, and it tends to produce horrible results. It is possible for a person to advance themselves under a great myriad of pressures and adject circumstances. The few can exist under this sort of long-term dehumanizing duress and emerge with some sense of humanity remaining, but anyone who has survived a prison experience knows, that it takes something from you, which cannot ever be returned.

Caging animals is a terrible idea. Caging humans is even worse. Somehow this nightmare was sold to us as a solution, and even more oddly, as most solutions require proof of efficacy, this one *has never worked*. Has never reduced crime …. Has never reduced the number of criminals …. Has never made any of our communities safer ….

And yet, continue arresting, sentencing, imprisoning ….

Act Boldly,
Be Courageous,
Stay True To Yourself ….

Respectfully,
Jason Vukovich

———————————————————

TABLE D1 Comparative punishment opinions of people who report being victims of sexual assault before their 18th birthday

	Not victim (n = 126)		Victim (n = 78)	
	Mean/ proportion	SD	Mean/ proportion	SD
Demographics				
Age	39.53	9.44	35.85	9.92
Men	0.55	0.50	0.51	0.50
White	0.82	0.39	0.89	0.31
Black	0.06	0.25	0.01	0.12
Asian	0.03	0.18	0.08	0.27
Other	0.08	0.27	0.01	0.12
College	0.69	0.46	0.97	0.17
Victim violent	0.31	0.46	0.46	0.50
Victim of sexual assault (as adult)	0.24	0.43	0.49	0.50
Victim of sexual assault (as minor)	0.21	0.41	0.46	0.50
Agreement with each statement in regards to sex offenders who victimize minors				
I believe that sex offenders can be treated	3.21	1.43	3.65	0.82
Treatment programs for sex offenders are effective	2.90	1.30	3.63	0.93
It is better to treat sex offenders because most of them will be released	3.47	1.25	3.79	0.87
Most sex offenders will not respond to treatment	3.26	1.17	3.74	0.90
I believe that all sex offenders should be chemically castrated	3.19	1.51	3.70	0.91
Regardless of treatment all sex offenders will eventually re-offend	3.27	1.32	3.58	0.83
Treatment doesn't work, sex offenders should be incarcerated for life	3.02	1.35	3.61	0.96
It is important that all sex offenders being released receive treatment	4.00	1.09	3.82	0.87
Sex offenders don't deserve another chance	3.18	1.30	3.70	0.97
Sex offenders don't need treatment since they chose to commit the crime(s)	2.76	1.34	3.57	1.04
Sex offenders should be executed	2.68	1.49	3.51	0.90
Sex offenders should never be released	2.85	1.33	3.68	0.97
The prison sentence sex offenders serve is enough, treatment is not necessary	2.45	1.26	3.58	1.02
Treatment should be conducted during incarceration	4.00	1.10	3.88	0.88
Agreement with each statement in regards to punishment orientations				
Punishment should be about looking forward to improve society, not backward, to address the criminal's misdeeds	3.77	1.08	3.79	0.71
When considering an appropriate punishment, the potential benefit to the public is more important than the need to avenge the particular crime	3.71	0.96	3.79	0.91
Punishment is more about addressing society's needs than serving out justice to a single individual	3.35	1.12	3.81	0.90
We should try to focus on how punishment can help the community instead of fixating on one person's wrongdoings	3.63	1.06	3.74	0.83
When punishing a person, it is better to take a step back to think about how that punishment will affect the community	3.58	0.93	3.77	0.86
It is better to let 10 guilty criminals go free than to punish one innocent person	3.58	1.27	3.72	0.89
It is more important to keep innocent people free from punishment than it is to ensure that all guilty persons are punished for their crimes	3.94	1.11	3.70	0.73
A punishment system should prioritize bringing offenders to justice, even at the risk of punishing the wrong person	3.39	1.42	2.32	0.85
Catching more guilty people isn't worth the expense of false convictions	3.74	1.23	3.75	0.91

(Continued)

TABLE D1 (Continued)

	Not victim (n = 126)		Victim (n = 78)	
	Mean/ proportion	SD	Mean/ proportion	SD
An overly harsh punishment may be necessary to prevent others from committing the same crime	3.06	1.19	3.87	0.78
If a crime has a low detection rate, we should punish those who are caught harshly to prevent others from thinking they can get away with it	2.97	1.14	3.89	0.73
Crimes that receive a great deal of publicity should be punished severely, even if the crime was not severe, so that society knows there is a strong response	2.63	1.07	3.73	0.81
We should err on the side of stricter punishments if it will result in greater public safety	3.03	1.24	3.74	0.83
Even if society would not benefit at all from punishing a guilty person, he should still be punished because he deserves it	3.21	1.06	3.75	0.87
Criminals are bad people and get what is coming to them	3.31	1.17	3.87	0.95
Punishment is necessary because it restores the balance of justice	3.44	1.18	3.94	0.82
It is more important to punish a guilty person because he deserves it than it is to punish him to benefit society	3.11	1.19	3.85	0.82
Do you think it is ever okay for a private citizen to violently harm a sex offender for revenge?				
Yes	0.24	0.43	0.43	0.50
Maybe	0.31	0.46	0.33	0.47
No	0.45	0.50	0.24	0.43

TABLE D2 Comparative punishment opinions of conservatives and liberals

	Conservative (n = 142)		Liberal (n = 62)	
	Mean/ proportion	SD	Mean/ proportion	SD
Demographics				
Age	35.85	9.92	39.53	9.44
Men	0.51	0.50	0.55	0.50
White	0.89	0.31	0.82	0.39
Black	0.01	0.12	0.06	0.25
Asian	0.08	0.27	0.03	0.18
Other	0.01	0.12	0.08	0.27
College	0.97	0.17	0.69	0.46
Victim violent	0.46	0.50	0.31	0.46
Victim of sexual assault (as adult)	0.49	0.50	0.24	0.43
Victim of sexual assault (as minor)	0.46	0.50	0.21	0.41
Agreement with each statement in regards to sex offenders who victimize adults				
I believe that sex offenders can be treated	3.70	0.78	3.08	1.38
Treatment programs for sex offenders are effective	3.75	0.97	2.95	1.29
It is better to treat sex offenders because most of them will be released	3.76	0.91	3.40	1.29
Most sex offenders will not respond to treatment	3.66	0.91	3.44	1.17

(Continued)

TABLE D2 (Continued)

	Conservative (n = 142)		Liberal (n = 62)	
	Mean/ proportion	SD	Mean/ proportion	SD
I believe that all sex offenders should be chemically castrated	3.81	0.93	2.95	1.41
Regardless of treatment all sex offenders will eventually re-offend	3.62	0.82	3.15	1.17
Treatment doesn't work, sex offenders should be incarcerated for life	3.61	0.83	2.90	1.33
It is important that all sex offenders being released receive treatment	3.78	0.86	3.76	1.25
Sex offenders don't deserve another chance	3.82	0.95	2.81	1.27
Sex offenders don't need treatment since they chose to commit the crime(s)	3.61	0.98	2.76	1.26
Sex offenders should be executed	3.54	0.92	2.66	1.50
Sex offenders should never be released	3.75	0.88	2.73	1.31
The prison sentence sex offenders serve is enough, treatment is not necessary	3.63	0.97	2.40	1.30
Treatment should be conducted during incarceration	3.85	0.91	3.94	1.08
Agreement with each statement in regards to sex offenders who victimize minors				
I believe that sex offenders can be treated	3.65	0.82	3.21	1.43
Treatment programs for sex offenders are effective	3.63	0.93	2.90	1.30
It is better to treat sex offenders because most of them will be released	3.79	0.87	3.47	1.25
Most sex offenders will not respond to treatment	3.74	0.90	3.26	1.17
I believe that all sex offenders should be chemically castrated	3.70	0.91	3.19	1.51
Regardless of treatment all sex offenders will eventually re-offend	3.58	0.83	3.27	1.32
Treatment doesn't work, sex offenders should be incarcerated for life	3.61	0.96	3.02	1.35
It is important that all sex offenders being released receive treatment	3.82	0.87	4.00	1.09
Sex offenders don't deserve another chance	3.70	0.97	3.18	1.30
Sex offenders don't need treatment since they chose to commit the crime(s)	3.57	1.04	2.76	1.34
Sex offenders should be executed	3.51	0.91	2.68	1.49
Sex offenders should never be released	3.68	0.97	2.85	1.33
The prison sentence sex offenders serve is enough, treatment is not necessary	3.58	1.02	2.45	1.26
Treatment should be conducted during incarceration.	3.88	0.88	4.00	1.10
Agreement with each statement in regards to punishment orientations				
Punishment should be about looking forward to improve society, not backward to address the criminal's misdeeds	3.79	0.71	3.77	1.08
When considering an appropriate punishment, the potential benefit to the public is more important than the need to avenge the particular crime	3.79	0.91	3.71	0.97
Punishment is more about addressing society's needs than serving out justice to a single individual	3.81	0.90	3.35	1.12
We should try to focus on how punishment can help the community instead of fixating on one person's wrongdoings	3.74	0.83	3.63	1.06
When punishing a person, it is better to take a step back to think about how that punishment will affect the community	3.77	0.86	3.58	0.93
It is better to let 10 guilty criminals go free than to punish one innocent person	3.72	0.89	3.58	1.28
It is more important to keep innocent people free from punishment than it is to ensure that all guilty persons are punished for their crimes	3.70	0.73	3.94	1.11
A punishment system should prioritize bringing offenders to justice, even at the risk of punishing the wrong person	2.32	0.85	3.39	1.42
Catching more guilty people isn't worth the expense of false convictions	3.75	0.91	3.74	1.23

(Continued)

TABLE D2 (Continued)

	Conservative (n = 142)		Liberal (n = 62)	
	Mean/ proportion	SD	Mean/ proportion	SD
An overly harsh punishment may be necessary to prevent others from committing the same crime	3.87	0.78	3.06	1.19
If a crime has a low detection rate, we should punish those who are caught harshly to prevent others from thinking they can get away with it	3.89	0.73	2.97	1.15
Crimes that receive a great deal of publicity should be punished severely, even if the crime was not severe, so that society knows there is a strong response	3.73	0.81	2.63	1.08
We should err on the side of stricter punishments if it will result in greater public safety	3.74	0.83	3.03	1.24
Even if society would not benefit at all from punishing a guilty person, he should still be punished because he deserves it	3.75	0.87	3.21	1.06
Criminals are bad people and get what is coming to them	3.87	0.95	3.31	1.17
Punishment is necessary because it restores the balance of justice	3.94	0.82	3.44	1.18
It is more important to punish a guilty person because he deserves it than it is to punish him to benefit society	3.85	0.82	3.11	1.19
Do you think it is ever okay for a private citizen to violently harm a sex offender for revenge?				
Yes	0.43	0.50	0.24	0.43
Maybe	0.33	0.47	0.31	0.46
No	0.24	0.43	0.45	0.50

INDEX

Made in the USA
Monee, IL
17 November 2023

46837945R00168